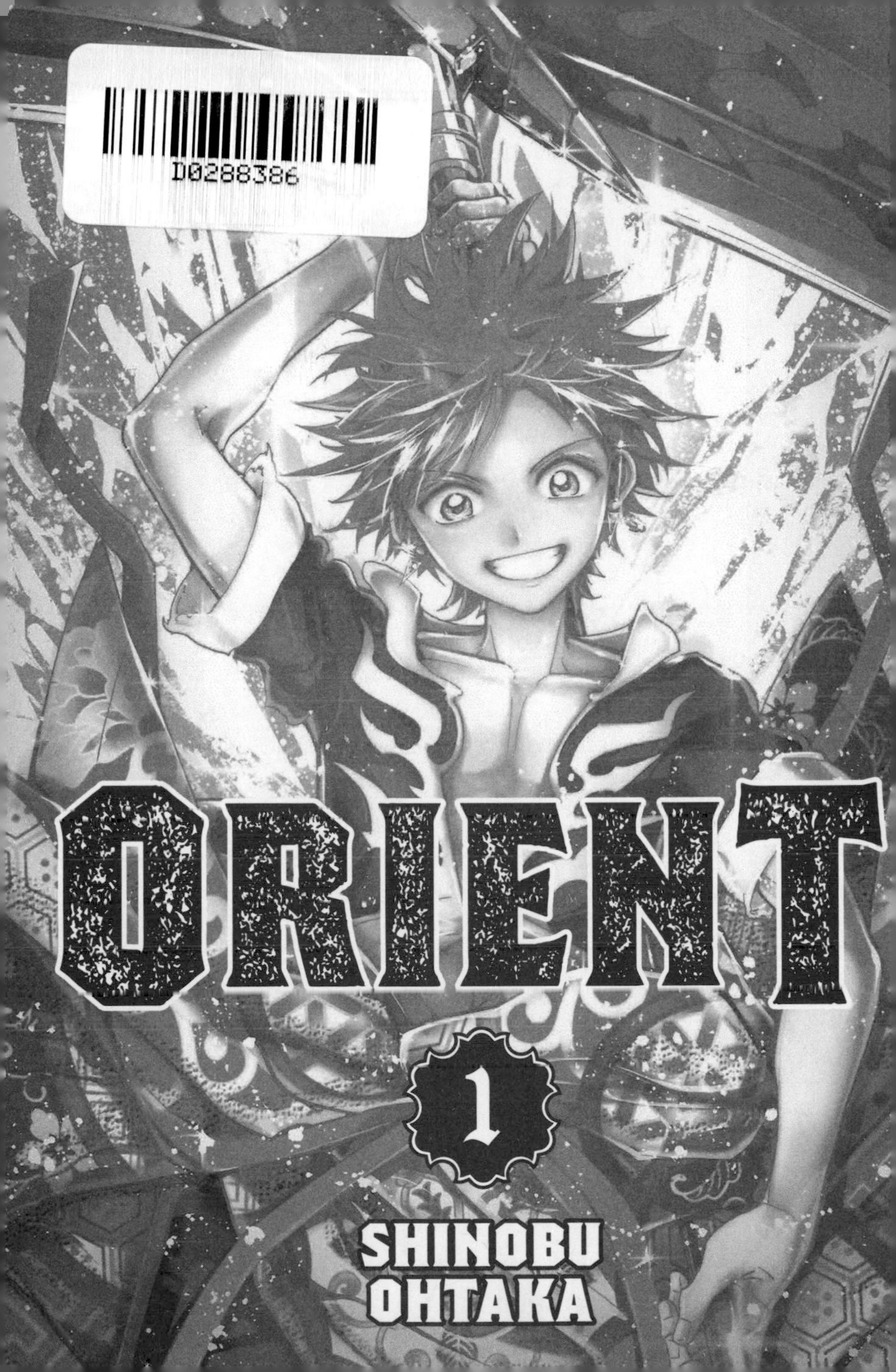
ORIENT
1
SHINOBU
OHTAKA

ORIENT

ORIENT

**SHINOBU
OHTAKA**

**CHAPTER 1:
MUSASHI AND
KOJIRO**
4

**CHAPTER 2:
THE
MALEVOLENT
GOD**
72

**CHAPTER 3:
BAND OF
SAMURAI**
121

**CHAPTER 4:
AZURE HEAVEN
CRANE WING**
157

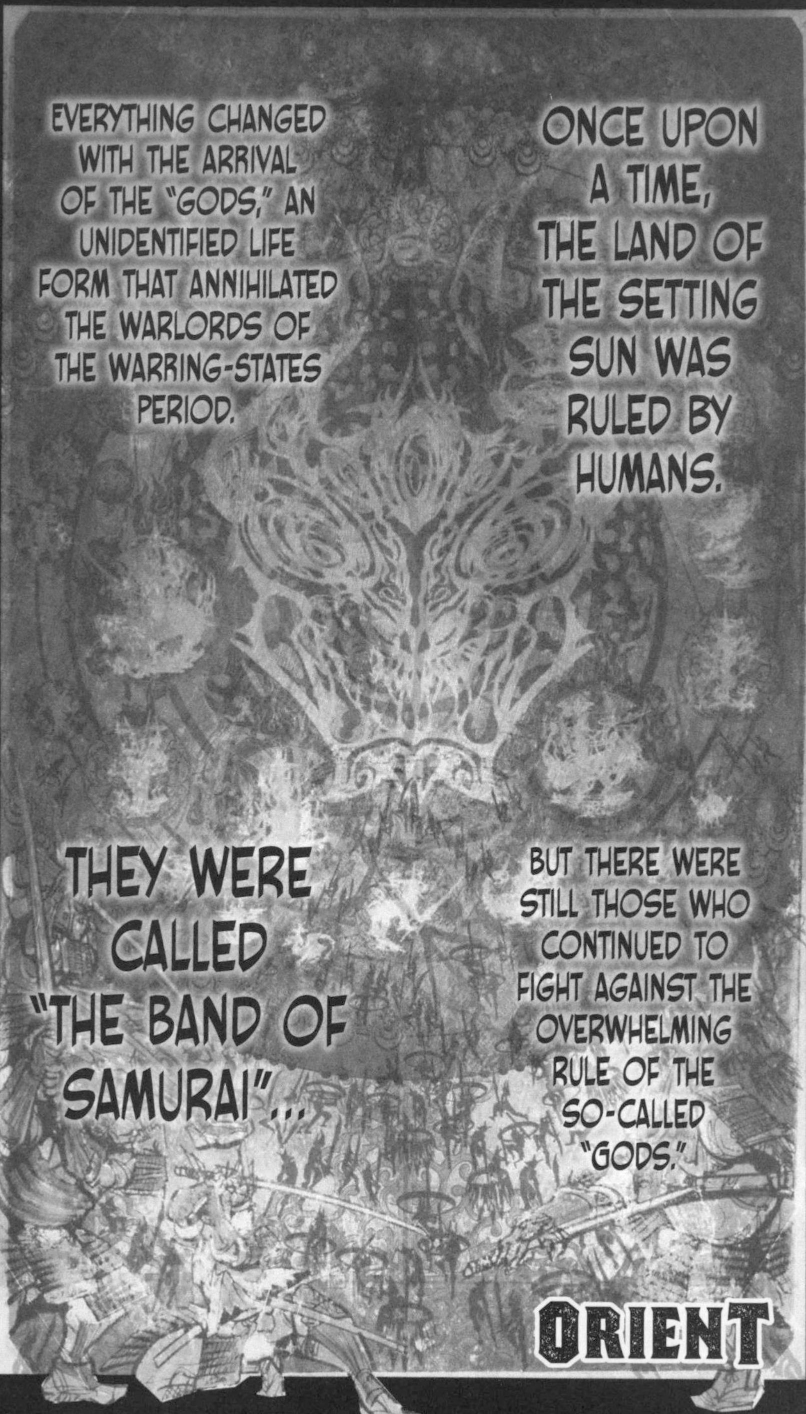
ONCE UPON A TIME, THE LAND OF THE SETTING SUN WAS RULED BY HUMANS.
EVERYTHING CHANGED WITH THE ARRIVAL OF THE "GODS," AN UNIDENTIFIED LIFE FORM THAT ANNIHILATED THE WARLORDS OF THE WARRING-STATES PERIOD.
BUT THERE WERE STILL THOSE WHO CONTINUED TO FIGHT AGAINST THE OVERWHELMING RULE OF THE SO-CALLED "GODS."
THEY WERE CALLED "THE BAND OF SAMURAI"...
ORIENT

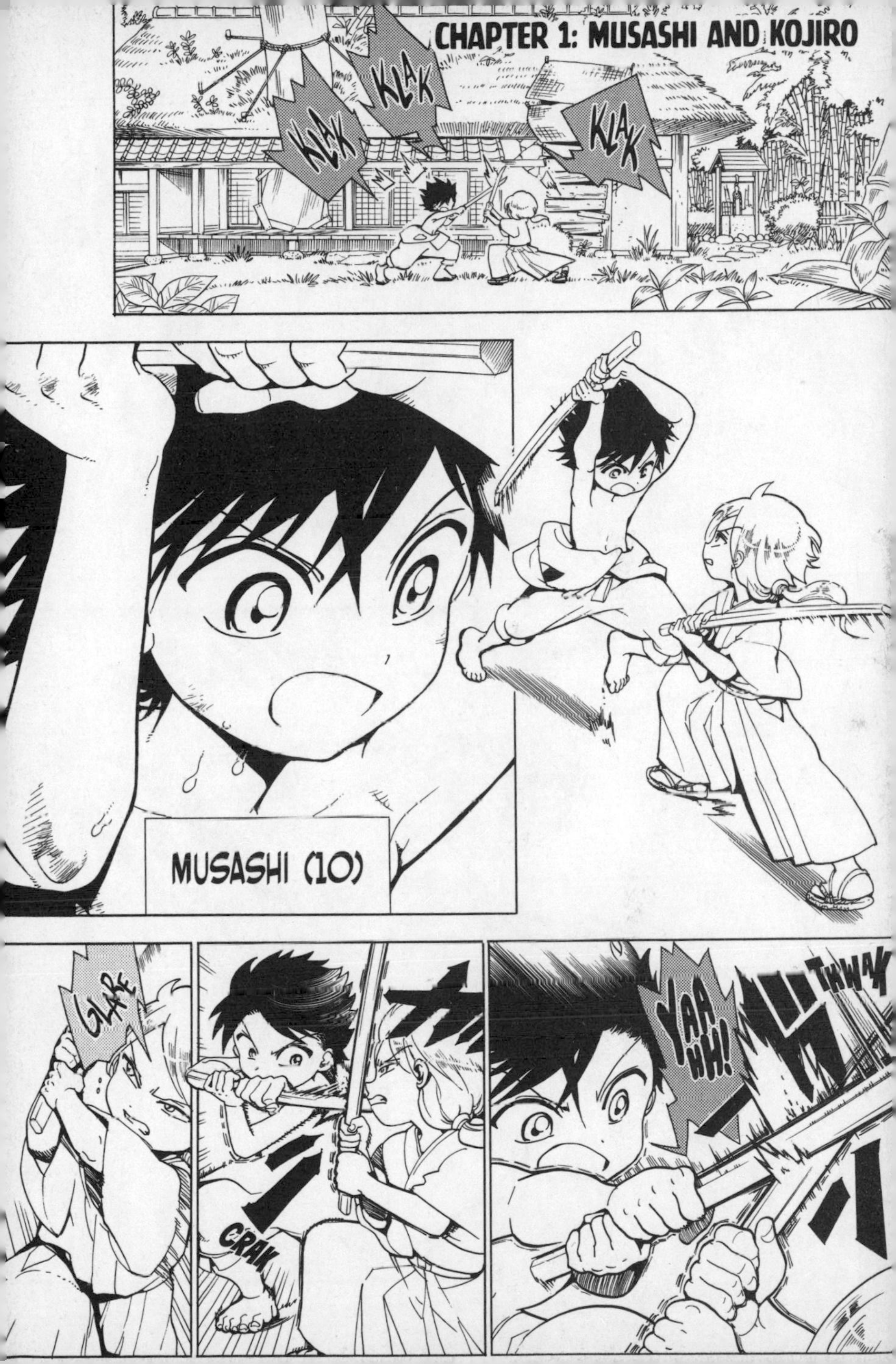
CHAPTER 1: MUSASHI AND KOJIRO
KLAK
KLAK
KLAK
MUSASHI (10)
YAAHH!
THWAK
CRAK
GLARE

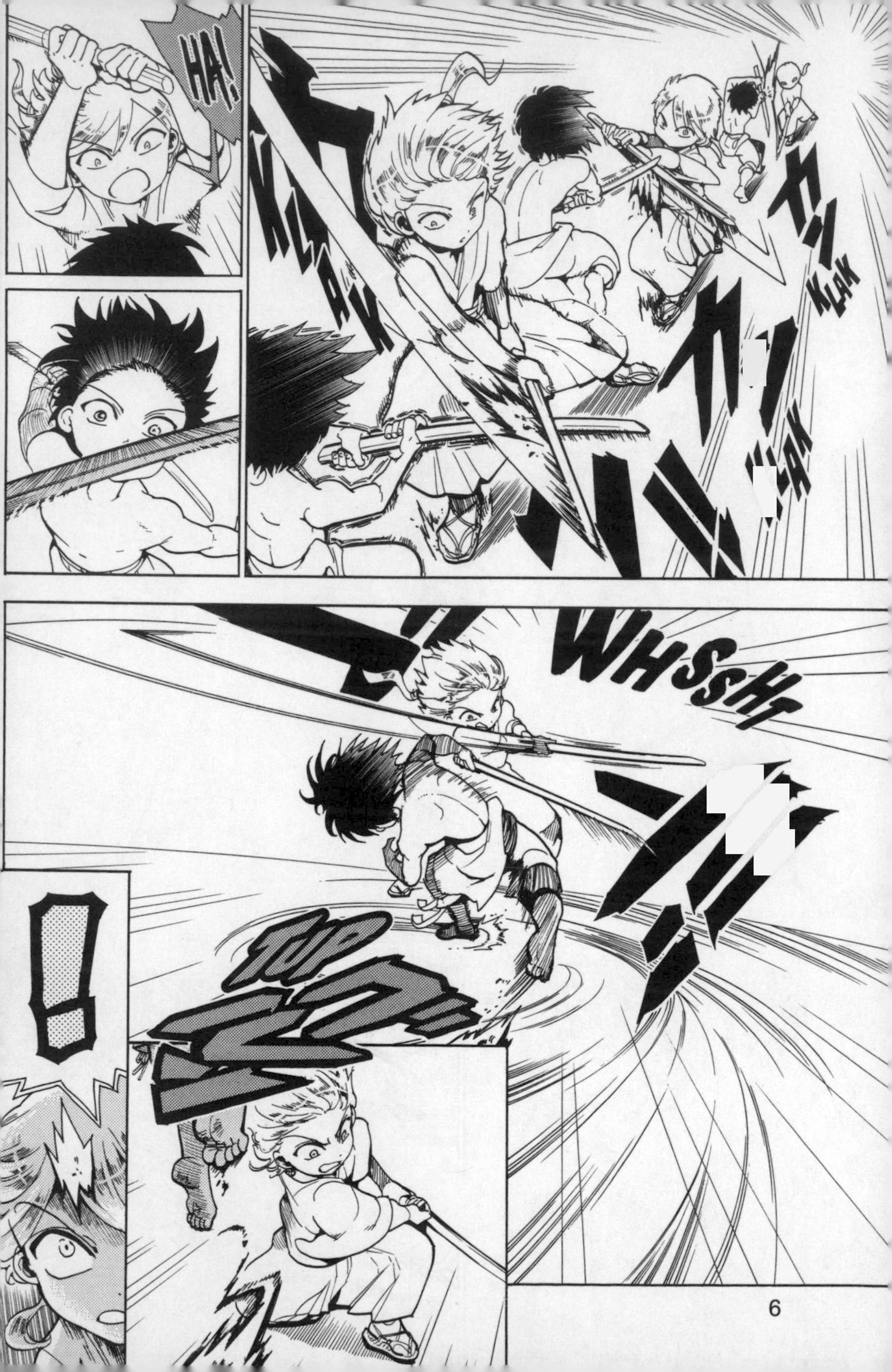
KLAK
KLAK
KLAK
HA!
WHSSHT
TUP
!

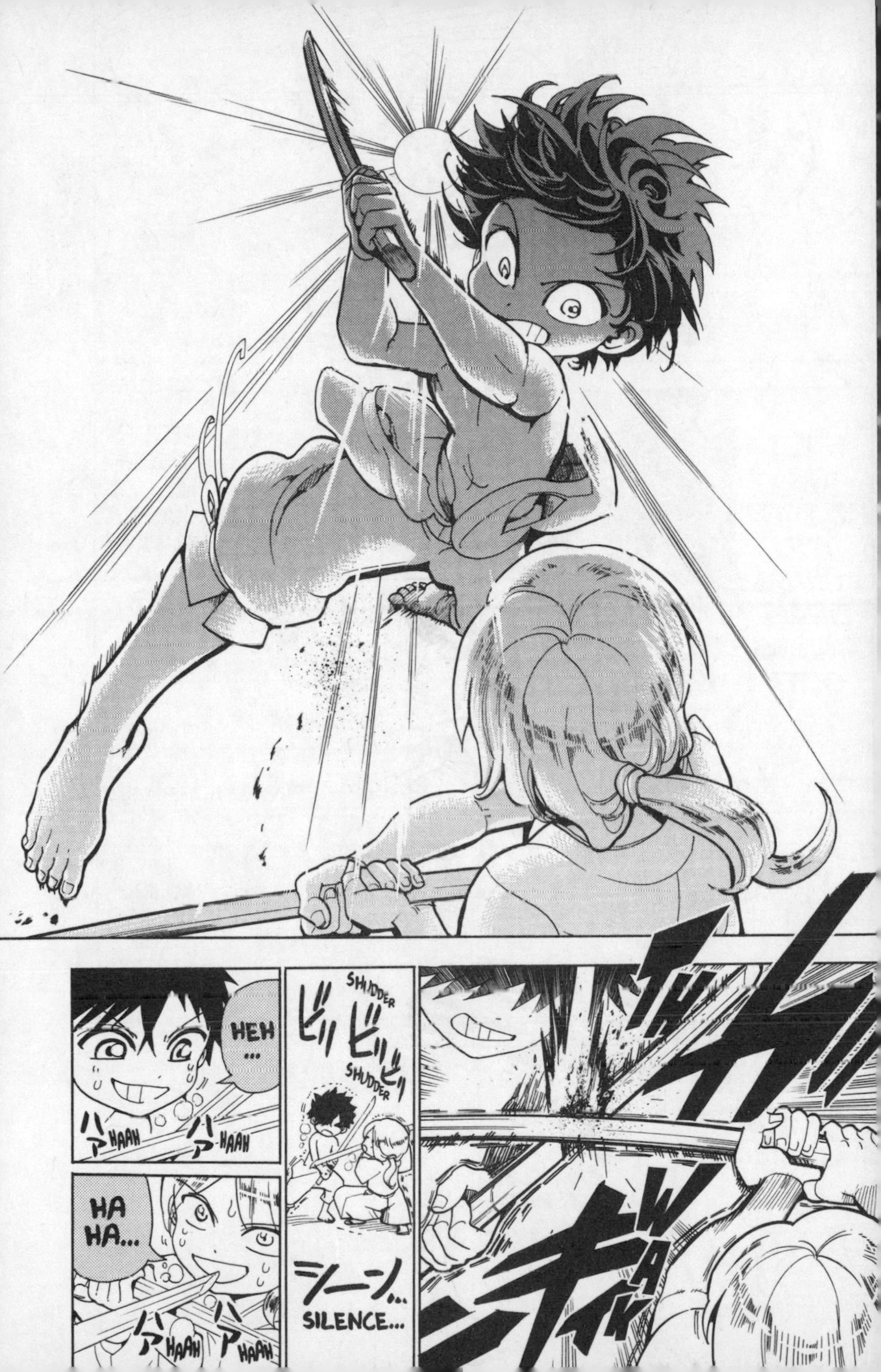

WAK
SHUDDER
SHUDDER
SILENCE...
HEH...
HAAH
HAAH
HA HA...
HAAH
HAAH

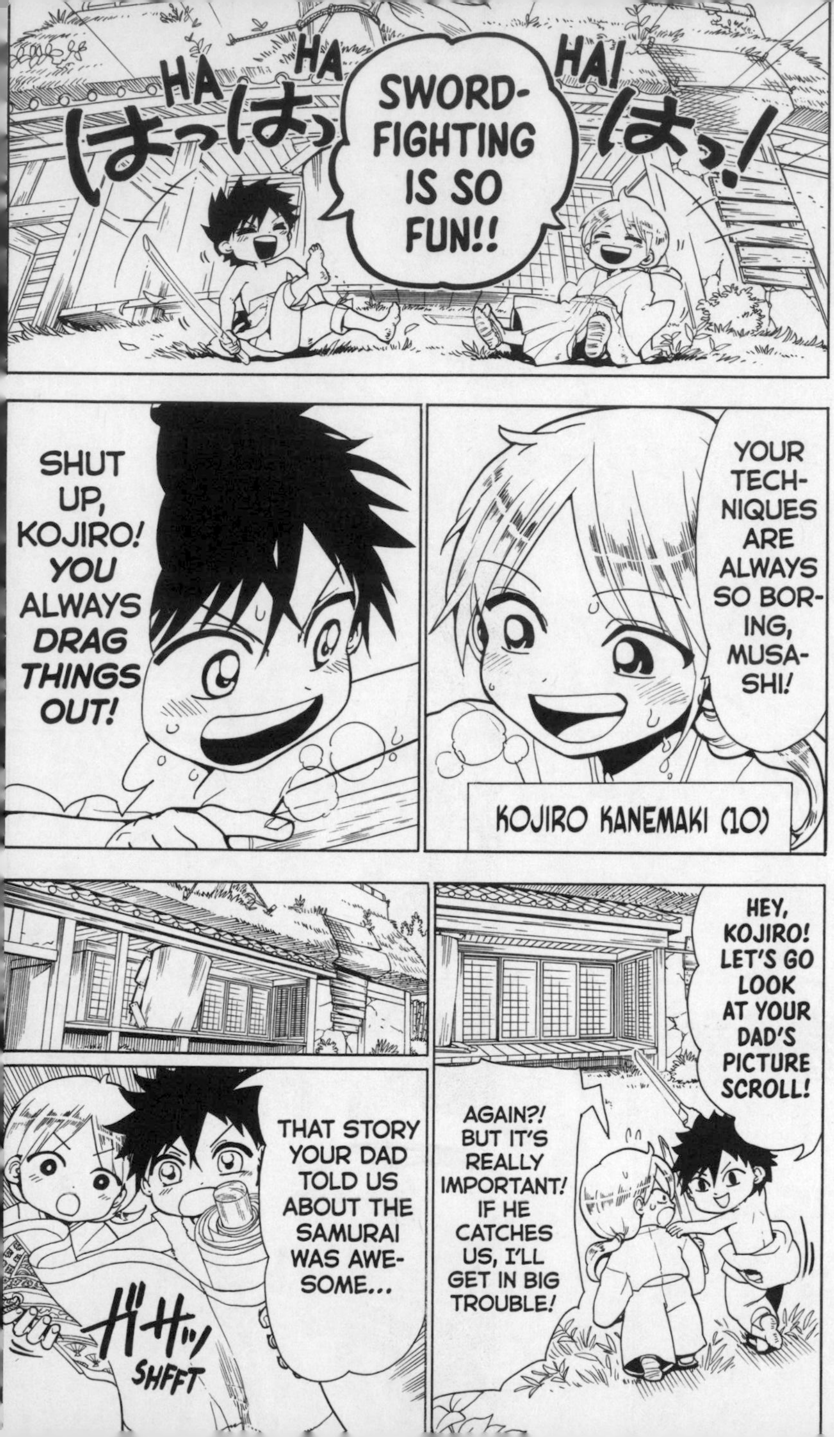
はっ! HA!
SWORD-FIGHTING IS SO FUN!!
はっはっ HA HA
YOUR TECH-NIQUES ARE ALWAYS SO BOR-ING, MUSA-SHI!
KOJIRO KANEMAKI (10)
SHUT UP, KOJIRO! *YOU* ALWAYS *DRAG* THINGS OUT!
HEY, KOJIRO! LET'S GO LOOK AT YOUR DAD'S PICTURE SCROLL!
AGAIN?! BUT IT'S REALLY IMPORTANT! IF HE CATCHES US, I'LL GET IN BIG TROUBLE!
THAT STORY YOUR DAD TOLD US ABOUT THE SAMURAI WAS AWE-SOME...
ガサッ SHFFT

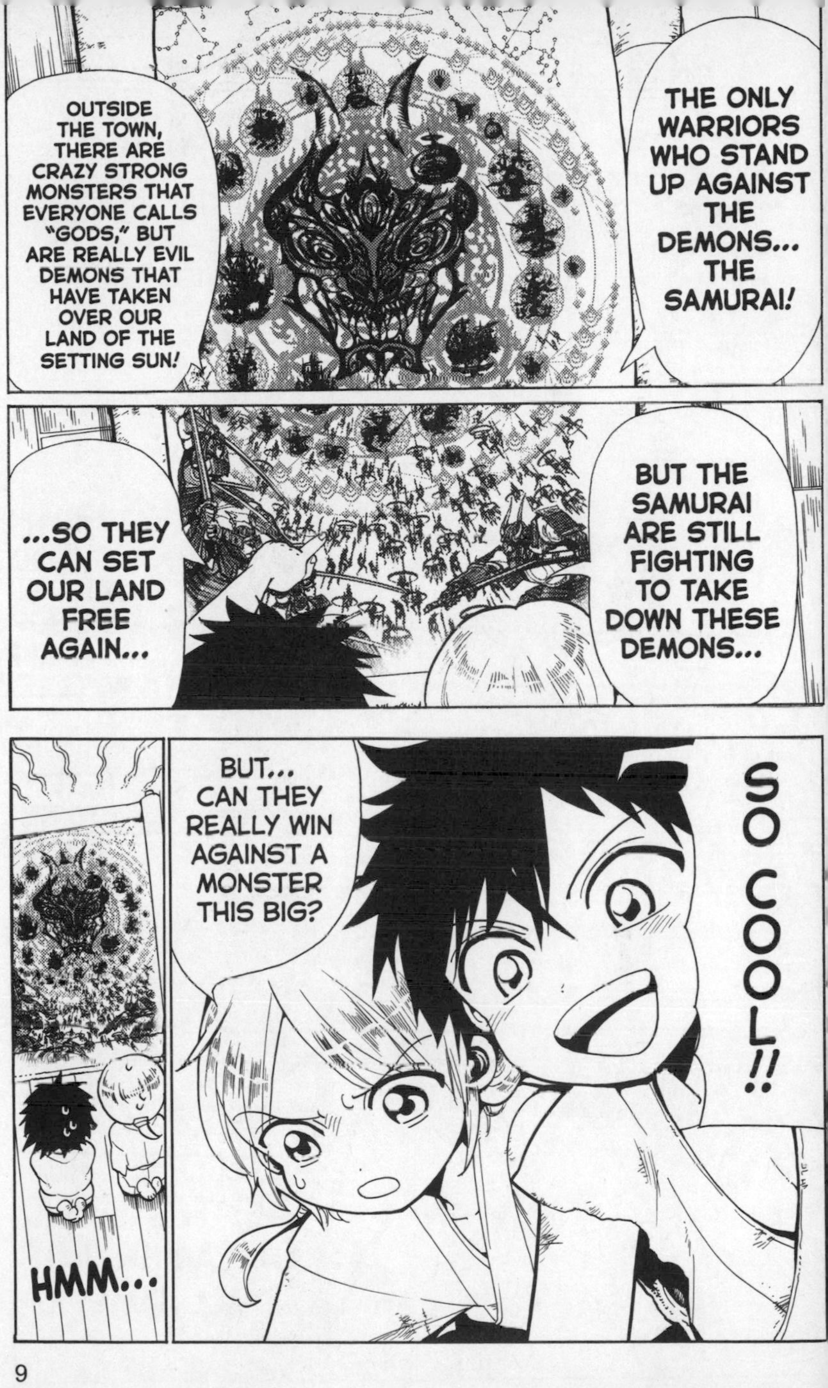
THE ONLY WARRIORS WHO STAND UP AGAINST THE DEMONS... THE SAMURAI!
OUTSIDE THE TOWN, THERE ARE CRAZY STRONG MONSTERS THAT EVERYONE CALLS "GODS," BUT ARE REALLY EVIL DEMONS THAT HAVE TAKEN OVER OUR LAND OF THE SETTING SUN!
BUT THE SAMURAI ARE STILL FIGHTING TO TAKE DOWN THESE DEMONS...
...SO THEY CAN SET OUR LAND FREE AGAIN...
SO COOL!!
BUT... CAN THEY REALLY WIN AGAINST A MONSTER THIS BIG?
HMM...

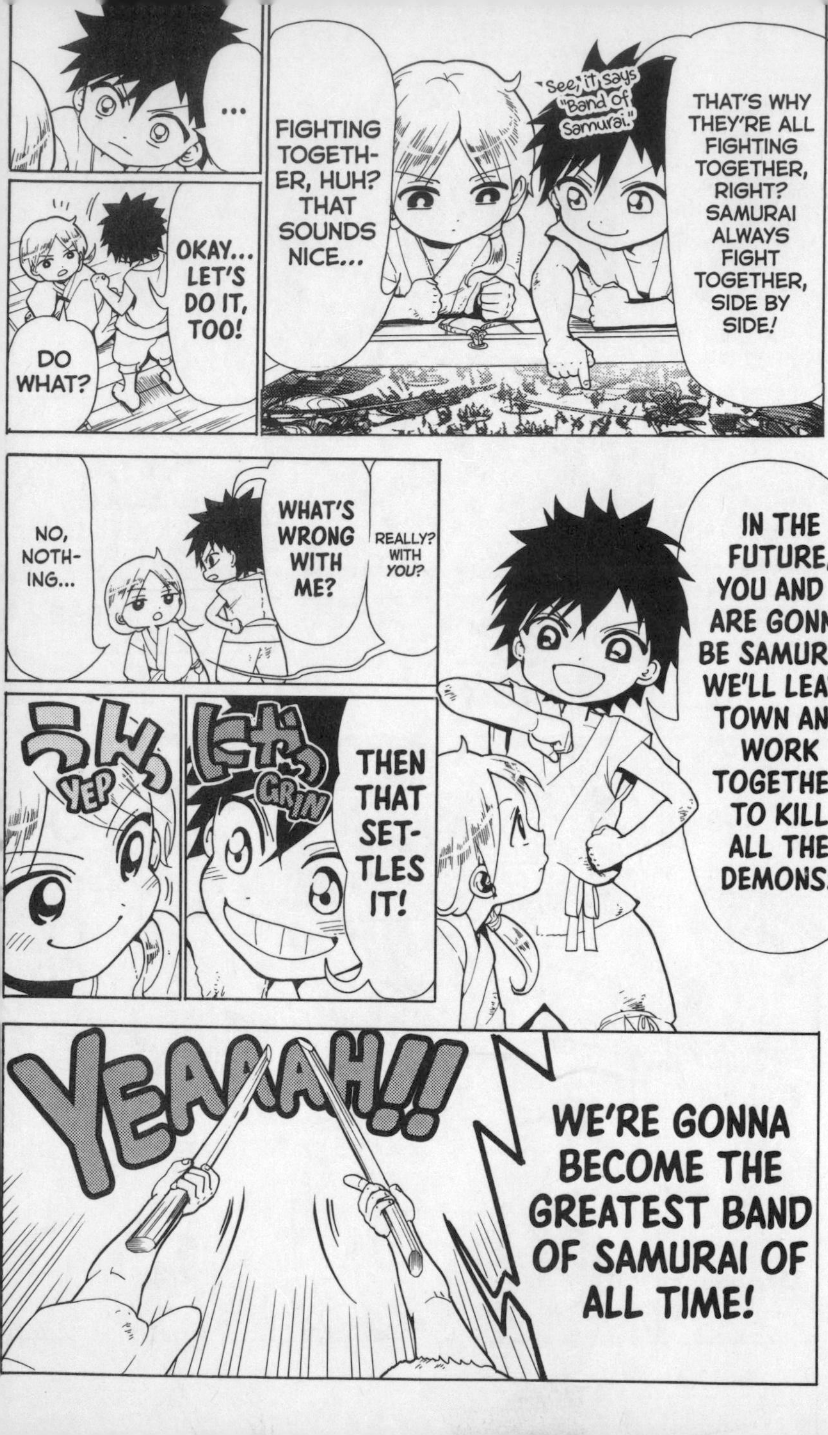

THAT'S WHY THEY'RE ALL FIGHTING TOGETHER, RIGHT? SAMURAI ALWAYS FIGHT TOGETHER, SIDE BY SIDE!
See, it says "Band of Samurai."
FIGHTING TOGETH-ER, HUH? THAT SOUNDS NICE...
...
OKAY... LET'S DO IT, TOO!
DO WHAT?
IN THE FUTURE, YOU AND I ARE GONNA BE SAMURAI! WE'LL LEAVE TOWN AND WORK TOGETHER TO KILL ALL THE DEMONS!
REALLY? WITH *YOU*?
WHAT'S WRONG WITH ME?
NO, NOTH-ING...
THEN THAT SET-TLES IT!
にやっ
GRIN
うんっ
YEP
WE'RE GONNA BECOME THE GREATEST BAND OF SAMURAI OF ALL TIME!
YEAAAH!!

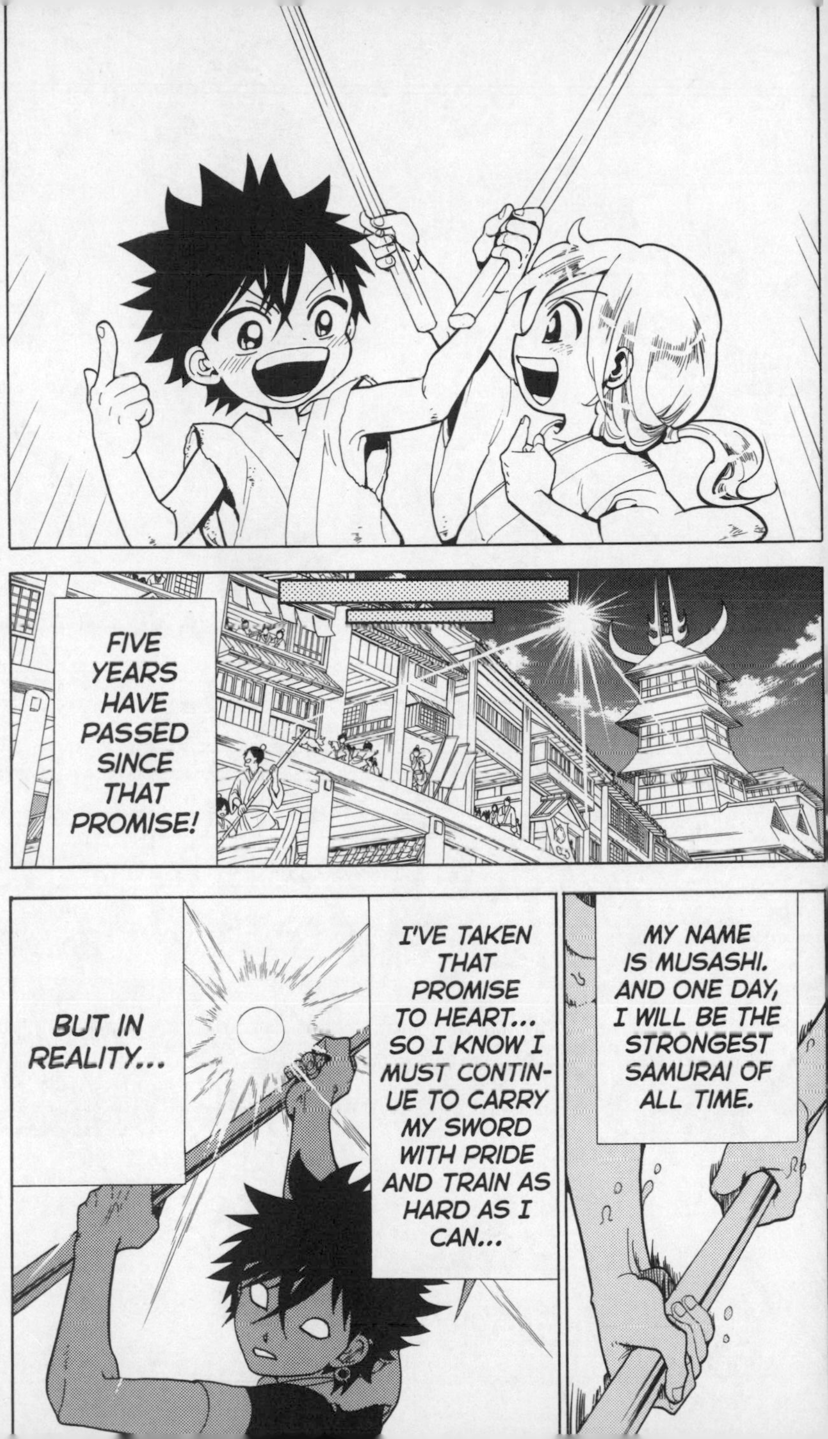
FIVE YEARS HAVE PASSED SINCE THAT PROMISE!
MY NAME IS MUSASHI. AND ONE DAY, I WILL BE THE STRONGEST SAMURAI OF ALL TIME.
I'VE TAKEN THAT PROMISE TO HEART... SO I KNOW I MUST CONTINUE TO CARRY MY SWORD WITH PRIDE AND TRAIN AS HARD AS I CAN...
BUT IN REALITY...

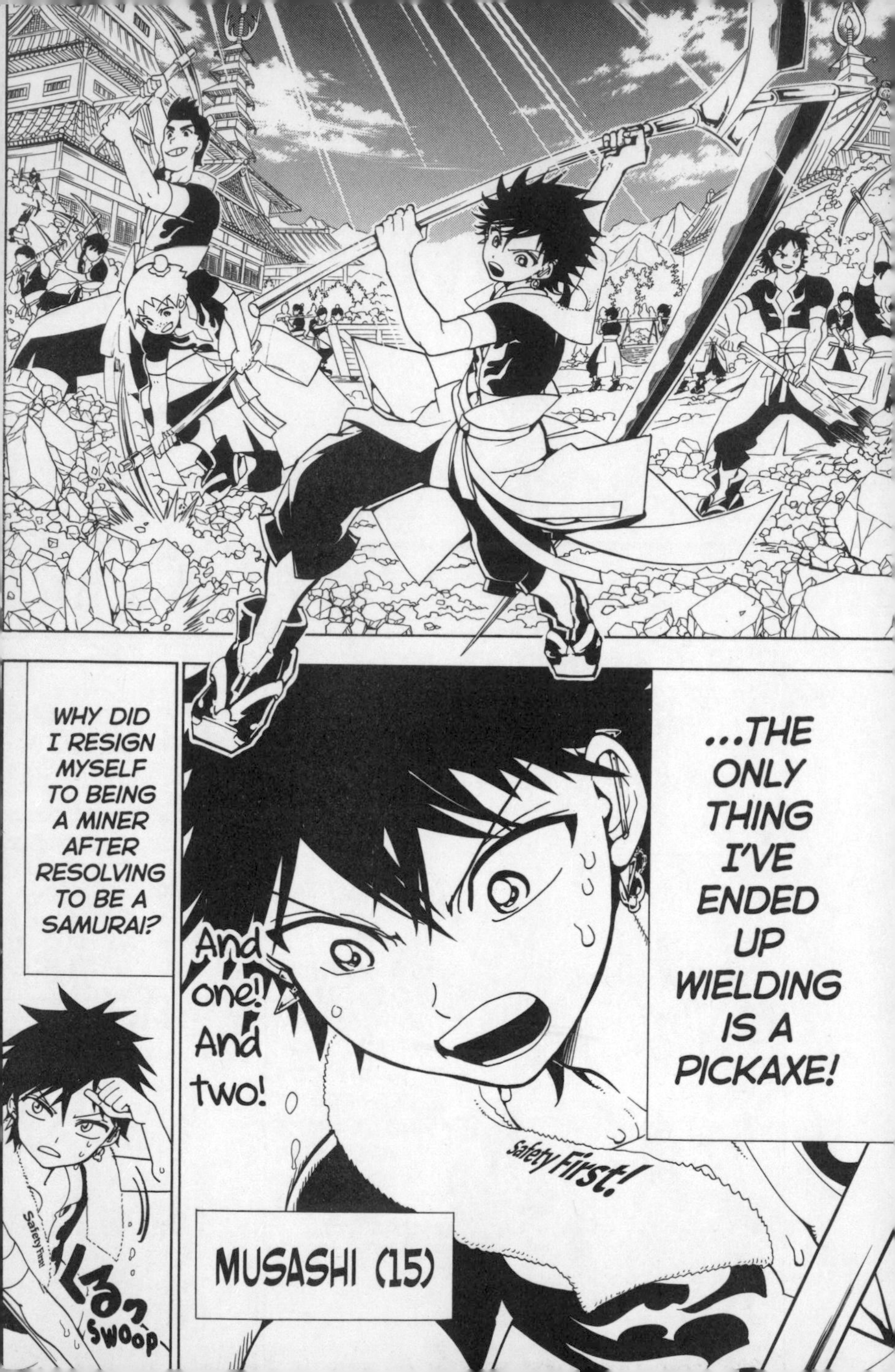
...THE ONLY THING I'VE ENDED UP WIELDING IS A PICKAXE!
And one! And two!
Safety First!
MUSASHI (15)
WHY DID I RESIGN MYSELF TO BEING A MINER AFTER RESOLVING TO BE A SAMURAI?
Safety First
くるっ
SWOOP

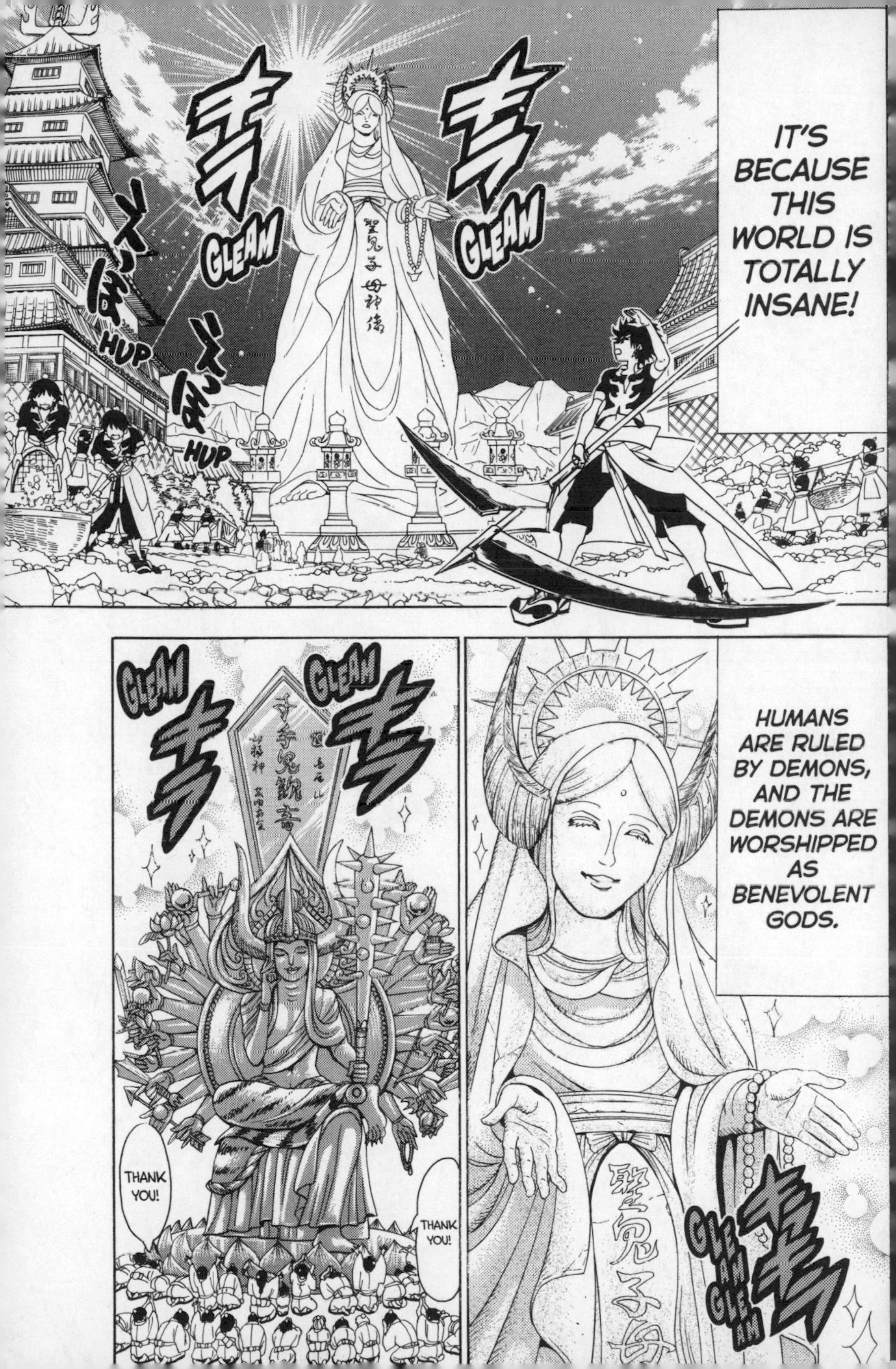
IT'S BECAUSE THIS WORLD IS TOTALLY INSANE!
GLEAM
GLEAM
HUP
HUP
HUMANS ARE RULED BY DEMONS, AND THE DEMONS ARE WORSHIPPED AS BENEVOLENT GODS.
GLEAM GLEAM GLEAM
GLEAM
GLEAM
THANK YOU!
THANK YOU!

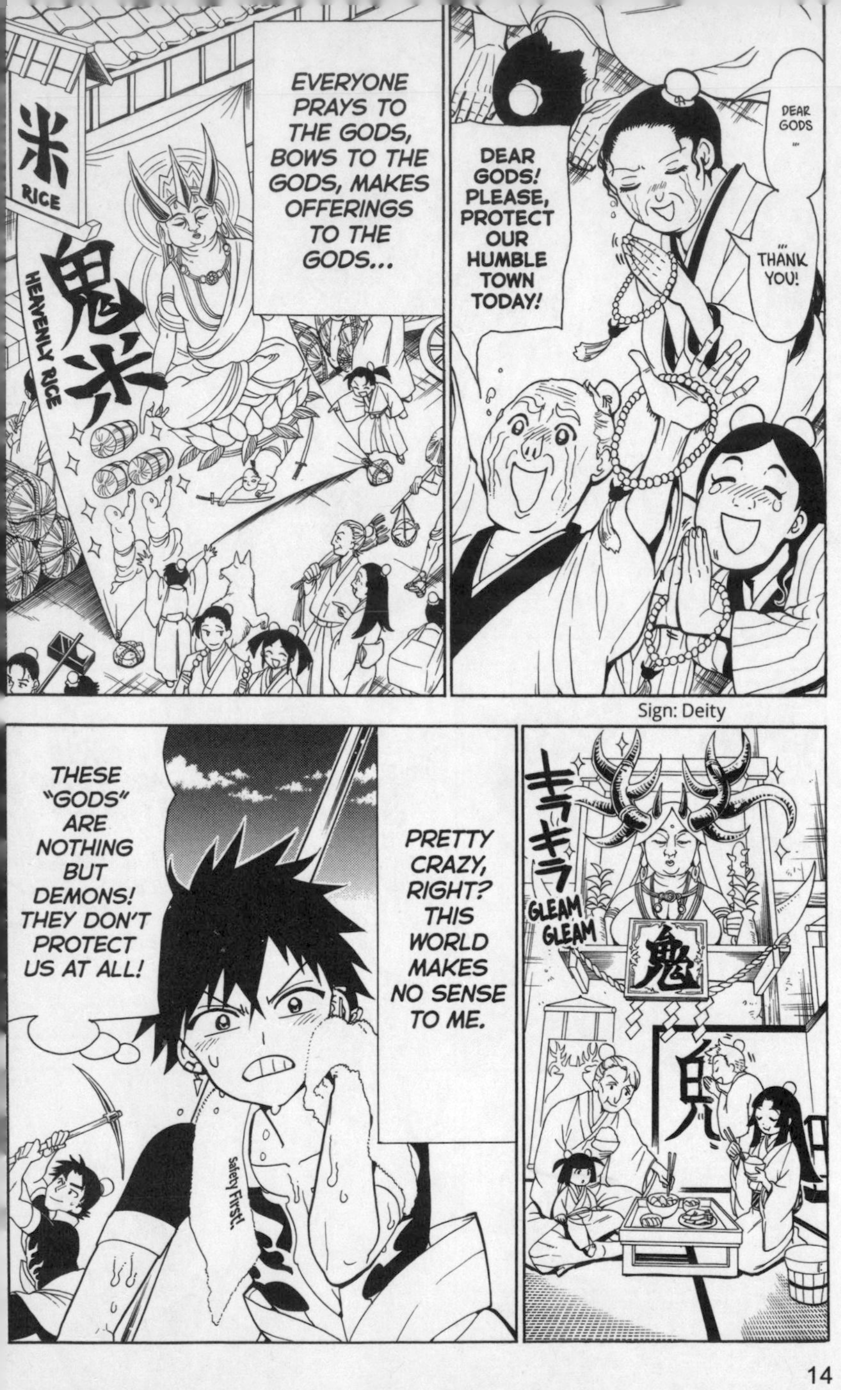
DEAR GODS …
… THANK YOU!
DEAR GODS! PLEASE, PROTECT OUR HUMBLE TOWN TODAY!
EVERYONE PRAYS TO THE GODS, BOWS TO THE GODS, MAKES OFFERINGS TO THE GODS...
米
RICE
鬼米
HEAVENLY RICE
Sign: Deity
キラキラ
GLEAM GLEAM
鬼
PRETTY CRAZY, RIGHT? THIS WORLD MAKES NO SENSE TO ME.
THESE "GODS" ARE NOTHING BUT DEMONS! THEY DON'T PROTECT US AT ALL!
Safety First!

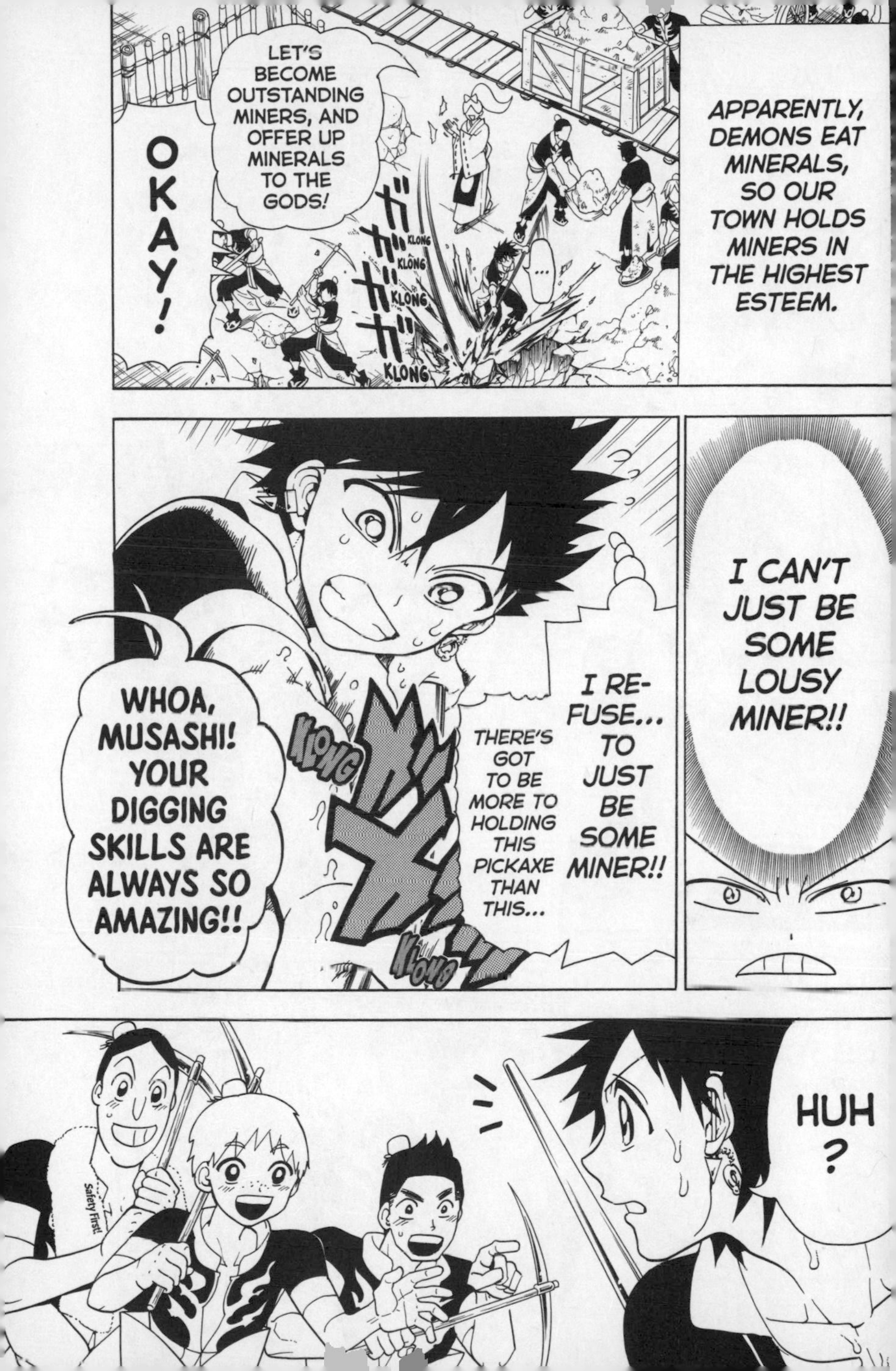
APPARENTLY, DEMONS EAT MINERALS, SO OUR TOWN HOLDS MINERS IN THE HIGHEST ESTEEM.
LET'S BECOME OUTSTANDING MINERS, AND OFFER UP MINERALS TO THE GODS!
OKAY!
...
KLONG
KLONG
KLONG
KLONG
I CAN'T JUST BE SOME LOUSY MINER!!
I RE-FUSE... TO JUST BE SOME MINER!!
THERE'S GOT TO BE MORE TO HOLDING THIS PICKAXE THAN THIS...
WHOA, MUSASHI! YOUR DIGGING SKILLS ARE ALWAYS SO AMAZING!!
KLONG
KLONG
HUH?
Safety First

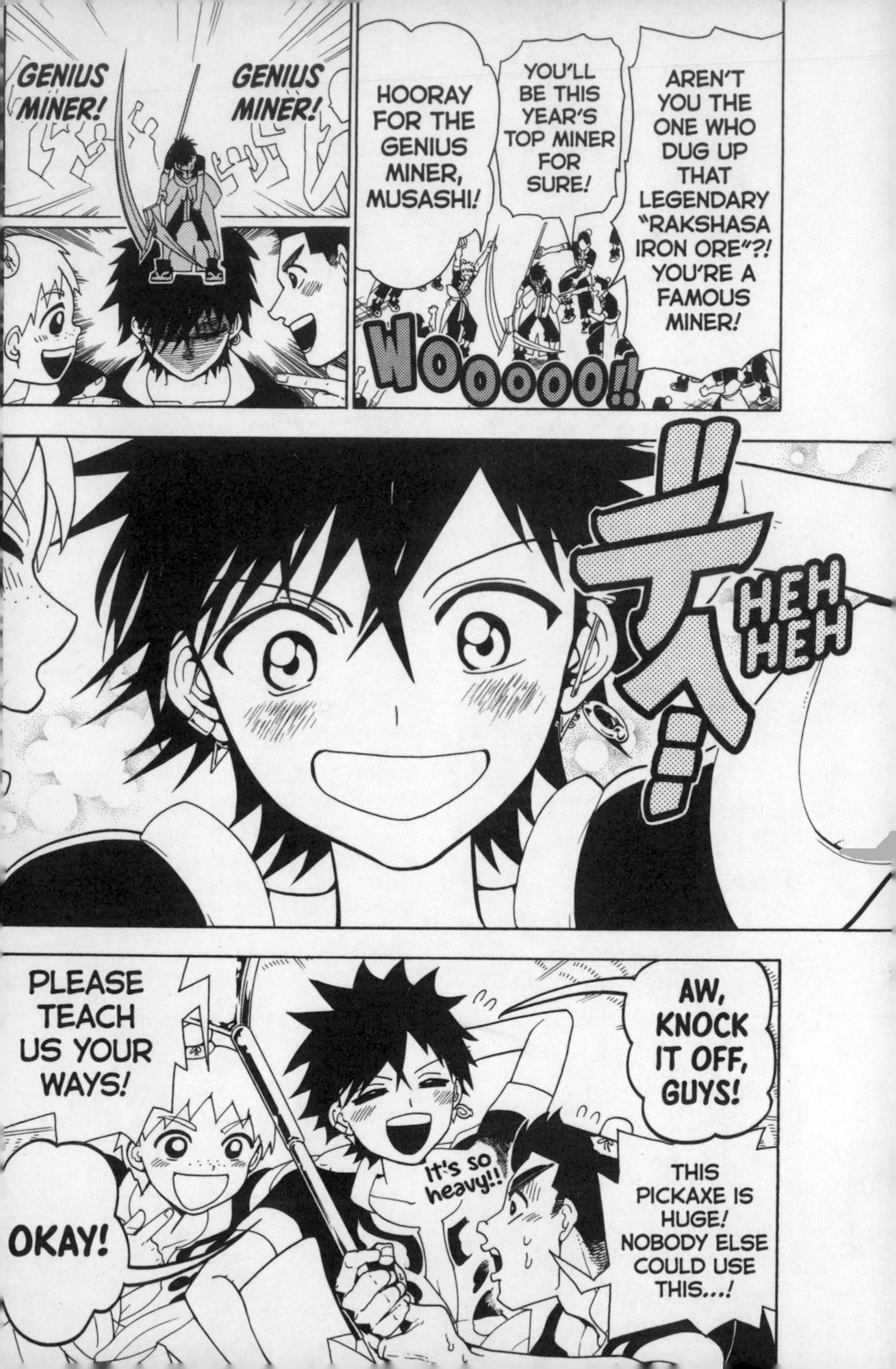
AREN'T YOU THE ONE WHO DUG UP THAT LEGENDARY "RAKSHASA IRON ORE"?! YOU'RE A FAMOUS MINER!
YOU'LL BE THIS YEAR'S TOP MINER FOR SURE!
HOORAY FOR THE GENIUS MINER, MUSASHI!
WOOOOO!!
GENIUS MINER!
GENIUS MINER!
HEH HEH
AW, KNOCK IT OFF, GUYS!
THIS PICKAXE IS HUGE! NOBODY ELSE COULD USE THIS...!
It's so heavy!!
PLEASE TEACH US YOUR WAYS!
OKAY!

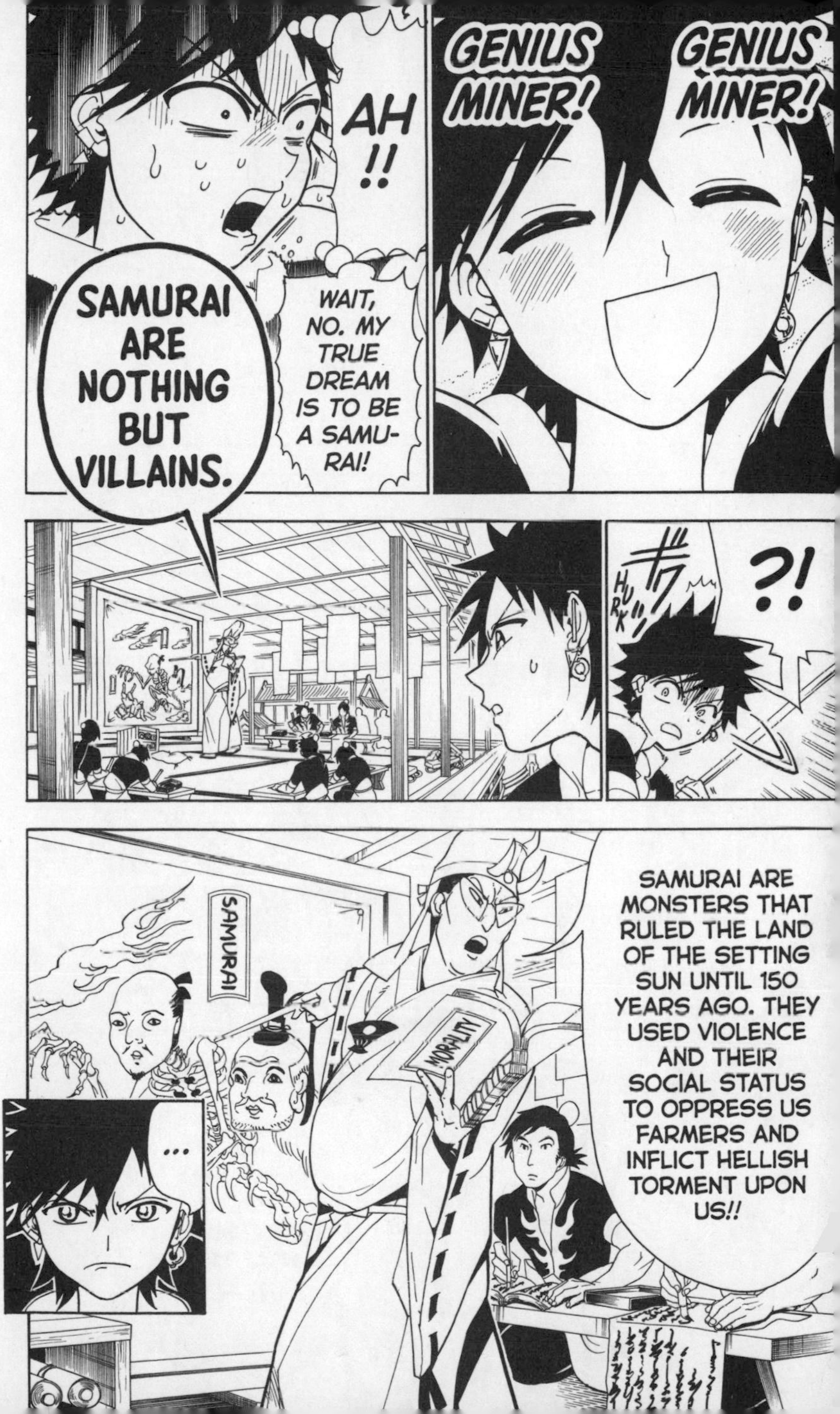
GENIUS MINER!
GENIUS MINER!
AH!!
WAIT, NO. MY TRUE DREAM IS TO BE A SAMURAI!
SAMURAI ARE NOTHING BUT VILLAINS.
HURK!!
?!
SAMURAI ARE MONSTERS THAT RULED THE LAND OF THE SETTING SUN UNTIL 150 YEARS AGO. THEY USED VIOLENCE AND THEIR SOCIAL STATUS TO OPPRESS US FARMERS AND INFLICT HELLISH TORMENT UPON US!!
SAMURAI
MORALITY
...

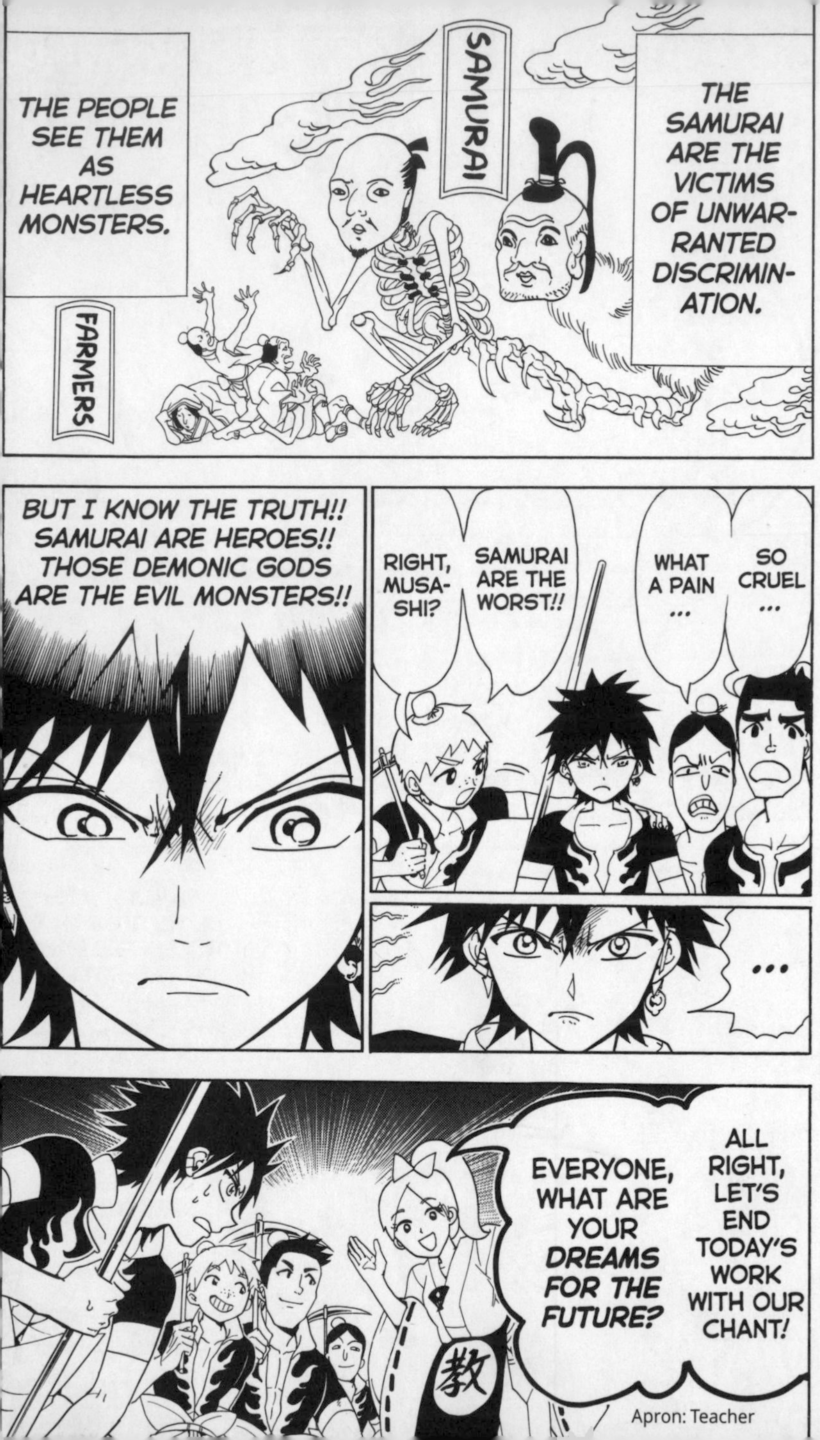
THE SAMURAI ARE THE VICTIMS OF UNWAR-RANTED DISCRIMIN-ATION.
SAMURAI
THE PEOPLE SEE THEM AS HEARTLESS MONSTERS.
FARMERS
SO CRUEL ...
WHAT A PAIN ...
SAMURAI ARE THE WORST!!
RIGHT, MUSA-SHI?
...
BUT I KNOW THE TRUTH!! SAMURAI ARE HEROES!! THOSE DEMONIC GODS ARE THE EVIL MONSTERS!!
ALL RIGHT, LET'S END TODAY'S WORK WITH OUR CHANT!
EVERYONE, WHAT ARE YOUR *DREAMS* FOR THE FUTURE?
教
Apron: Teacher

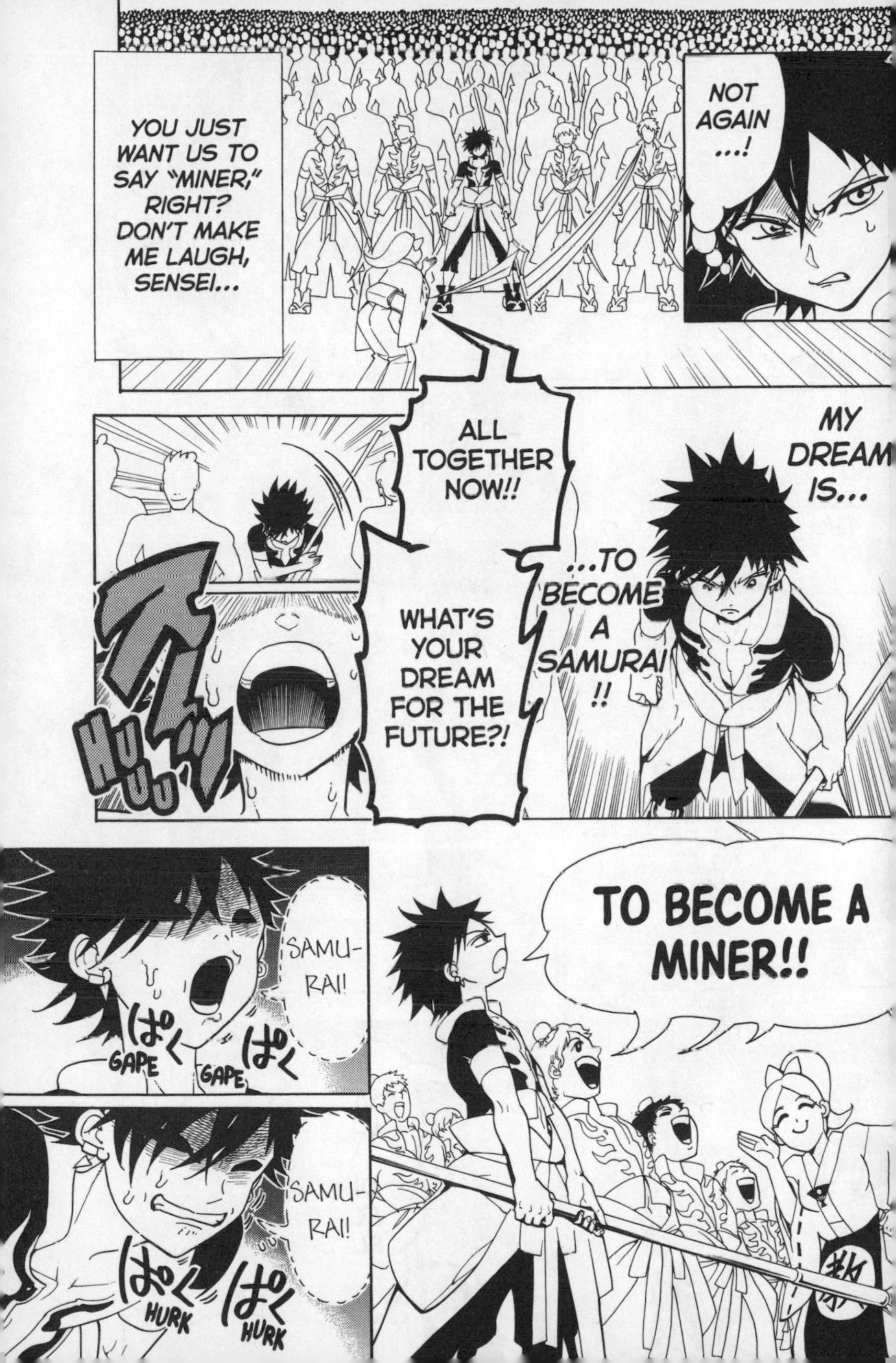
NOT AGAIN ...!
YOU JUST WANT US TO SAY "MINER," RIGHT? DON'T MAKE ME LAUGH, SENSEI...
MY DREAM IS...
...TO BECOME A SAMURAI !!
ALL TOGETHER NOW!!
WHAT'S YOUR DREAM FOR THE FUTURE?!
HUUU
TO BECOME A MINER!!
SAMU-RAI!
ぱく GAPE
ぱく GAPE
SAMU-RAI!
ぱく HURK
ぱく HURK

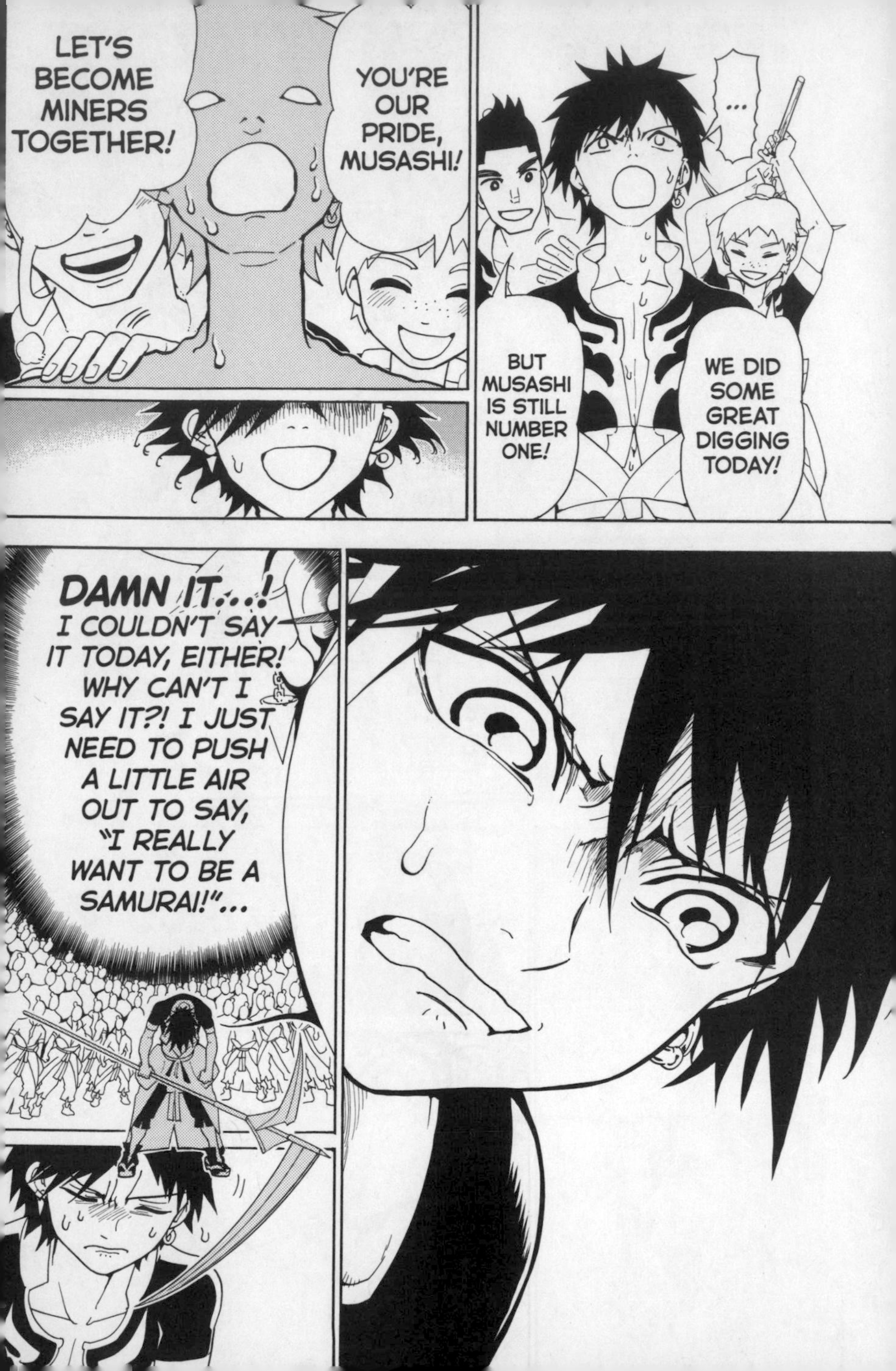
...
WE DID SOME GREAT DIGGING TODAY!
BUT MUSASHI IS STILL NUMBER ONE!
YOU'RE OUR PRIDE, MUSASHI!
LET'S BECOME MINERS TOGETHER!
DAMN IT...! I COULDN'T SAY IT TODAY, EITHER! WHY CAN'T I SAY IT?! I JUST NEED TO PUSH A LITTLE AIR OUT TO SAY, "I REALLY WANT TO BE A SAMURAI!"...

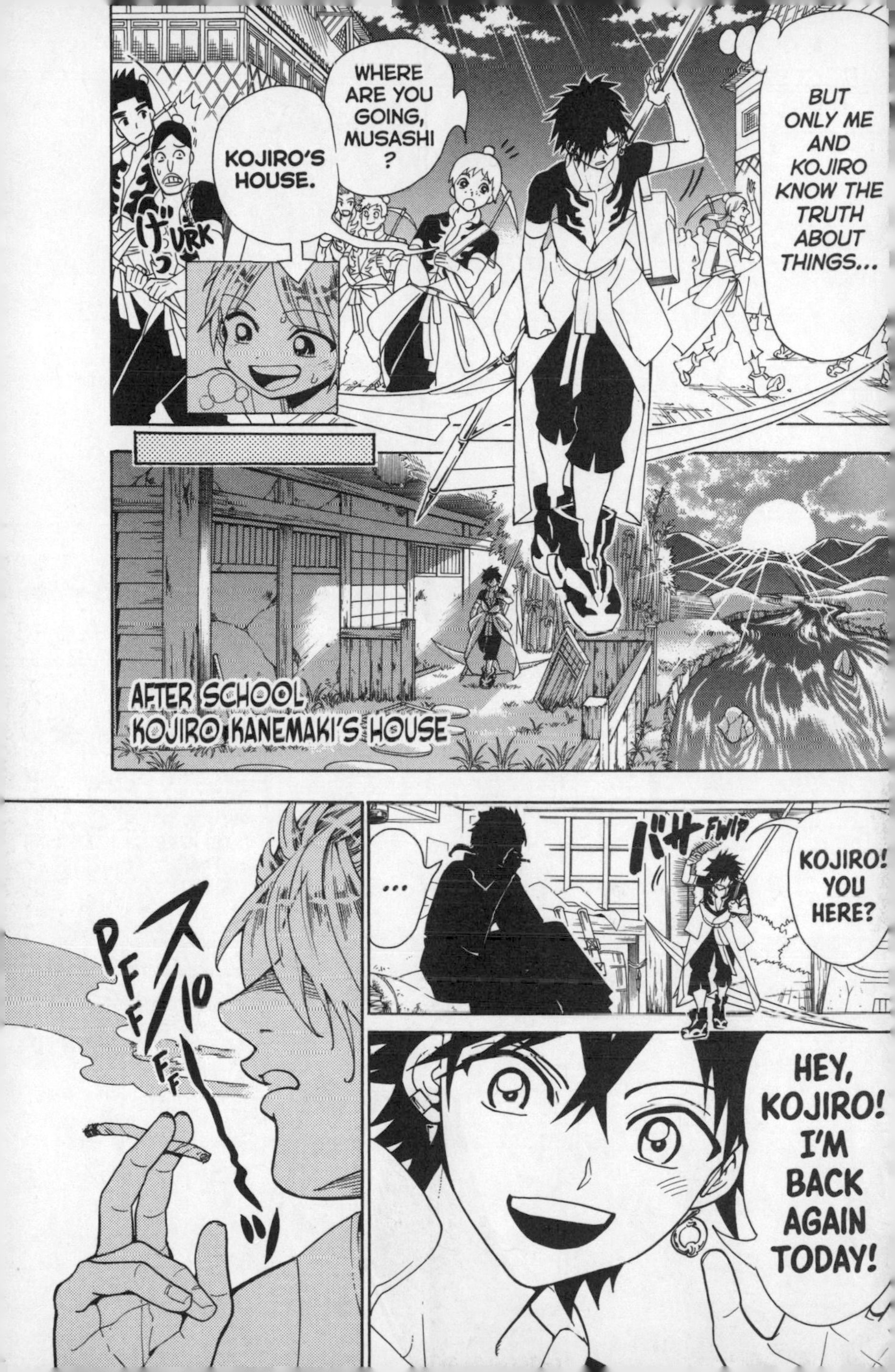
BUT ONLY ME AND KOJIRO KNOW THE TRUTH ABOUT THINGS...
WHERE ARE YOU GOING, MUSASHI?
KOJIRO'S HOUSE.
URK
AFTER SCHOOL
KOJIRO KANEMAKI'S HOUSE
FWIP
KOJIRO! YOU HERE?
...
HEY, KOJIRO! I'M BACK AGAIN TODAY!
PFFFF

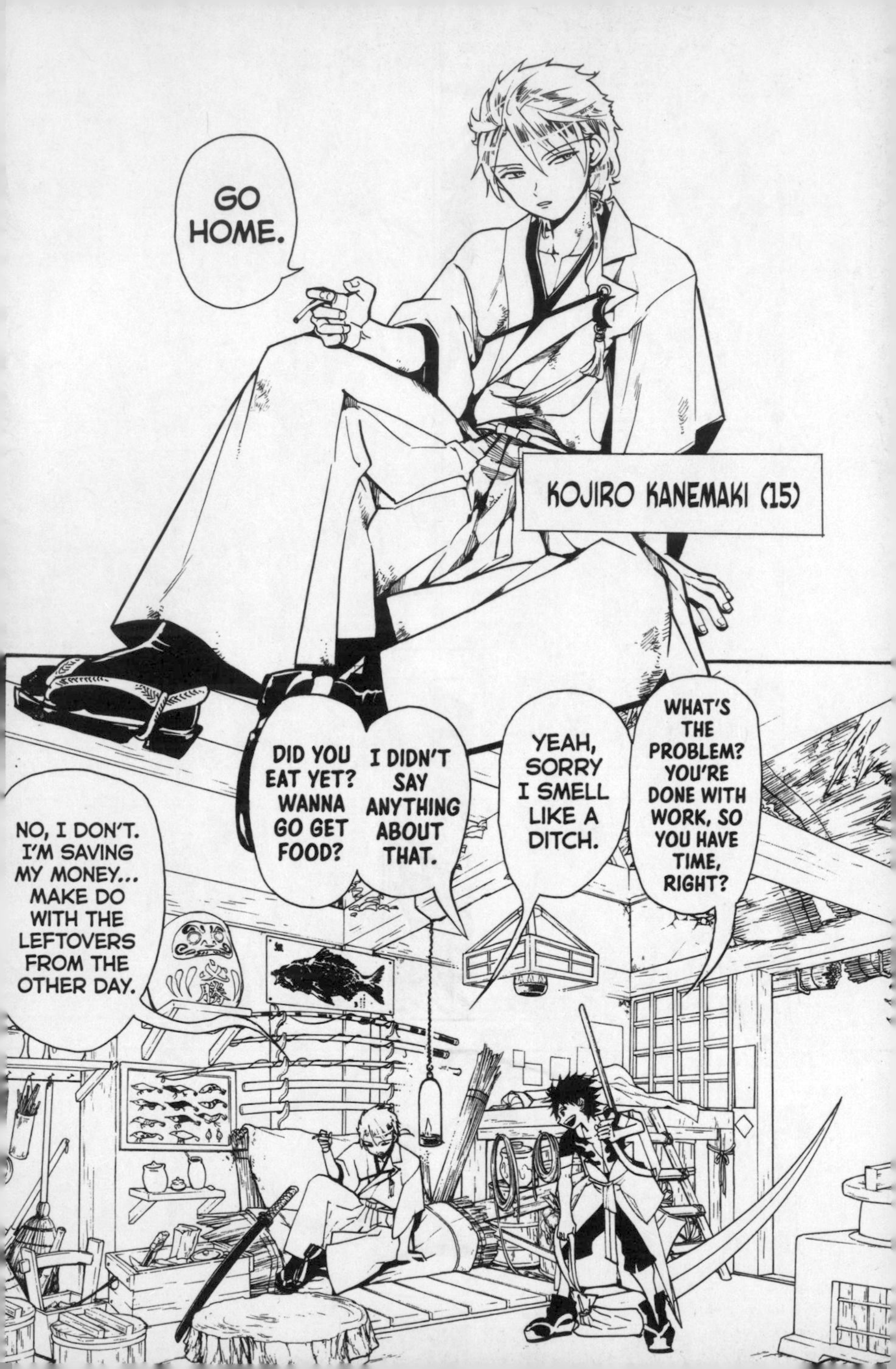
GO HOME.
KOJIRO KANEMAKI (15)
WHAT'S THE PROBLEM? YOU'RE DONE WITH WORK, SO YOU HAVE TIME, RIGHT?
YEAH, SORRY I SMELL LIKE A DITCH.
I DIDN'T SAY ANYTHING ABOUT THAT.
DID YOU EAT YET? WANNA GO GET FOOD?
NO, I DON'T. I'M SAVING MY MONEY... MAKE DO WITH THE LEFTOVERS FROM THE OTHER DAY.

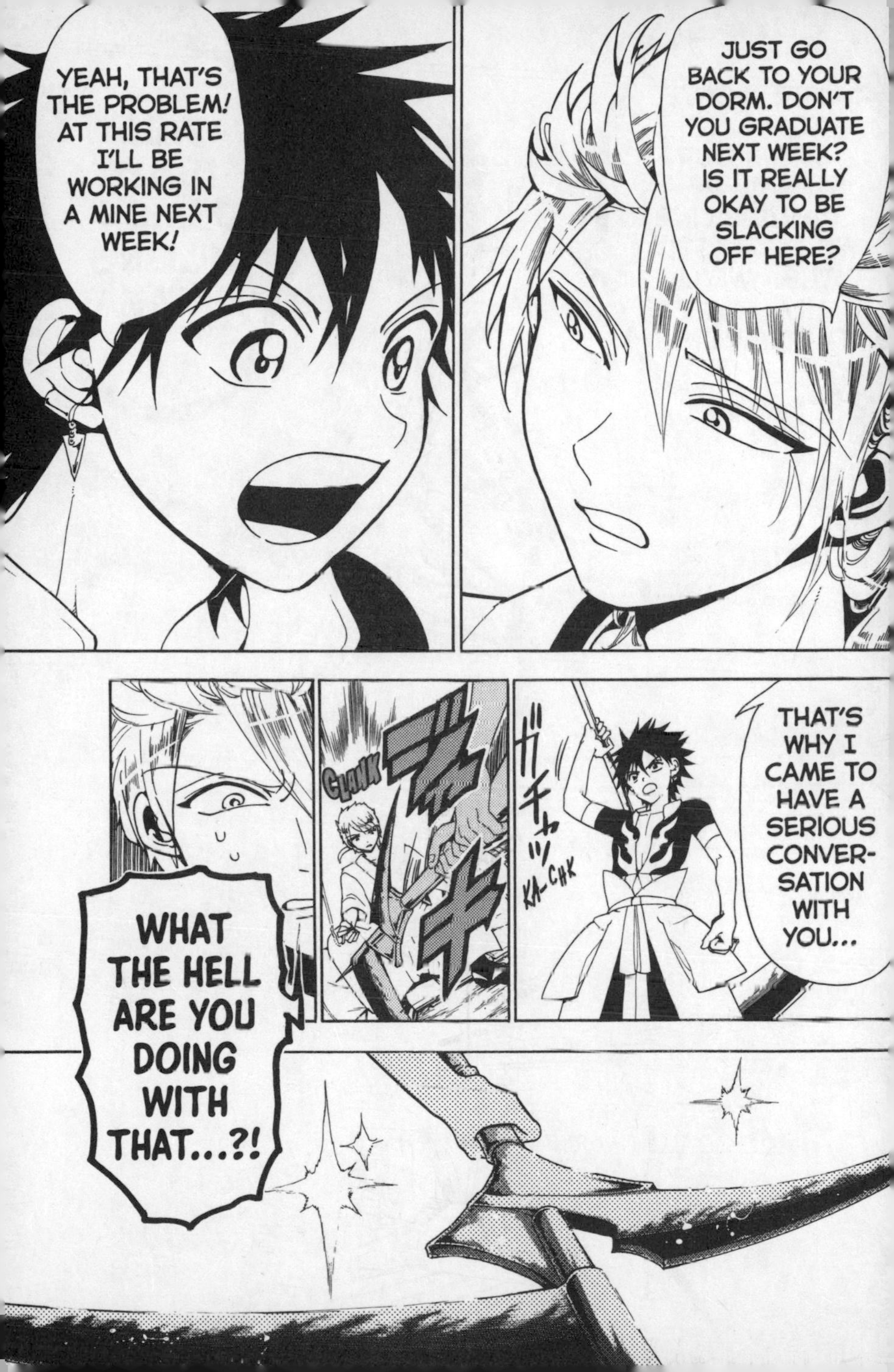
JUST GO BACK TO YOUR DORM. DON'T YOU GRADUATE NEXT WEEK? IS IT REALLY OKAY TO BE SLACKING OFF HERE?
YEAH, THAT'S THE PROBLEM! AT THIS RATE I'LL BE WORKING IN A MINE NEXT WEEK!
THAT'S WHY I CAME TO HAVE A SERIOUS CONVER-SATION WITH YOU...
KA-CHK
CLANK
WHAT THE HELL ARE YOU DOING WITH THAT...?!

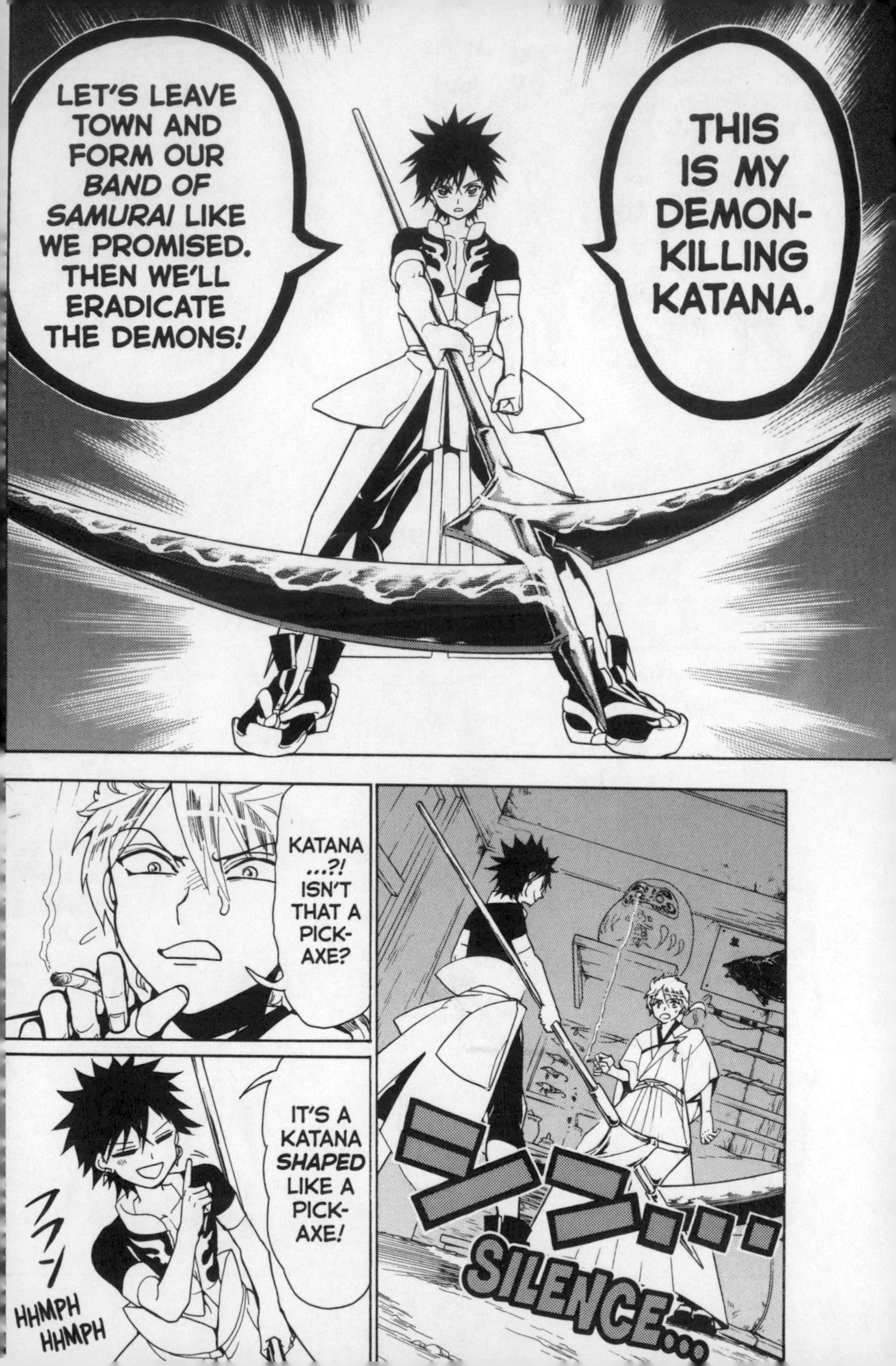

THIS IS MY DEMON-KILLING KATANA.
LET'S LEAVE TOWN AND FORM OUR *BAND OF SAMURAI* LIKE WE PROMISED. THEN WE'LL ERADICATE THE DEMONS!
SILENCE...
KATANA ...?! ISN'T THAT A PICK-AXE?
IT'S A KATANA *SHAPED* LIKE A PICK-AXE!
HHMPH HHMPH

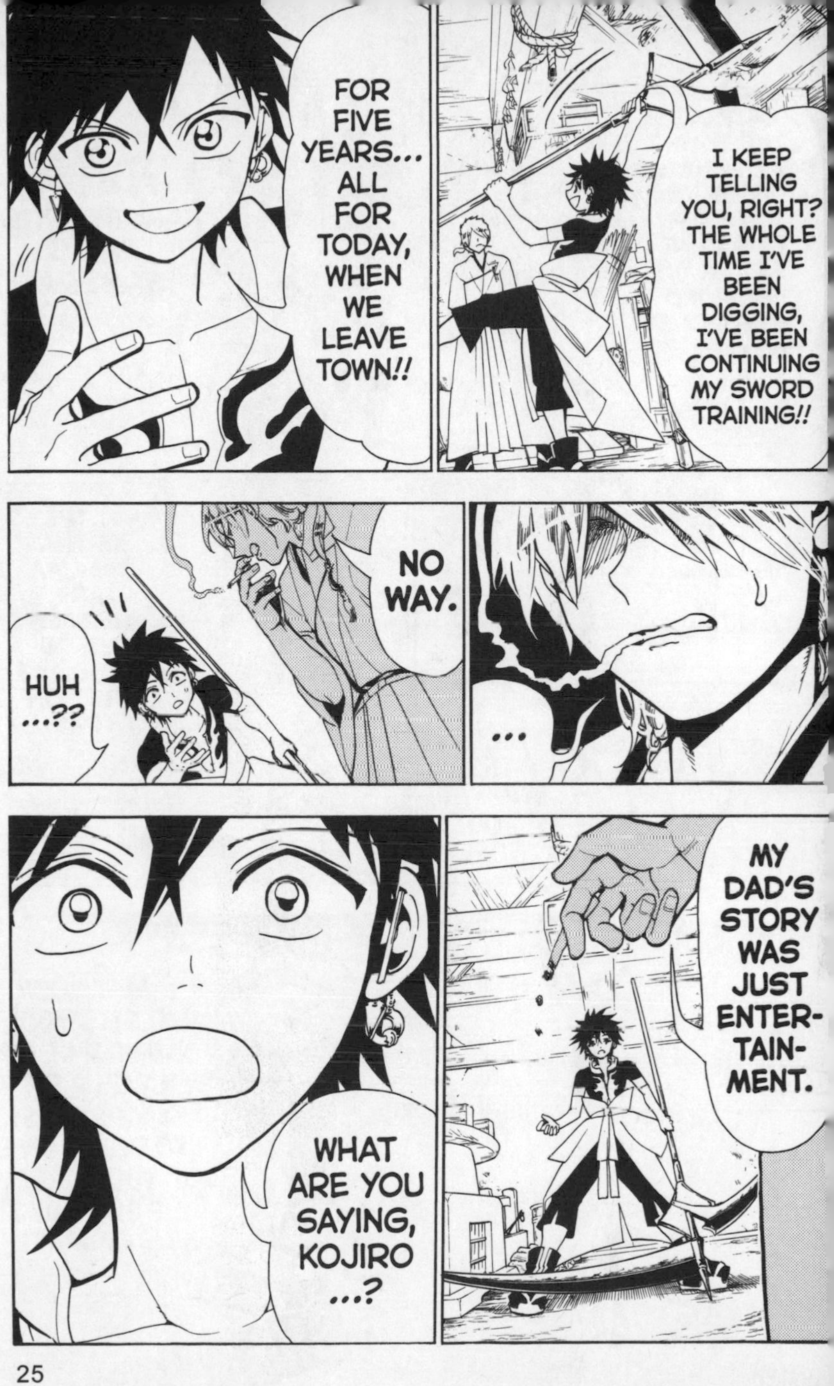
I KEEP TELLING YOU, RIGHT? THE WHOLE TIME I'VE BEEN DIGGING, I'VE BEEN CONTINUING MY SWORD TRAINING!!
FOR FIVE YEARS... ALL FOR TODAY, WHEN WE LEAVE TOWN!!
...
NO WAY.
HUH ...??
MY DAD'S STORY WAS JUST ENTER-TAIN-MENT.
WHAT ARE YOU SAYING, KOJIRO ...?

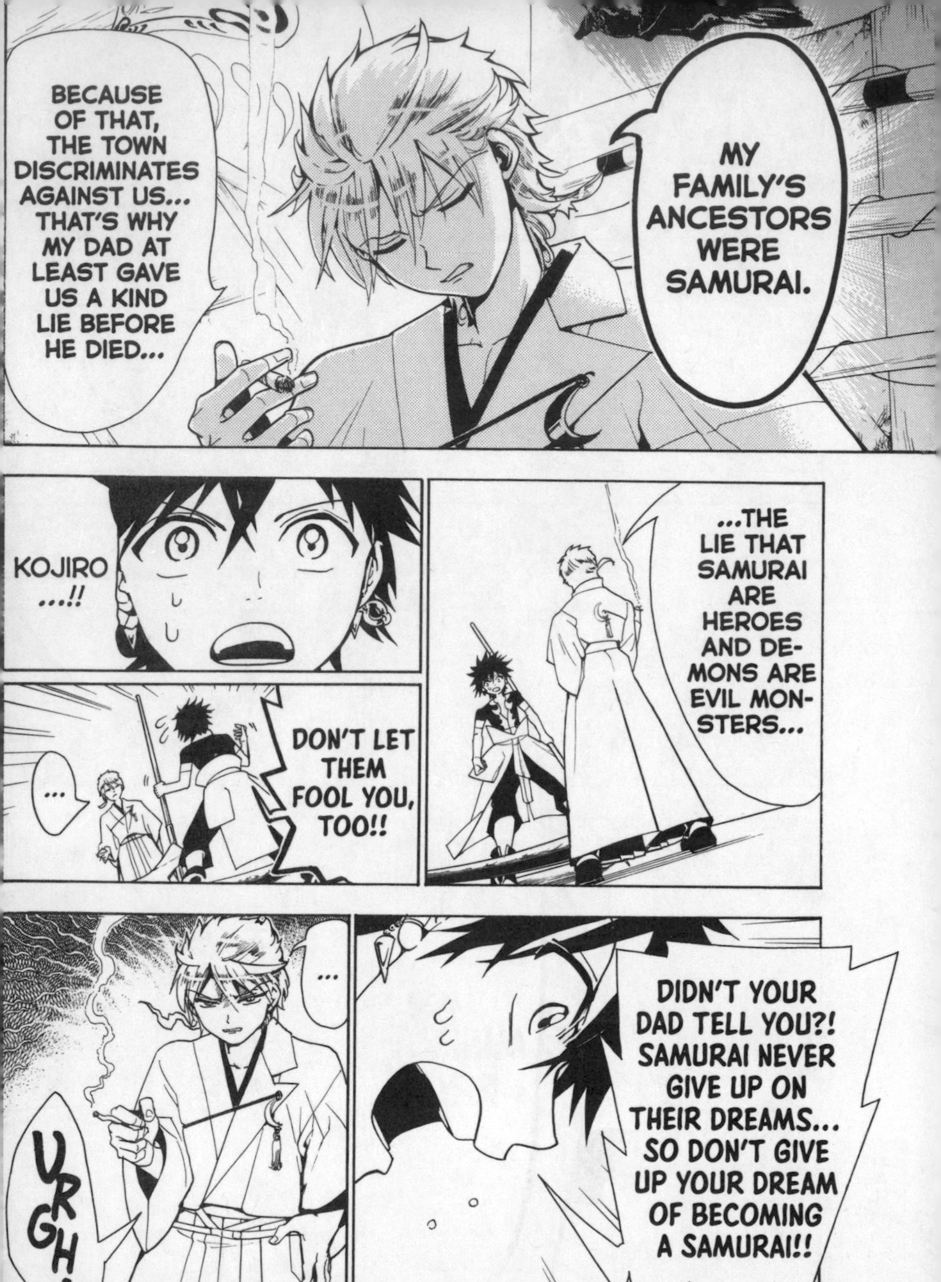
MY FAMILY'S ANCESTORS WERE SAMURAI.
BECAUSE OF THAT, THE TOWN DISCRIMINATES AGAINST US... THAT'S WHY MY DAD AT LEAST GAVE US A KIND LIE BEFORE HE DIED...
...THE LIE THAT SAMURAI ARE HEROES AND DE-MONS ARE EVIL MON-STERS...
KOJIRO ...!!
DON'T LET THEM FOOL YOU, TOO!!
...
DIDN'T YOUR DAD TELL YOU?! SAMURAI NEVER GIVE UP ON THEIR DREAMS... SO DON'T GIVE UP YOUR DREAM OF BECOMING A SAMURAI!!
...
URGH...

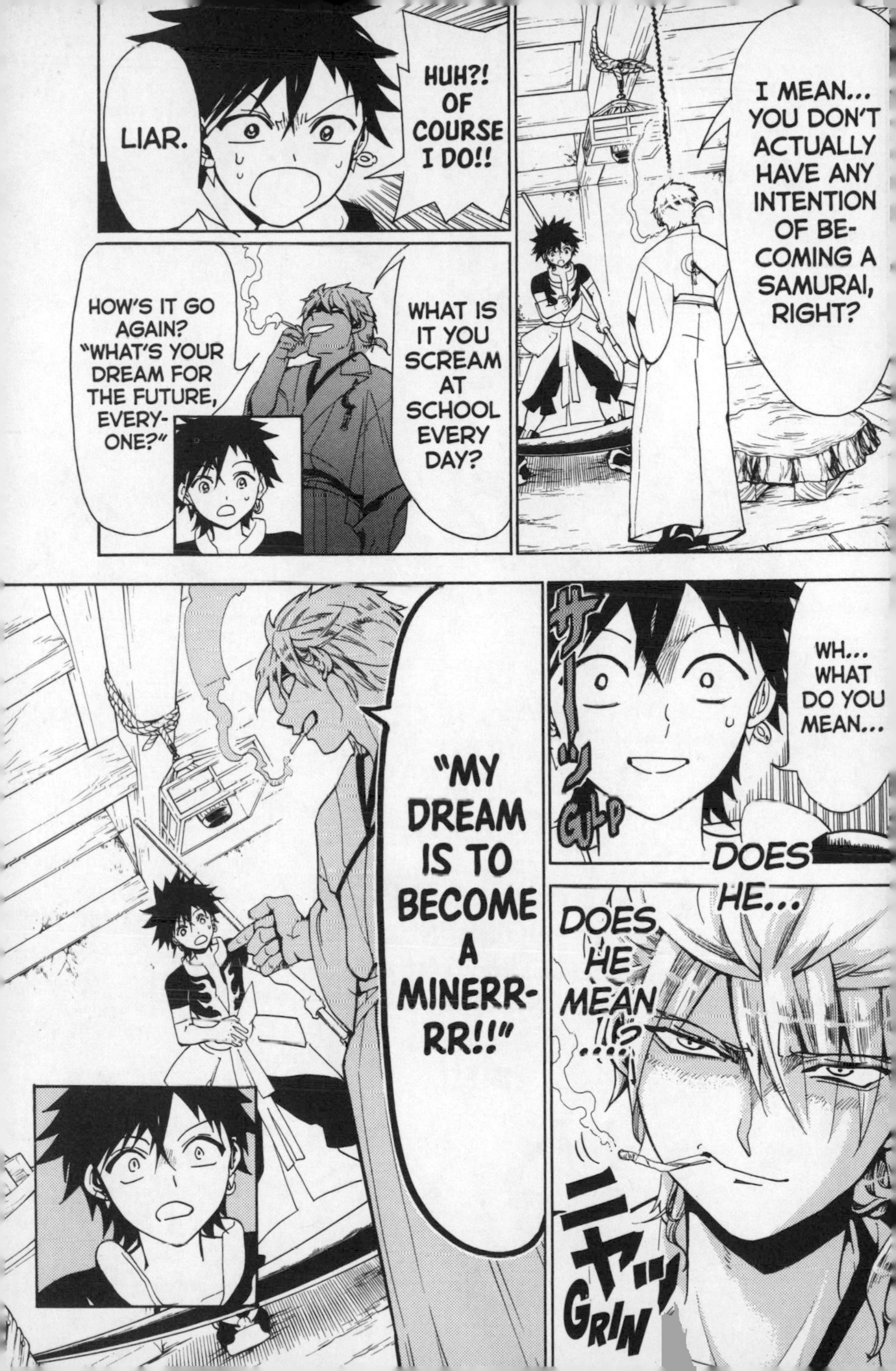
I MEAN... YOU DON'T ACTUALLY HAVE ANY INTENTION OF BECOMING A SAMURAI, RIGHT?
HUH?! OF COURSE I DO!!
LIAR.
WHAT IS IT YOU SCREAM AT SCHOOL EVERY DAY?
HOW'S IT GO AGAIN? "WHAT'S YOUR DREAM FOR THE FUTURE, EVERYONE?"
WH... WHAT DO YOU MEAN...
GULP
DOES HE...
DOES HE MEAN...!?
GRIN
"MY DREAM IS TO BECOME A MINERRRR!!"

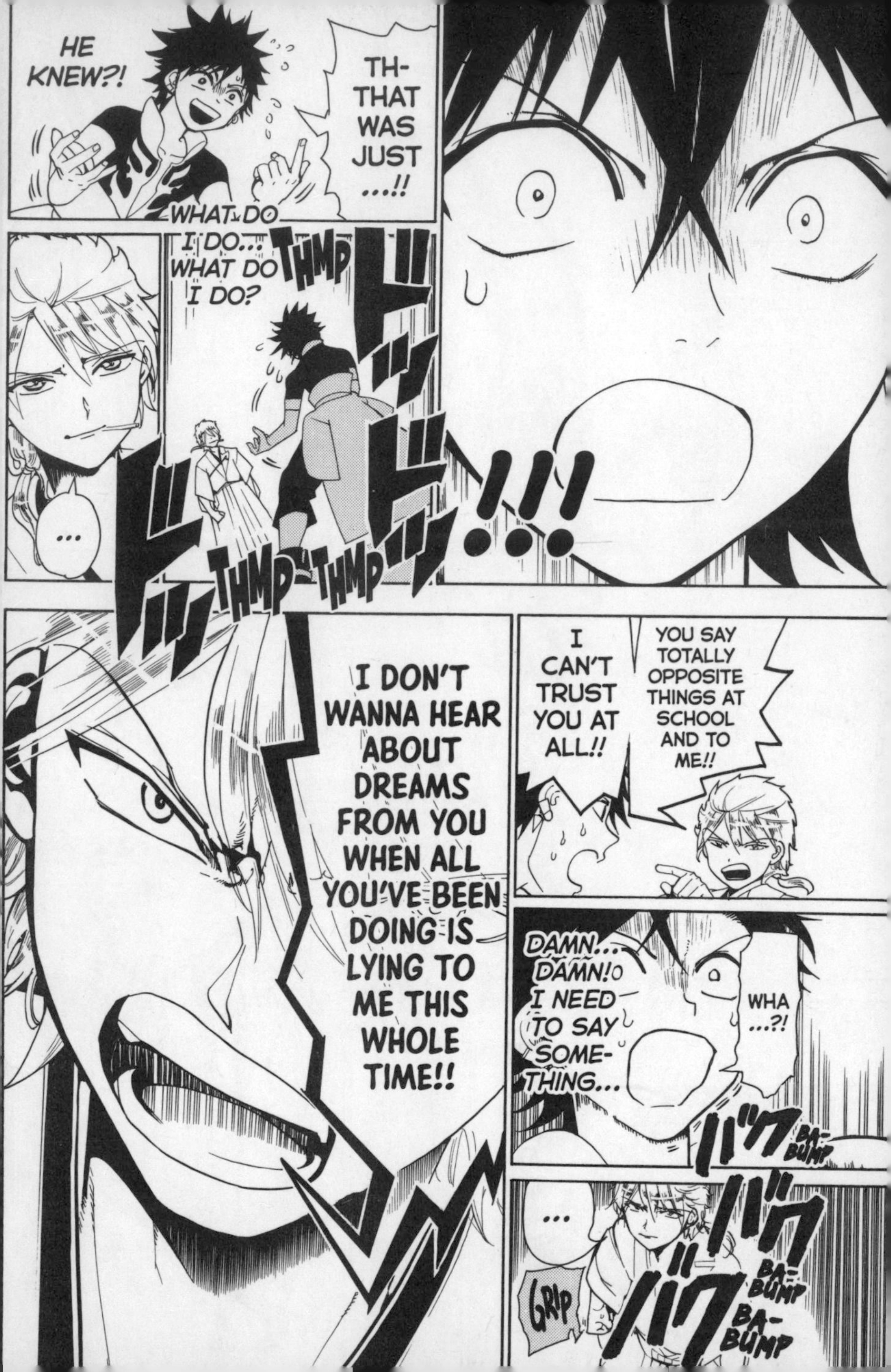
!!!
TH- THAT WAS JUST ...!!
HE KNEW?!
WHAT DO I DO... WHAT DO I DO?
THMP
THMP THMP
...
YOU SAY TOTALLY OPPOSITE THINGS AT SCHOOL AND TO ME!!
I CAN'T TRUST YOU AT ALL!!
WHA ...?!
DAMN... DAMN! I NEED TO SAY SOME- THING...
BA- BUMP
...
BA- BUMP
BA- BUMP
GRIP
I DON'T WANNA HEAR ABOUT DREAMS FROM YOU WHEN ALL YOU'VE BEEN DOING IS LYING TO ME THIS WHOLE TIME!!

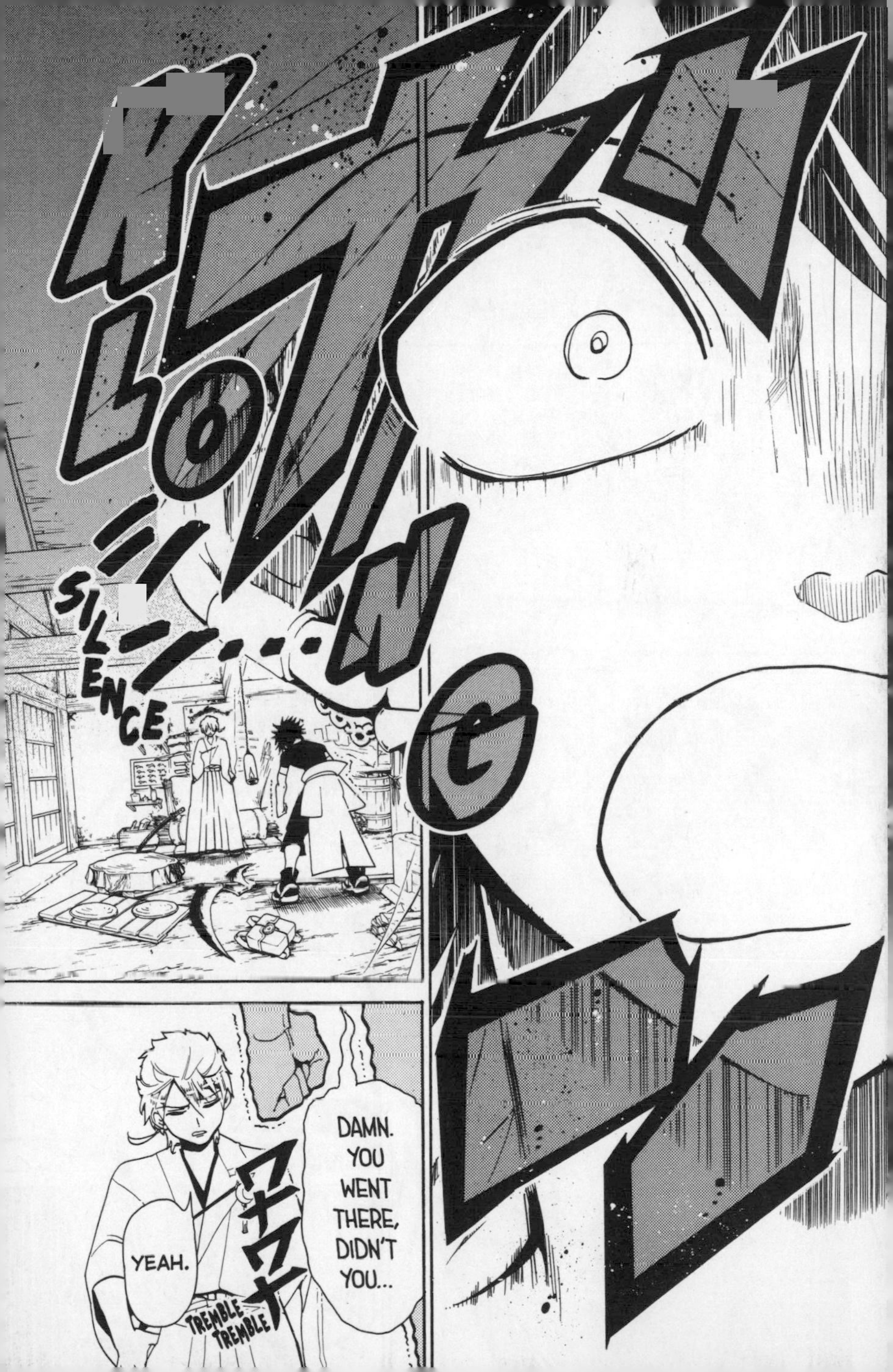
SILENCE
DAMN. YOU WENT THERE, DIDN'T YOU...
ワナワナ
TREMBLE TREMBLE
YEAH.

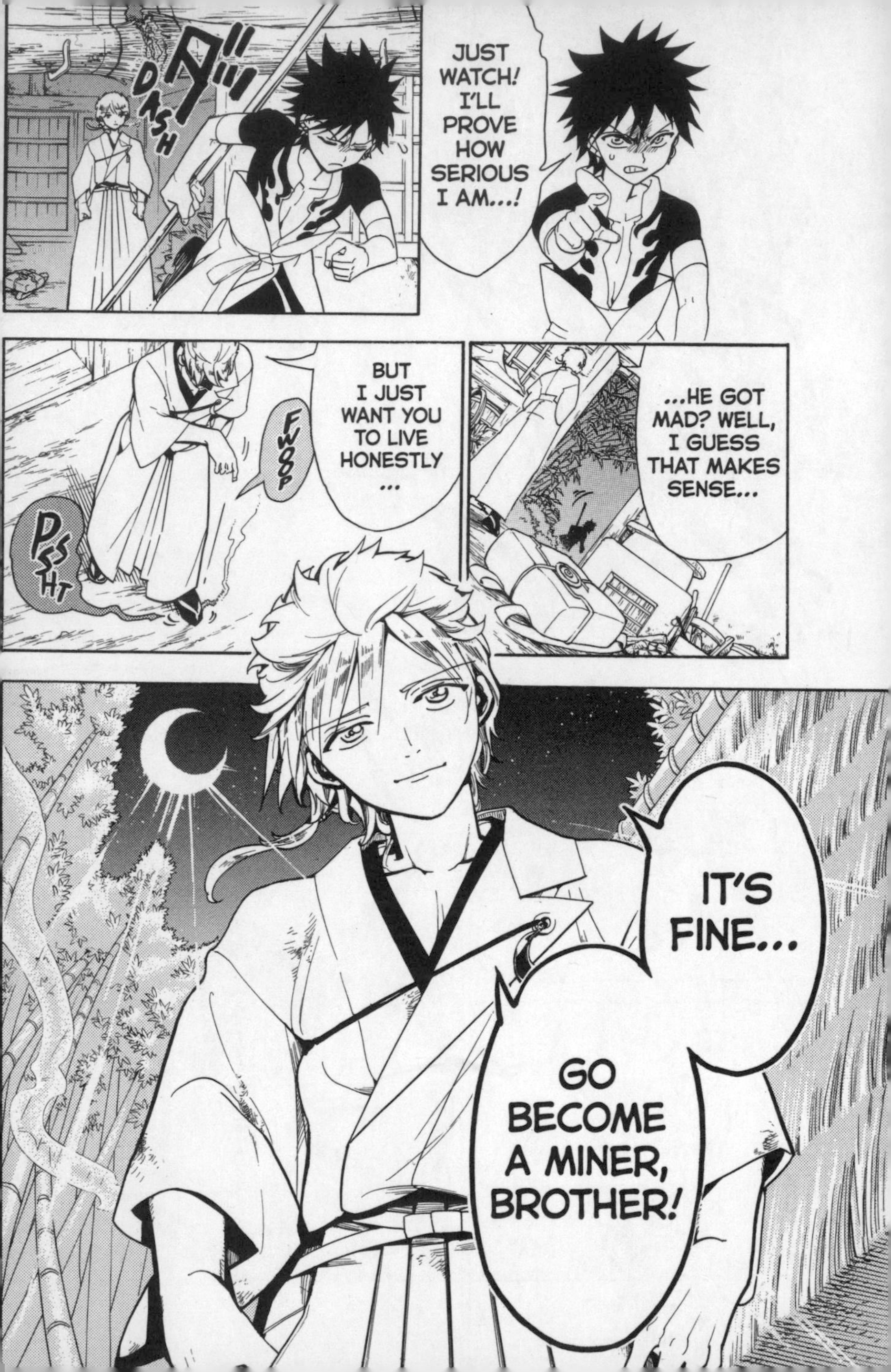
JUST WATCH! I'LL PROVE HOW SERIOUS I AM...!
DASH
...HE GOT MAD? WELL, I GUESS THAT MAKES SENSE...
BUT I JUST WANT YOU TO LIVE HONESTLY...
FWOOP
PSSHT
IT'S FINE...
GO BECOME A MINER, BROTHER!

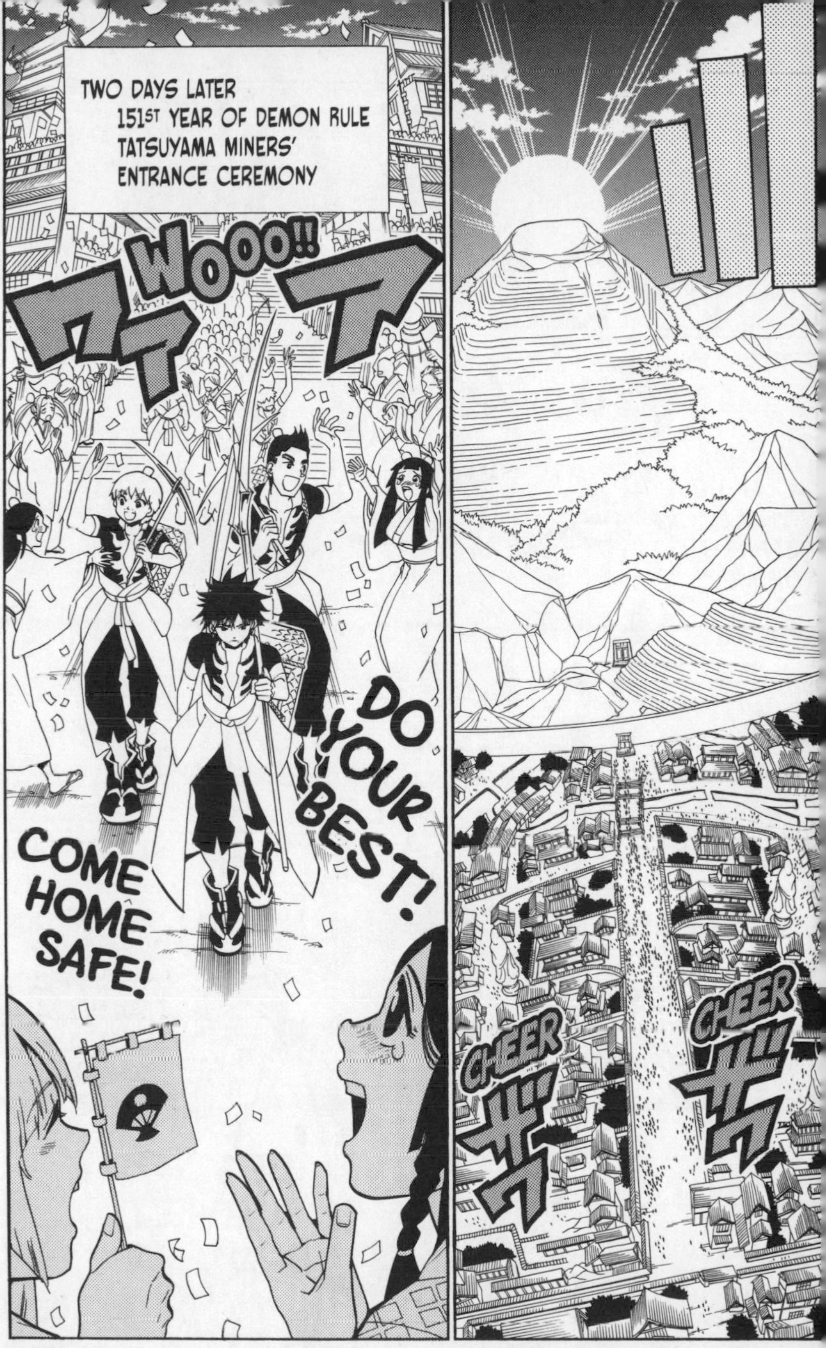
CHEER
CHEER
TWO DAYS LATER
151ST YEAR OF DEMON RULE
TATSUYAMA MINERS' ENTRANCE CEREMONY
WOOO!!
DO YOUR BEST!
COME HOME SAFE!

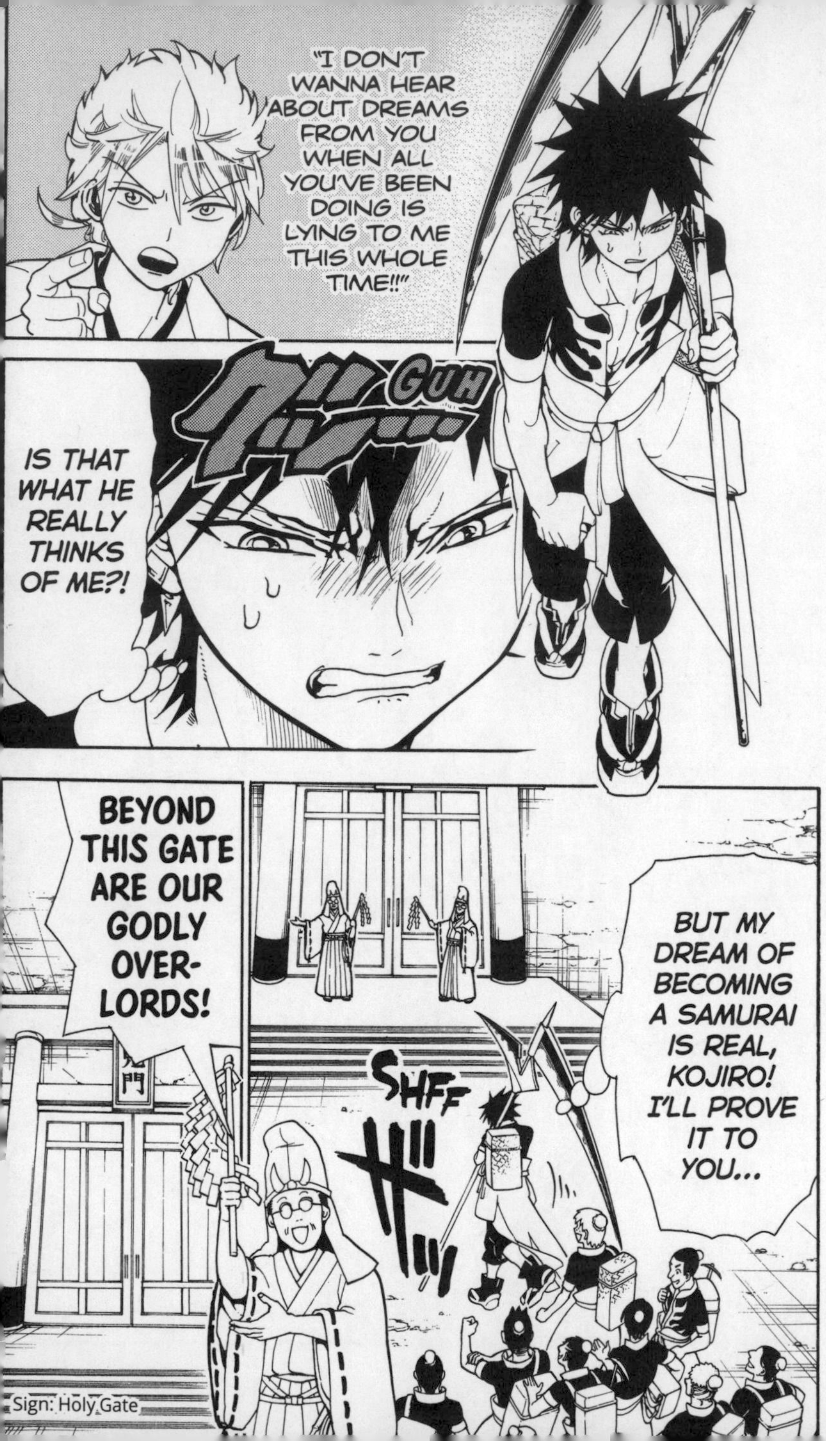
"I DON'T WANNA HEAR ABOUT DREAMS FROM YOU WHEN ALL YOU'VE BEEN DOING IS LYING TO ME THIS WHOLE TIME!!"
GUH
IS THAT WHAT HE REALLY THINKS OF ME?!
BUT MY DREAM OF BECOMING A SAMURAI IS REAL, KOJIRO! I'LL PROVE IT TO YOU...
SHFF
BEYOND THIS GATE ARE OUR GODLY OVER-LORDS!
Sign: Holy Gate

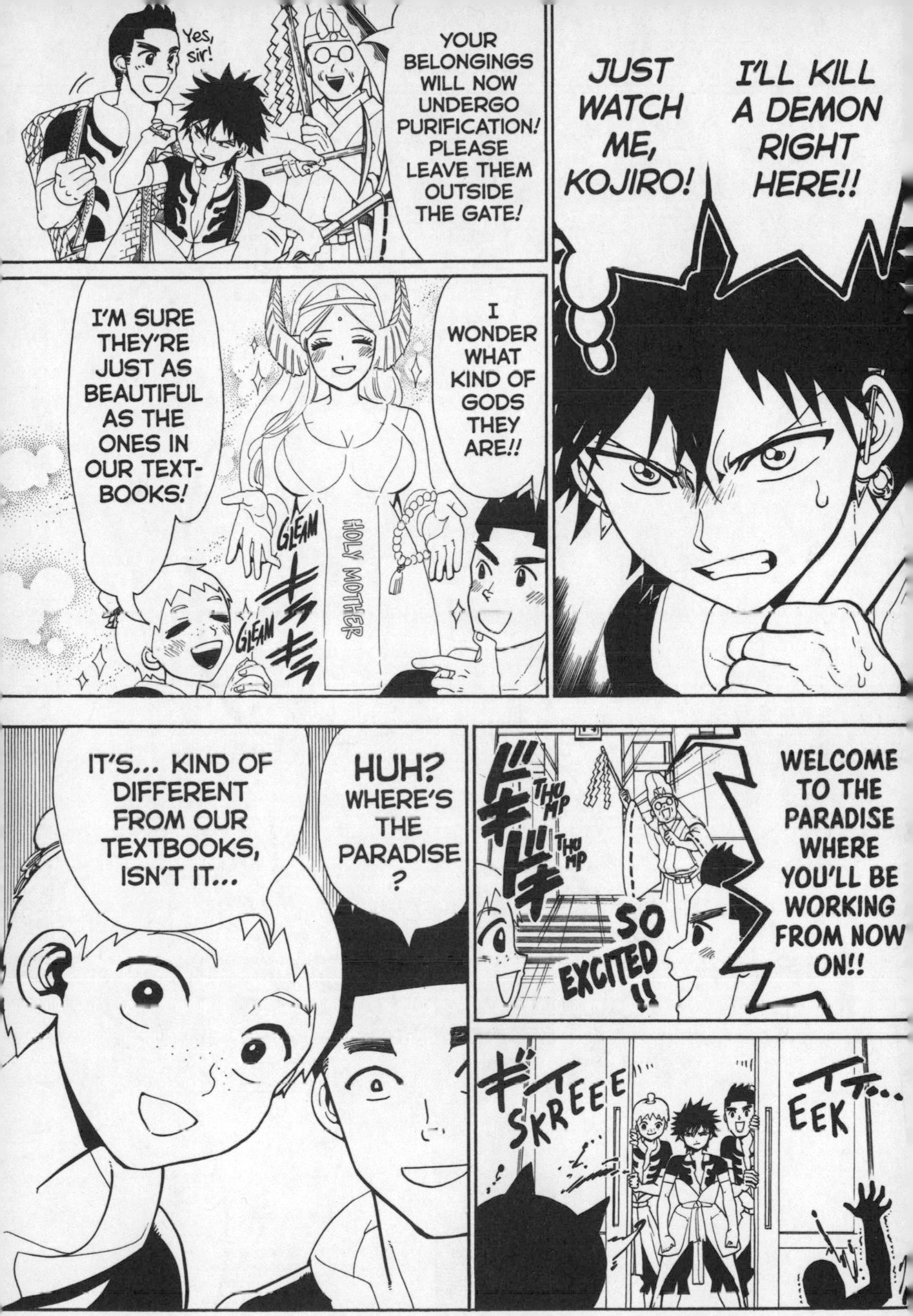
JUST WATCH ME, KOJIRO! I'LL KILL A DEMON RIGHT HERE!!
YOUR BELONGINGS WILL NOW UNDERGO PURIFICATION! PLEASE LEAVE THEM OUTSIDE THE GATE!
Yes, sir!
I WONDER WHAT KIND OF GODS THEY ARE!!
GLEAM
HOLY MOTHER
GLEAM
I'M SURE THEY'RE JUST AS BEAUTIFUL AS THE ONES IN OUR TEXT-BOOKS!
WELCOME TO THE PARADISE WHERE YOU'LL BE WORKING FROM NOW ON!!
THUMP
THUMP
SO EXCITED!!
EEK
SKREEE
HUH? WHERE'S THE PARADISE?
IT'S... KIND OF DIFFERENT FROM OUR TEXTBOOKS, ISN'T IT...

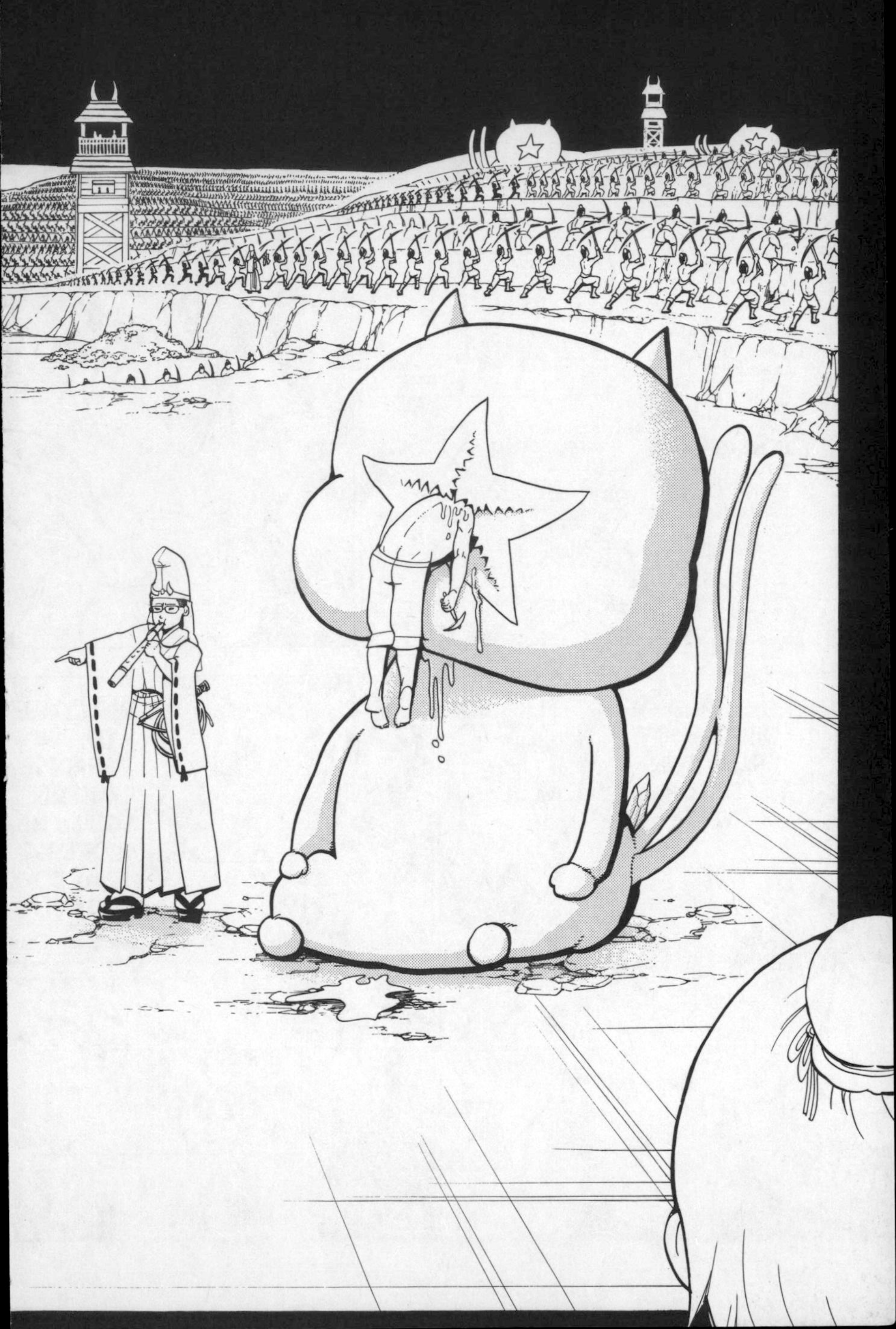

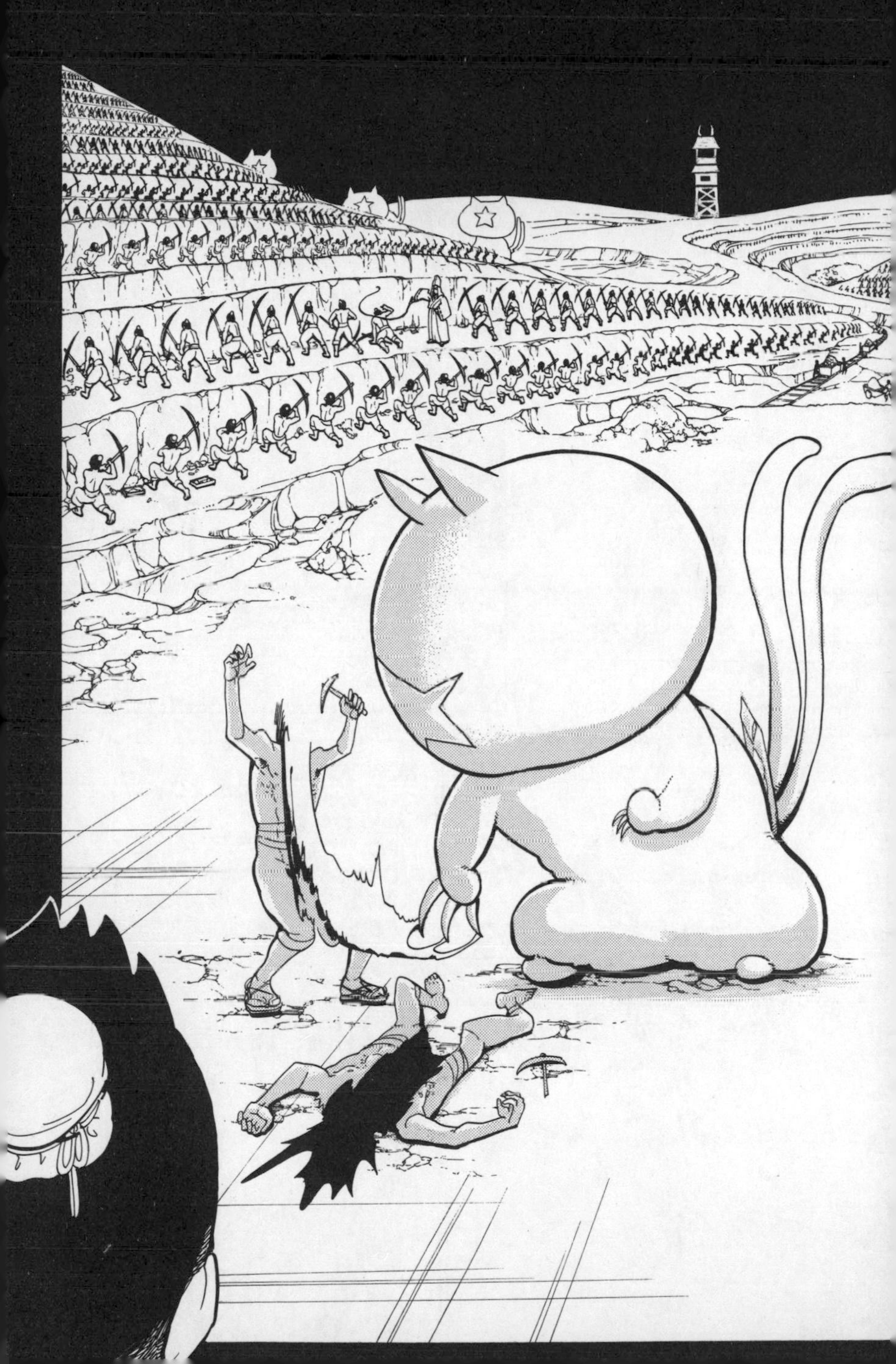

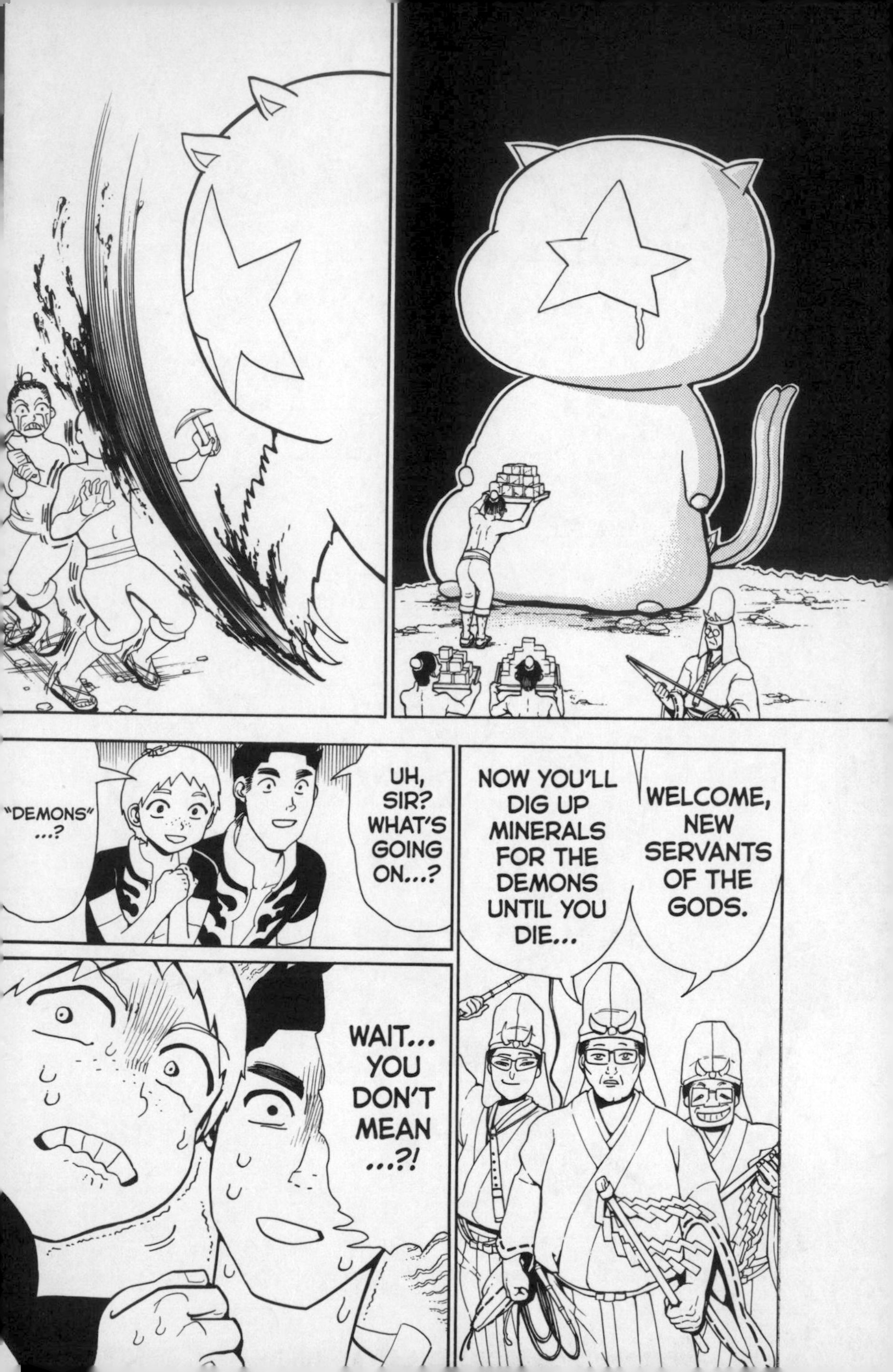
WELCOME, NEW SERVANTS OF THE GODS.
NOW YOU'LL DIG UP MINERALS FOR THE DEMONS UNTIL YOU DIE...
UH, SIR? WHAT'S GOING ON...?
"DEMONS" ...?
WAIT... YOU DON'T MEAN ...?!

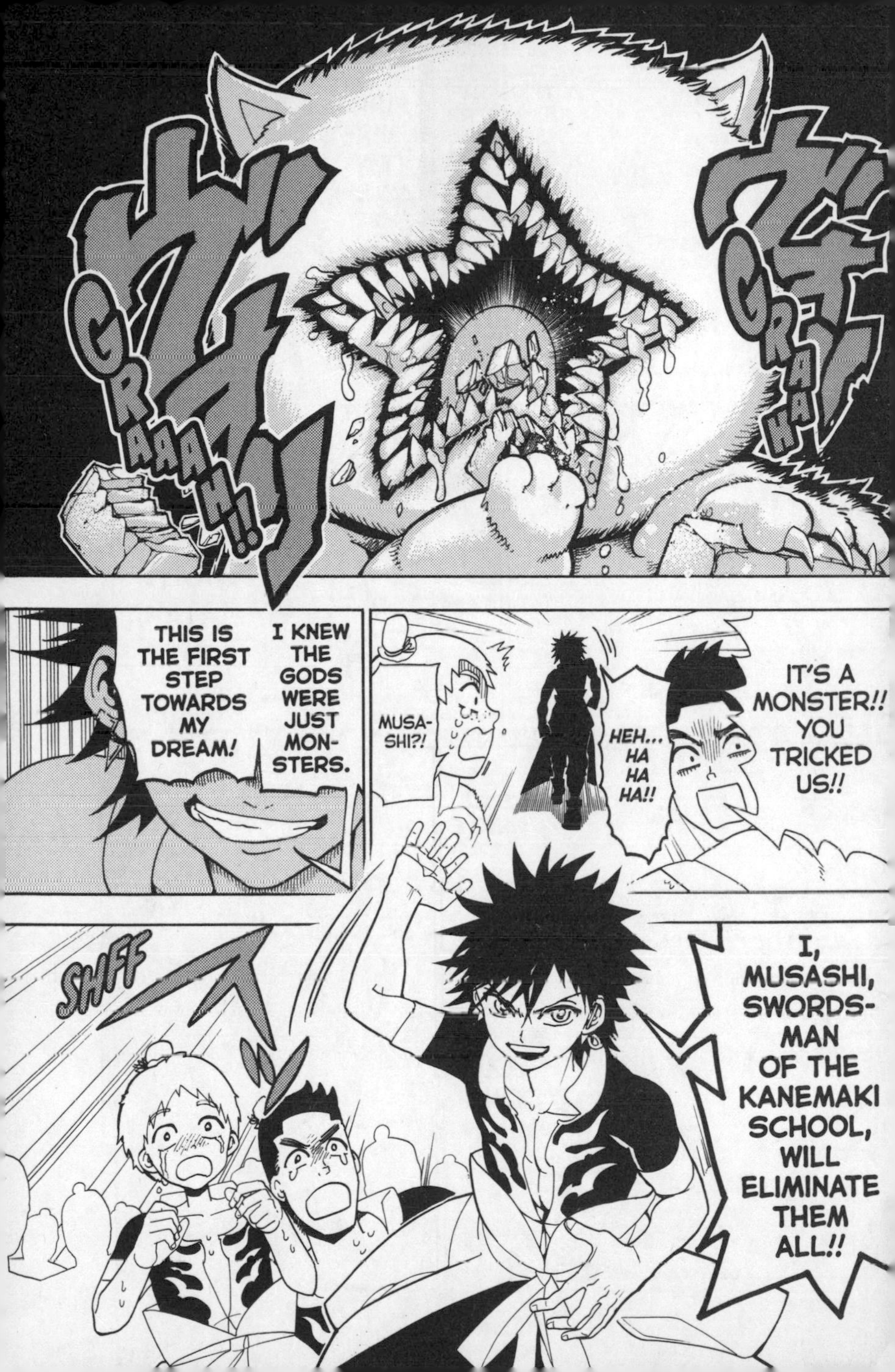
GRAAH
GRAAAAH!!
IT'S A MONSTER!! YOU TRICKED US!!
HEH... HA HA HA!!
MUSA-SHI?!
I KNEW THE GODS WERE JUST MON-STERS.
THIS IS THE FIRST STEP TOWARDS MY DREAM!
I, MUSASHI, SWORDS-MAN OF THE KANEMAKI SCHOOL, WILL ELIMINATE THEM ALL!!
SHFF

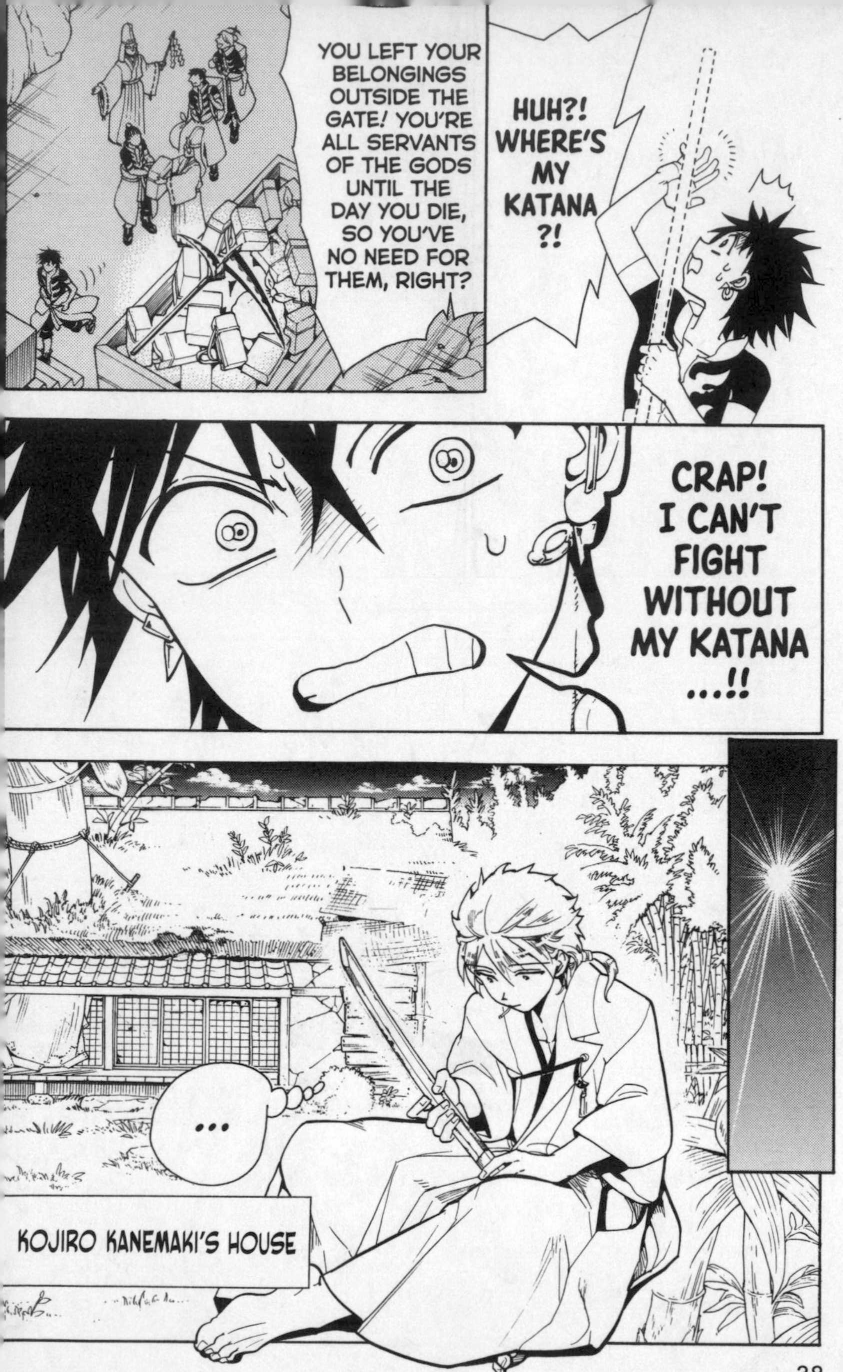
HUH?! WHERE'S MY KATANA ?!
YOU LEFT YOUR BELONGINGS OUTSIDE THE GATE! YOU'RE ALL SERVANTS OF THE GODS UNTIL THE DAY YOU DIE, SO YOU'VE NO NEED FOR THEM, RIGHT?
CRAP! I CAN'T FIGHT WITHOUT MY KATANA ...!!
...
KOJIRO KANEMAKI'S HOUSE

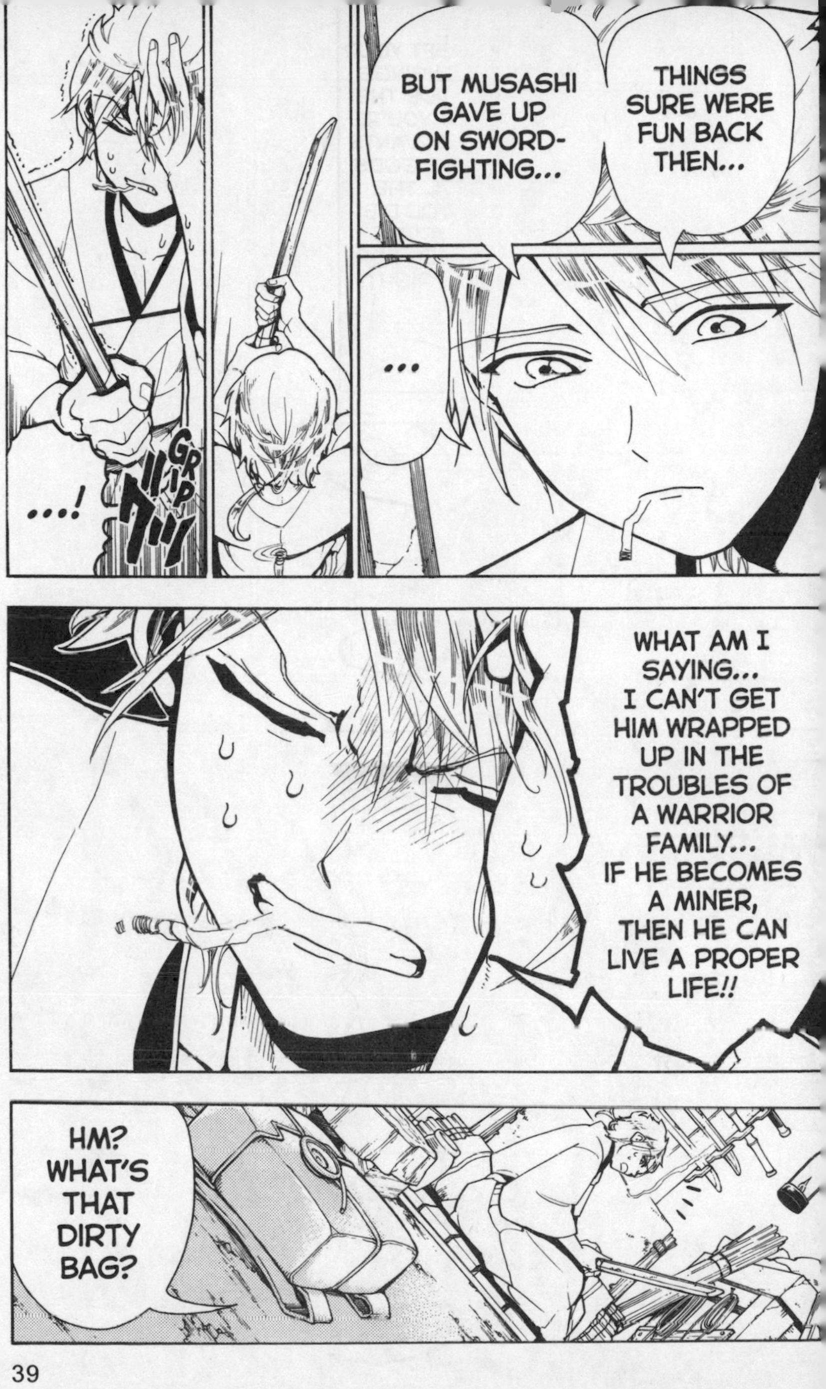
THINGS SURE WERE FUN BACK THEN...
BUT MUSASHI GAVE UP ON SWORD-FIGHTING...
...
GRIP
...!
WHAT AM I SAYING... I CAN'T GET HIM WRAPPED UP IN THE TROUBLES OF A WARRIOR FAMILY... IF HE BECOMES A MINER, THEN HE CAN LIVE A PROPER LIFE!!
HM? WHAT'S THAT DIRTY BAG?

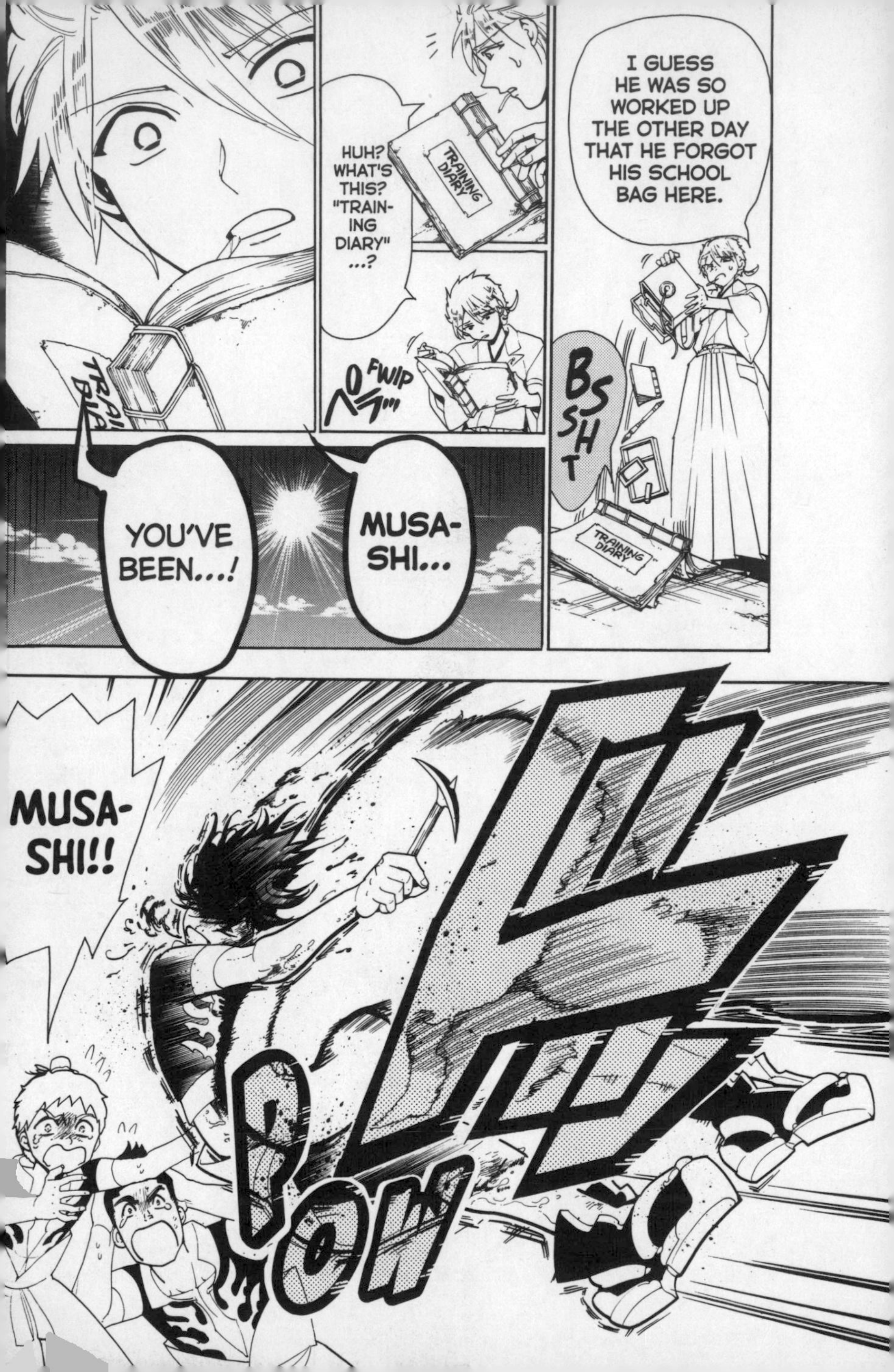
I GUESS HE WAS SO WORKED UP THE OTHER DAY THAT HE FORGOT HIS SCHOOL BAG HERE.
BSSHT
TRAINING DIARY
TRAINING DIARY
HUH? WHAT'S THIS? "TRAIN-ING DIARY" ...?
FWIP
MUSA-SHI...
YOU'VE BEEN...!
MUSA-SHI!!
POW

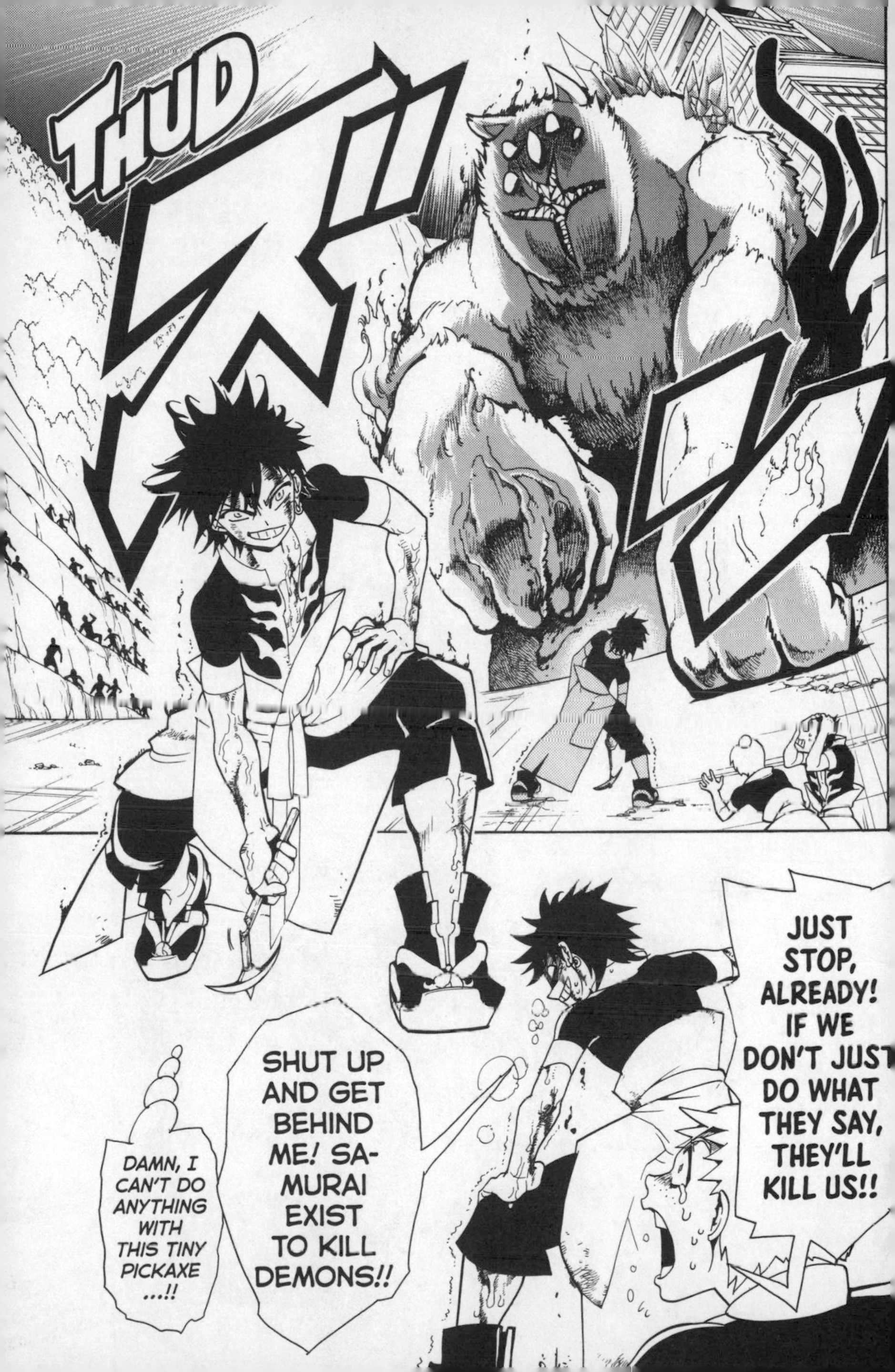
THUD
JUST STOP, ALREADY! IF WE DON'T JUST DO WHAT THEY SAY, THEY'LL KILL US!!
SHUT UP AND GET BEHIND ME! SA-MURAI EXIST TO KILL DEMONS!!
DAMN, I CAN'T DO ANYTHING WITH THIS TINY PICKAXE ...!!

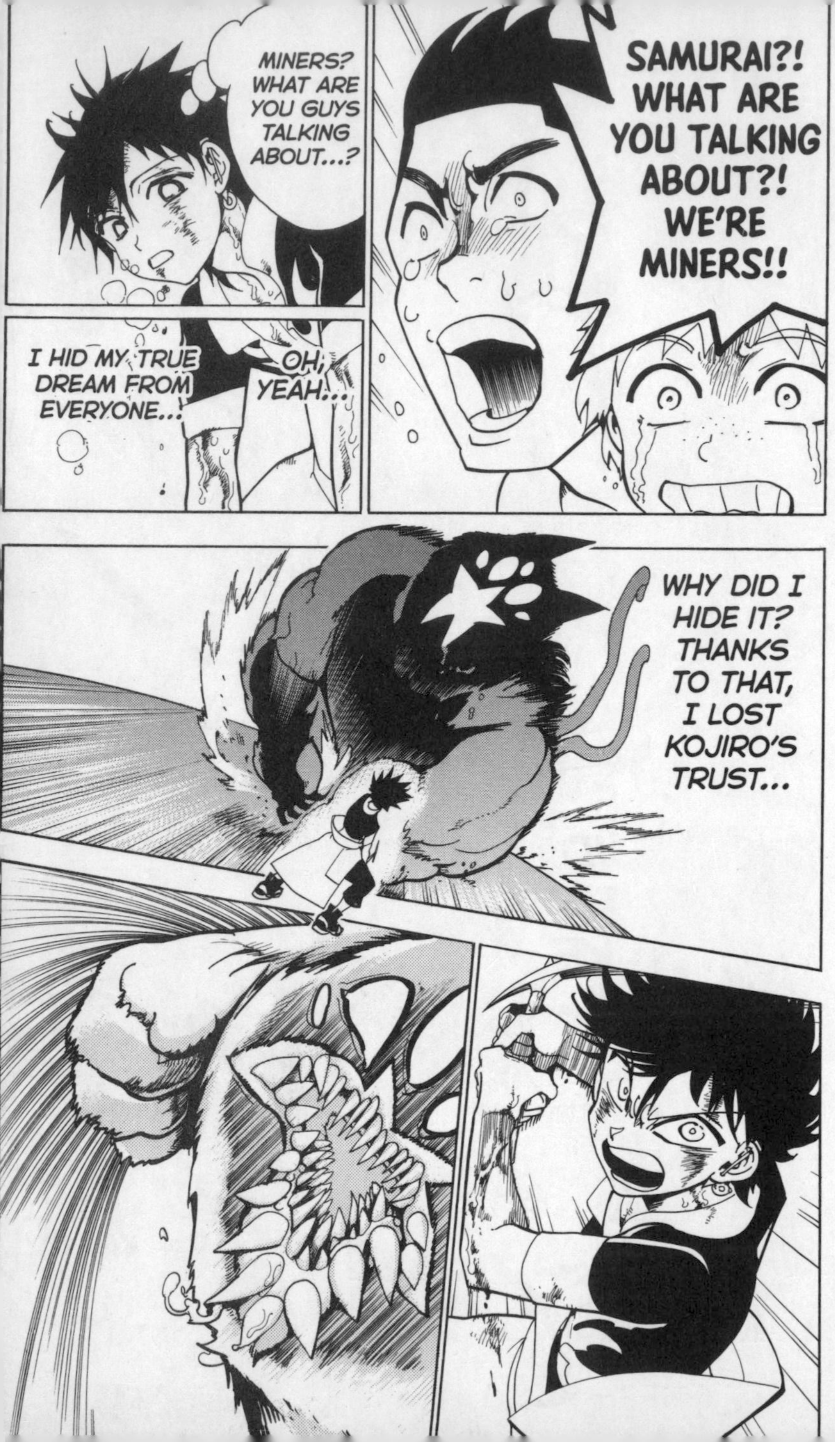
SAMURAI?! WHAT ARE YOU TALKING ABOUT?! WE'RE MINERS!!
MINERS? WHAT ARE YOU GUYS TALKING ABOUT...?
OH, YEAH...
I HID MY TRUE DREAM FROM EVERYONE...
WHY DID I HIDE IT? THANKS TO THAT, I LOST KOJIRO'S TRUST...

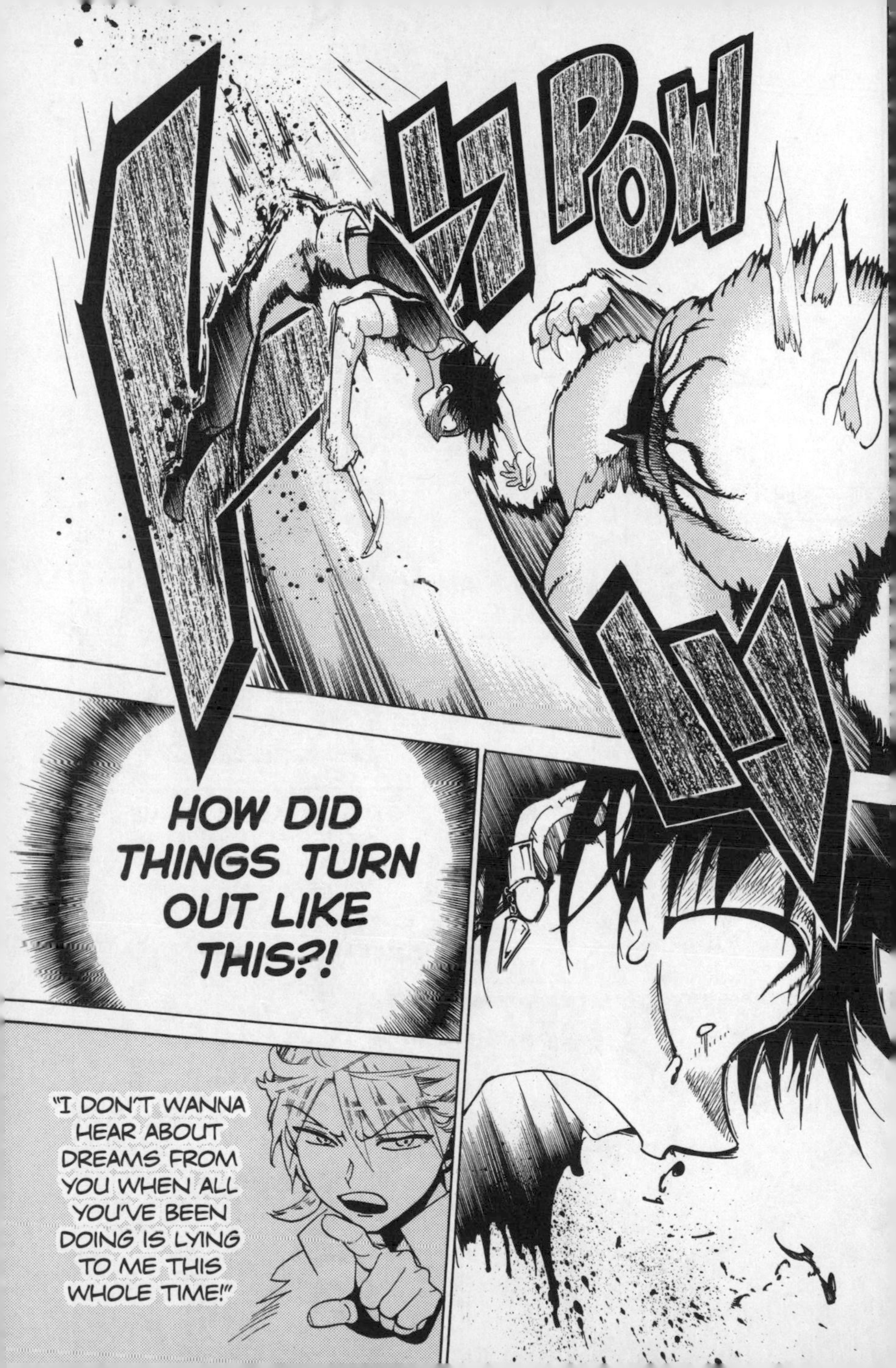
POW
HOW DID THINGS TURN OUT LIKE THIS?!
"I DON'T WANNA HEAR ABOUT DREAMS FROM YOU WHEN ALL YOU'VE BEEN DOING IS LYING TO ME THIS WHOLE TIME!"

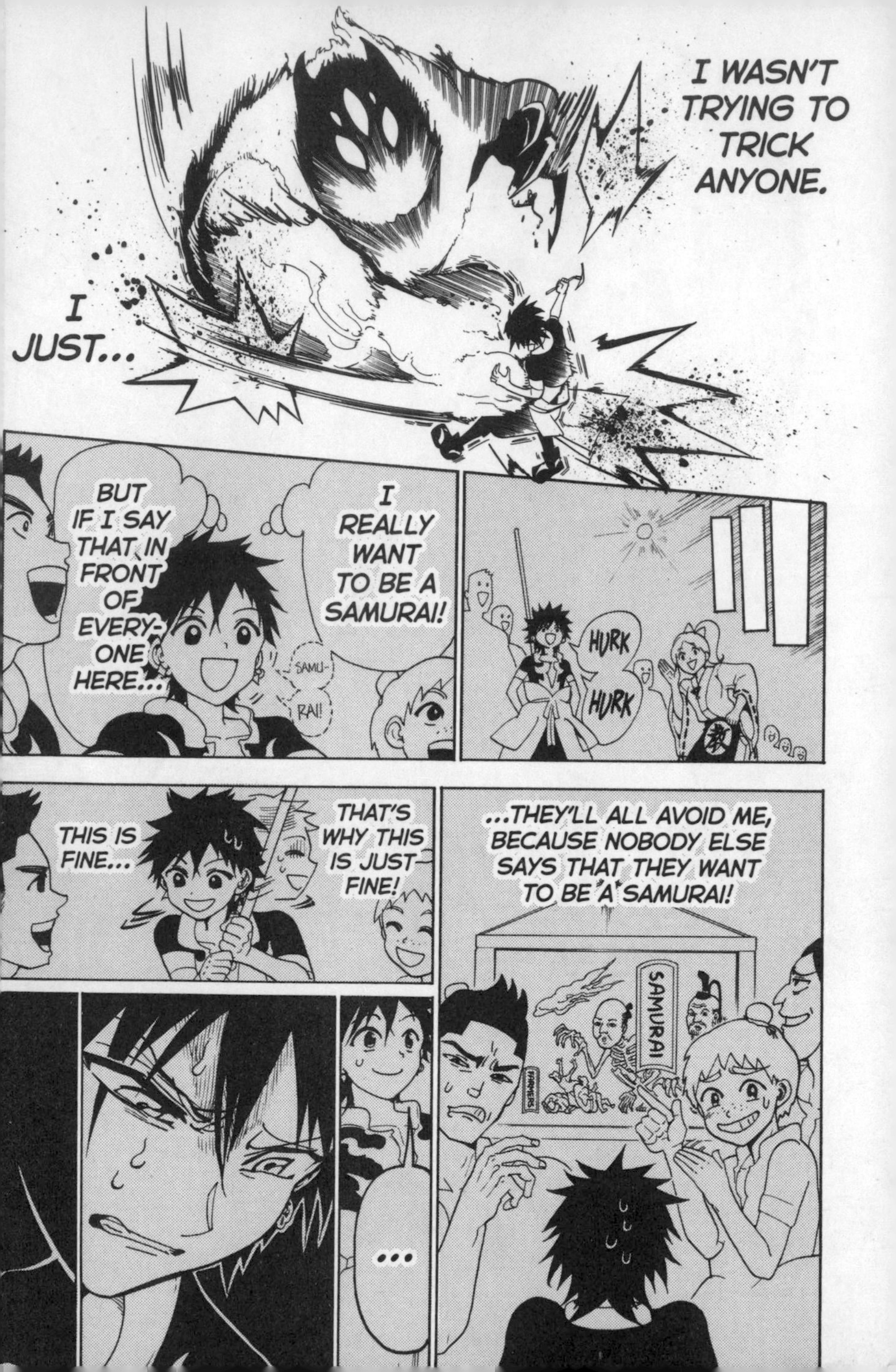

I WASN'T TRYING TO TRICK ANYONE.
I JUST...
HURK
HURK
I REALLY WANT TO BE A SAMURAI!
SAMU- RAI!
BUT IF I SAY THAT IN FRONT OF EVERYONE HERE...
...THEY'LL ALL AVOID ME, BECAUSE NOBODY ELSE SAYS THAT THEY WANT TO BE A SAMURAI!
SAMURAI
FARMERS
THAT'S WHY THIS IS JUST FINE!
THIS IS FINE...
...

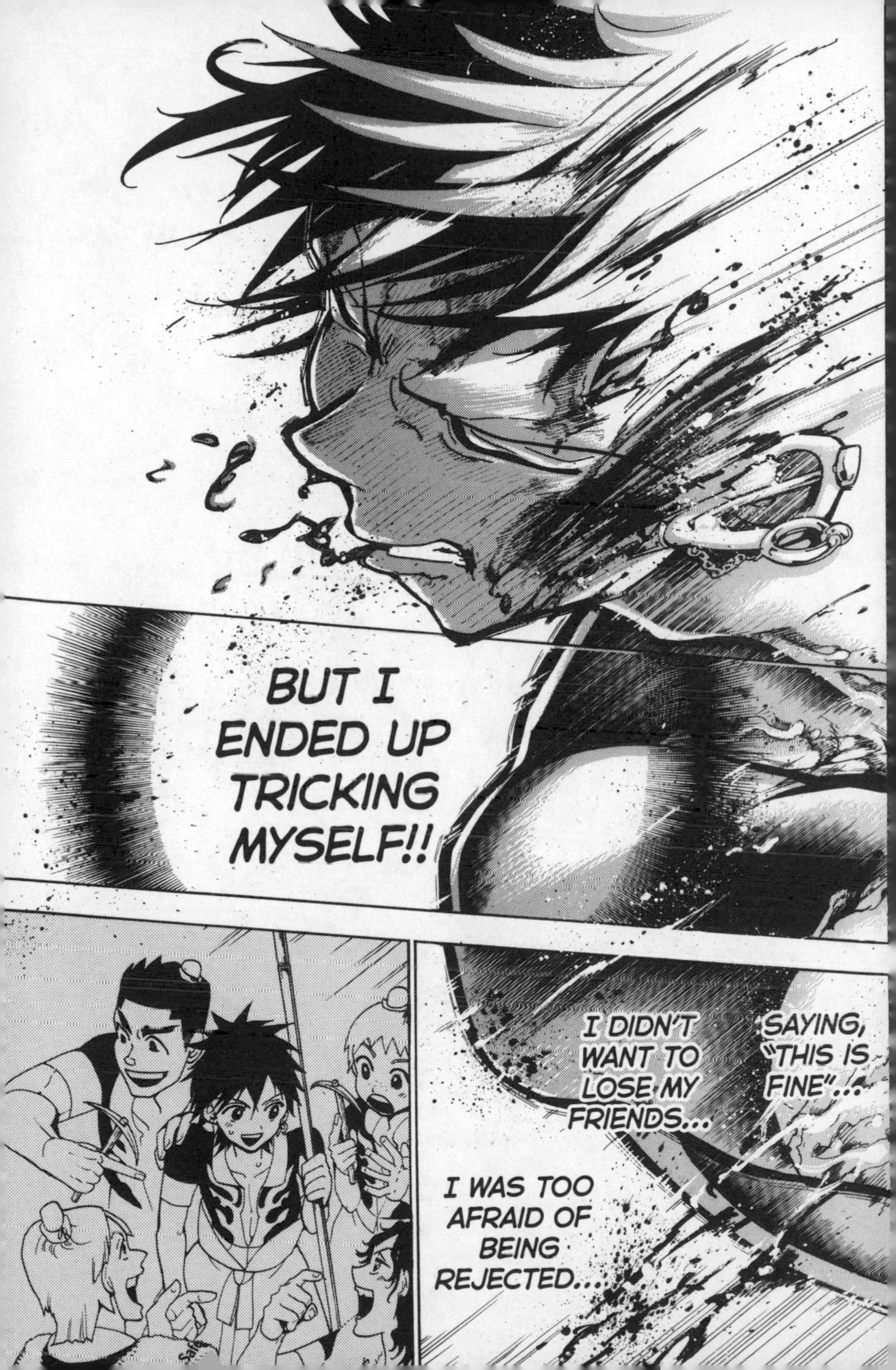
BUT I ENDED UP TRICKING MYSELF!!
SAYING, "THIS IS FINE"...
I DIDN'T WANT TO LOSE MY FRIENDS...
I WAS TOO AFRAID OF BEING REJECTED...

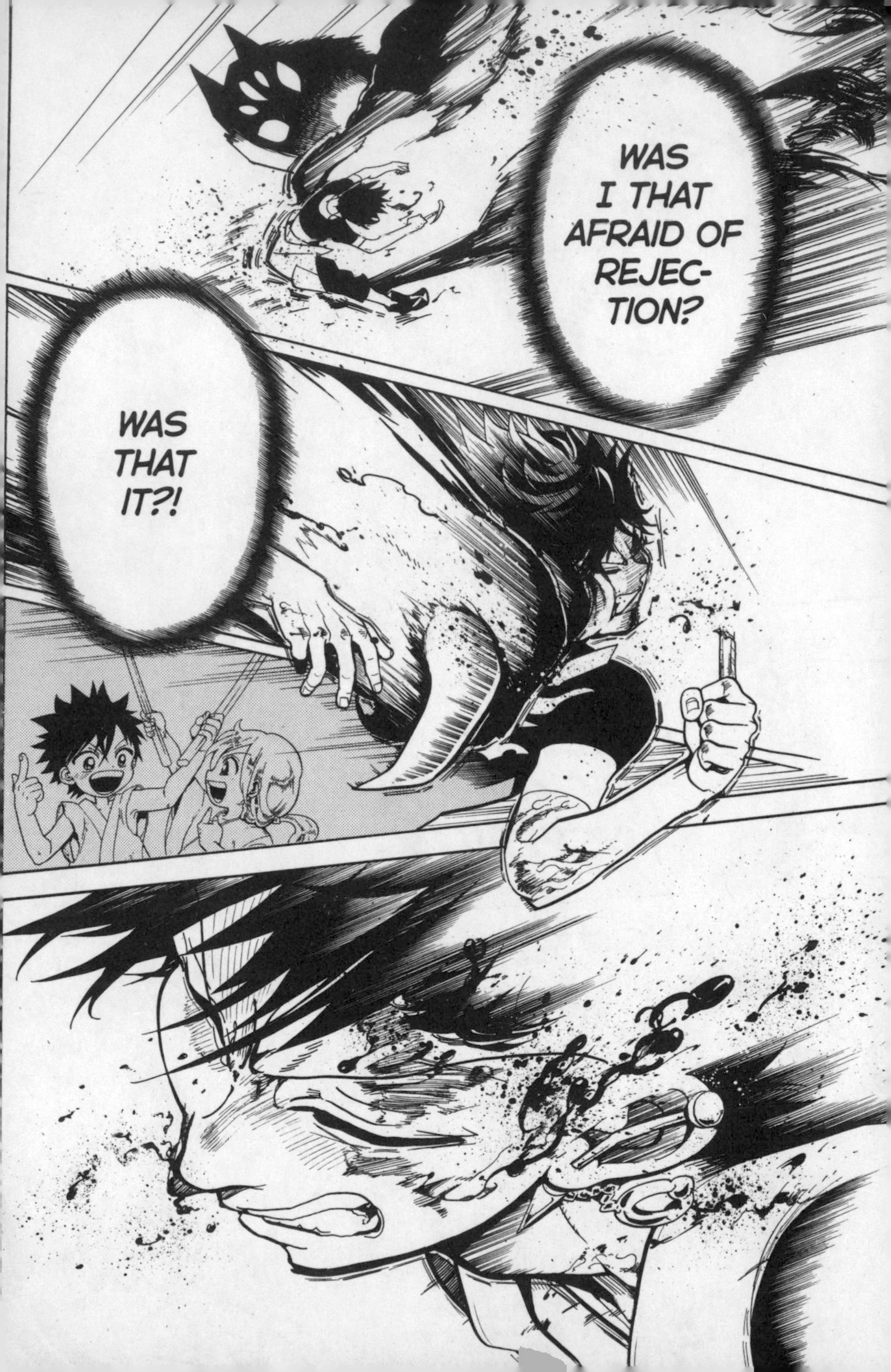
WAS I THAT AFRAID OF REJEC-TION?
WAS THAT IT?!

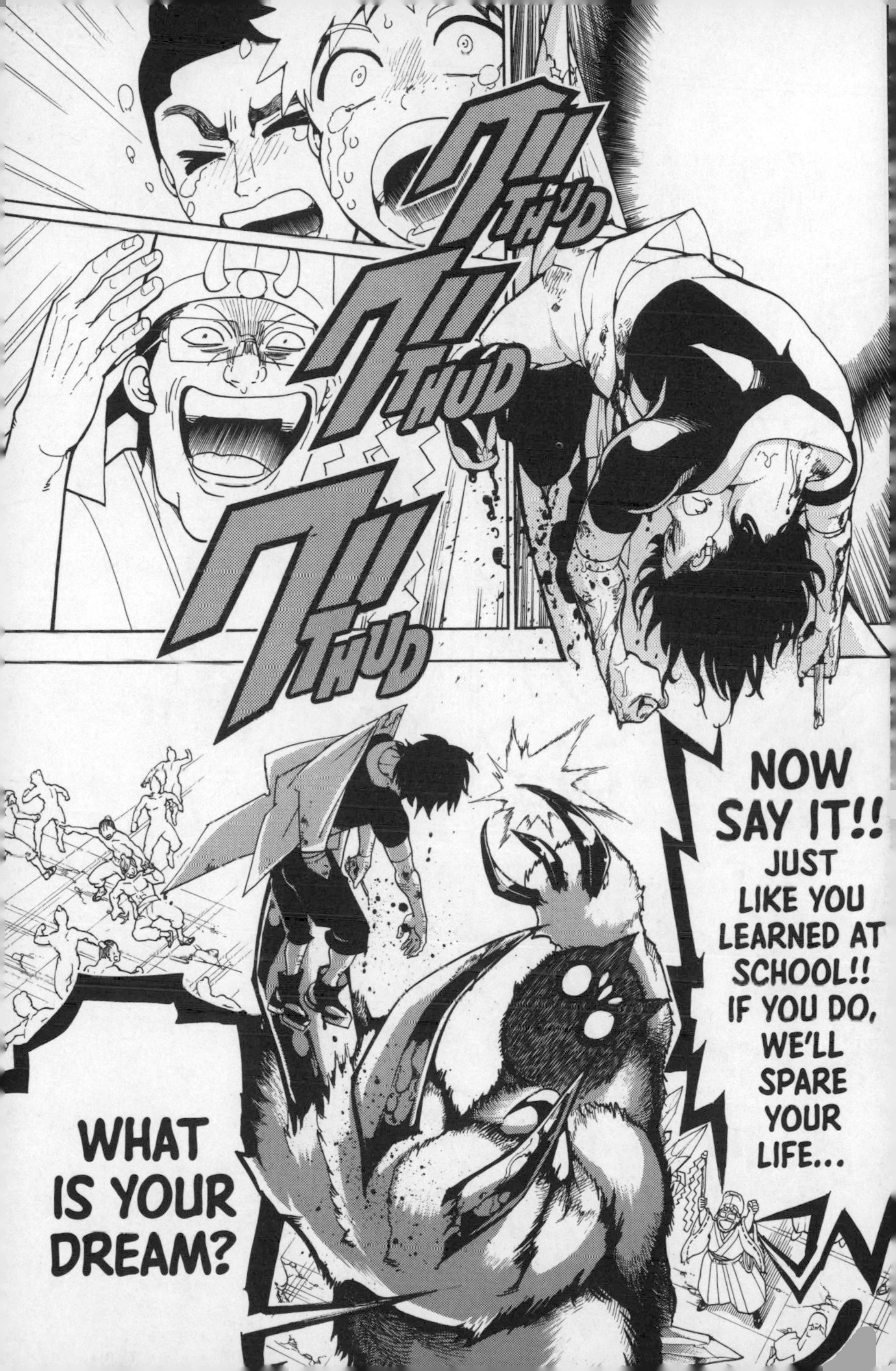
THUD
THUD
THUD
NOW SAY IT!! JUST LIKE YOU LEARNED AT SCHOOL!! IF YOU DO, WE'LL SPARE YOUR LIFE...
WHAT IS YOUR DREAM?

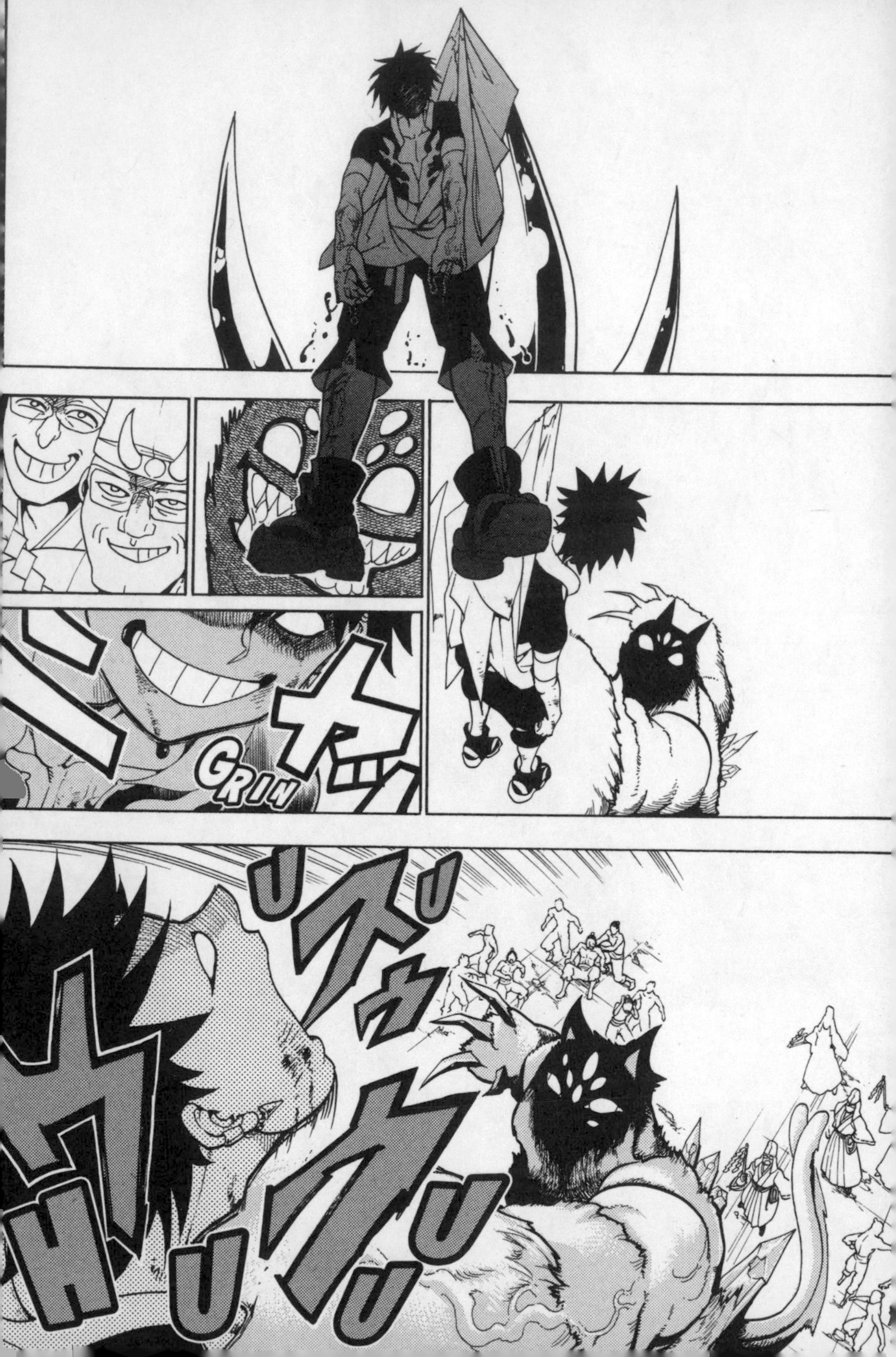
GRIN

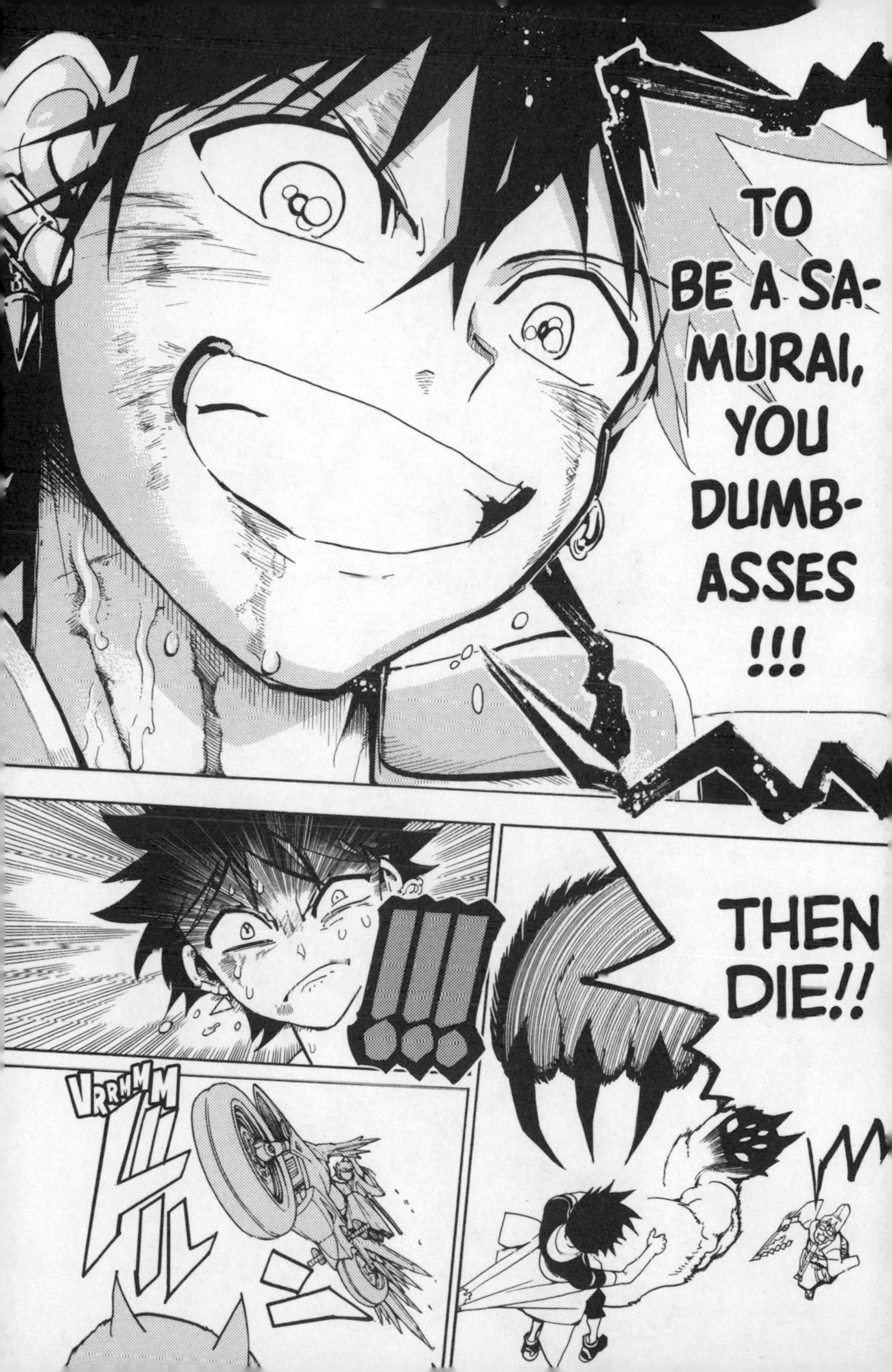
TO BE A SAMURAI, YOU DUMBASSES!!!
THEN DIE!!
VRRMMMM

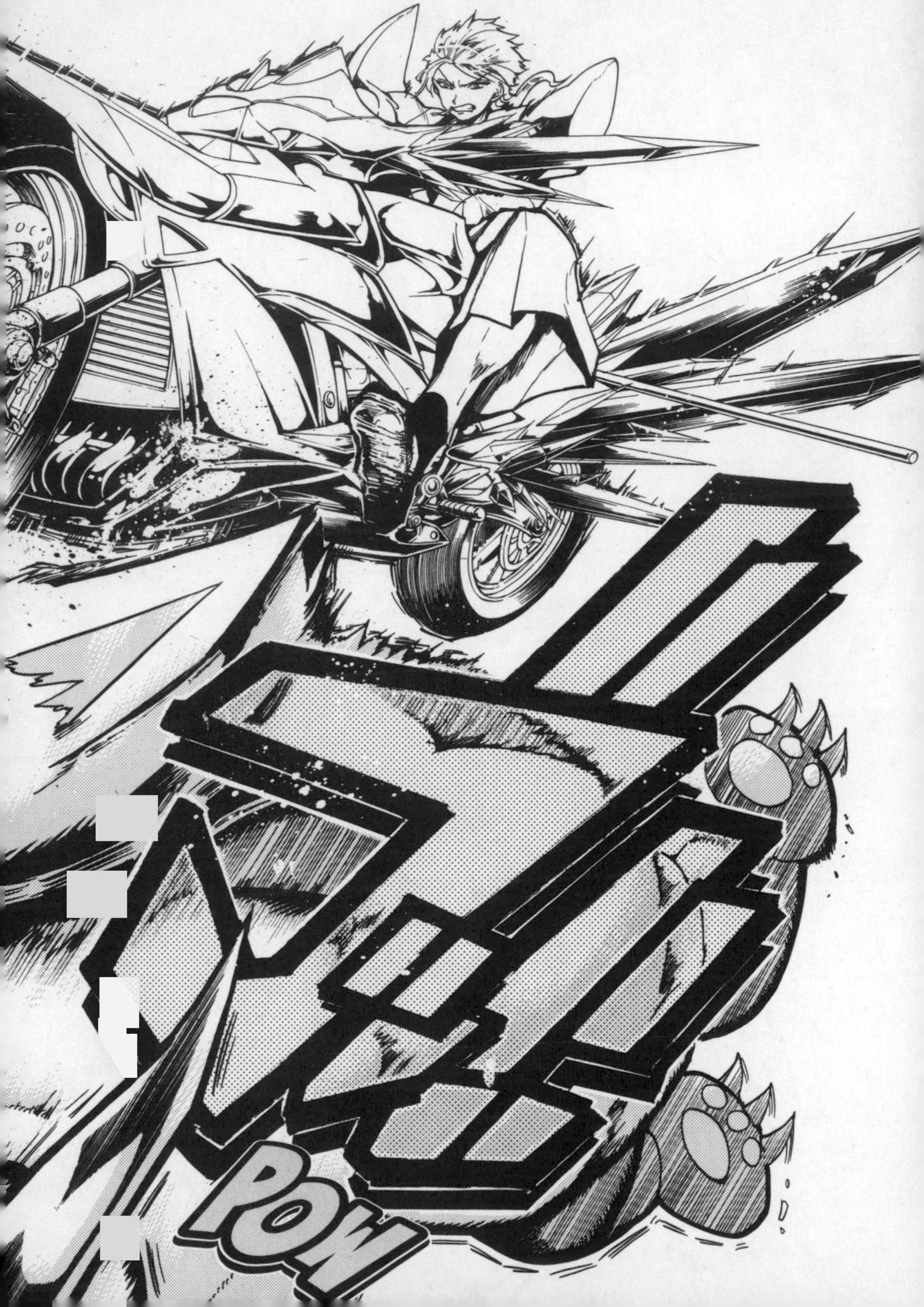
POW

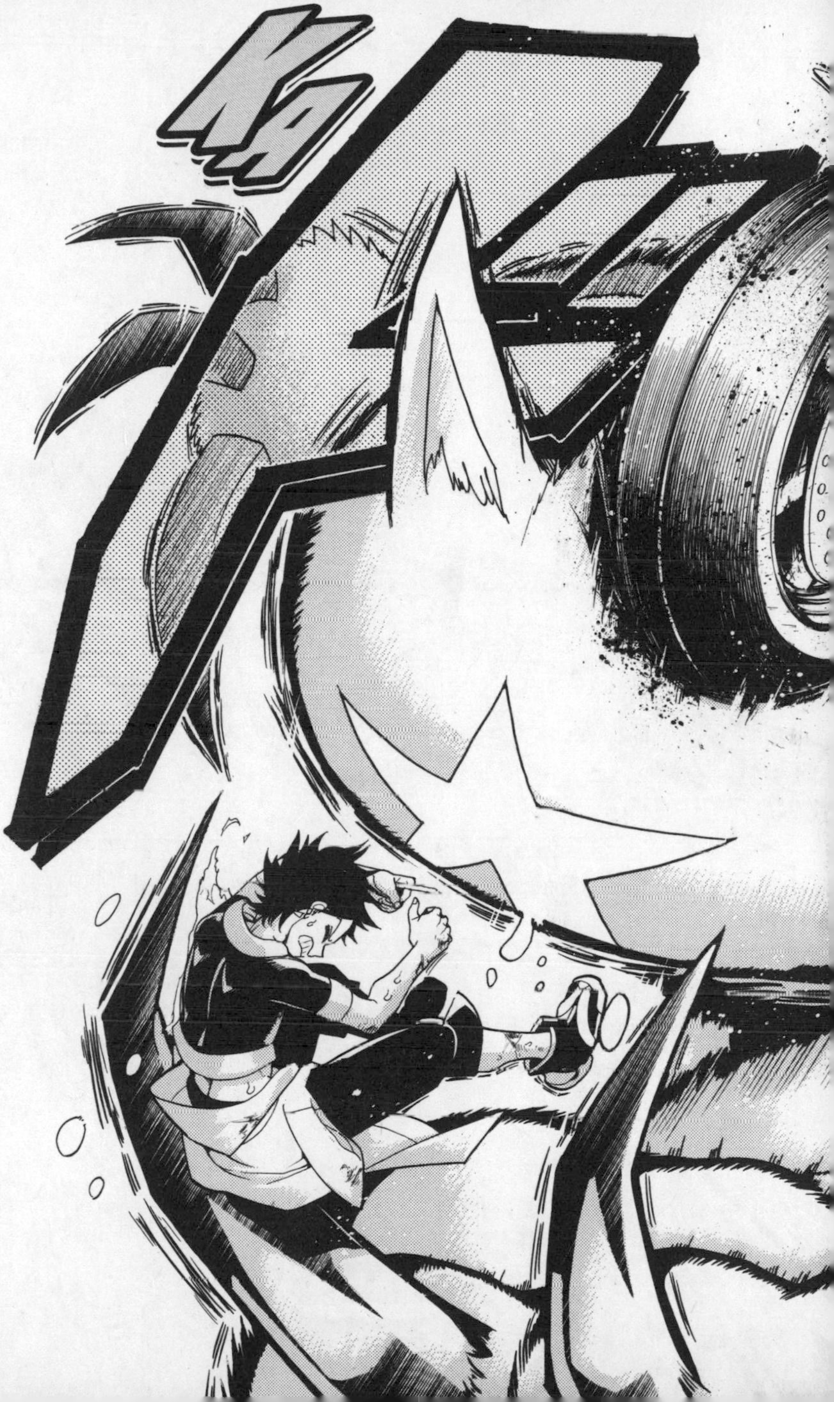

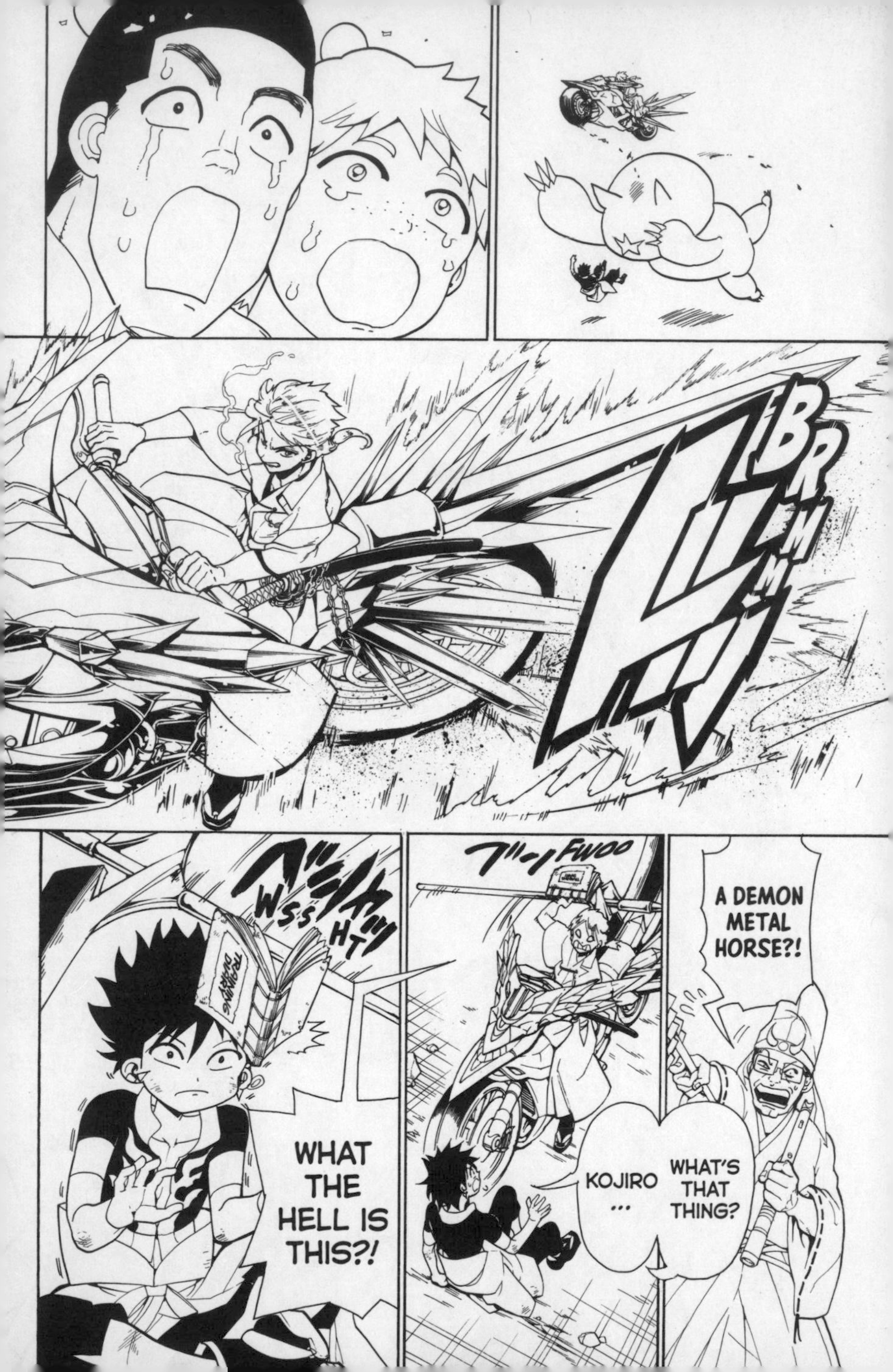
BRMMM
A DEMON METAL HORSE?!
FWOO
WHAT'S THAT THING?
KOJIRO ...
WSSHT
TRAINING DIARY
WHAT THE HELL IS THIS?!

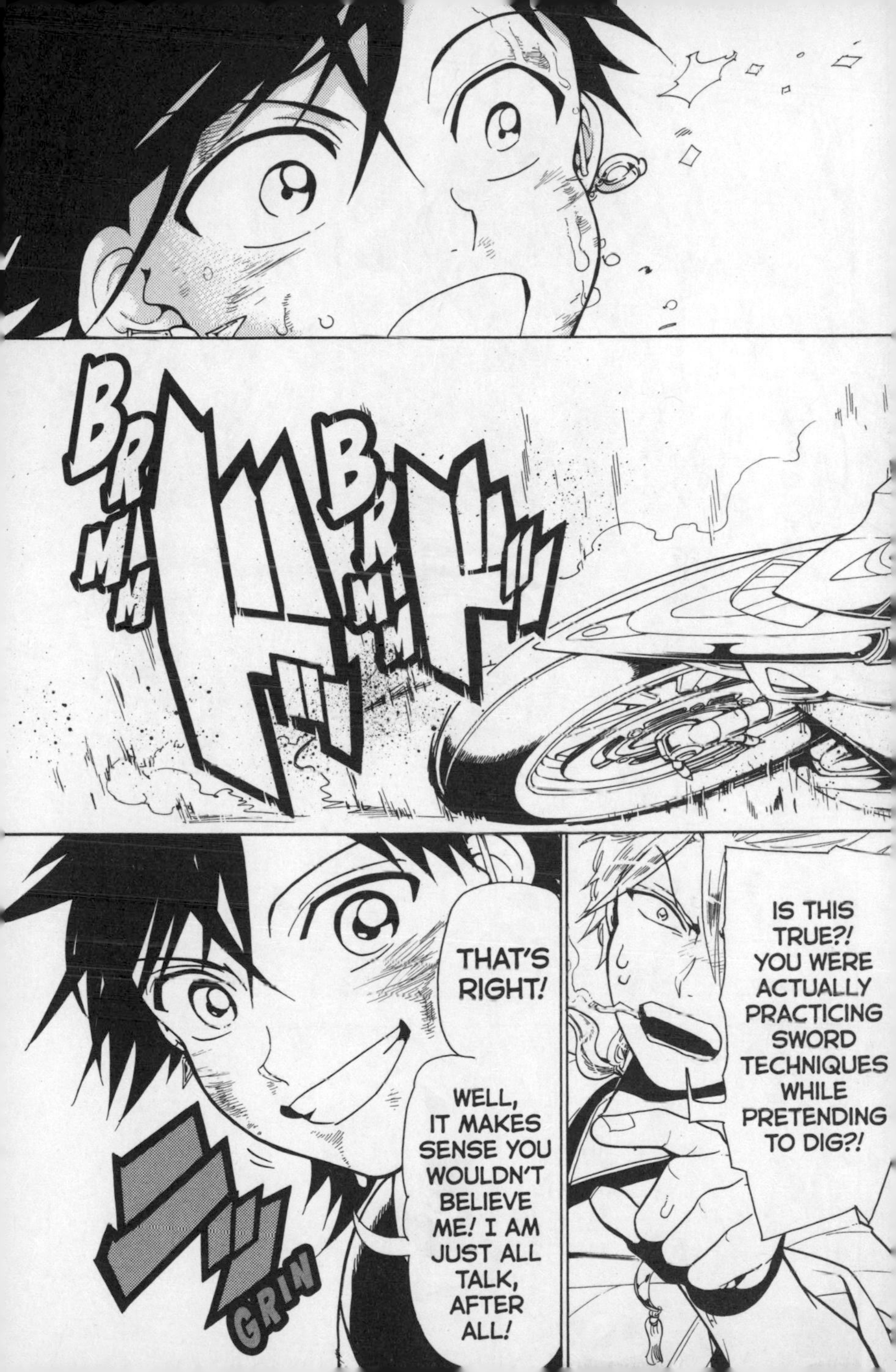
BRMM
BRMM
IS THIS TRUE?! YOU WERE ACTUALLY PRACTICING SWORD TECHNIQUES WHILE PRETENDING TO DIG?!
THAT'S RIGHT!
WELL, IT MAKES SENSE YOU WOULDN'T BELIEVE ME! I AM JUST ALL TALK, AFTER ALL!
GRIN

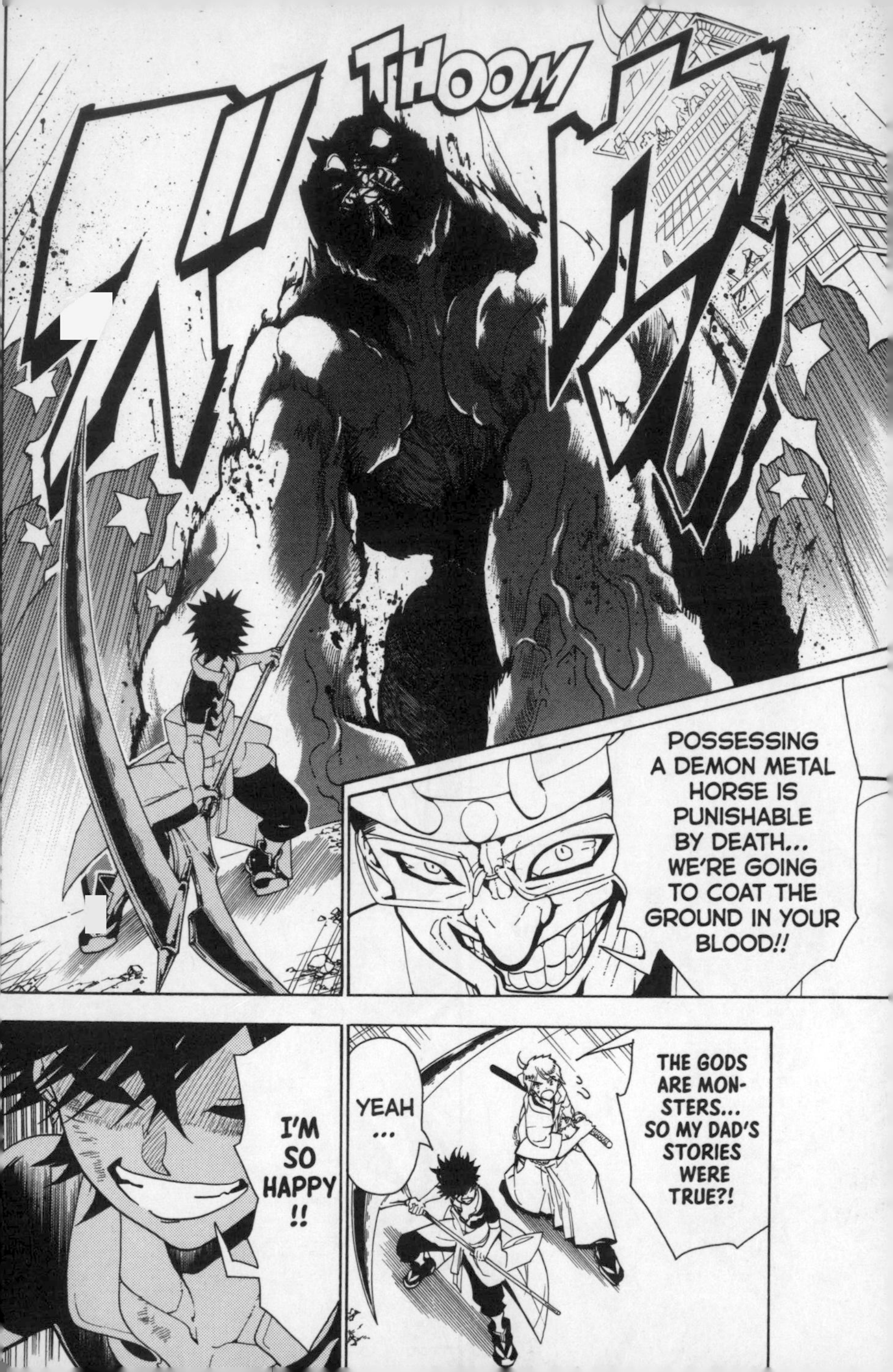
THOOM
POSSESSING A DEMON METAL HORSE IS PUNISHABLE BY DEATH... WE'RE GOING TO COAT THE GROUND IN YOUR BLOOD!!
THE GODS ARE MON-STERS... SO MY DAD'S STORIES WERE TRUE?!
YEAH ...
I'M SO HAPPY !!

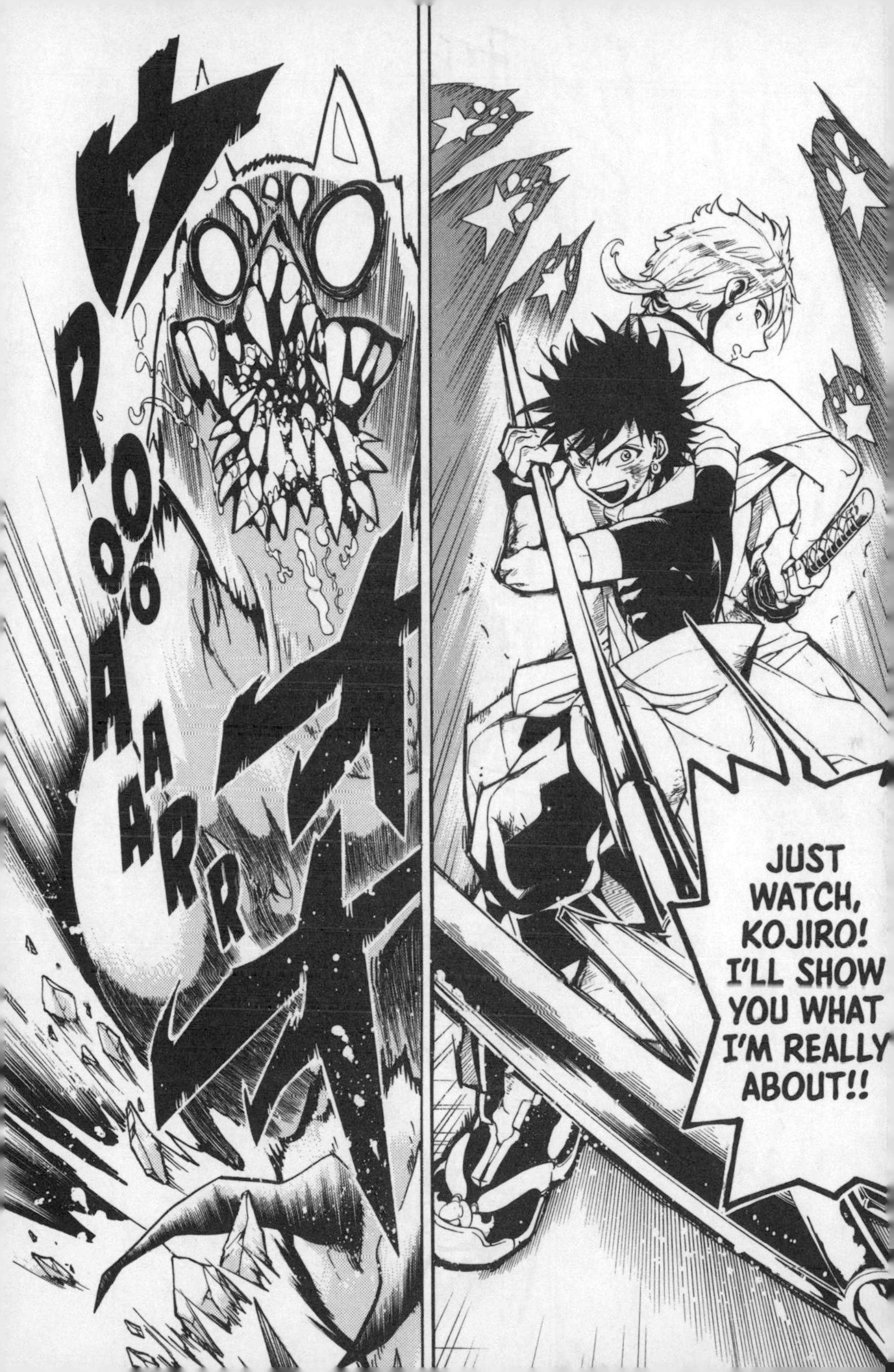
JUST WATCH, KOJIRO! I'LL SHOW YOU WHAT I'M REALLY ABOUT!!
ROOOAAARR

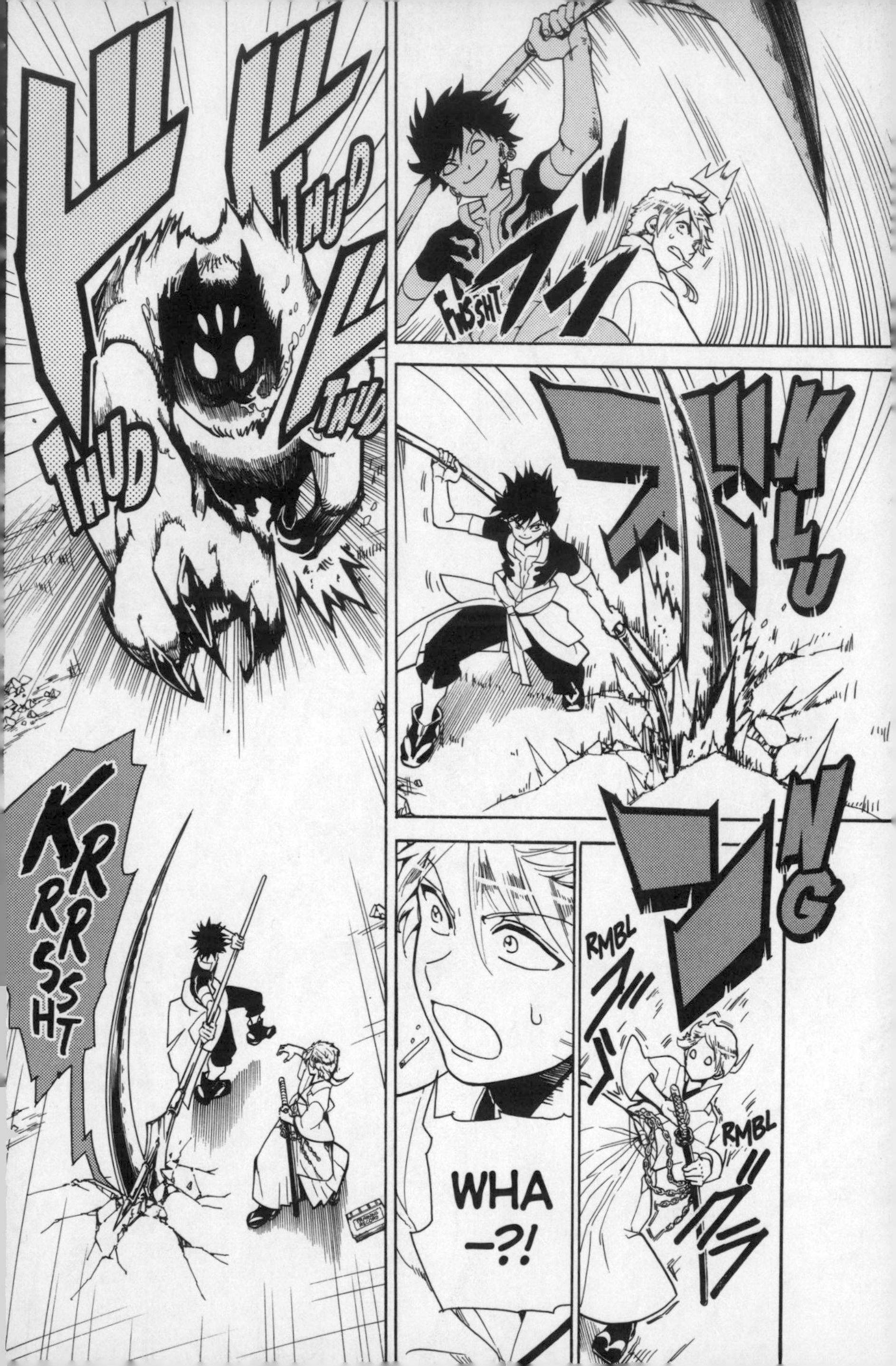
FWSSHT
KLUNG
RMBL
RMBL
WHA
—?!
THUD
THUD
THUD
KRRRRSSHT

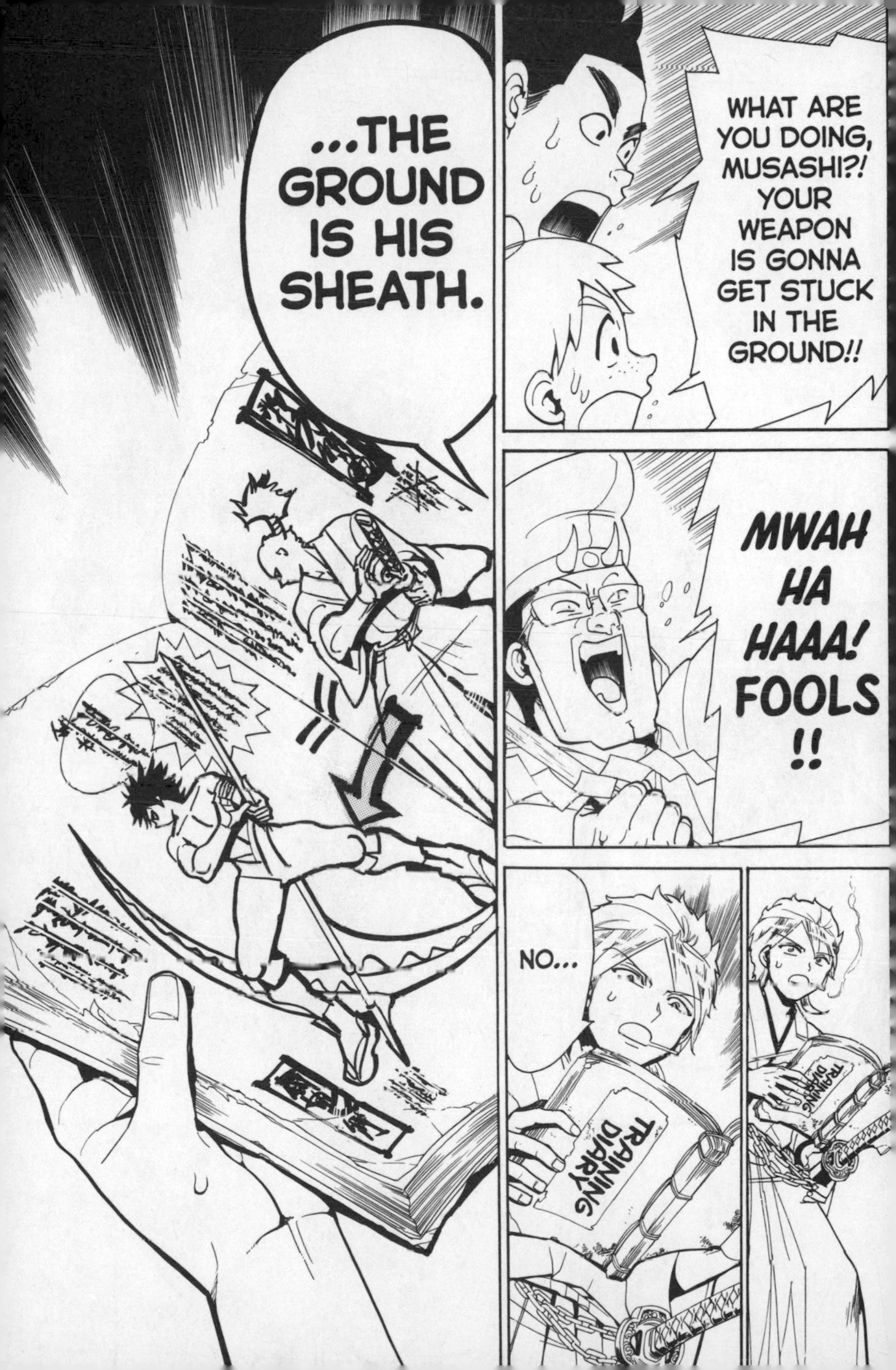
WHAT ARE YOU DOING, MUSASHI?! YOUR WEAPON IS GONNA GET STUCK IN THE GROUND!!
MWAH HA HAAA! FOOLS!!
NO...
TRAINING DIARY
TRAINING DIARY
...THE GROUND IS HIS SHEATH.

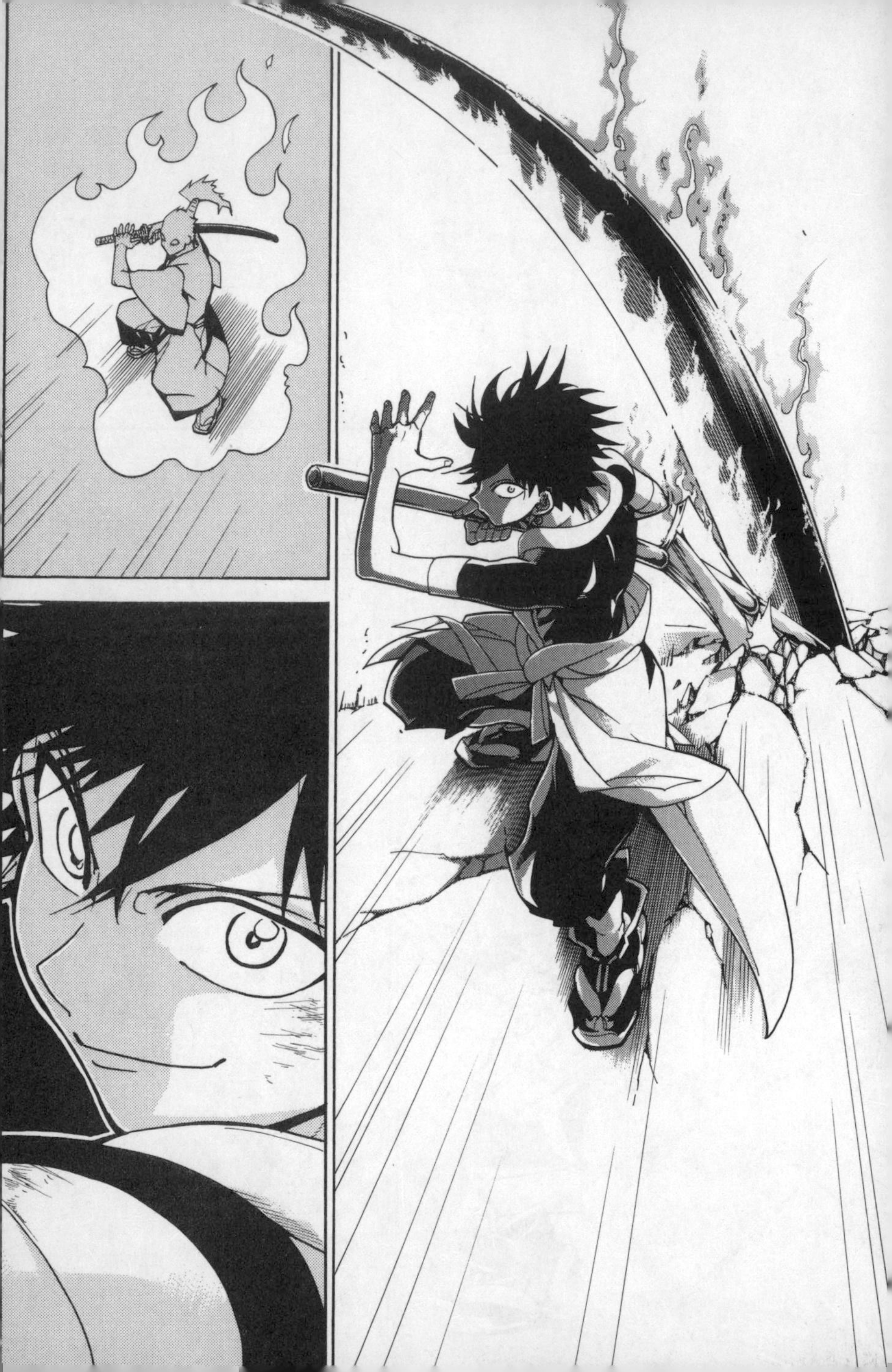

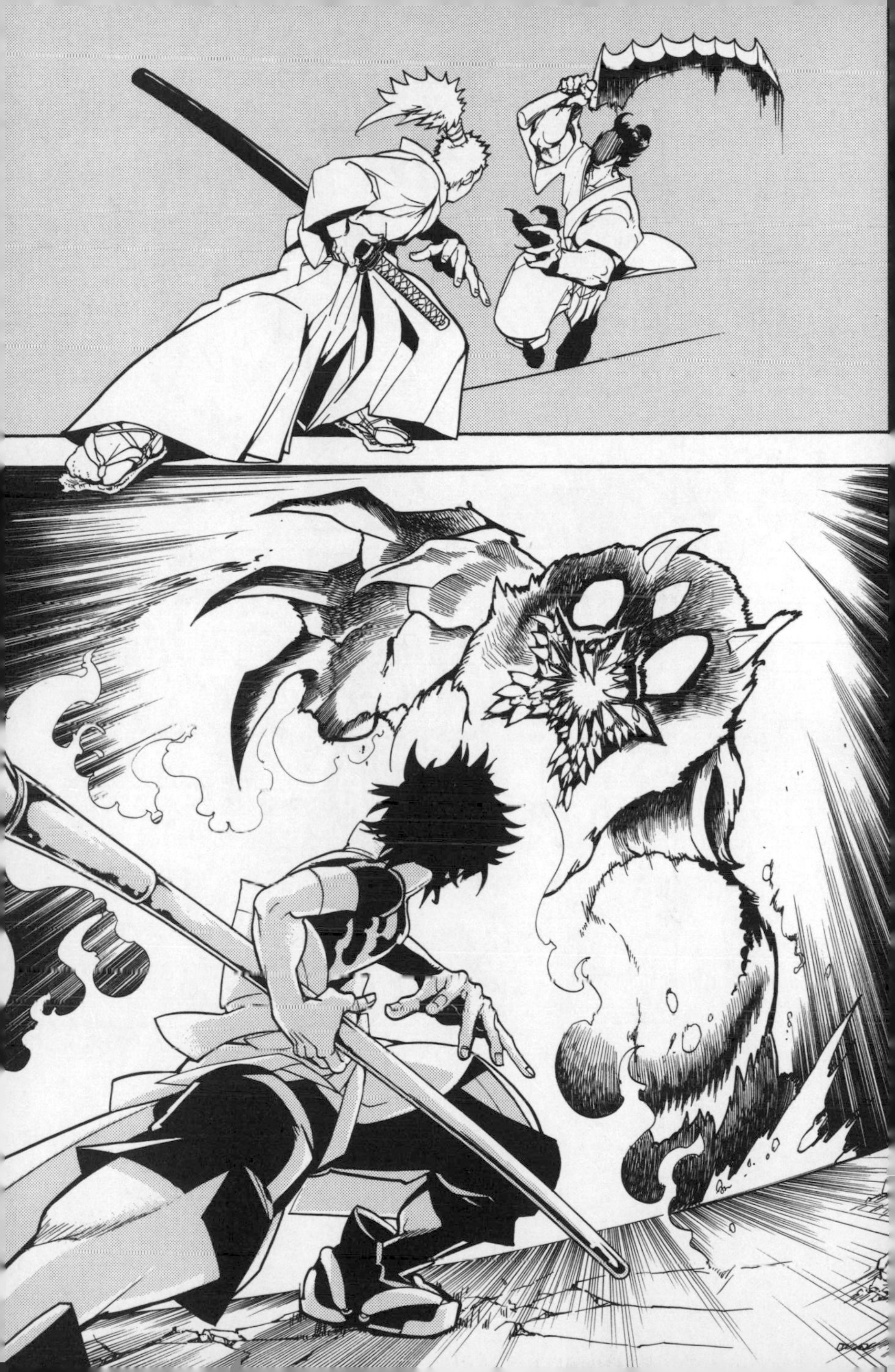

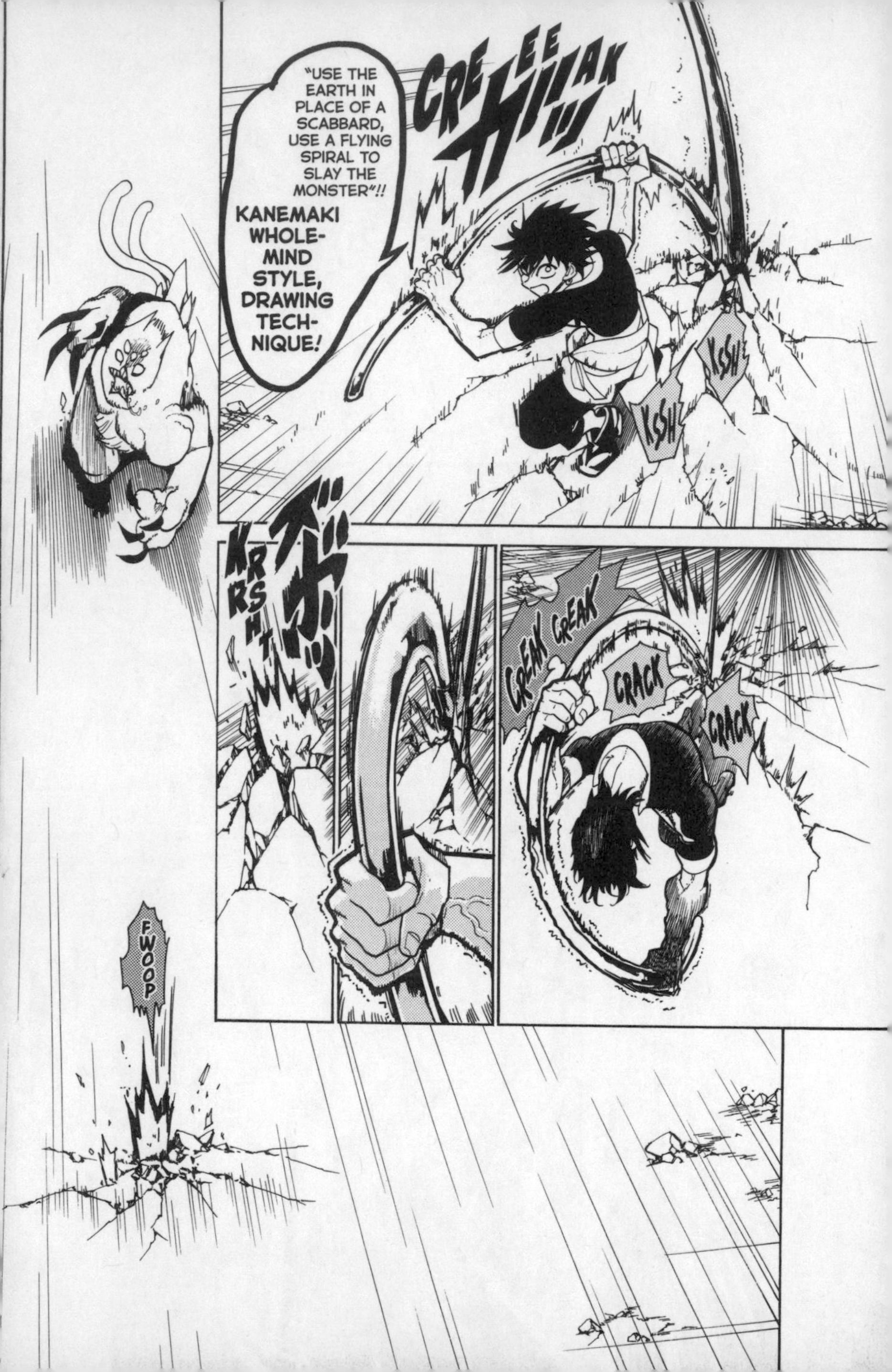
"USE THE EARTH IN PLACE OF A SCABBARD, USE A FLYING SPIRAL TO SLAY THE MONSTER"!! KANEMAKI WHOLE-MIND STYLE, DRAWING TECHNIQUE!
CREEEAK
KSH
KSH
CREAK CREAK
CRACK
CRACK
KRRSHT
FWOOP

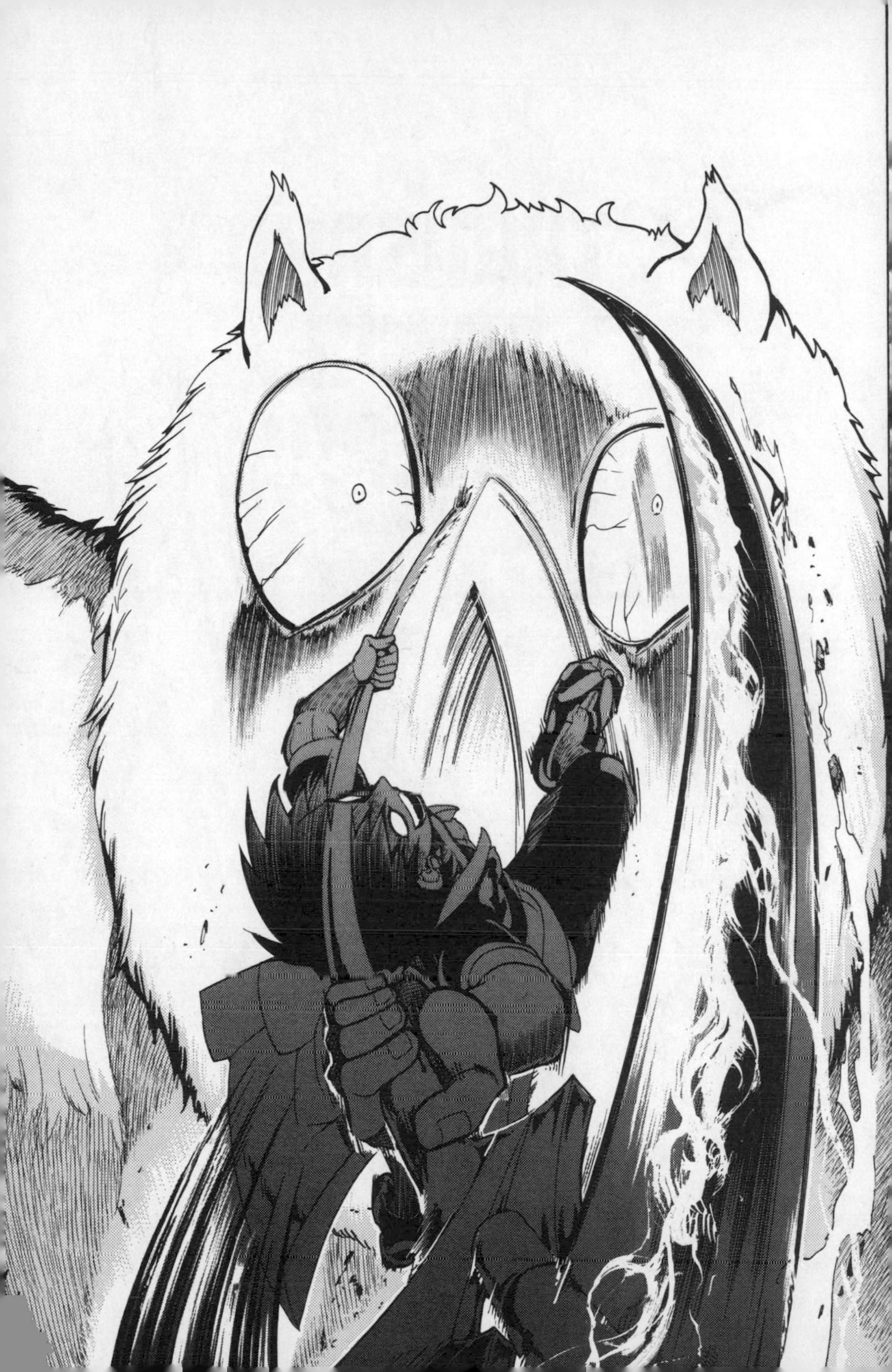

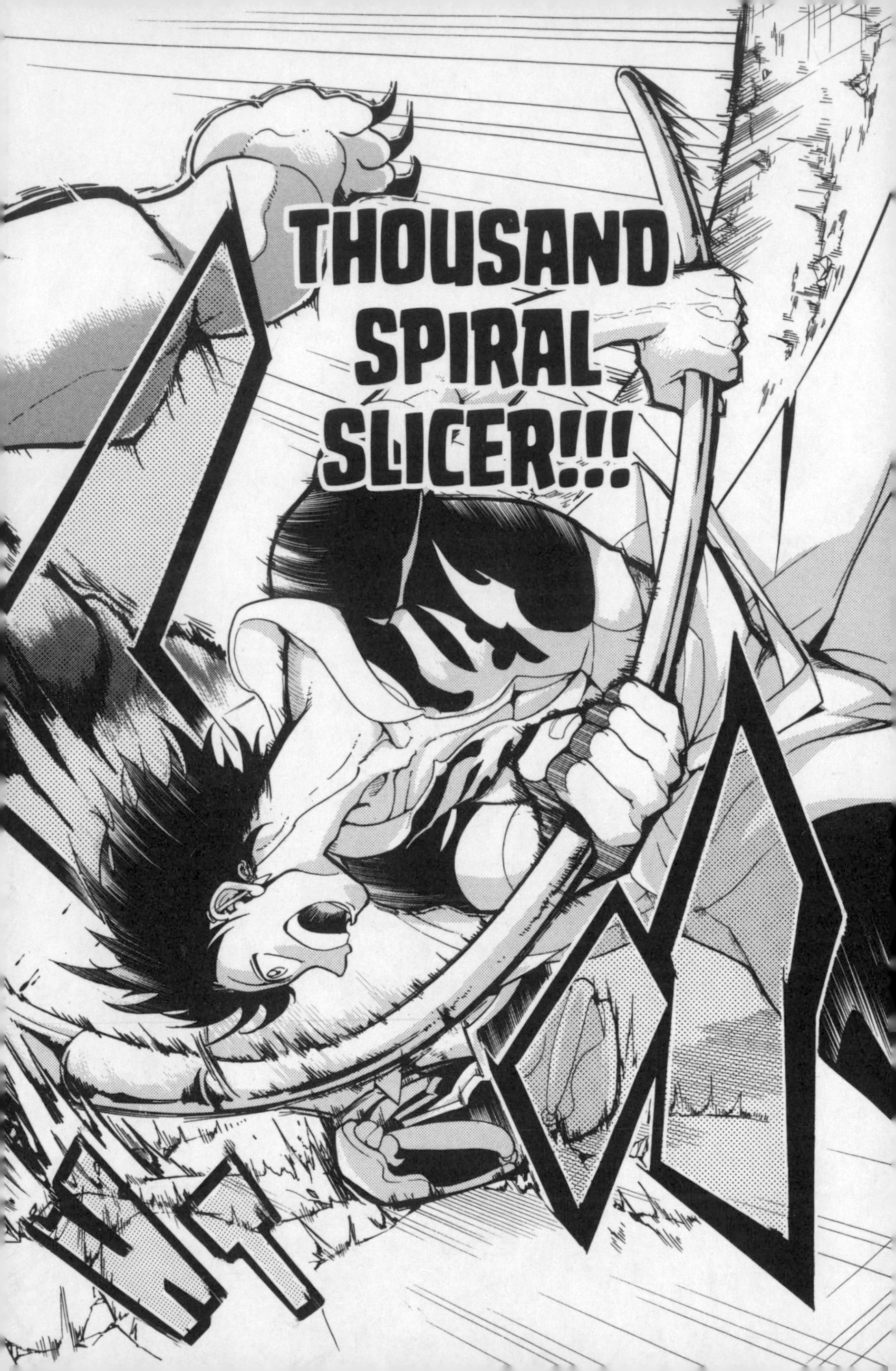
THOUSAND SPIRAL SLICER!!!

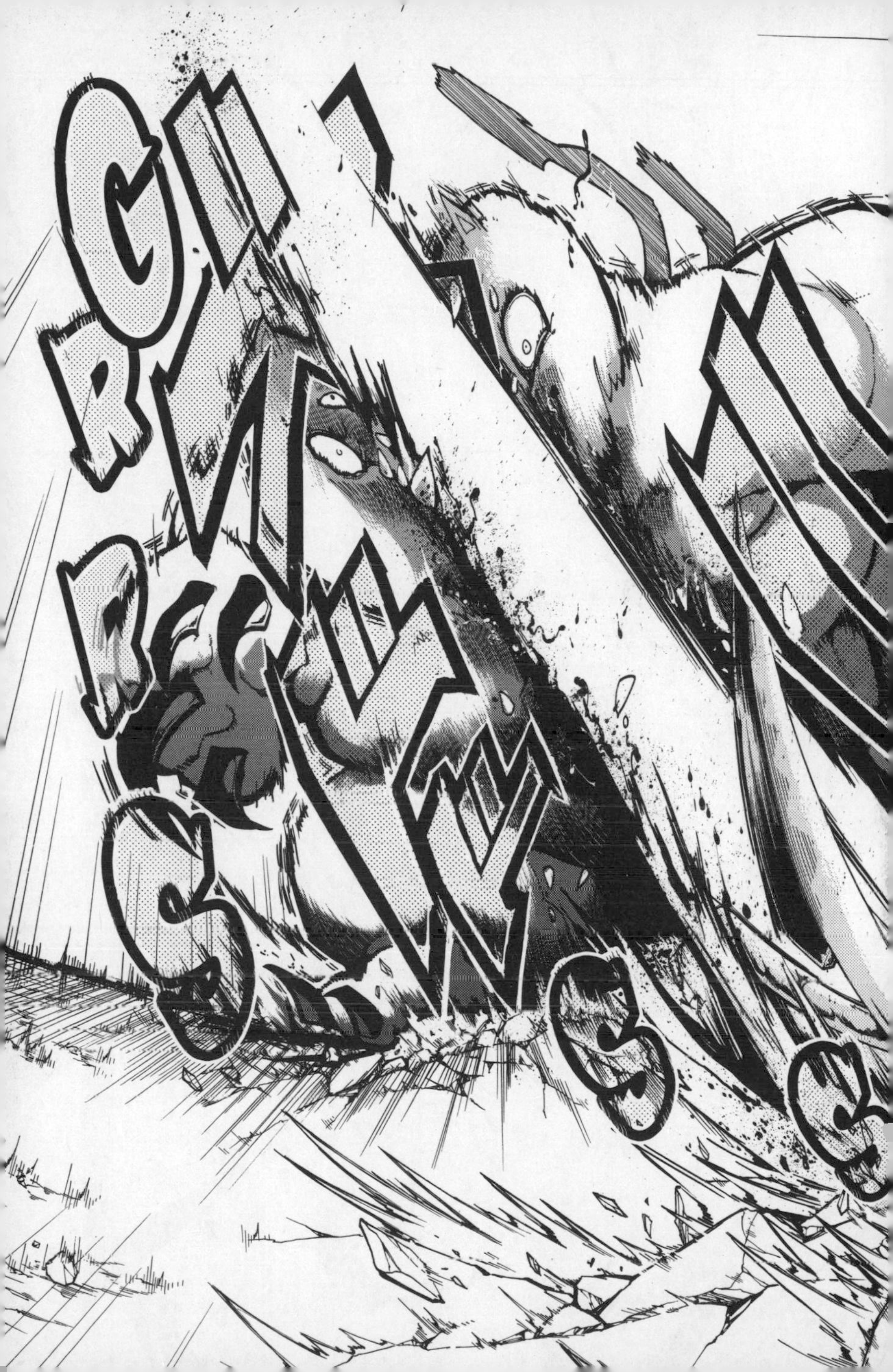

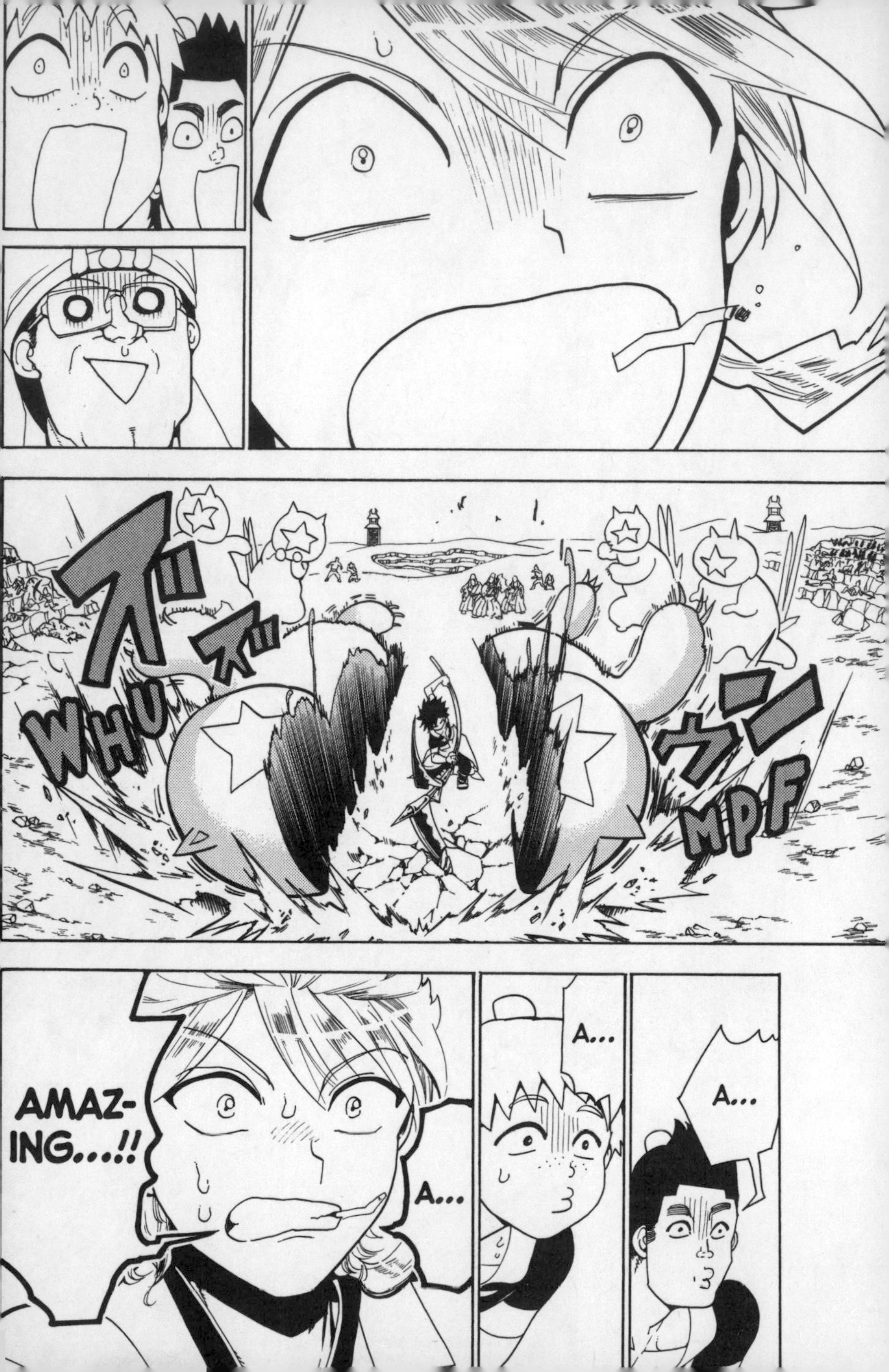

ズズ
WHU
ヴーン
MPF
A...
A...
AMAZ-
ING...!!
A...

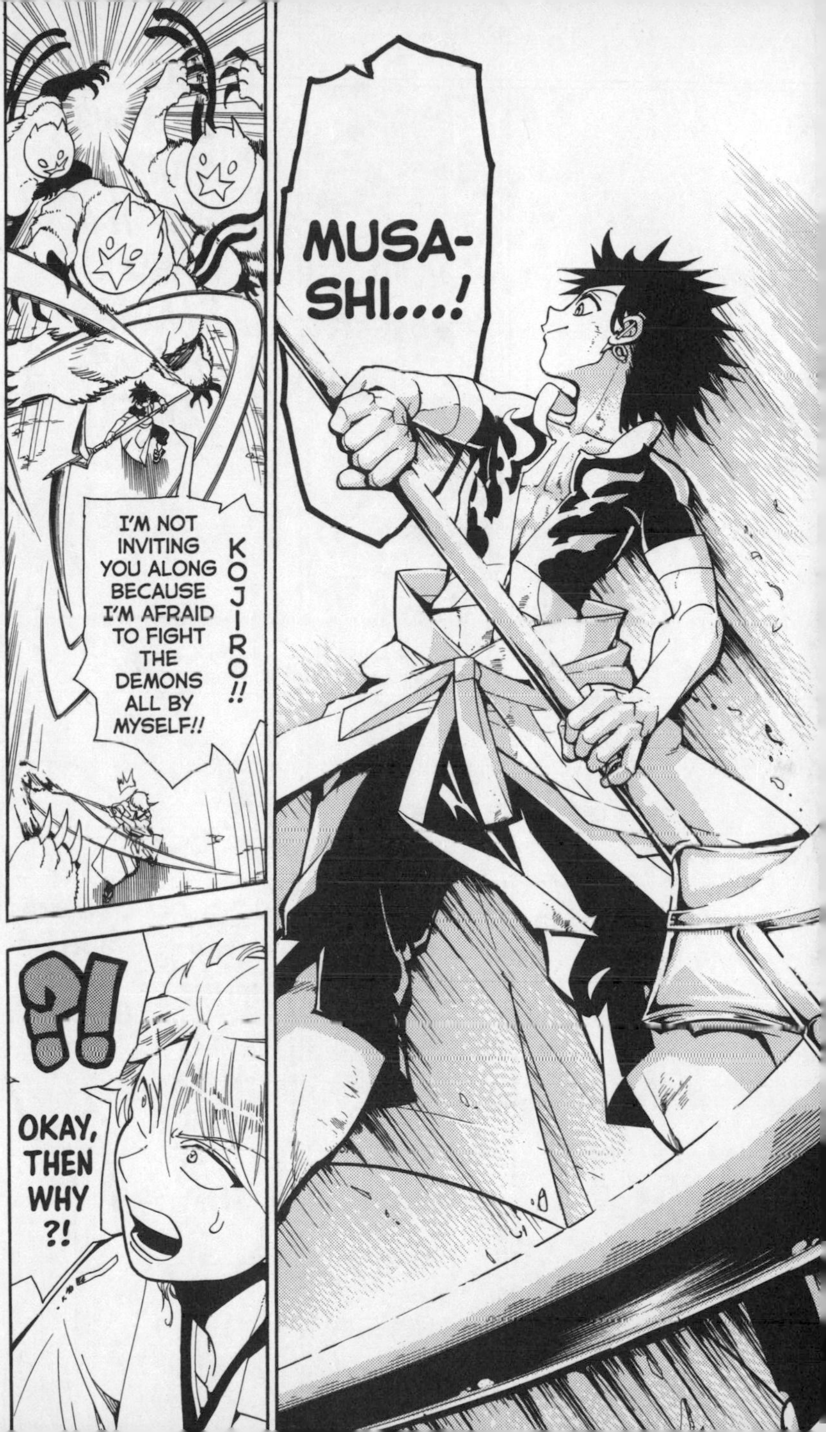
MUSA-SHI...!
I'M NOT INVITING YOU ALONG BECAUSE I'M AFRAID TO FIGHT THE DEMONS ALL BY MYSELF!!
KOJIRO!!
?!
OKAY, THEN WHY?!

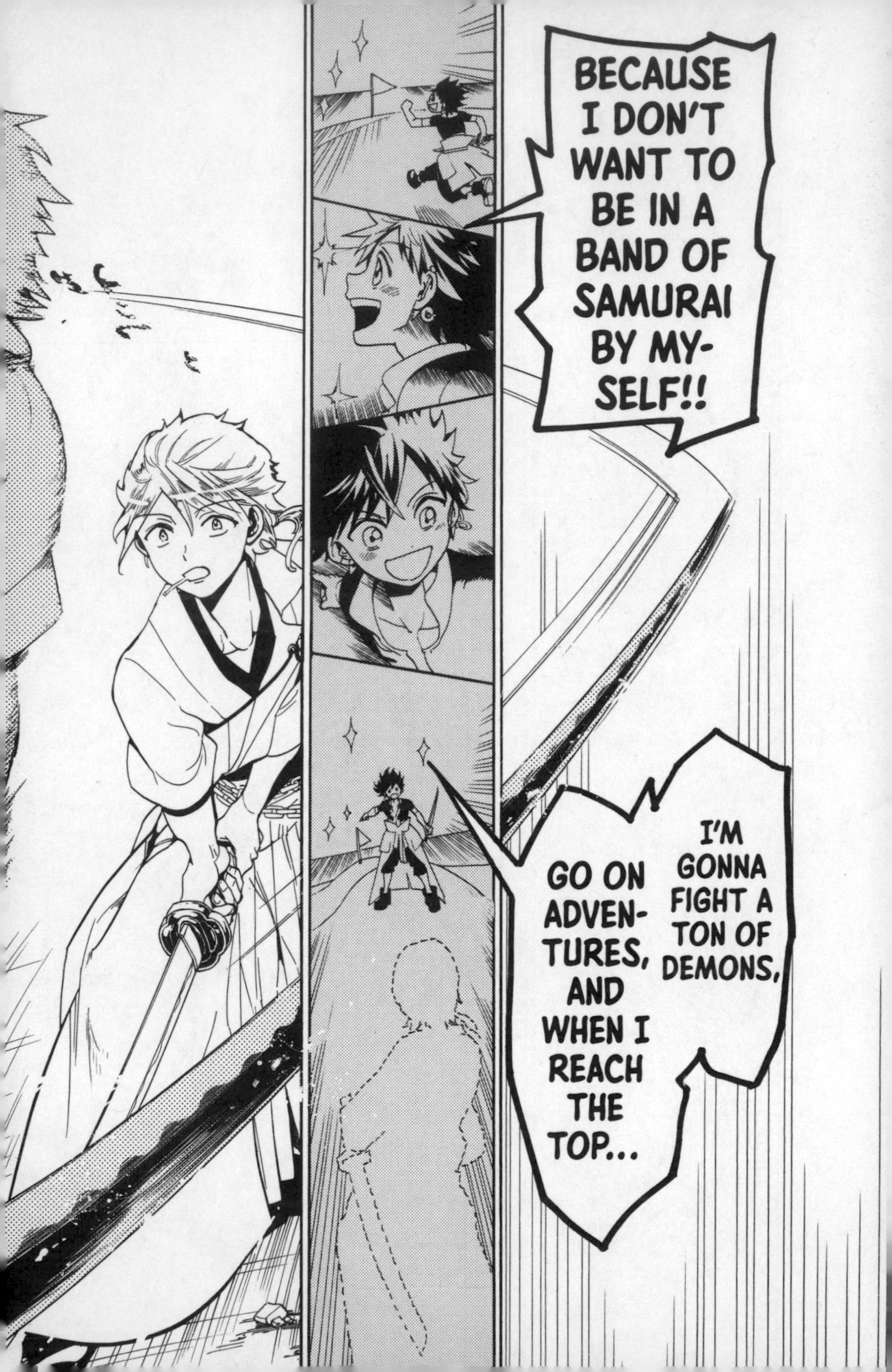
BECAUSE I DON'T WANT TO BE IN A BAND OF SAMURAI BY MY-SELF!!
I'M GONNA FIGHT A TON OF DEMONS,
GO ON ADVEN-TURES, AND WHEN I REACH THE TOP...

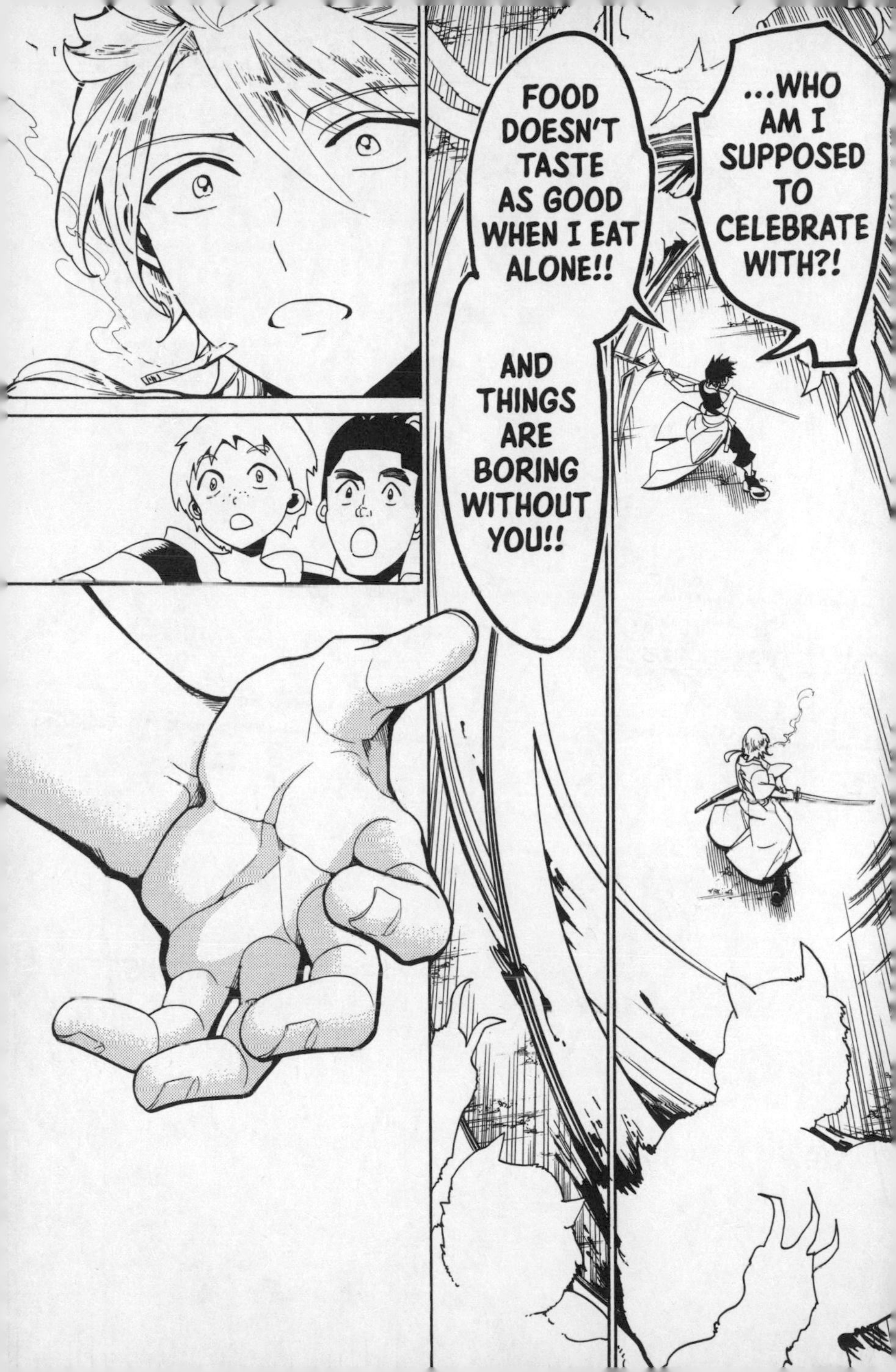
...WHO AM I SUPPOSED TO CELEBRATE WITH?!
FOOD DOESN'T TASTE AS GOOD WHEN I EAT ALONE!!
AND THINGS ARE BORING WITHOUT YOU!!

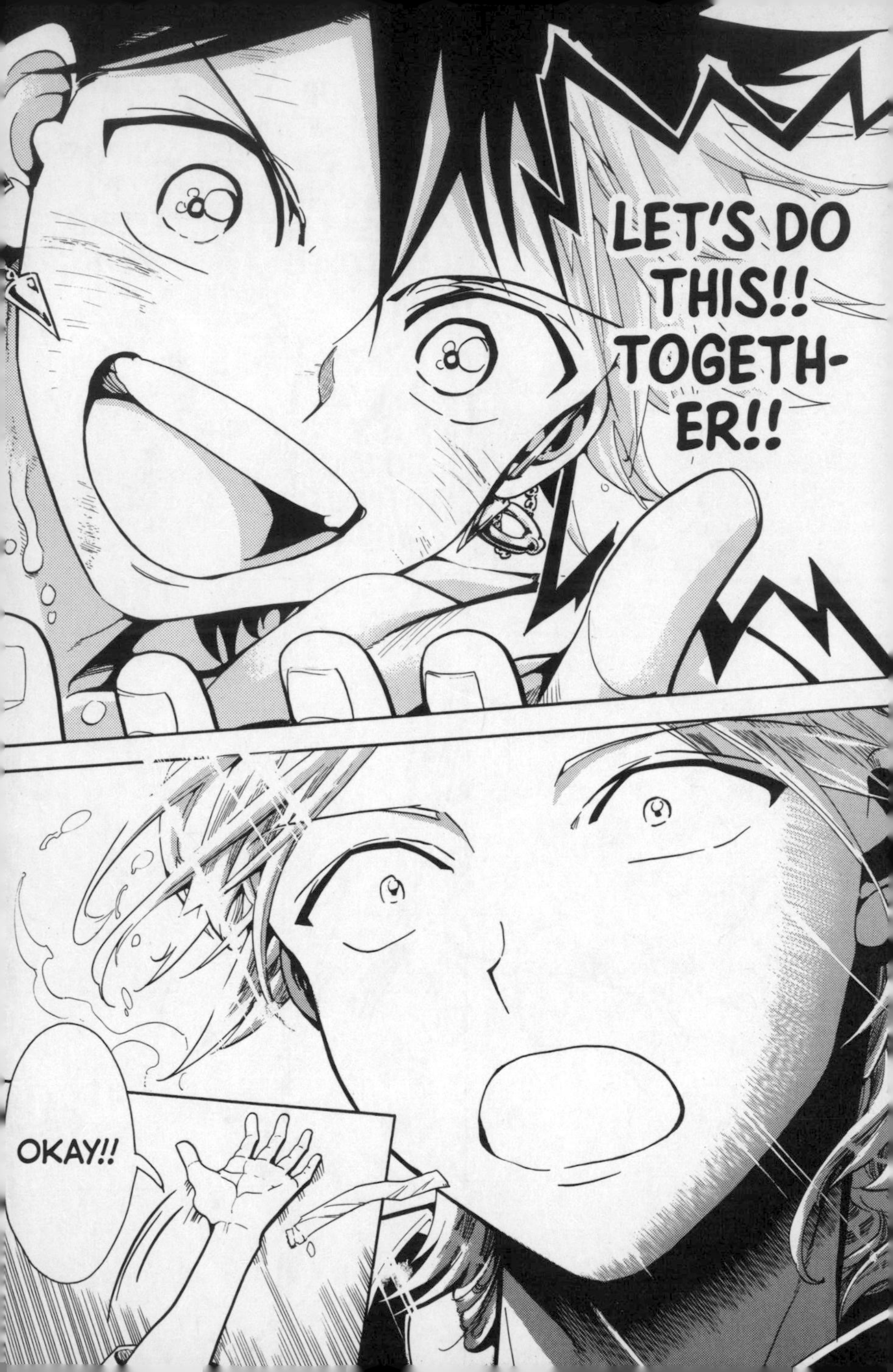
LET'S DO THIS!! TOGETH-ER!!
OKAY!!

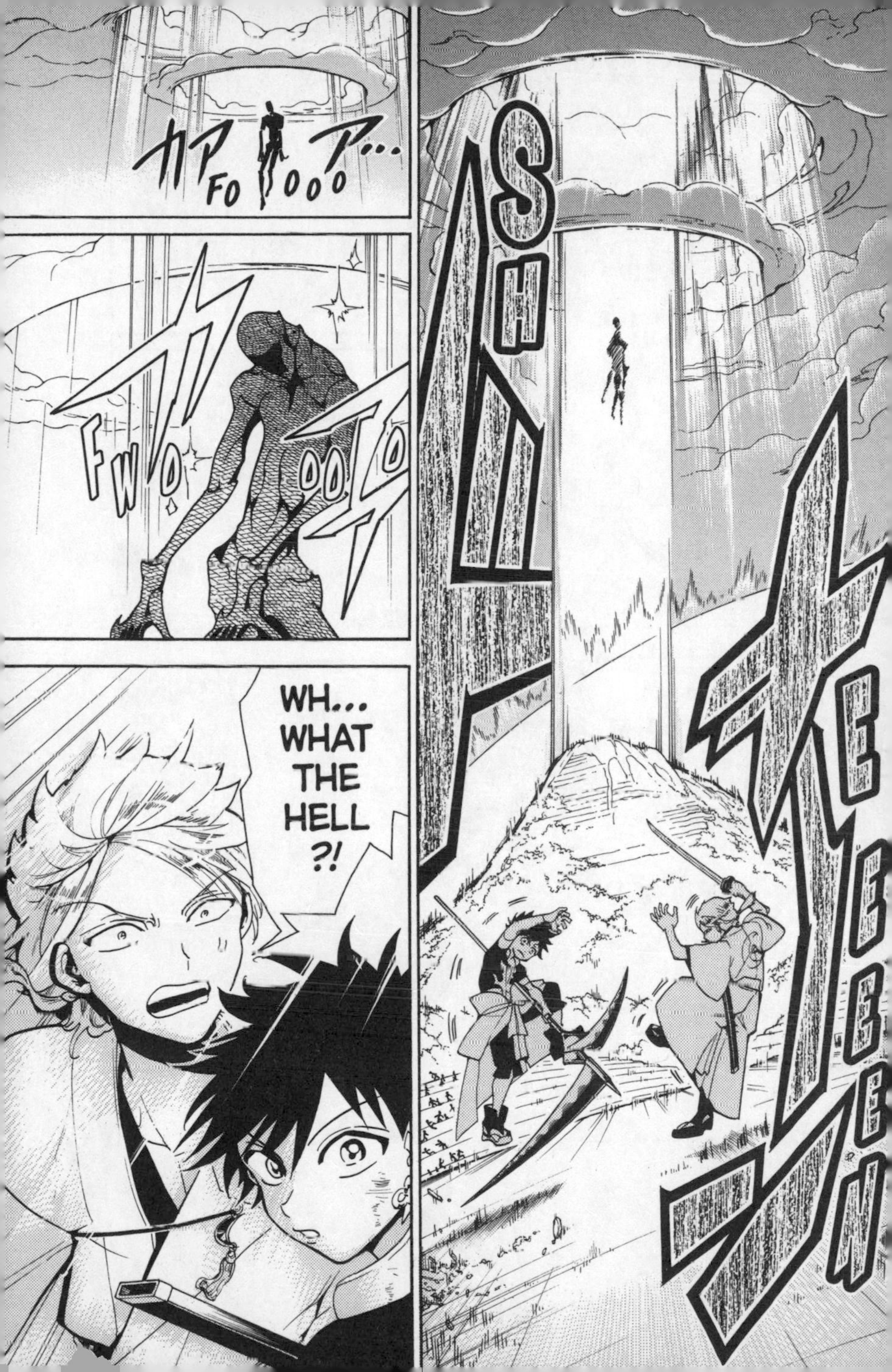
SH
EEEEN
カア…ア…
FOOOO
FWOOOO
WH… WHAT THE HELL ?!

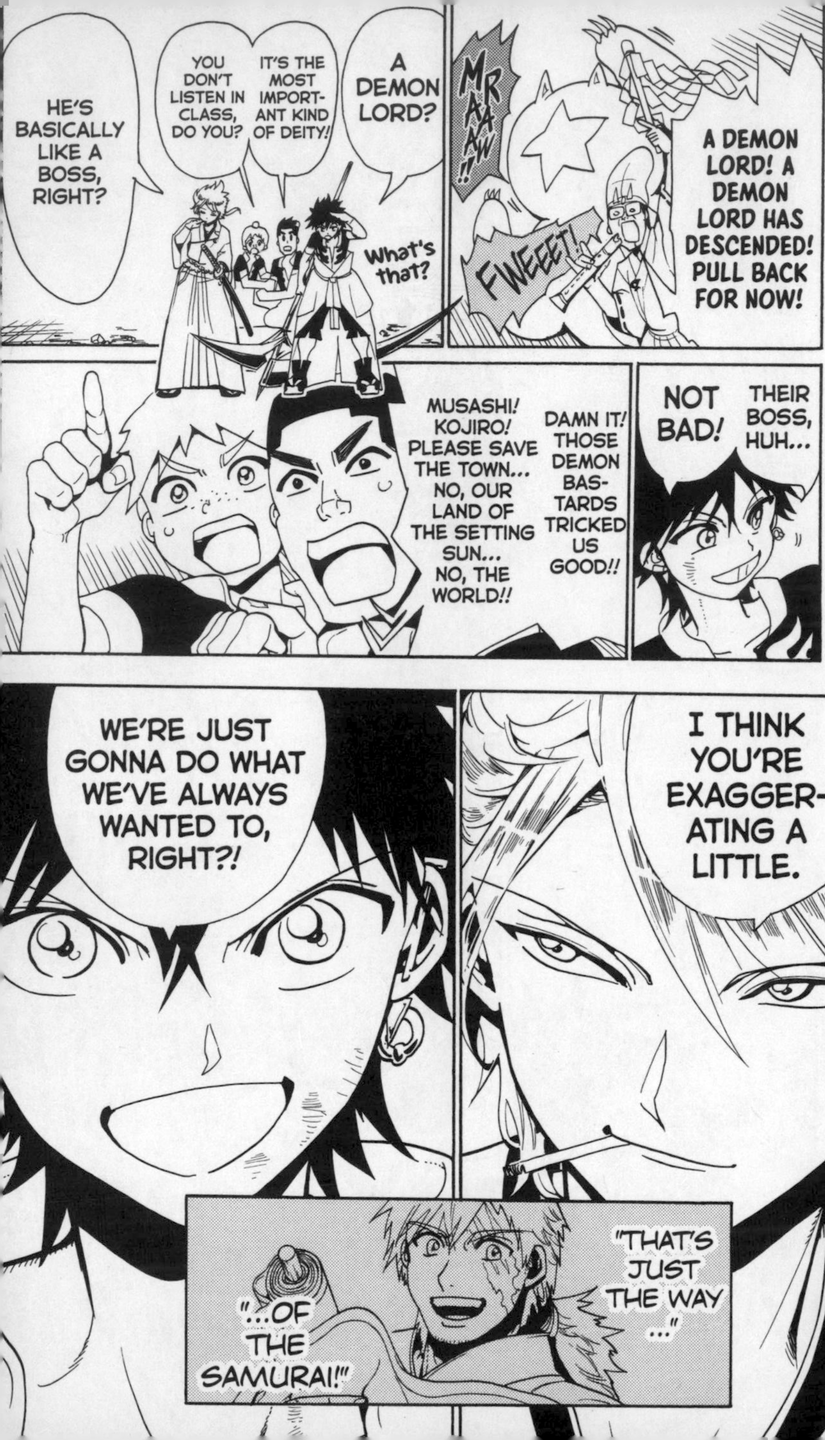
MRAAAW!!
FWEEET!
A DEMON LORD! A DEMON LORD HAS DESCENDED! PULL BACK FOR NOW!
A DEMON LORD?
IT'S THE MOST IMPORTANT KIND OF DEITY!
YOU DON'T LISTEN IN CLASS, DO YOU?
HE'S BASICALLY LIKE A BOSS, RIGHT?
What's that?
THEIR BOSS, HUH...
NOT BAD!
DAMN IT! THOSE DEMON BASTARDS TRICKED US GOOD!!
MUSASHI! KOJIRO! PLEASE SAVE THE TOWN... NO, OUR LAND OF THE SETTING SUN... NO, THE WORLD!!
I THINK YOU'RE EXAGGERATING A LITTLE.
WE'RE JUST GONNA DO WHAT WE'VE ALWAYS WANTED TO, RIGHT?!
"THAT'S JUST THE WAY ..."
"...OF THE SAMURAI!"

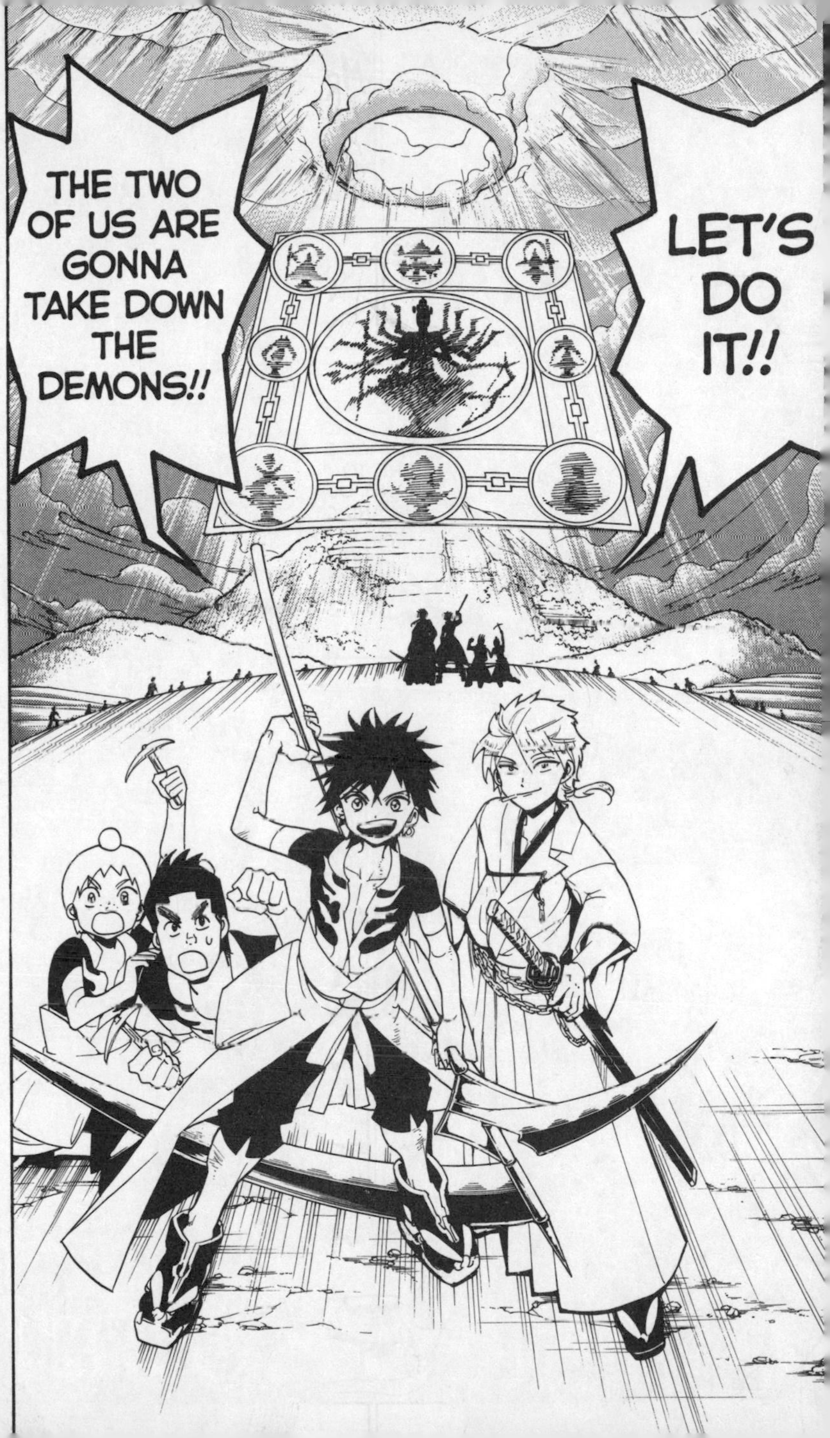
LET'S DO IT!!
THE TWO OF US ARE GONNA TAKE DOWN THE DEMONS!!

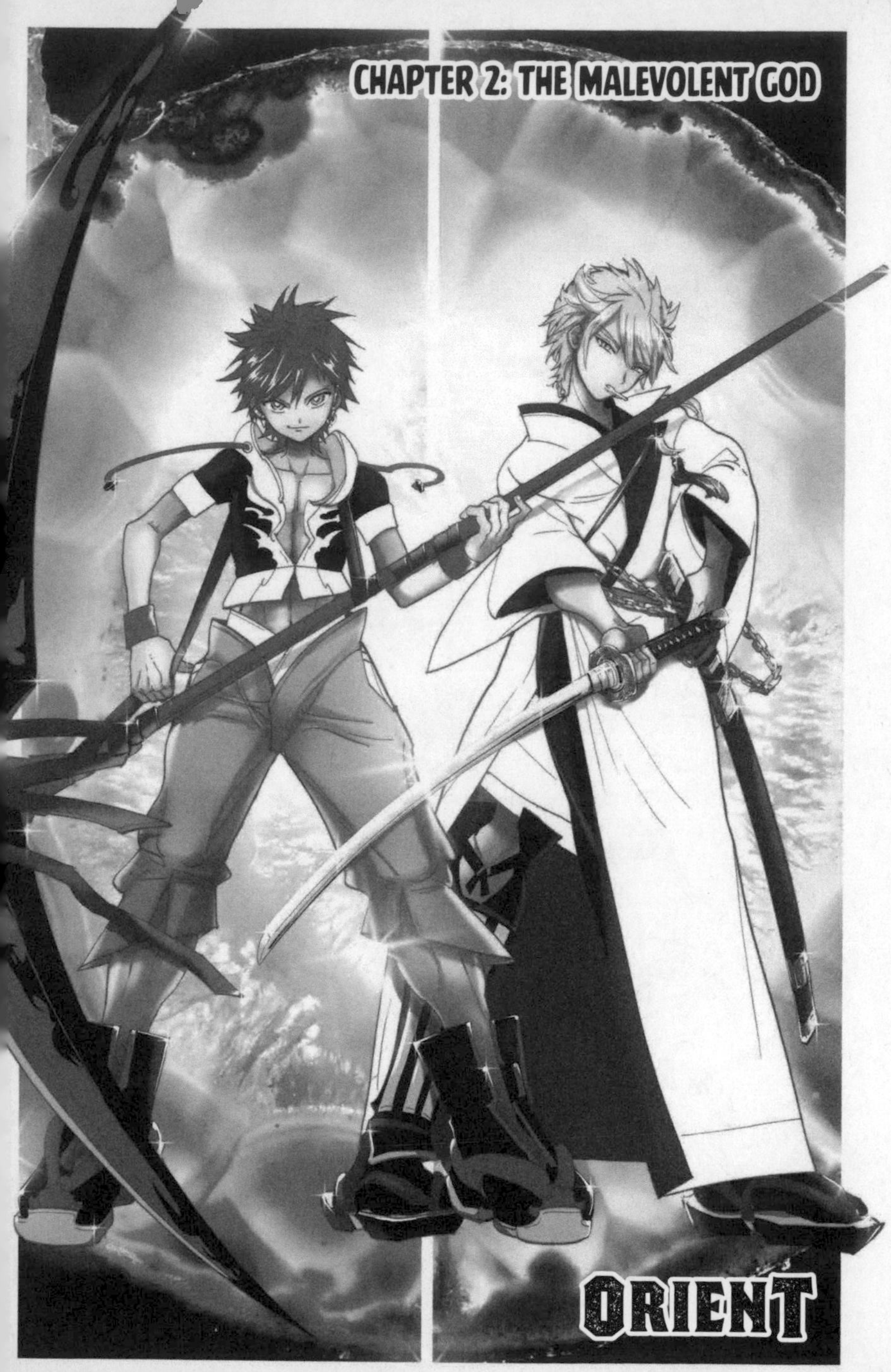
CHAPTER 2: THE MALEVOLENT GOD
ORIENT

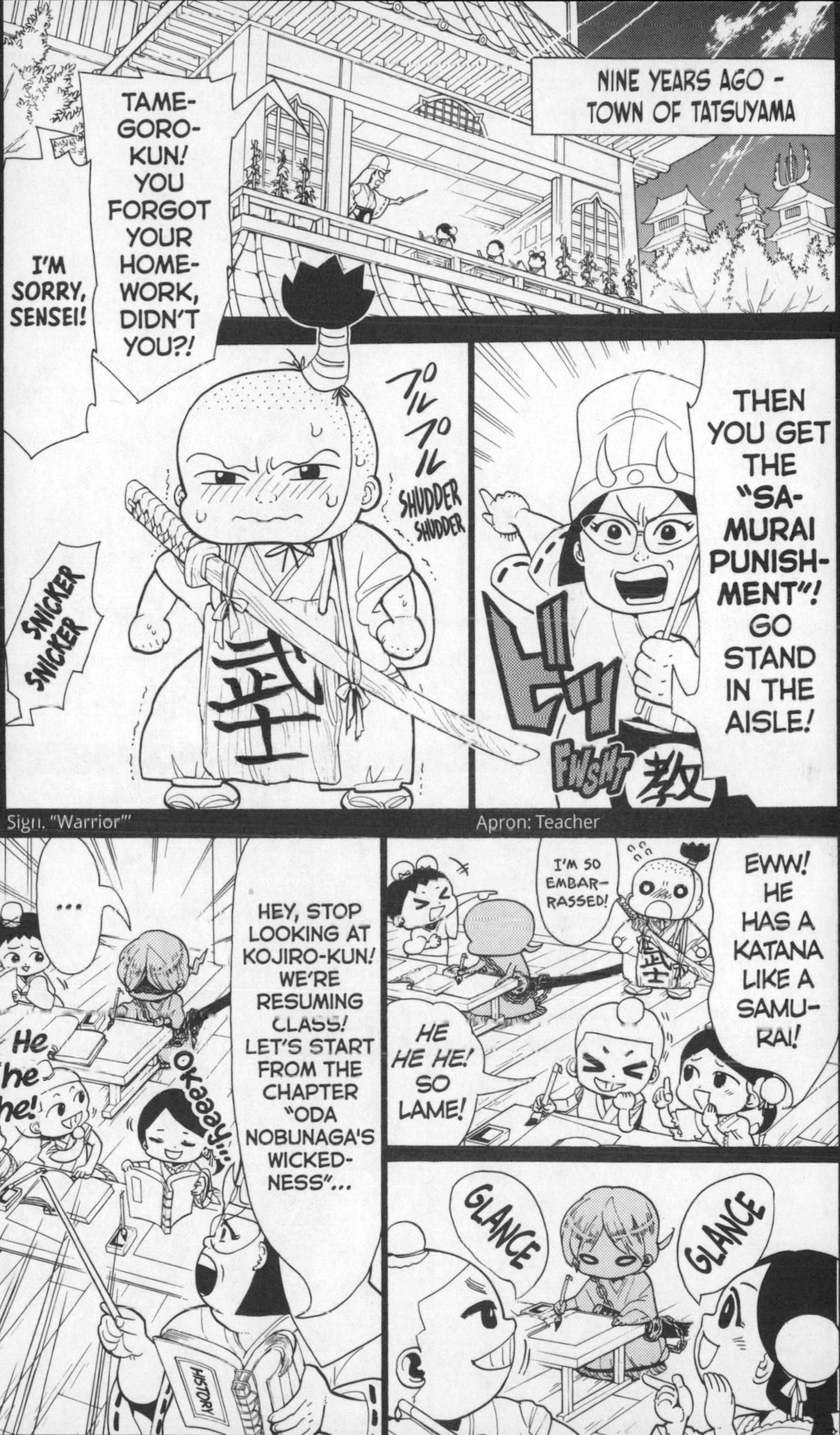
NINE YEARS AGO - TOWN OF TATSUYAMA
TAME-GORO-KUN! YOU FORGOT YOUR HOME-WORK, DIDN'T YOU?!
I'M SORRY, SENSEI!
THEN YOU GET THE "SA-MURAI PUNISH-MENT"! GO STAND IN THE AISLE!
ビッ
FWSHT
教
プルプル
SHUDDER SHUDDER
武士
SNICKER SNICKER
EWW! HE HAS A KATANA LIKE A SAMU-RAI!
I'M SO EMBAR-RASSED!
HE HE HE! SO LAME!
HEY, STOP LOOKING AT KOJIRO-KUN! WE'RE RESUMING CLASS! LET'S START FROM THE CHAPTER "ODA NOBUNAGA'S WICKED-NESS"...
...
He he he!
Okaaay!!
HISTORY
GLANCE
GLANCE

Sign: "Warrior"

Apron: Teacher

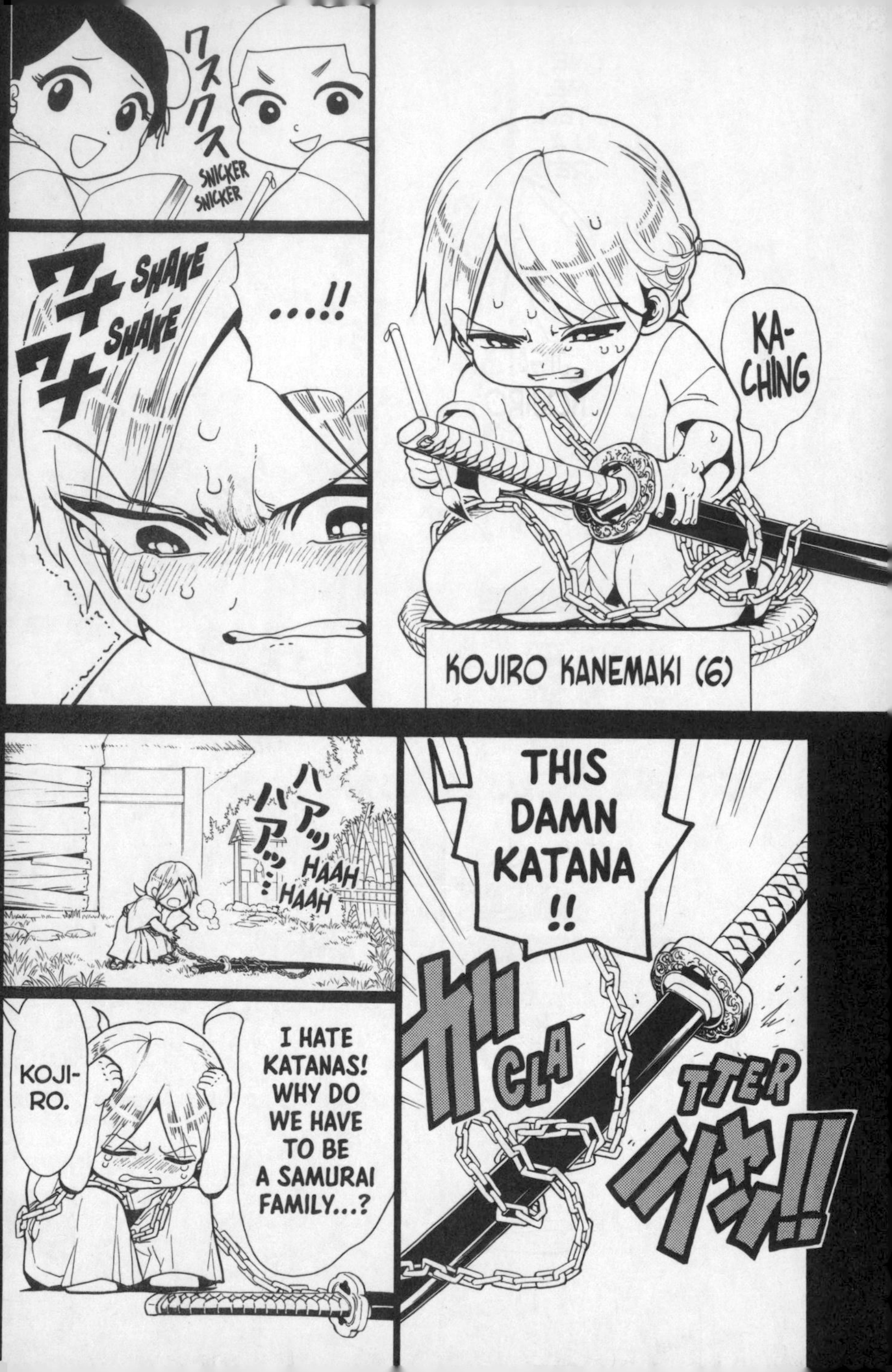
KA-CHING
KOJIRO KANEMAKI (6)
クスクス
SNICKER SNICKER
ワナワナ
SHAKE SHAKE
...!!
THIS DAMN KATANA !!
ガシャッ!!
CLA
TTER
ハァッハァッ…
HAAH HAAH
KOJI-RO.
I HATE KATANAS! WHY DO WE HAVE TO BE A SAMURAI FAMILY...?

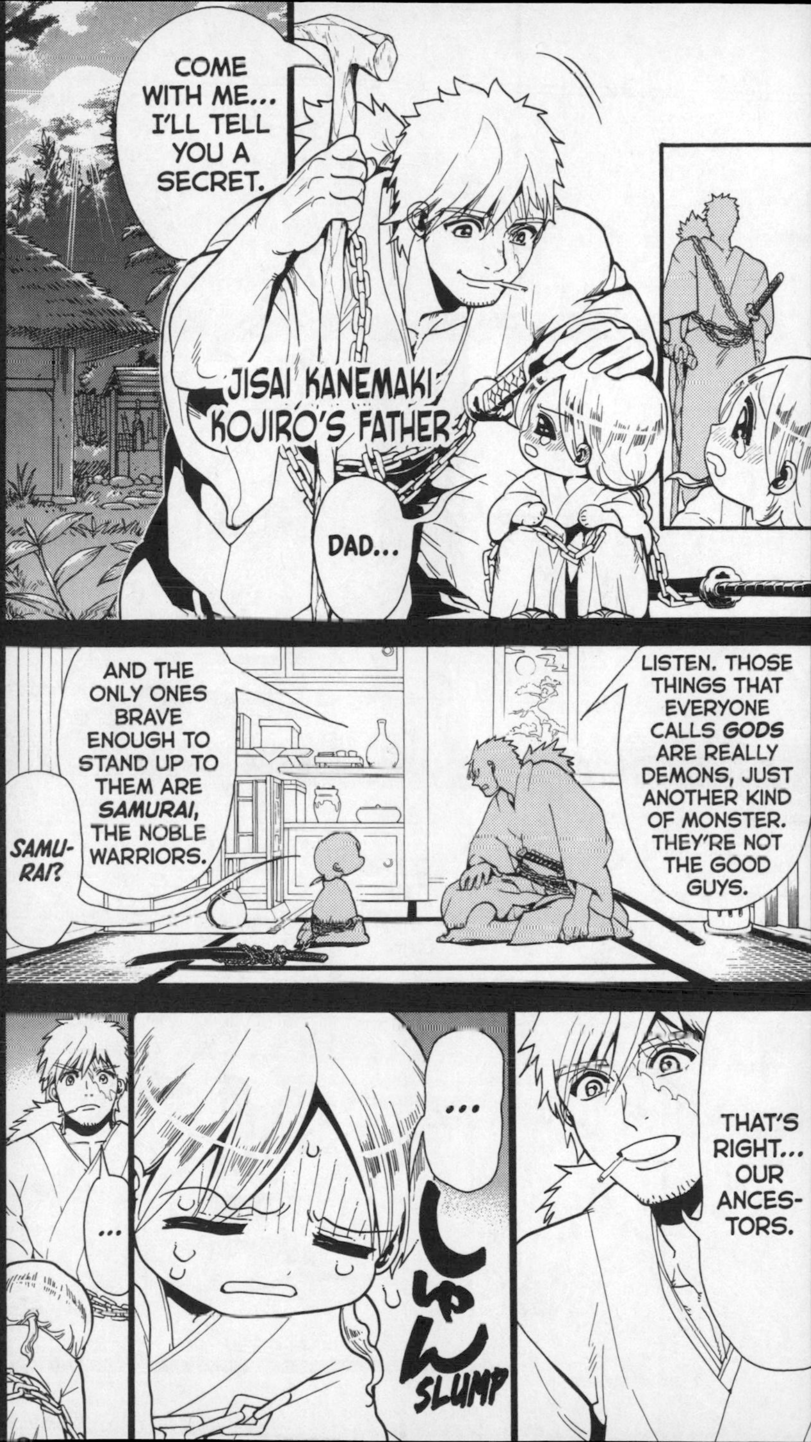
COME WITH ME... I'LL TELL YOU A SECRET.
JISAI KANEMAKI
KOJIRO'S FATHER
DAD...
LISTEN. THOSE THINGS THAT EVERYONE CALLS *GODS* ARE REALLY DEMONS, JUST ANOTHER KIND OF MONSTER. THEY'RE NOT THE GOOD GUYS.
AND THE ONLY ONES BRAVE ENOUGH TO STAND UP TO THEM ARE *SAMURAI*, THE NOBLE WARRIORS.
SAMURAI?
THAT'S RIGHT... OUR ANCESTORS.
...
SLUMP
...

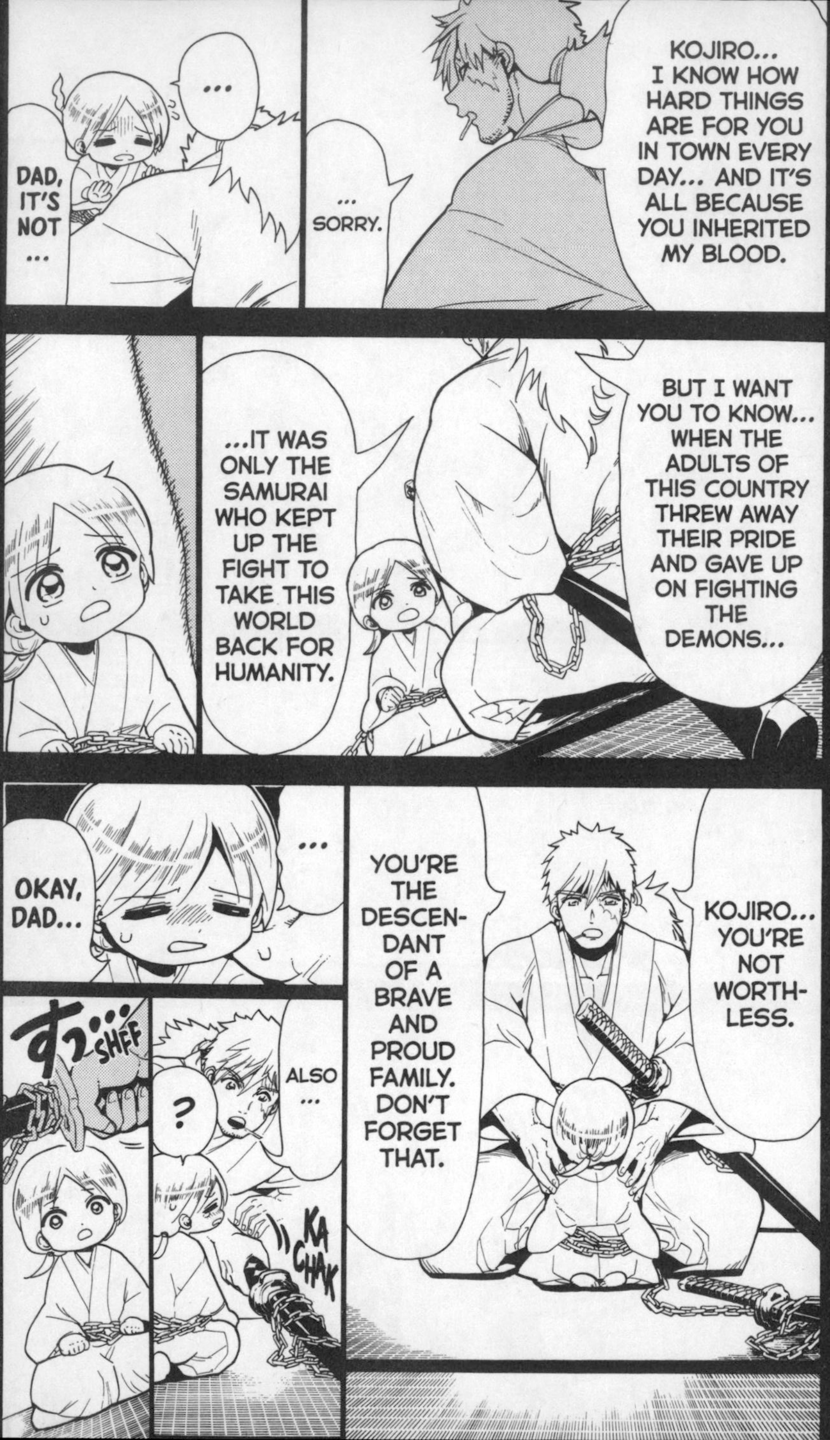
KOJIRO... I KNOW HOW HARD THINGS ARE FOR YOU IN TOWN EVERY DAY... AND IT'S ALL BECAUSE YOU INHERITED MY BLOOD.
... SORRY.
...
DAD, IT'S NOT ...
BUT I WANT YOU TO KNOW... WHEN THE ADULTS OF THIS COUNTRY THREW AWAY THEIR PRIDE AND GAVE UP ON FIGHTING THE DEMONS...
...IT WAS ONLY THE SAMURAI WHO KEPT UP THE FIGHT TO TAKE THIS WORLD BACK FOR HUMANITY.
KOJIRO... YOU'RE NOT WORTH-LESS.
YOU'RE THE DESCEN-DANT OF A BRAVE AND PROUD FAMILY. DON'T FORGET THAT.
...
OKAY, DAD...
ALSO ...
?
すっ… SHFF
KA CHAK

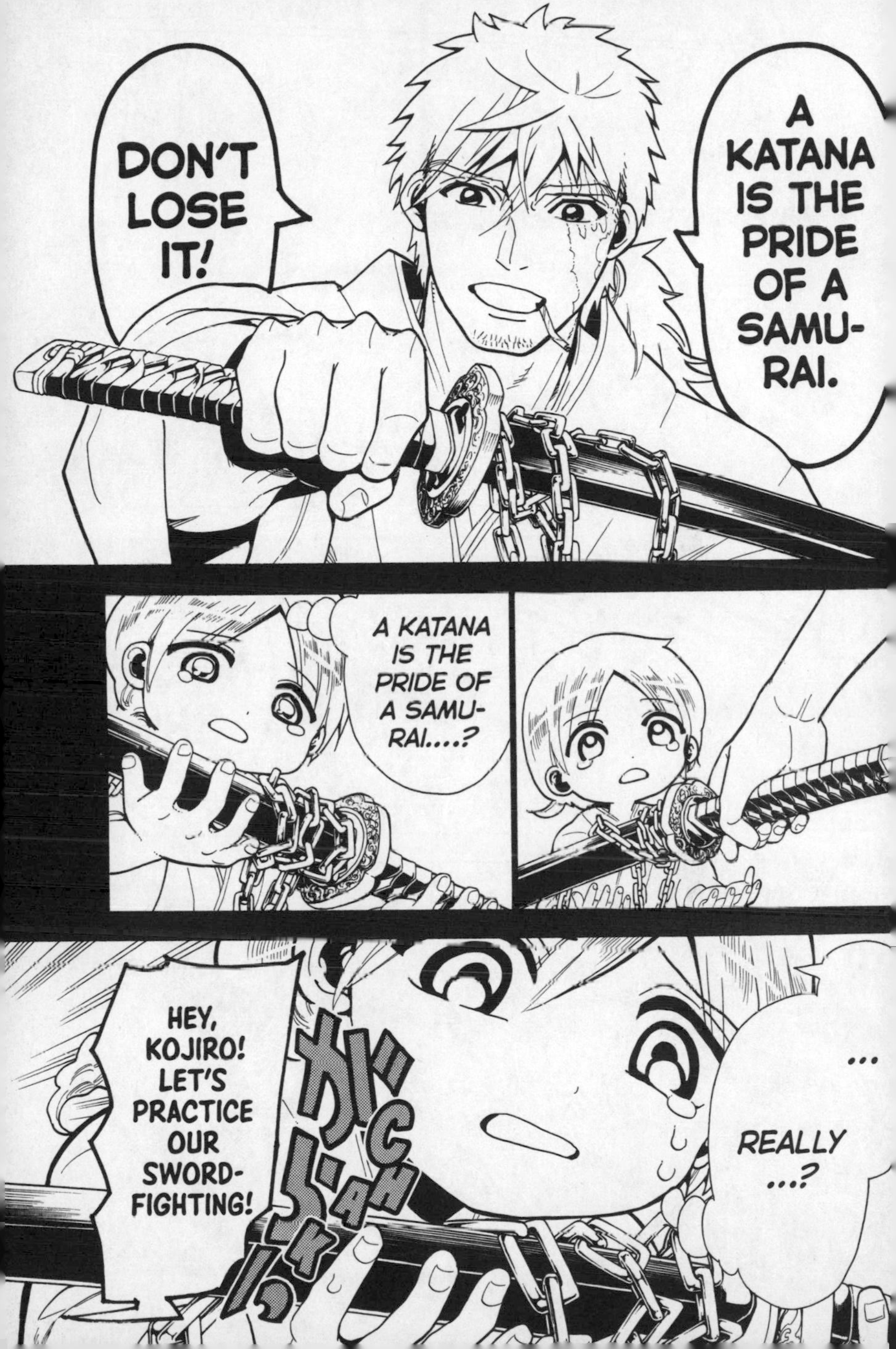
A KATANA IS THE PRIDE OF A SAMU-RAI.
DON'T LOSE IT!
A KATANA IS THE PRIDE OF A SAMU-RAI....?
... REALLY ...?
CHAK
HEY, KOJIRO! LET'S PRACTICE OUR SWORD-FIGHTING!

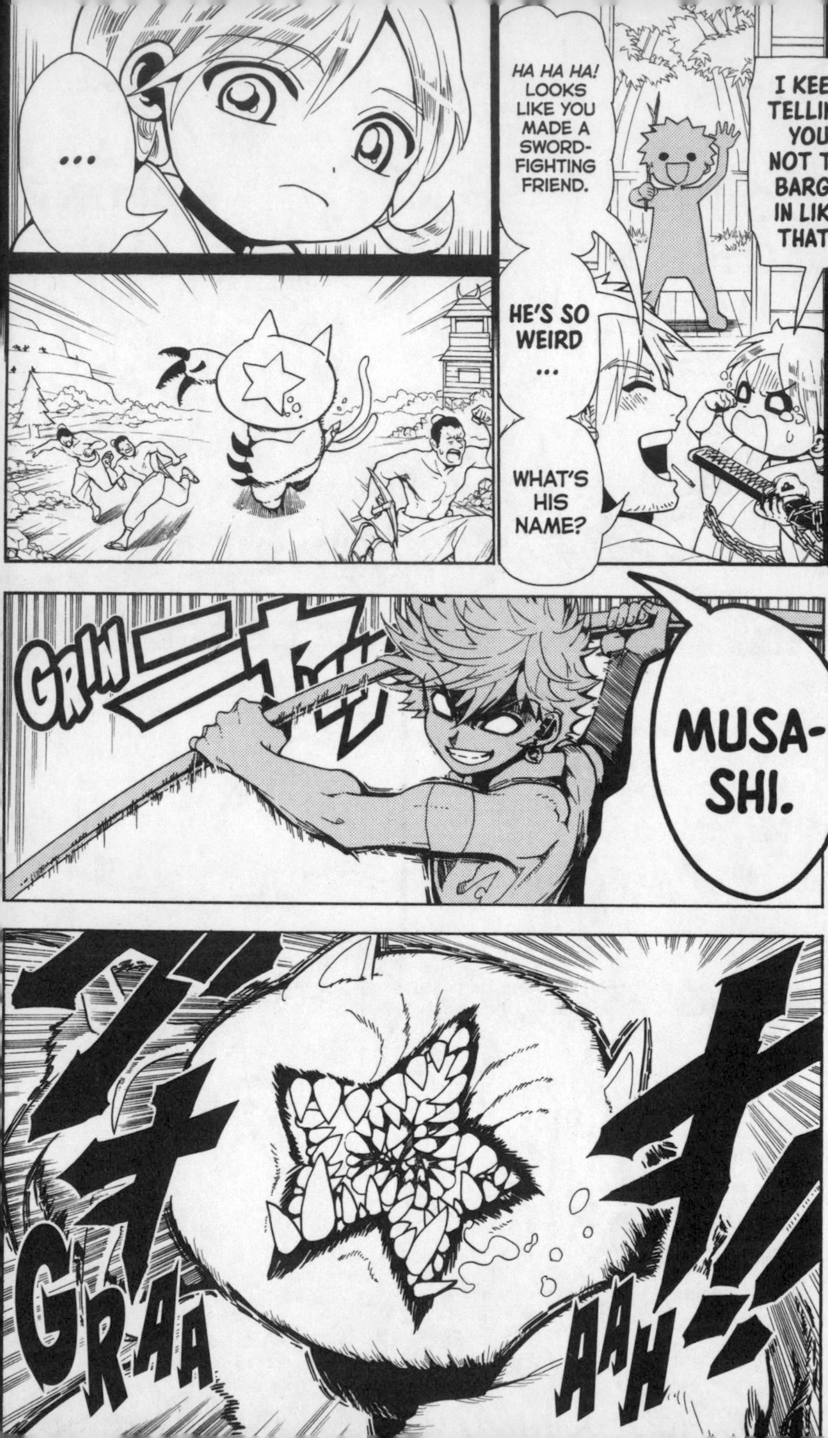
I KEEP TELLING YOU NOT TO BARGE IN LIKE THAT!
HA HA HA! LOOKS LIKE YOU MADE A SWORD-FIGHTING FRIEND.
HE'S SO WEIRD ...
WHAT'S HIS NAME?
...
MUSA-SHI.
GRIN
GRAA
AAH!!

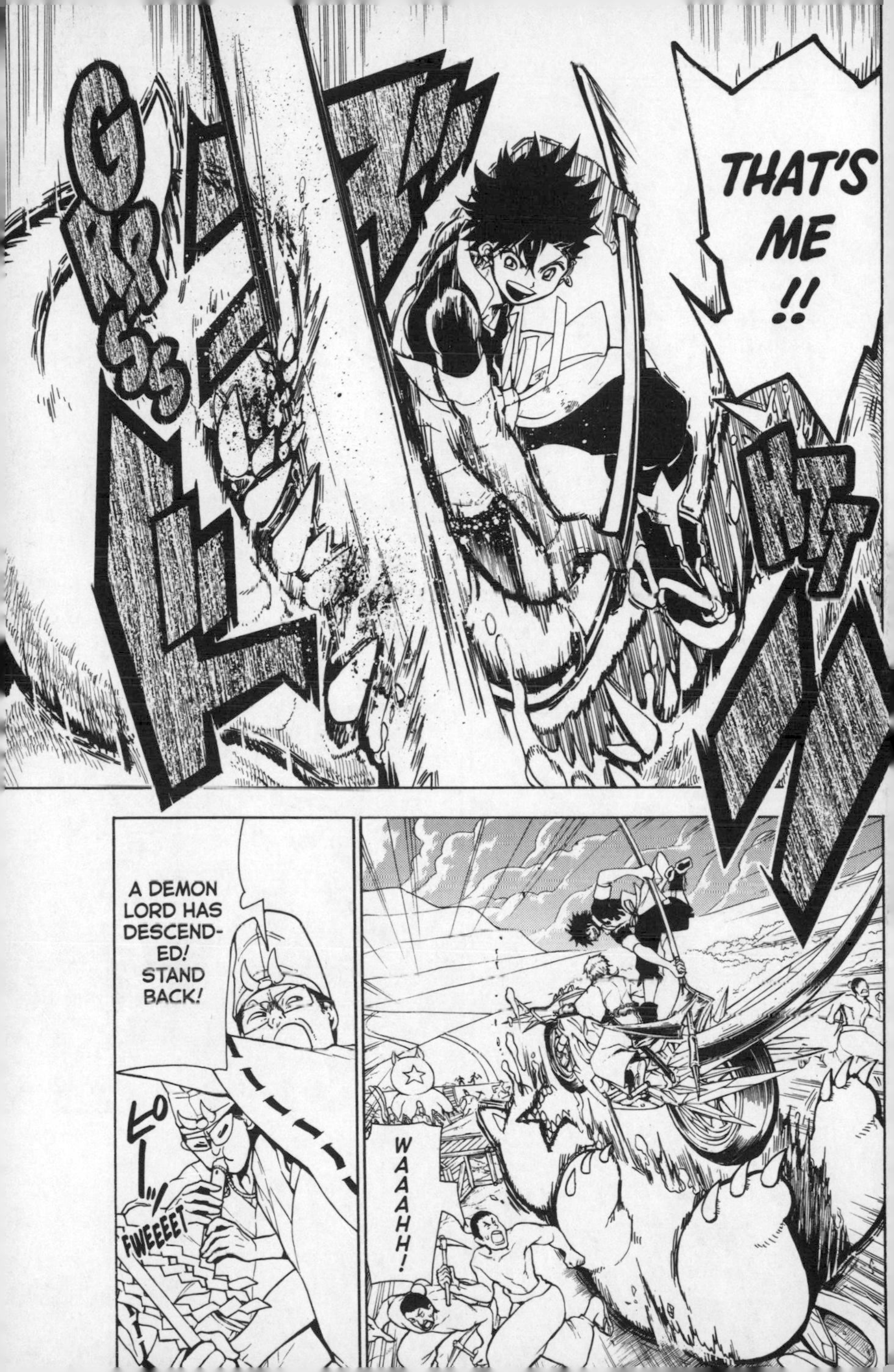
THAT'S ME !!
WAAAAHH!
A DEMON LORD HAS DESCENDED! STAND BACK!
FWEEEET

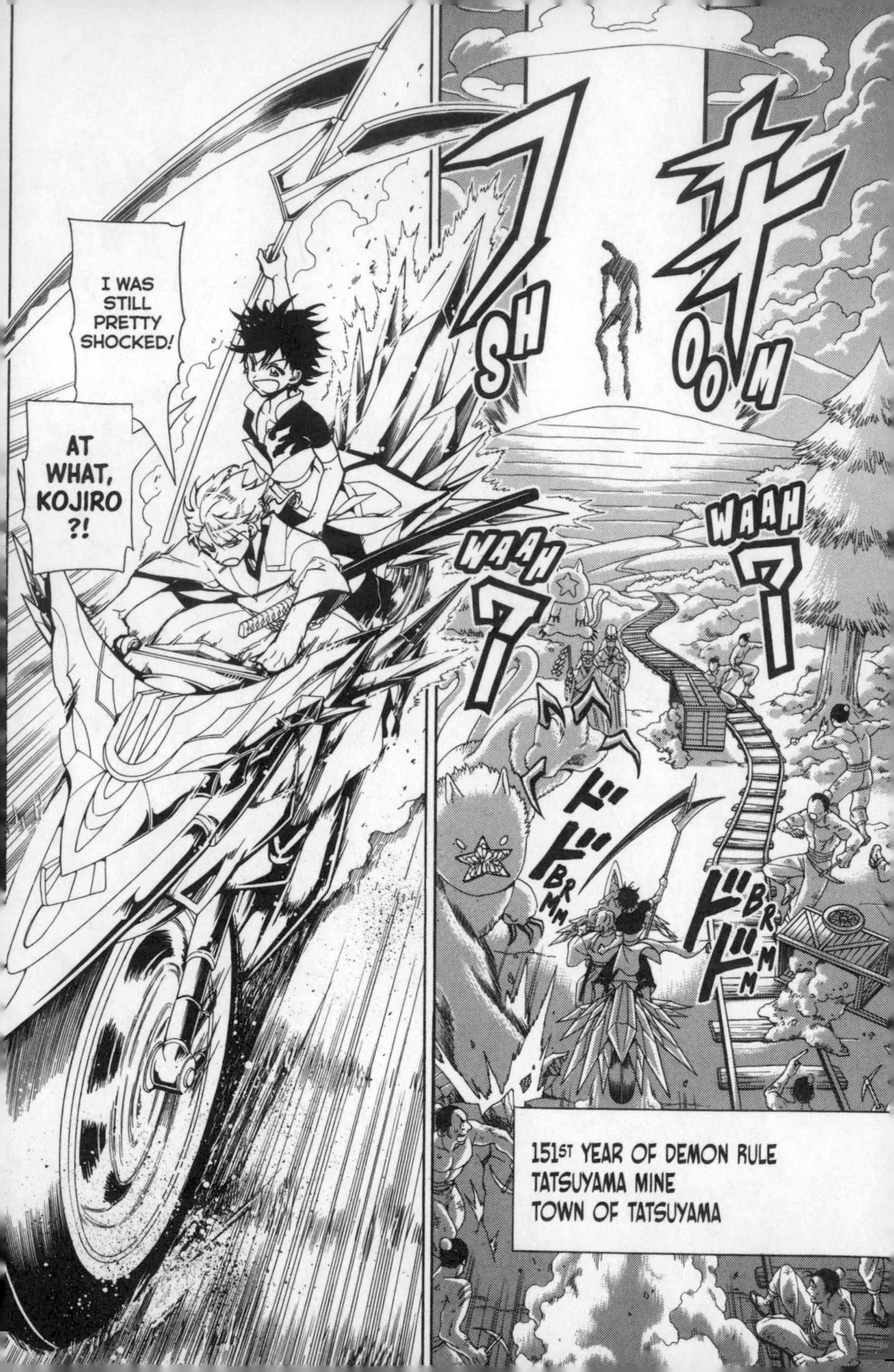

SHOOM
WAAH
WAAH
BRMM
BRRMM
151st YEAR OF DEMON RULE
TATSUYAMA MINE
TOWN OF TATSUYAMA
I WAS STILL PRETTY SHOCKED!
AT WHAT, KOJIRO?!

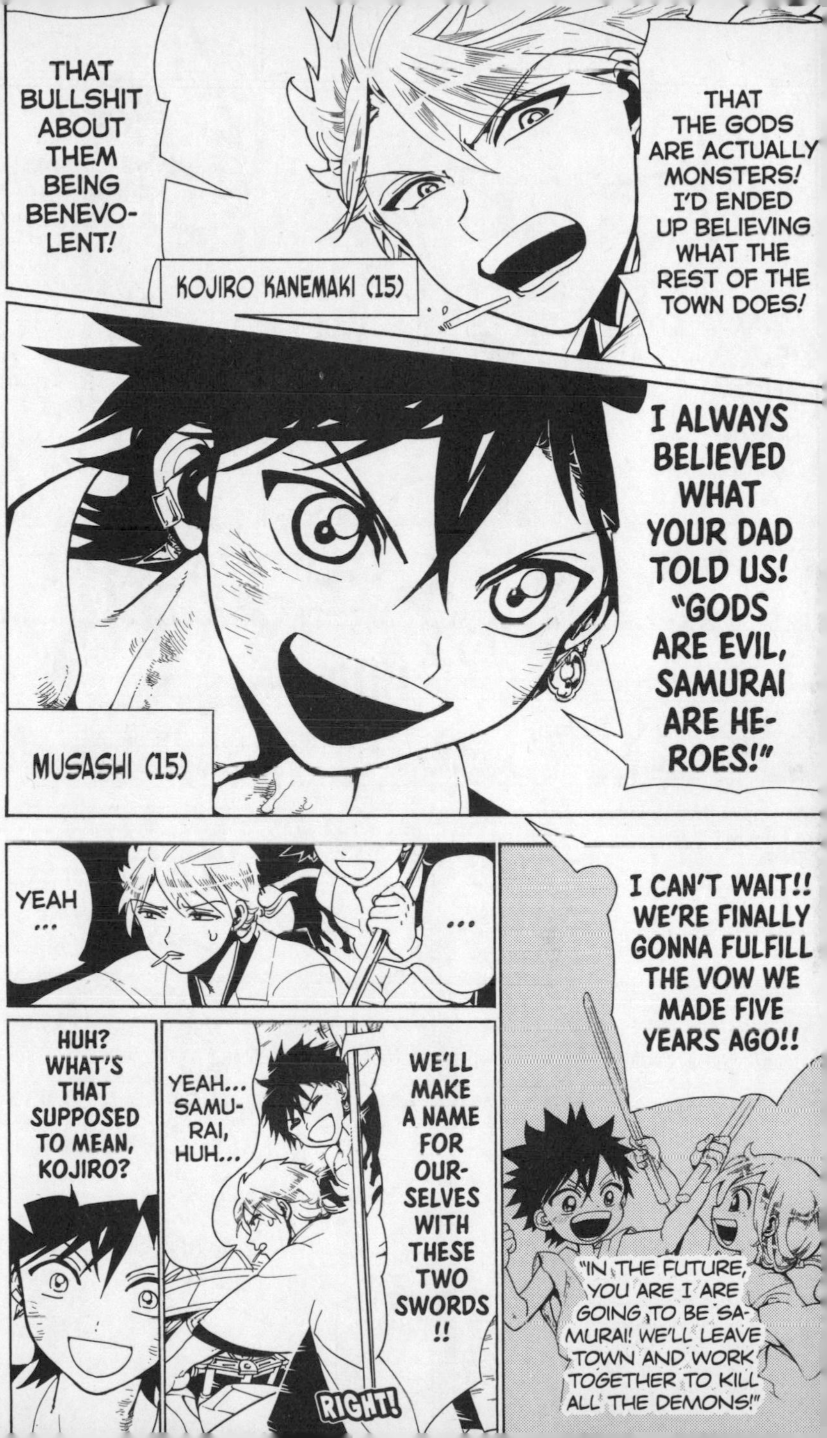
THAT THE GODS ARE ACTUALLY MONSTERS! I'D ENDED UP BELIEVING WHAT THE REST OF THE TOWN DOES!
THAT BULLSHIT ABOUT THEM BEING BENEVO-LENT!
KOJIRO KANEMAKI (15)
I ALWAYS BELIEVED WHAT YOUR DAD TOLD US! "GODS ARE EVIL, SAMURAI ARE HE-ROES!"
MUSASHI (15)
I CAN'T WAIT!! WE'RE FINALLY GONNA FULFILL THE VOW WE MADE FIVE YEARS AGO!!
"IN THE FUTURE, YOU ARE I ARE GOING TO BE SA-MURAI! WE'LL LEAVE TOWN AND WORK TOGETHER TO KILL ALL THE DEMONS!"
...
YEAH ...
WE'LL MAKE A NAME FOR OUR-SELVES WITH THESE TWO SWORDS !!
YEAH... SAMU-RAI, HUH...
RIGHT!
HUH? WHAT'S THAT SUPPOSED TO MEAN, KOJIRO?

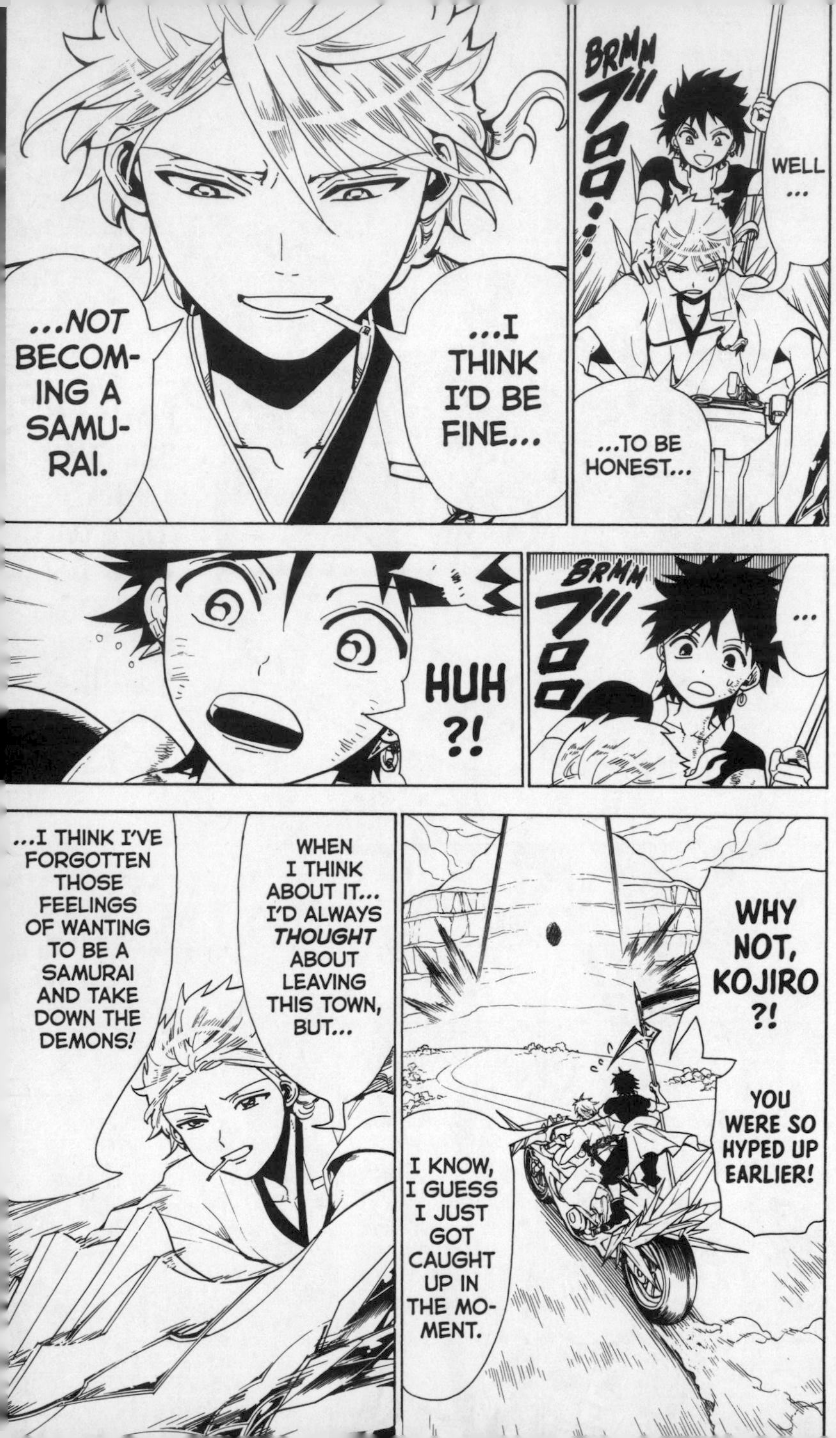
BRMN
ブロロ・・・
WELL ...
...TO BE HONEST...
...I THINK I'D BE FINE...
...NOT BECOMING A SAMURAI.
BRMM
ブロロ
...
HUH ?!
WHY NOT, KOJIRO ?!
YOU WERE SO HYPED UP EARLIER!
I KNOW, I GUESS I JUST GOT CAUGHT UP IN THE MOMENT.
WHEN I THINK ABOUT IT... I'D ALWAYS *THOUGHT* ABOUT LEAVING THIS TOWN, BUT...
...I THINK I'VE FORGOTTEN THOSE FEELINGS OF WANTING TO BE A SAMURAI AND TAKE DOWN THE DEMONS!

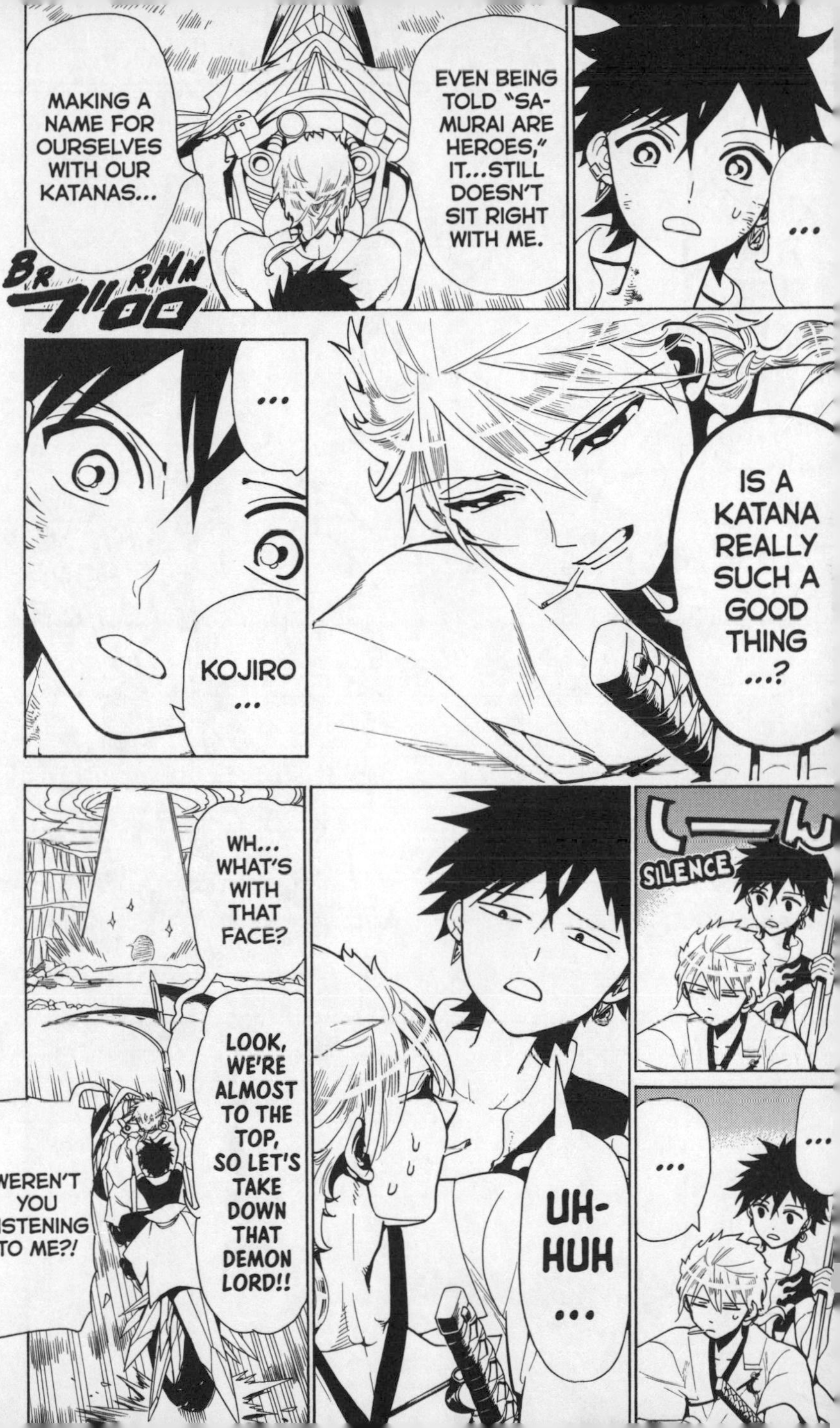
...
EVEN BEING TOLD "SAMURAI ARE HEROES," IT...STILL DOESN'T SIT RIGHT WITH ME.
MAKING A NAME FOR OURSELVES WITH OUR KATANAS...
BRRMN
IS A KATANA REALLY SUCH A GOOD THING ...?
...
KOJIRO ...
しーん
SILENCE
...
...
UH-HUH ...
WH... WHAT'S WITH THAT FACE?
LOOK, WE'RE ALMOST TO THE TOP, SO LET'S TAKE DOWN THAT DEMON LORD!!
WEREN'T YOU LISTENING TO ME?!

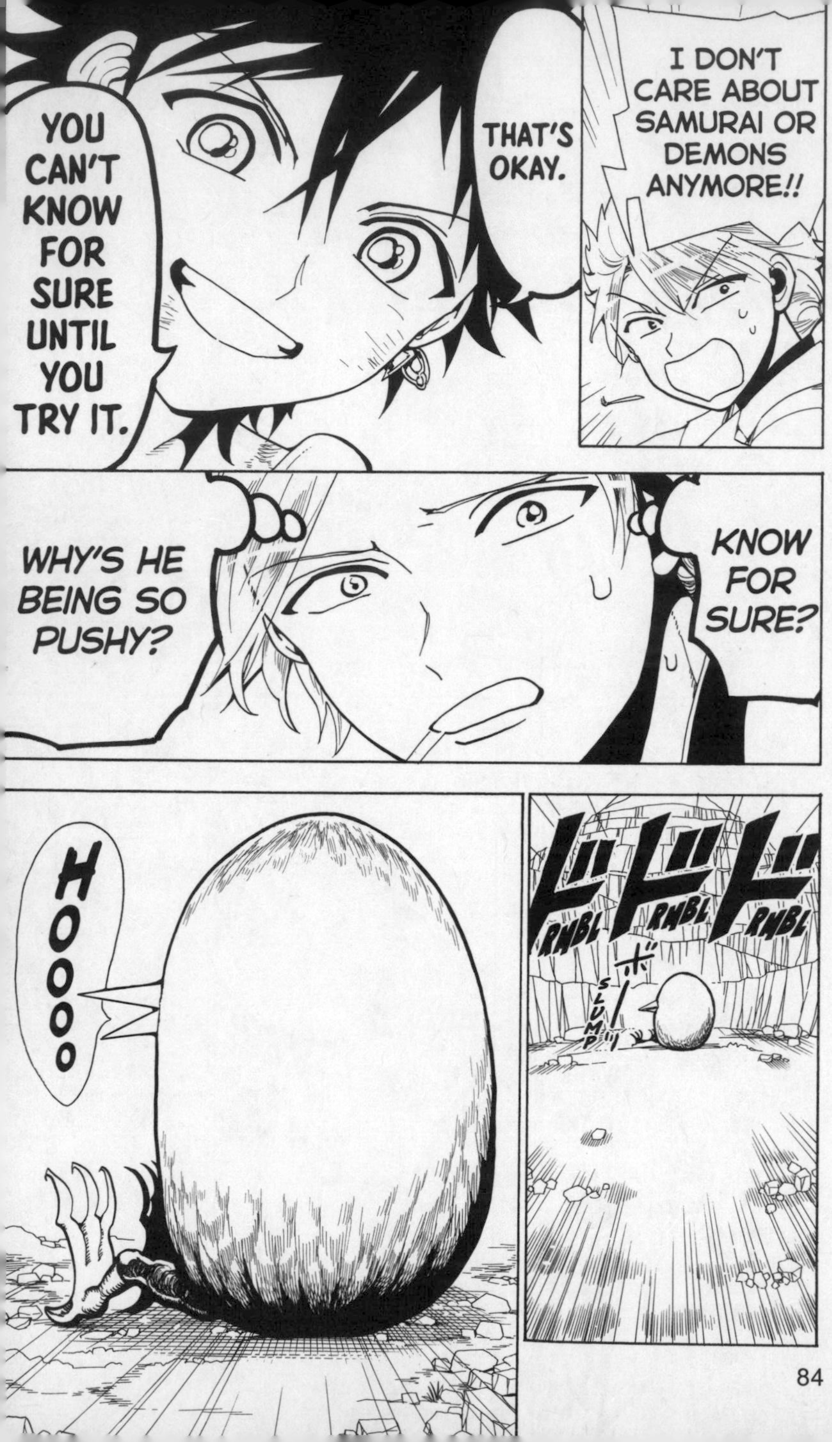
I DON'T CARE ABOUT SAMURAI OR DEMONS ANYMORE!!
THAT'S OKAY.
YOU CAN'T KNOW FOR SURE UNTIL YOU TRY IT.
KNOW FOR SURE?
WHY'S HE BEING SO PUSHY?
RMBL
RMBL
RMBL
SLUMP
HOOOOO

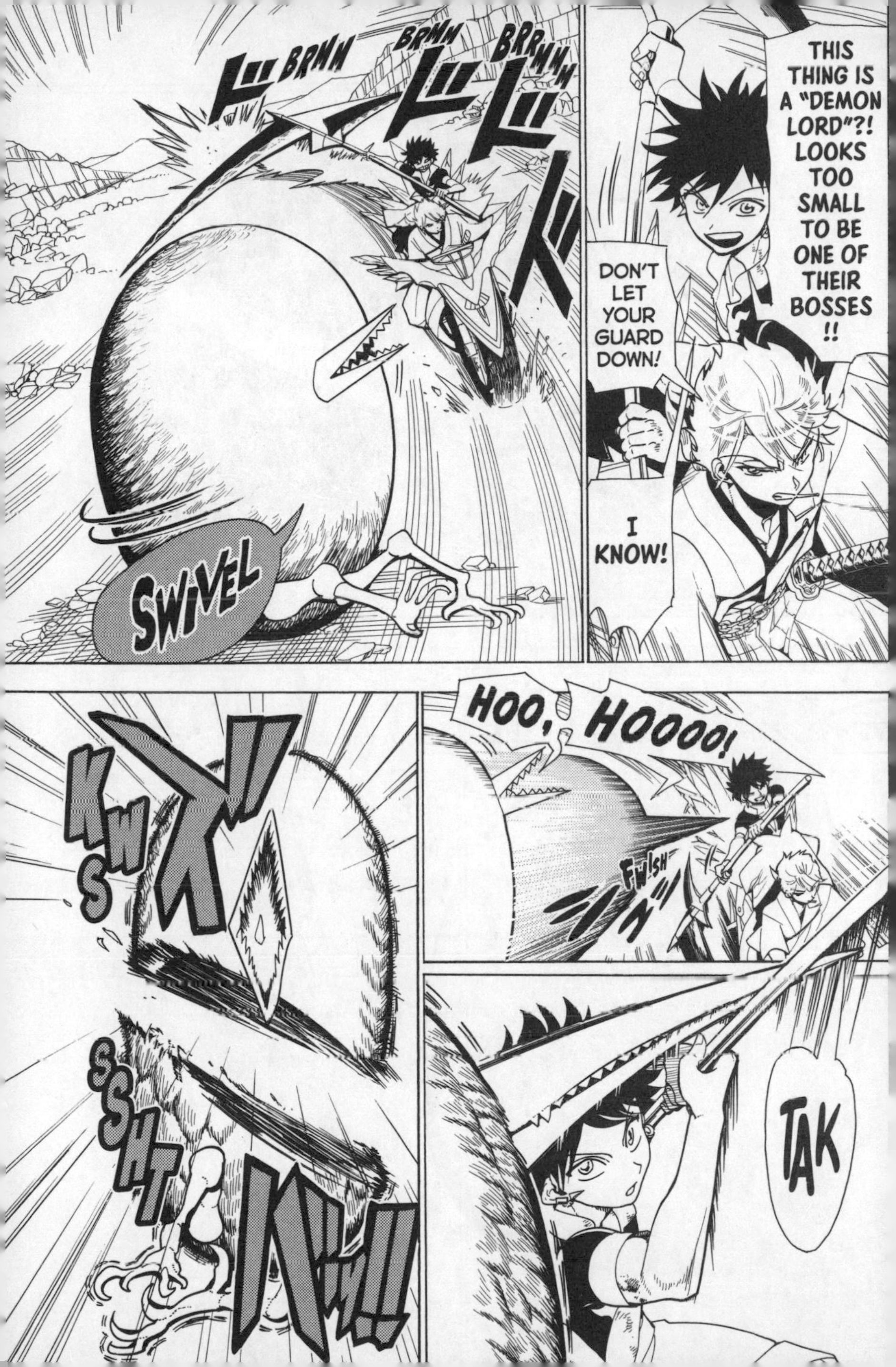
THIS THING IS A "DEMON LORD"?! LOOKS TOO SMALL TO BE ONE OF THEIR BOSSES !!
DON'T LET YOUR GUARD DOWN!
I KNOW!
BRRMMMM
BRMM
BRMM
SWIVEL
HOO, HOOOOO!
FWISH
TAK
KWSS
SSHT

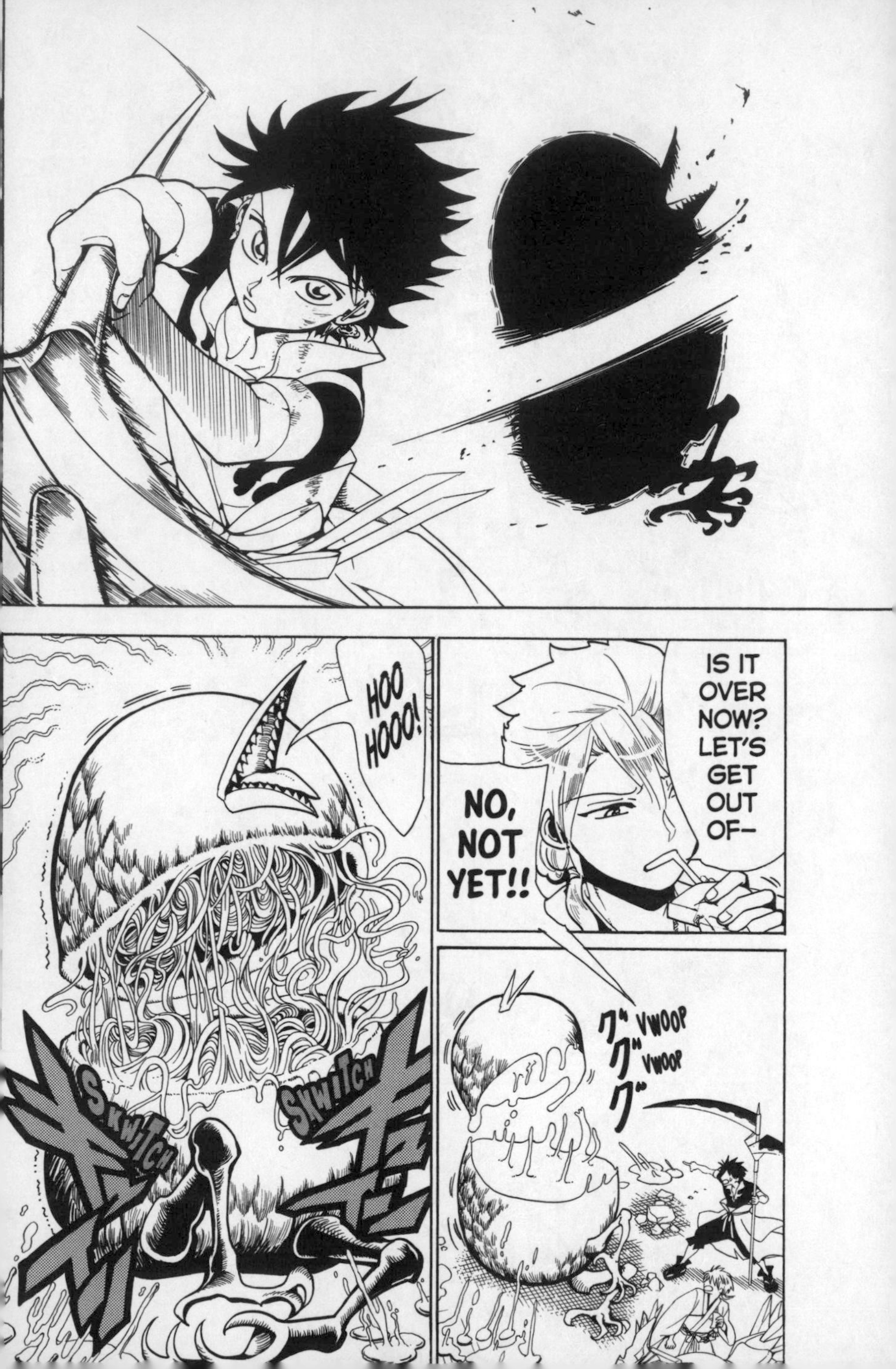

IS IT OVER NOW? LET'S GET OUT OF–
NO, NOT YET!!
グ VWOOP
ググ VWOOP
HOO HOOO!
SKWITCH
SKWITCH

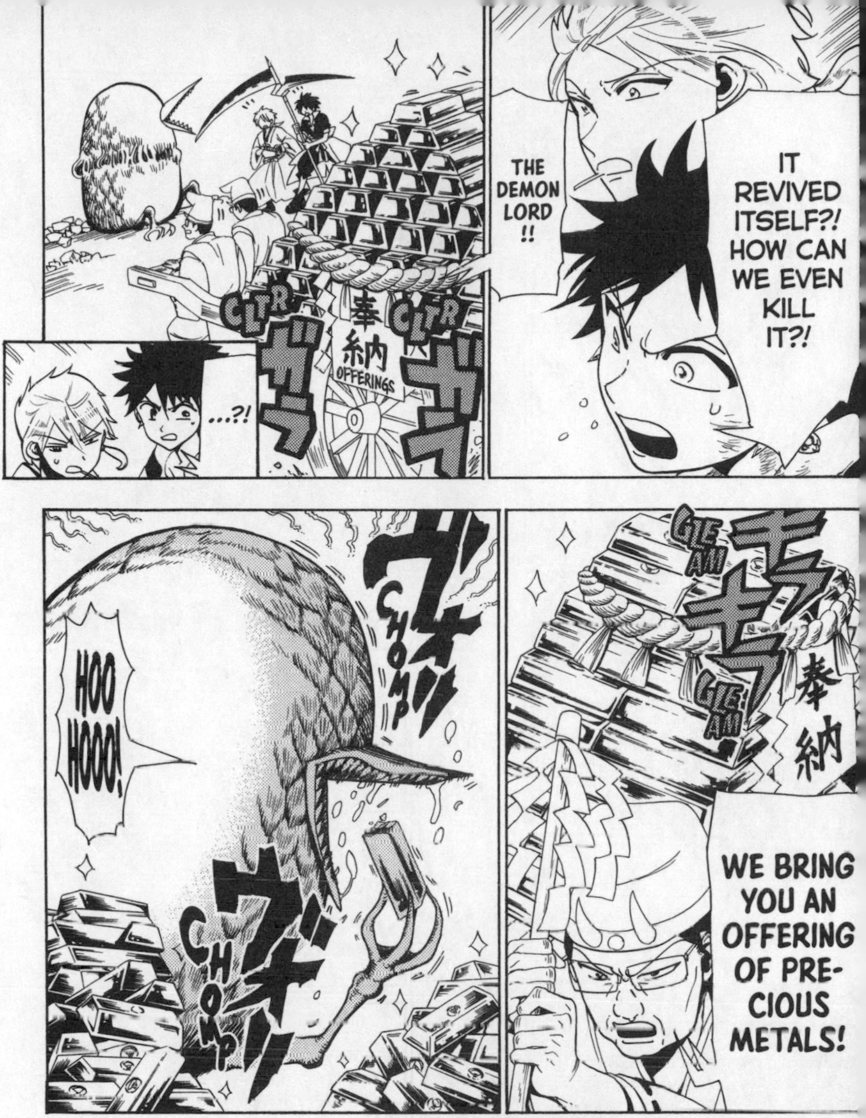
IT REVIVED ITSELF?! HOW CAN WE EVEN KILL IT?!
THE DEMON LORD!!
CLTR
CLTR
奉納
OFFERINGS
...?!
GLEAM
GLEAM
奉納
WE BRING YOU AN OFFERING OF PRECIOUS METALS!
CHOMP
CHOMP
HOO HOOO!
Sign: Offerings

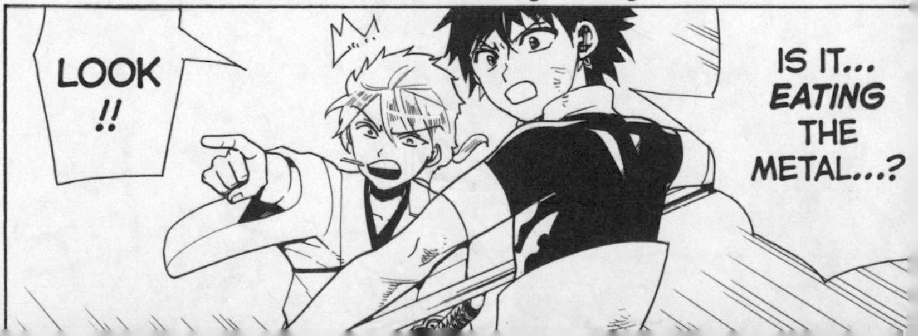
IS IT... EATING THE METAL...?
LOOK!!

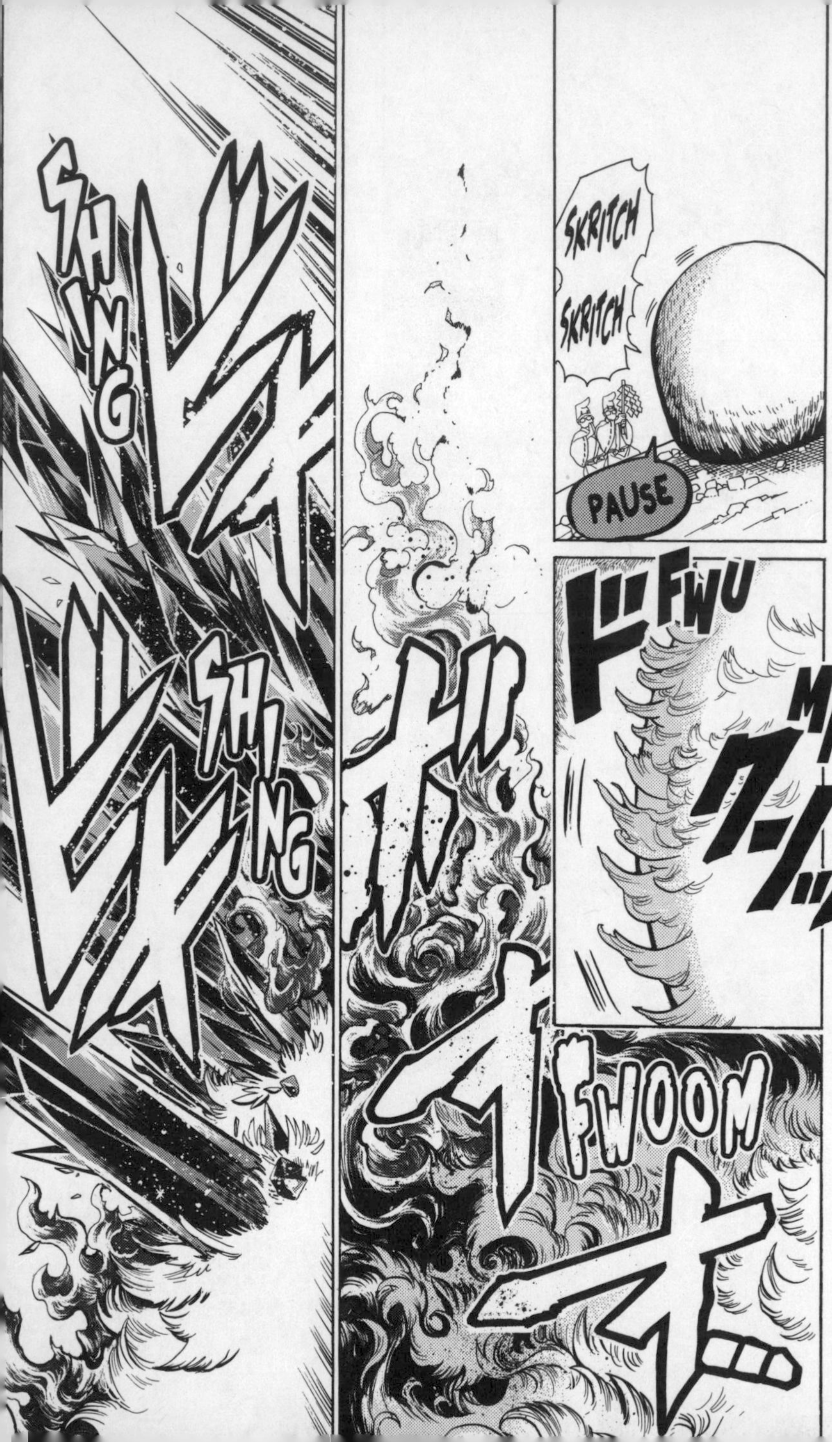
SKRITCH
SKRITCH
PAUSE
FWUMP
FWOOM
SHING
SHING

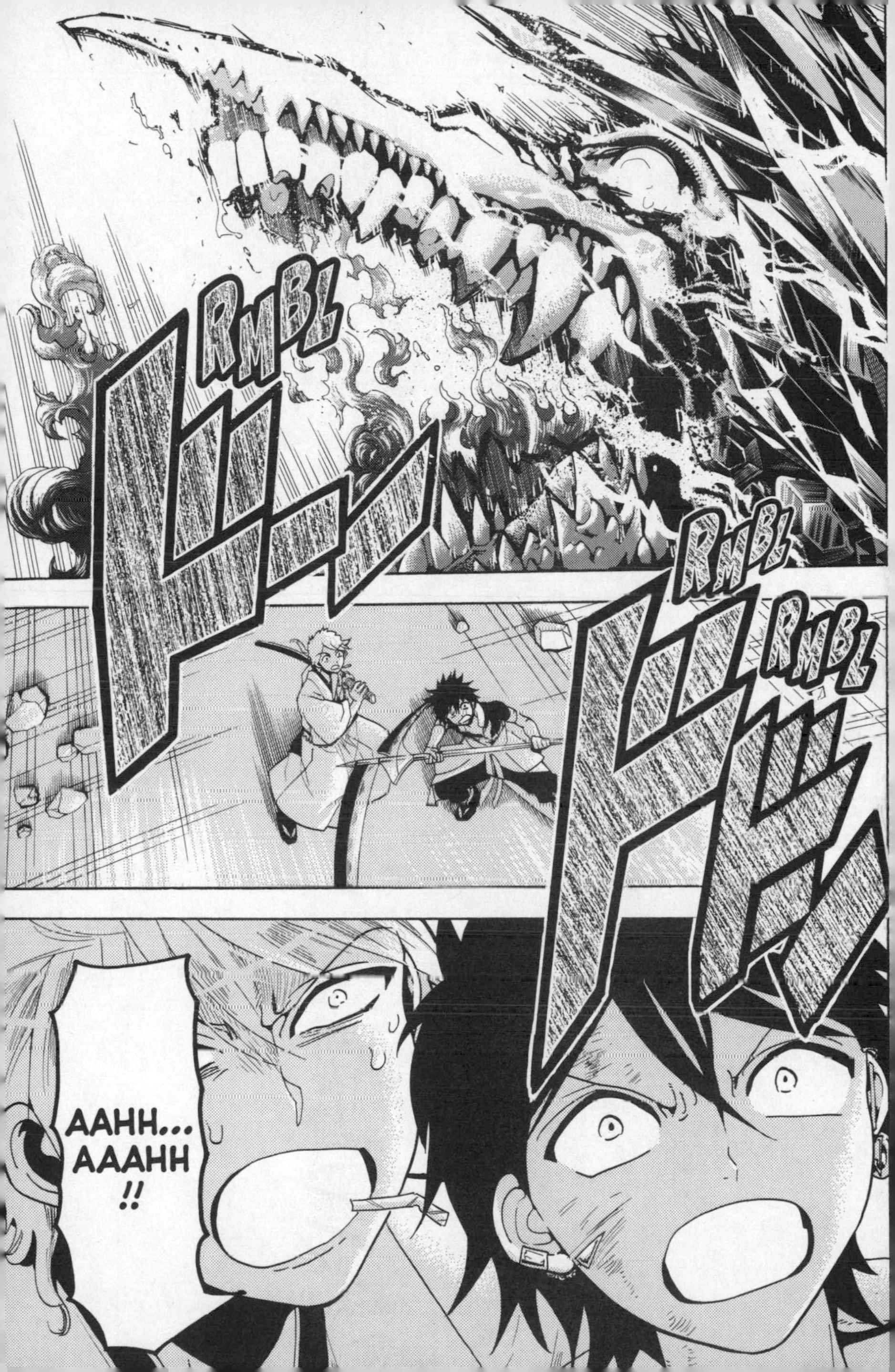
RMBL
RMBL
RMBL
AAHH... AAAHH !!

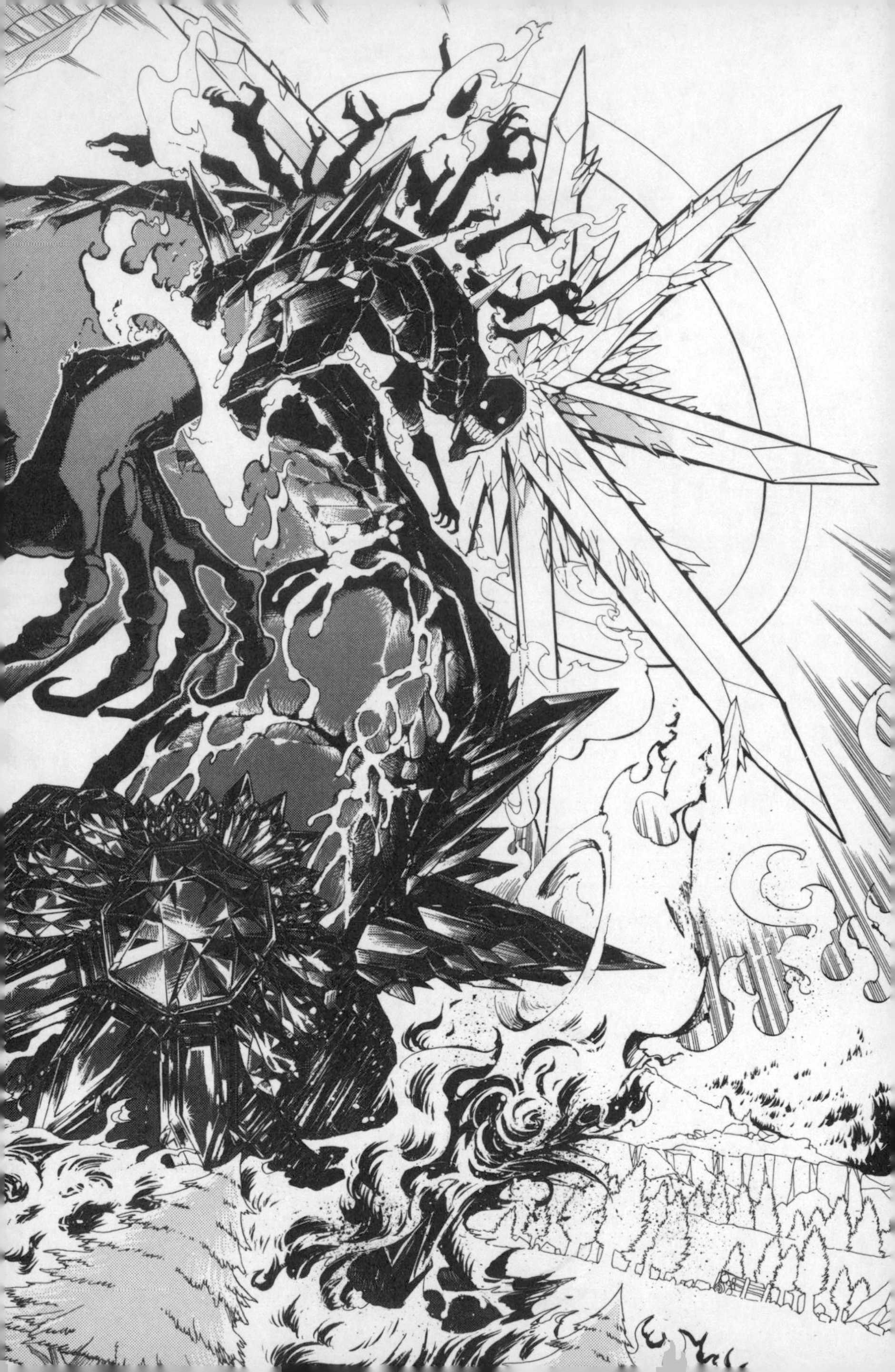

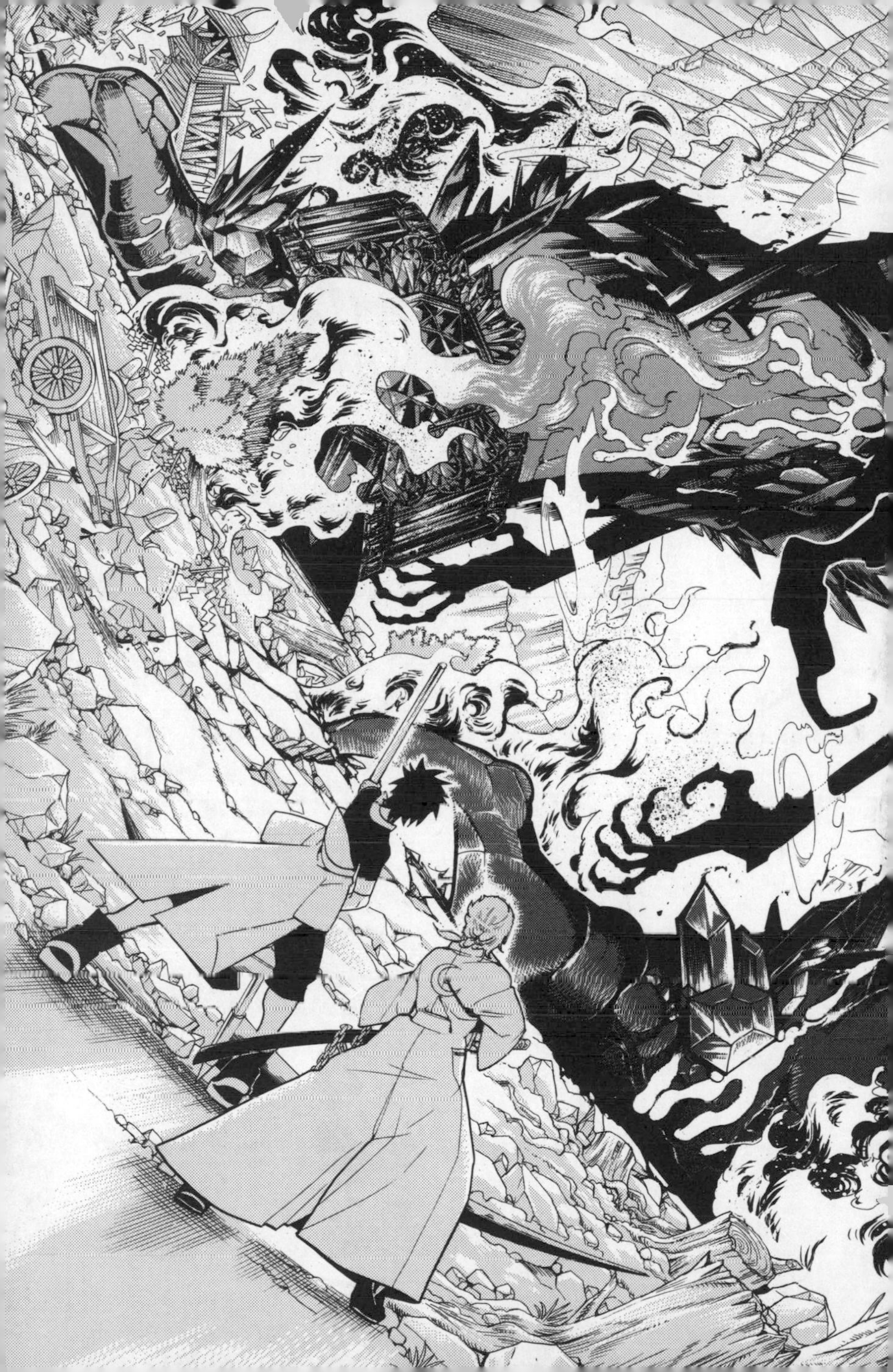

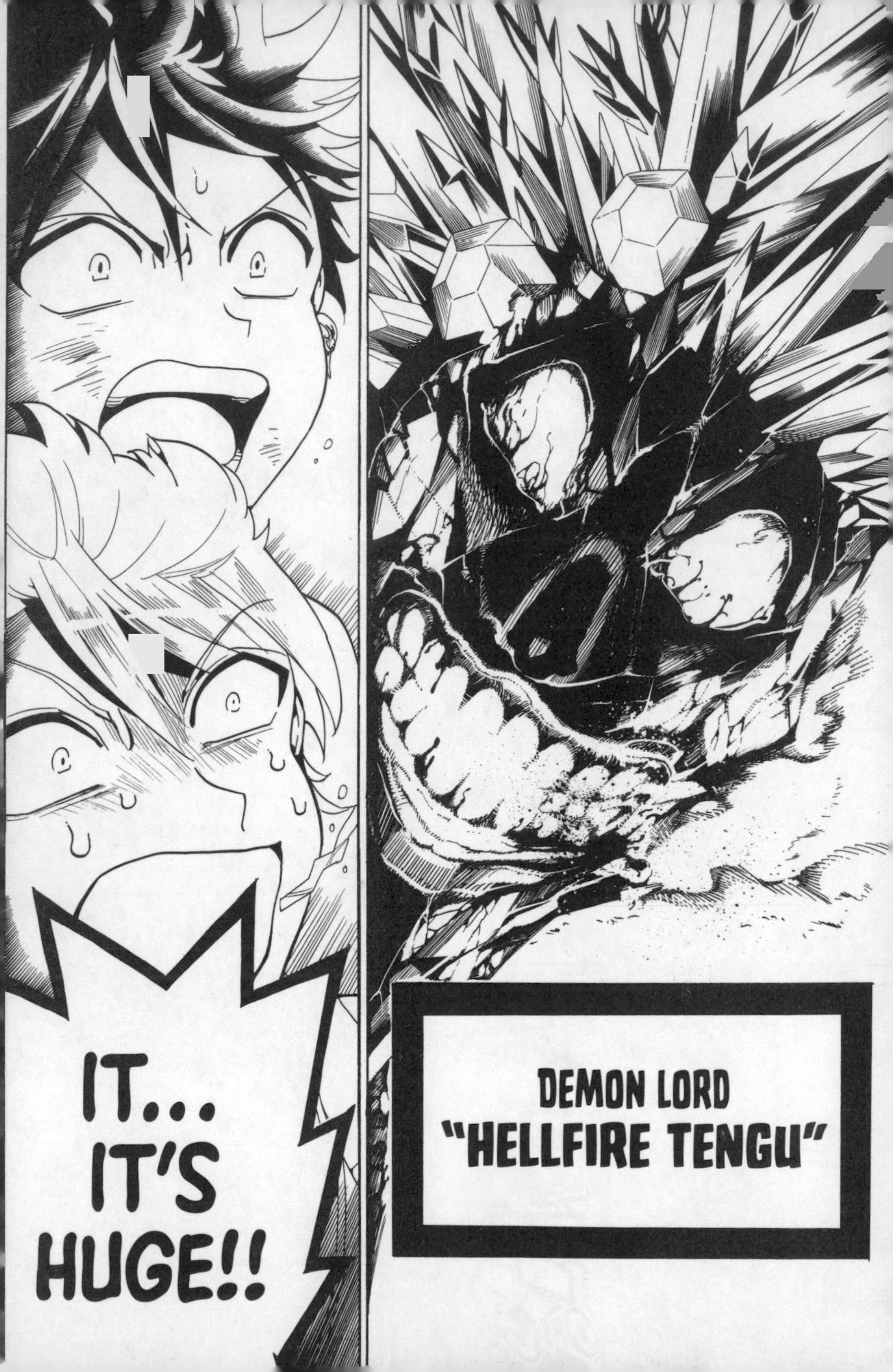
DEMON LORD
"HELLFIRE TENGU"
IT... IT'S HUGE!!

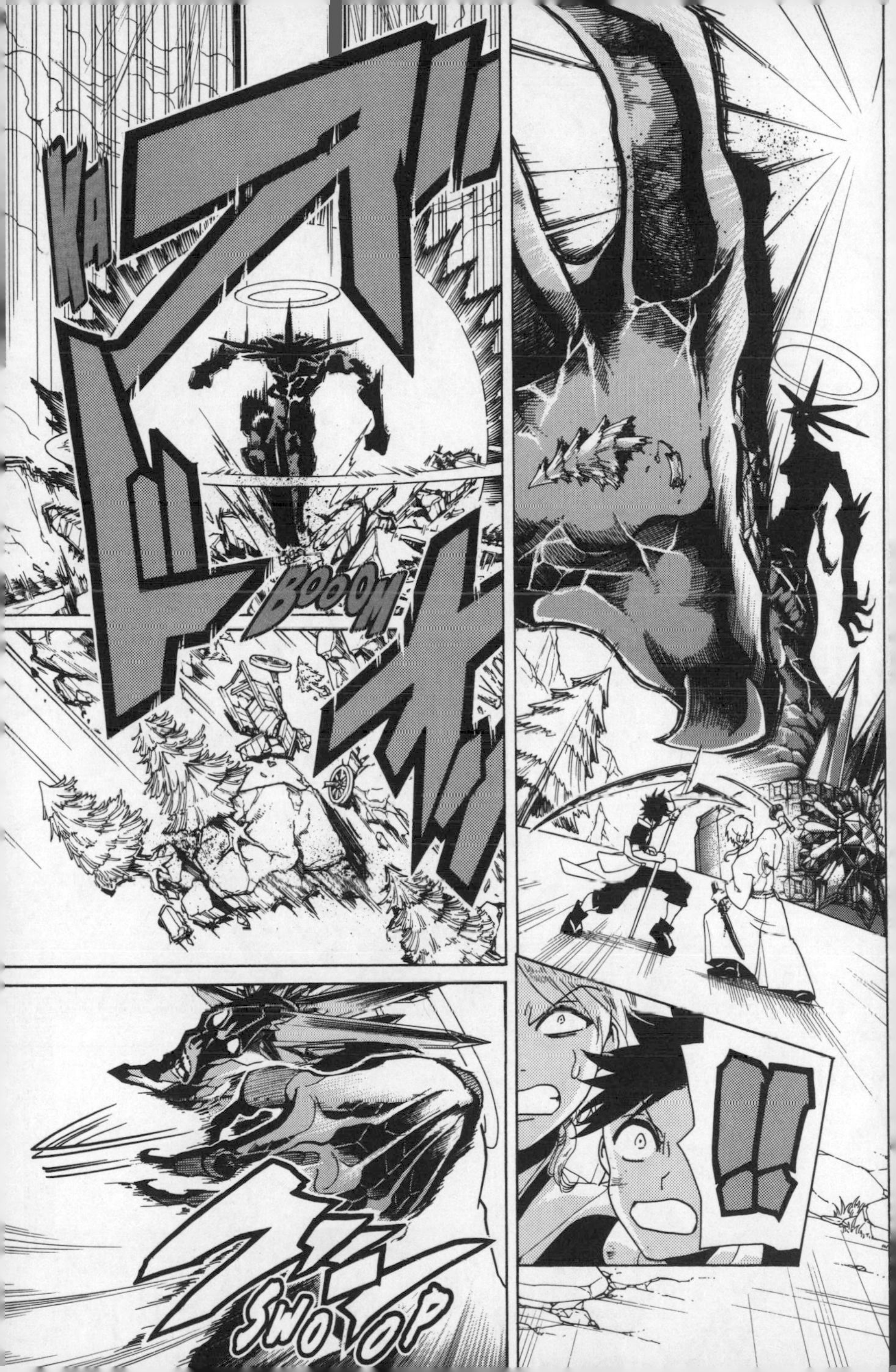
KA
BOOOM
!!
SWOOP

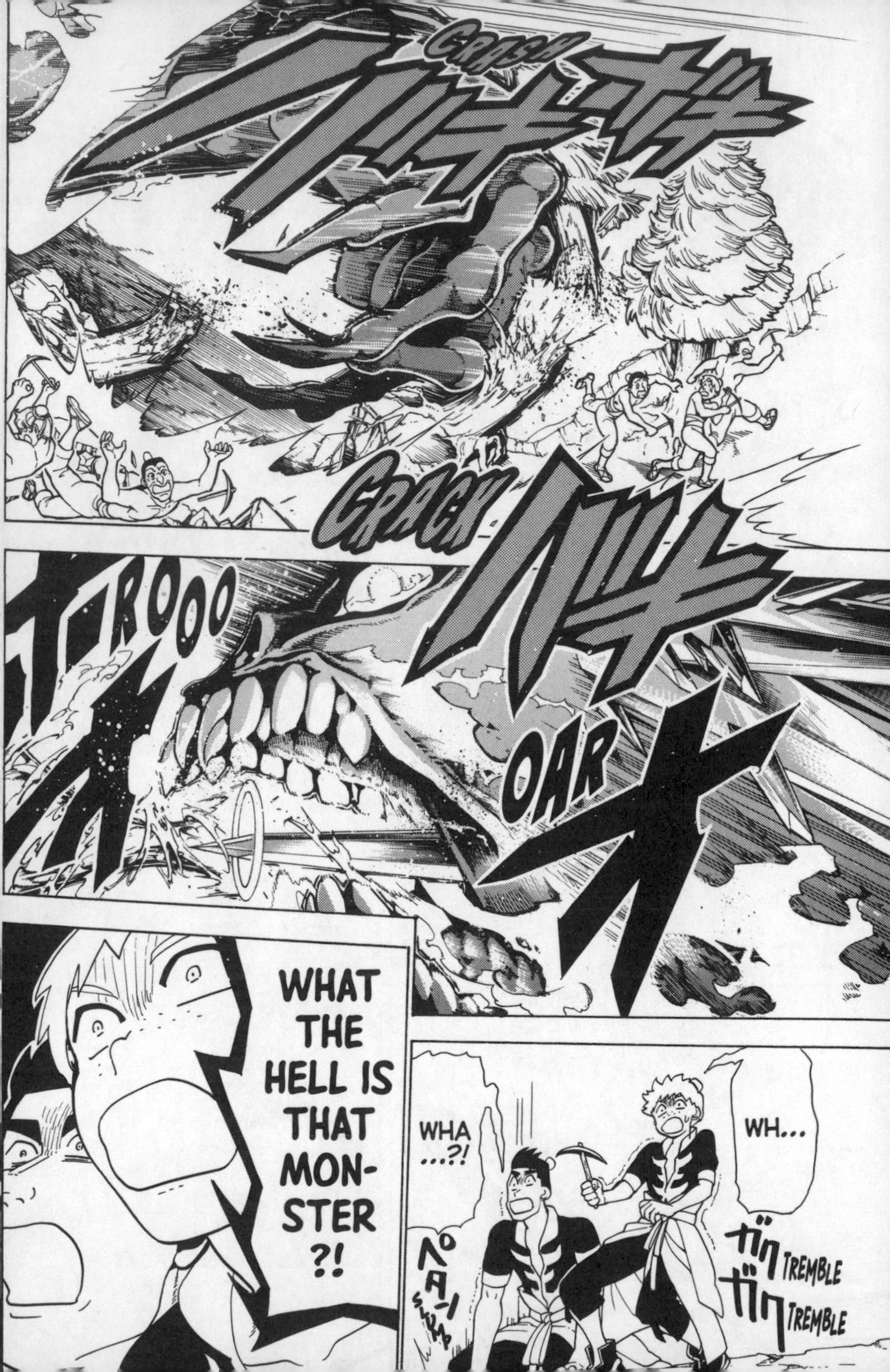
CRASH
CRACK
ROOO
OAR
WH...
WHA ...?!
TREMBLE
TREMBLE
WHAT THE HELL IS THAT MONSTER?!

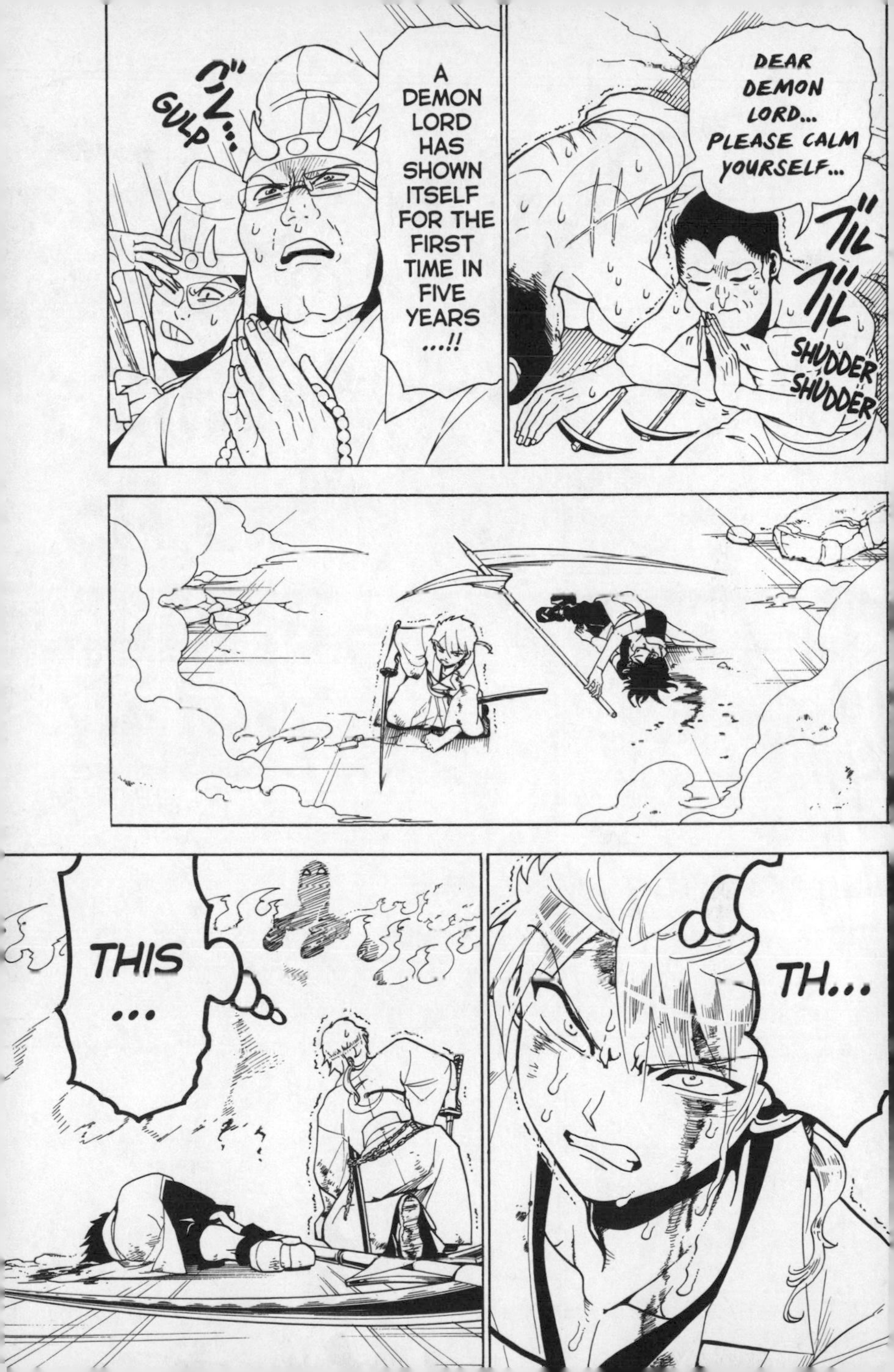
DEAR DEMON LORD... PLEASE CALM YOURSELF...
ブル ブル
SHUDDER SHUDDER
A DEMON LORD HAS SHOWN ITSELF FOR THE FIRST TIME IN FIVE YEARS ...!!
GULP
TH...
THIS ...

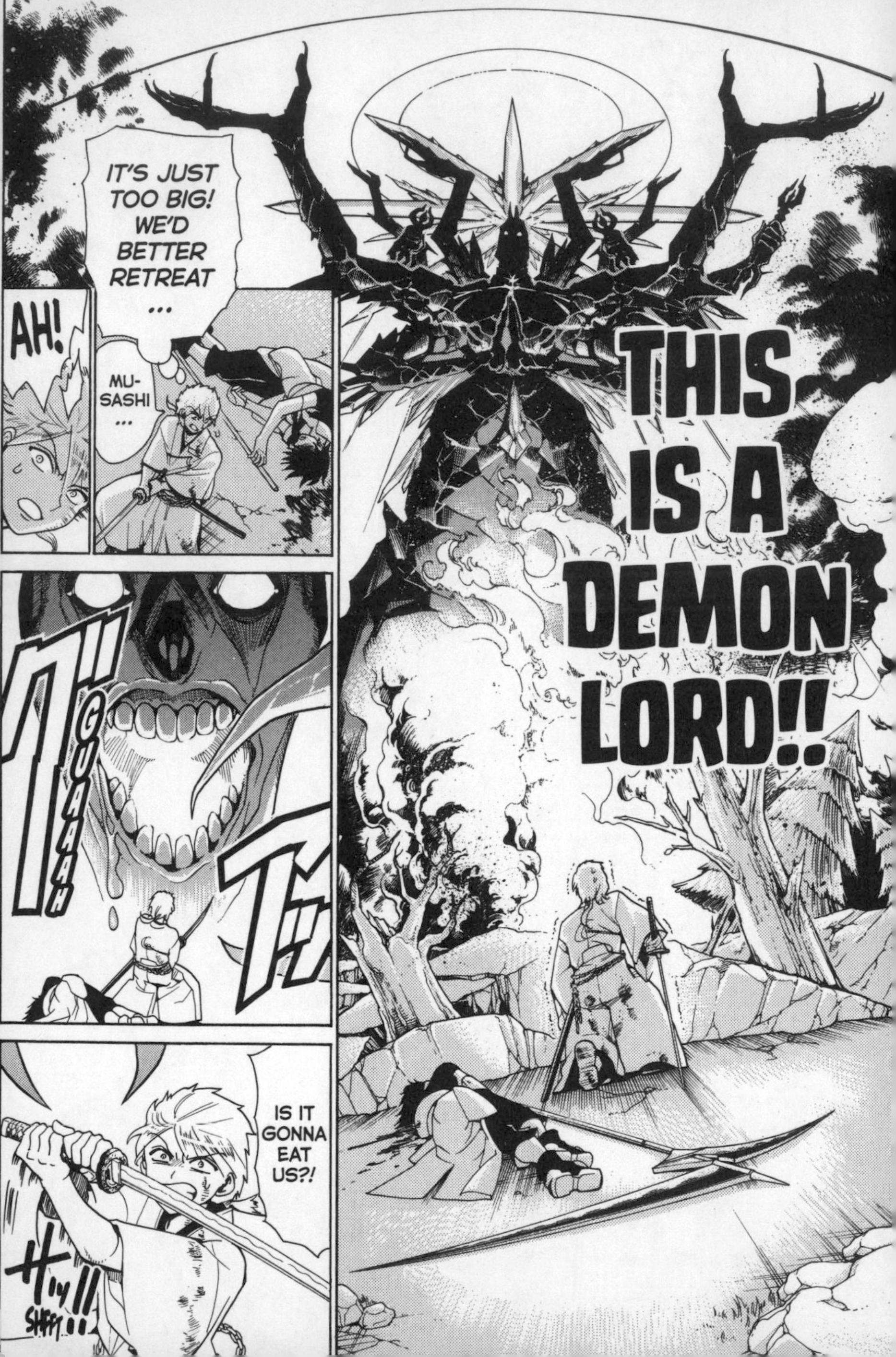
THIS IS A DEMON LORD!!
IT'S JUST TOO BIG! WE'D BETTER RETREAT ...
MU-SASHI ...
AH!
GUAAAAAH
IS IT GONNA EAT US?!
SHFFT!!

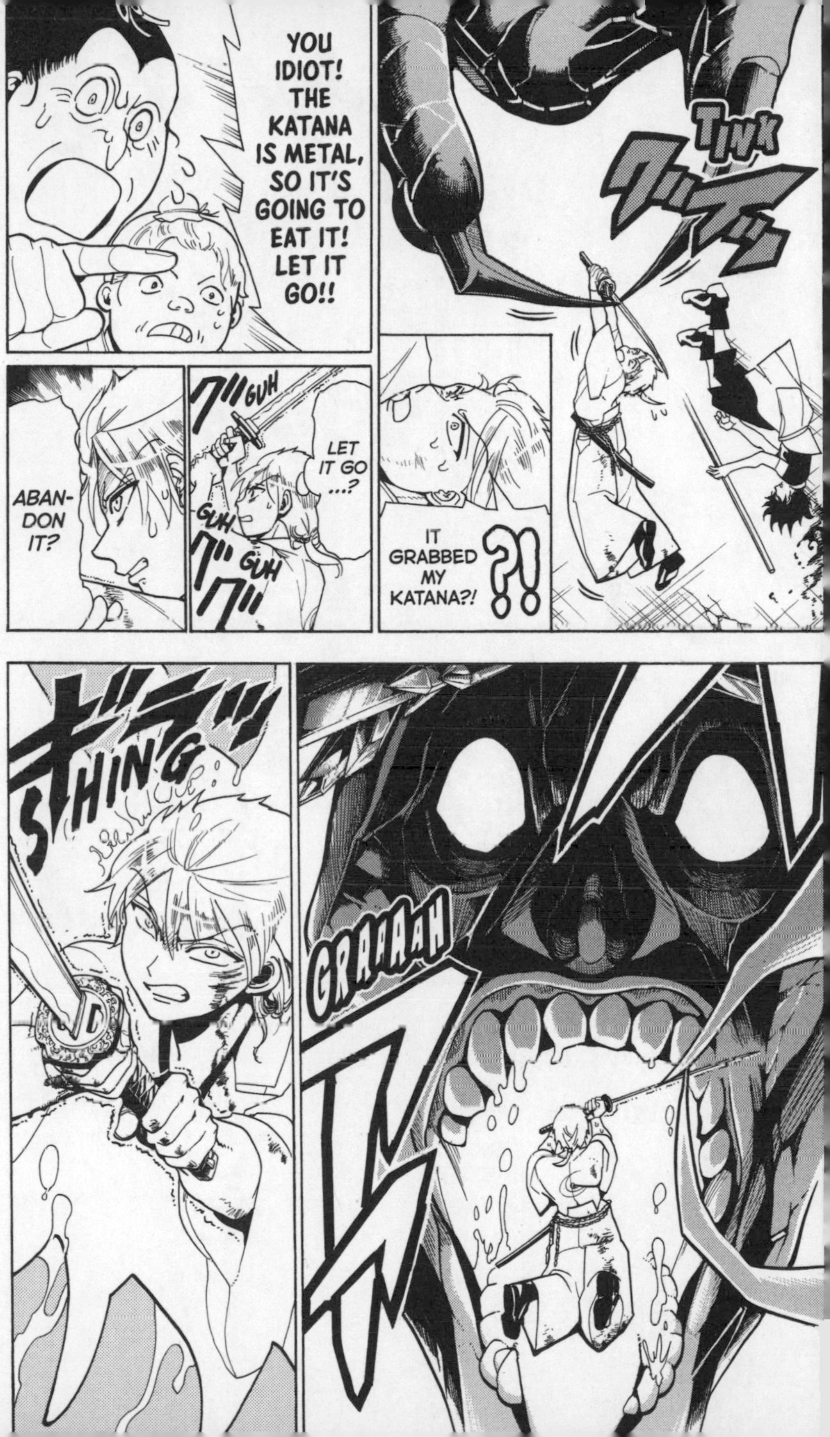
TINK
IT GRABBED MY KATANA?!
?!
YOU IDIOT! THE KATANA IS METAL, SO IT'S GOING TO EAT IT! LET IT GO!!
LET IT GO ...?
GUH
GUH
GUH
ABAN-DON IT?
GRAAAAH
SHING

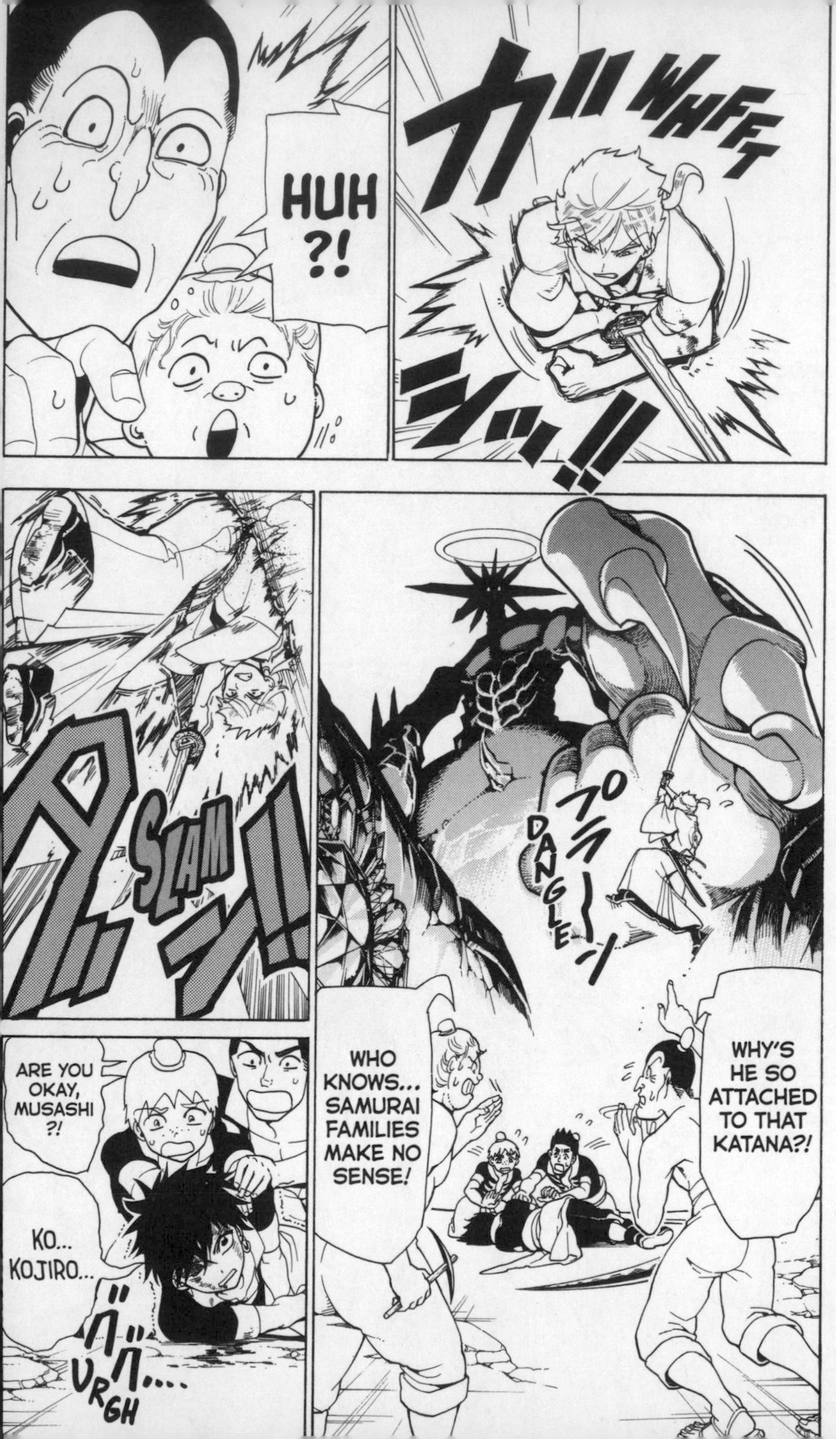
WHFFT
HUH ?!
DANGLE
SLAM
WHY'S HE SO ATTACHED TO THAT KATANA?!
WHO KNOWS... SAMURAI FAMILIES MAKE NO SENSE!
ARE YOU OKAY, MUSASHI ?!
KO... KOJIRO...
URGH

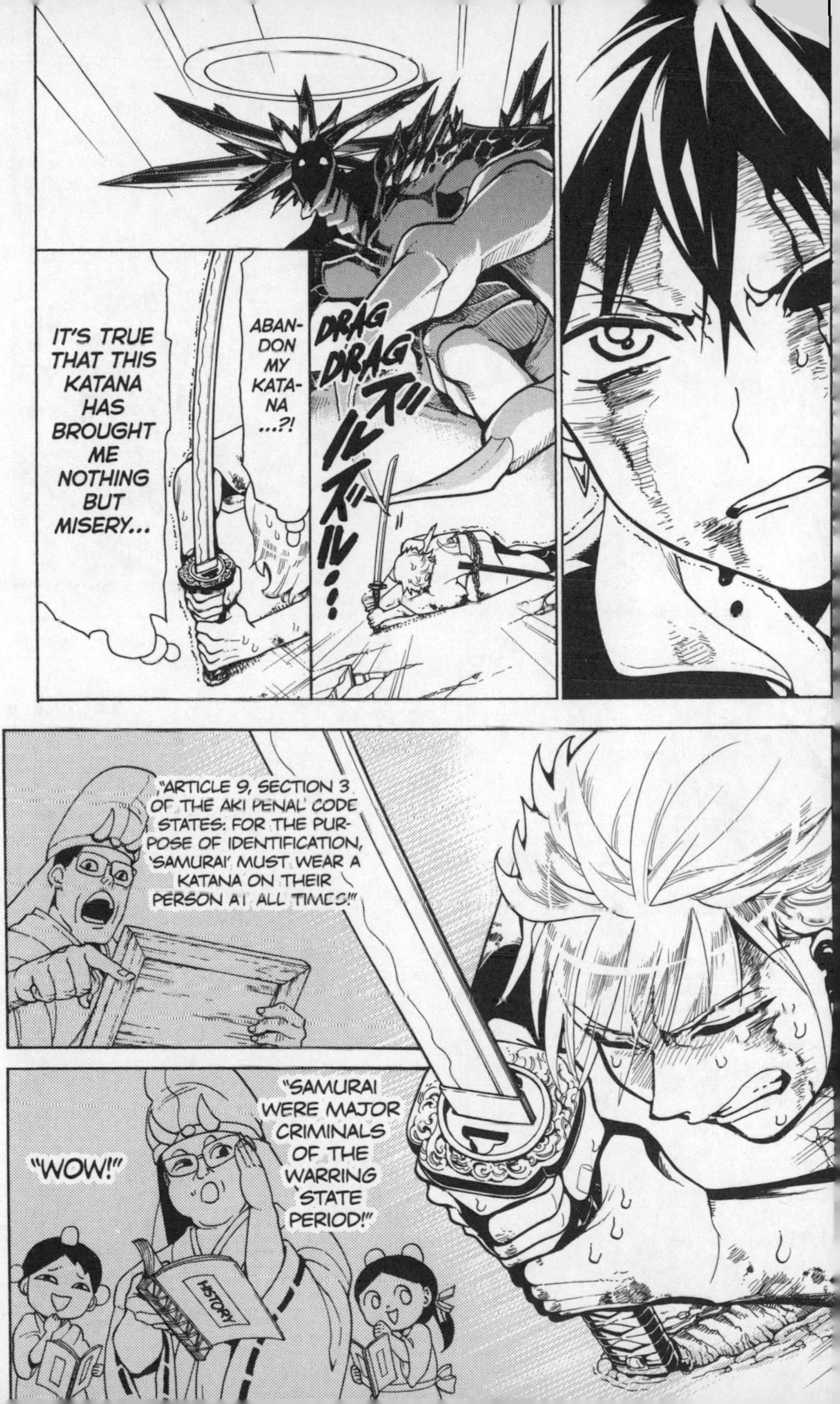
ABAN-
DON
MY
KATA-
NA
...?!
DRAG
DRAG
ズルズル...
IT'S TRUE THAT THIS KATANA HAS BROUGHT ME NOTHING BUT MISERY...
"ARTICLE 9, SECTION 3 OF THE AKI PENAL CODE STATES: FOR THE PURPOSE OF IDENTIFICATION, 'SAMURAI' MUST WEAR A KATANA ON THEIR PERSON AT ALL TIMES!"
"SAMURAI WERE MAJOR CRIMINALS OF THE WARRING STATE PERIOD!"
"WOW!"
HISTORY

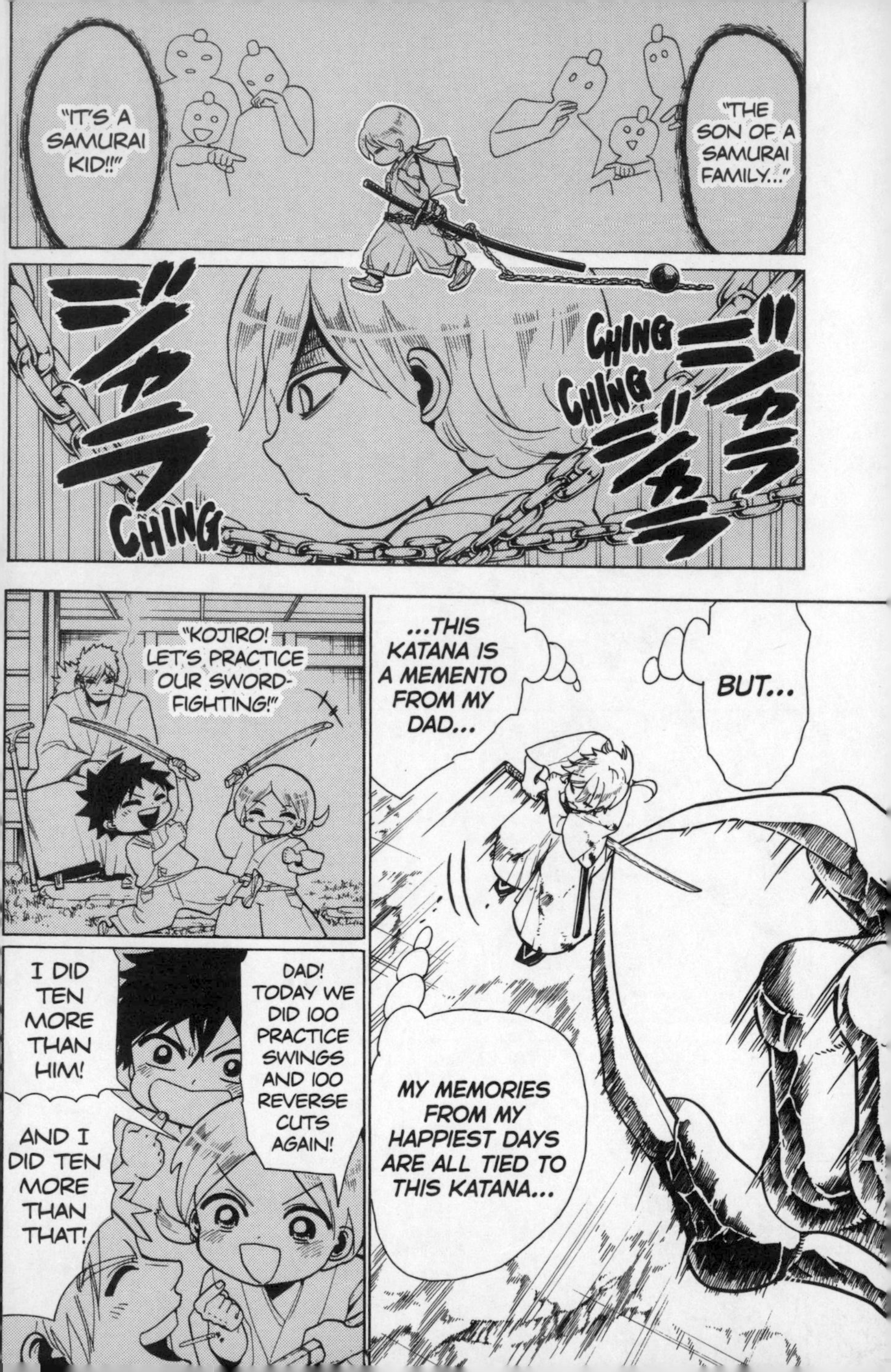
"THE SON OF A SAMURAI FAMILY..."
"IT'S A SAMURAI KID!!"
ジャラ
ジャラ
CHING CHING
ジャラ
CHING
...THIS KATANA IS A MEMENTO FROM MY DAD...
MY MEMORIES FROM MY HAPPIEST DAYS ARE ALL TIED TO THIS KATANA...
BUT...
"KOJIRO! LET'S PRACTICE OUR SWORD-FIGHTING!"
DAD! TODAY WE DID 100 PRACTICE SWINGS AND 100 REVERSE CUTS AGAIN!
I DID TEN MORE THAN HIM!
AND I DID TEN MORE THAN THAT!

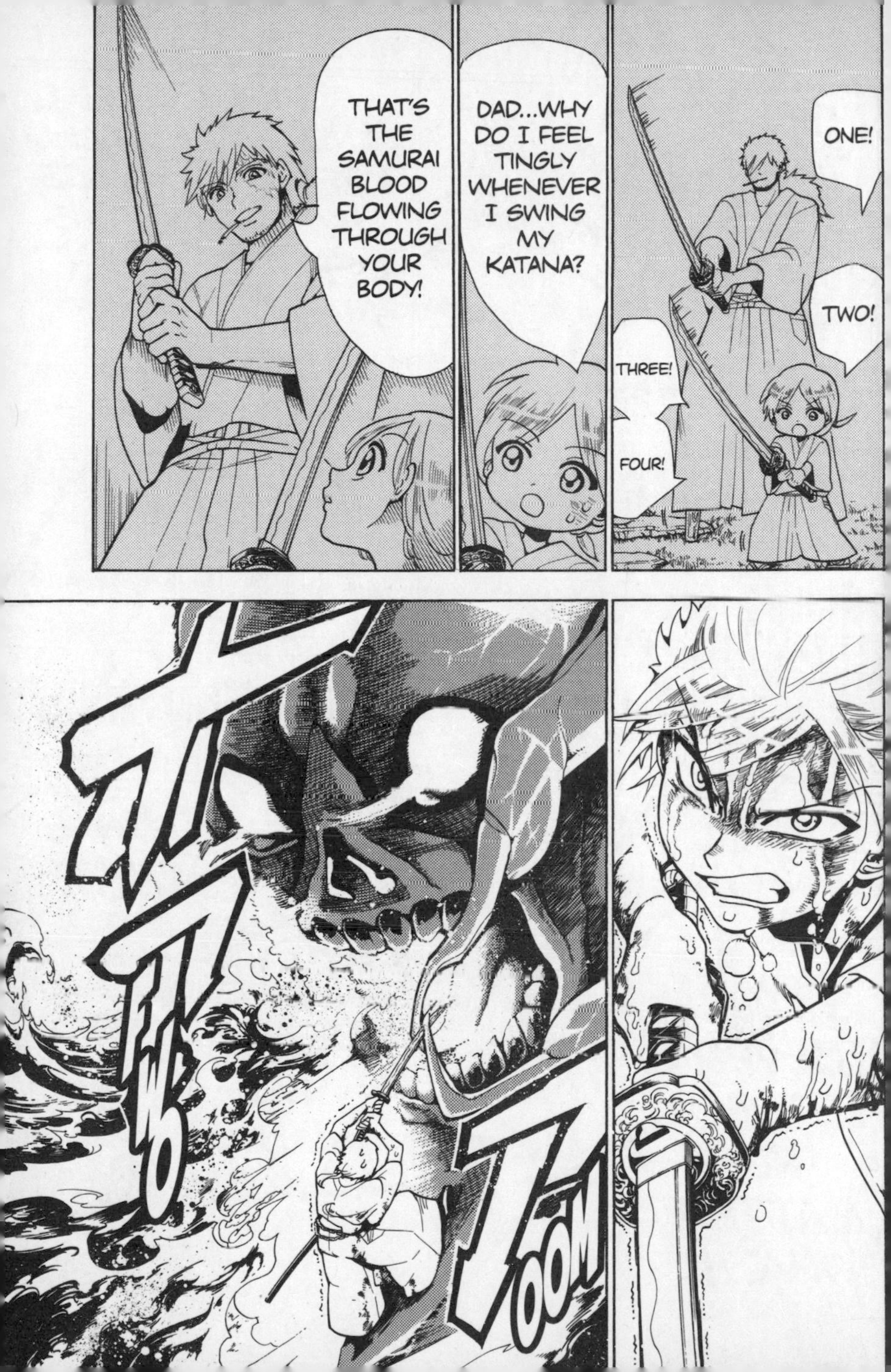
ONE!
TWO!
THREE!
FOUR!
DAD...WHY DO I FEEL TINGLY WHENEVER I SWING MY KATANA?
THAT'S THE SAMURAI BLOOD FLOWING THROUGH YOUR BODY!
ZOOM

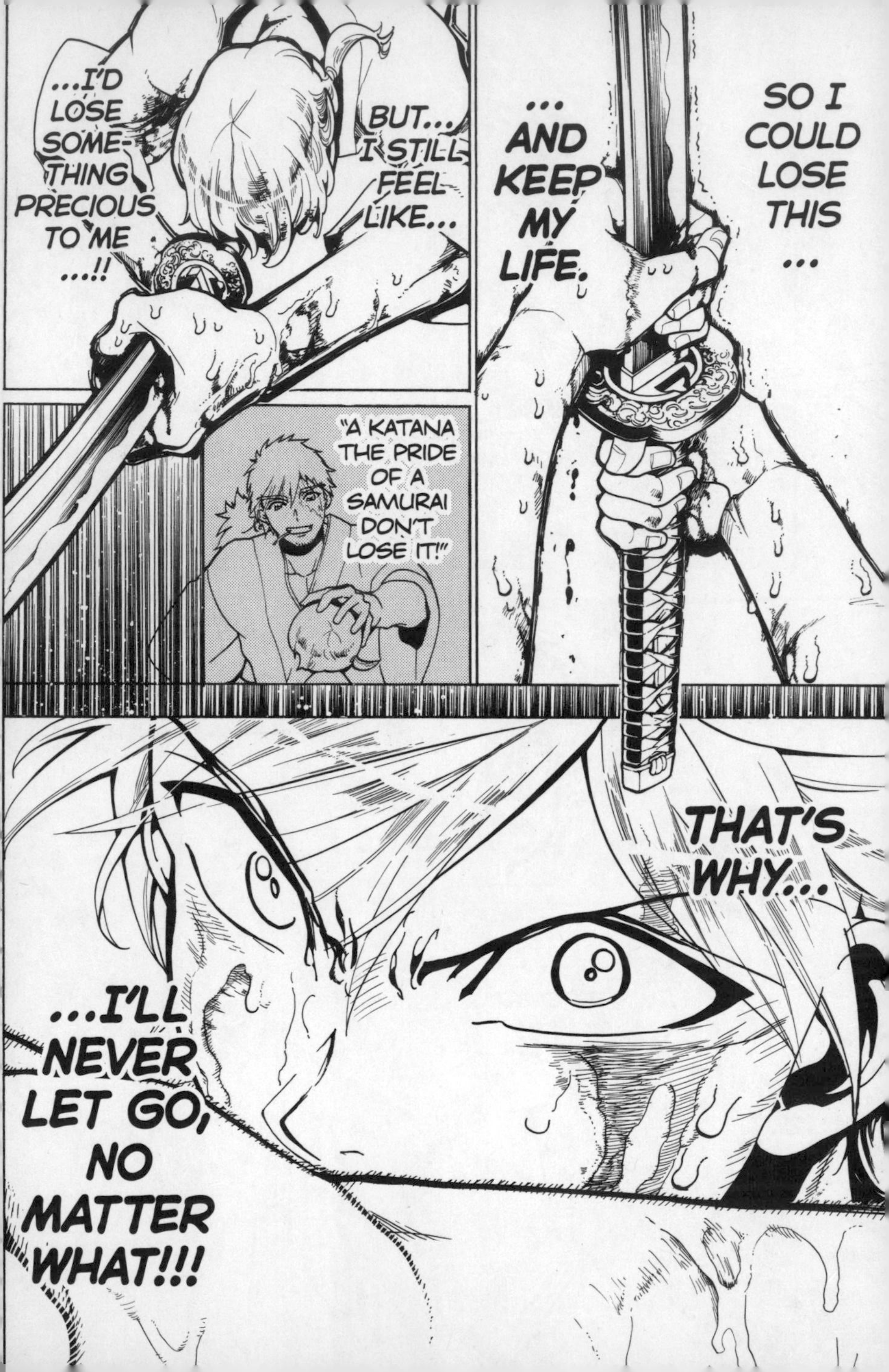
SO I COULD LOSE THIS ...
... AND KEEP MY LIFE.
BUT... I STILL FEEL LIKE...
...I'D LOSE SOME-THING PRECIOUS TO ME ...!!
"A KATANA THE PRIDE OF A SAMURAI DON'T LOSE IT!"
THAT'S WHY...
...I'LL NEVER LET GO, NO MATTER WHAT!!!

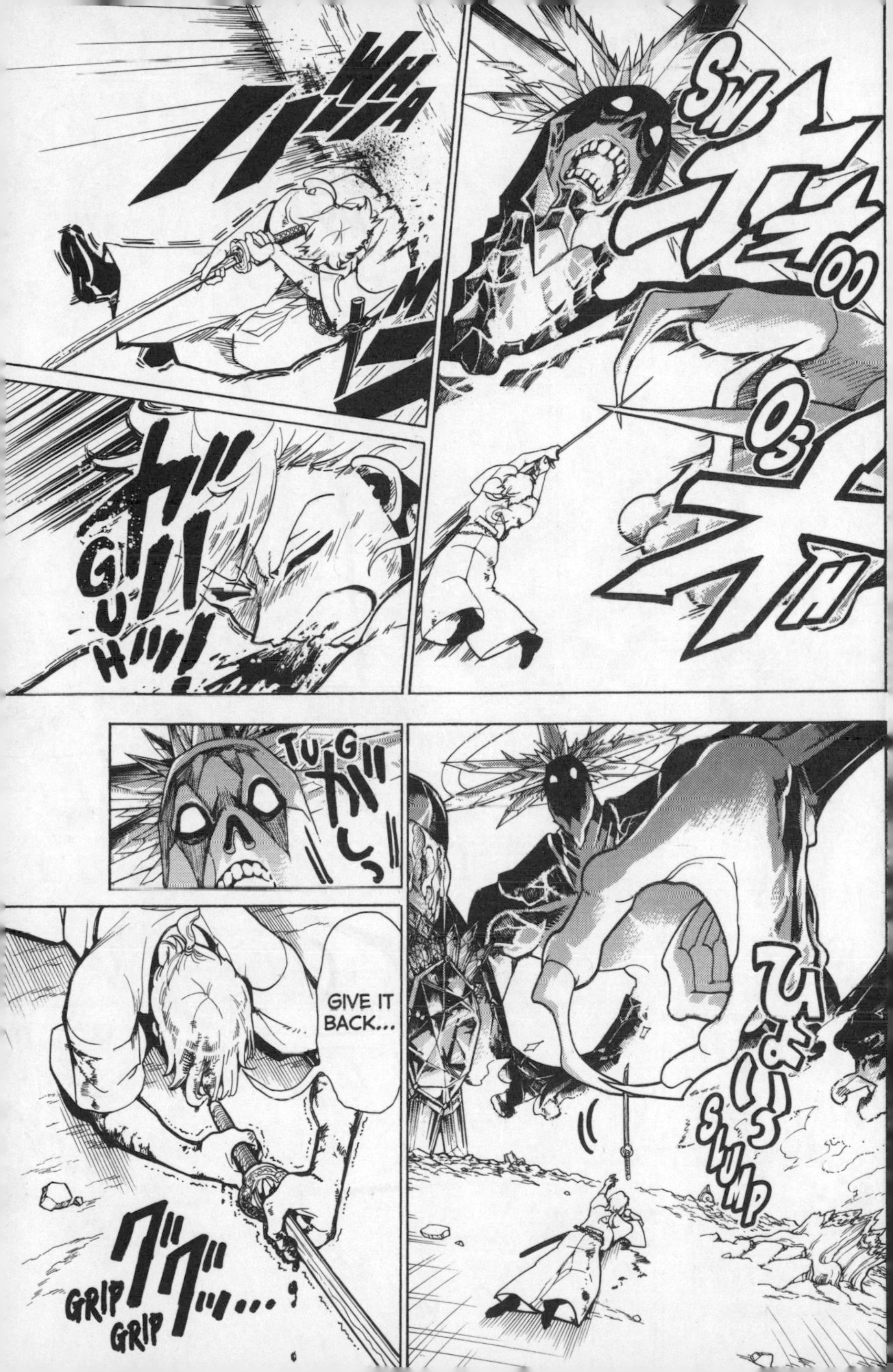
SWOOOSH
WHAM
GUH
TUG
SLUMP
GIVE IT BACK...
GRIP GRIP

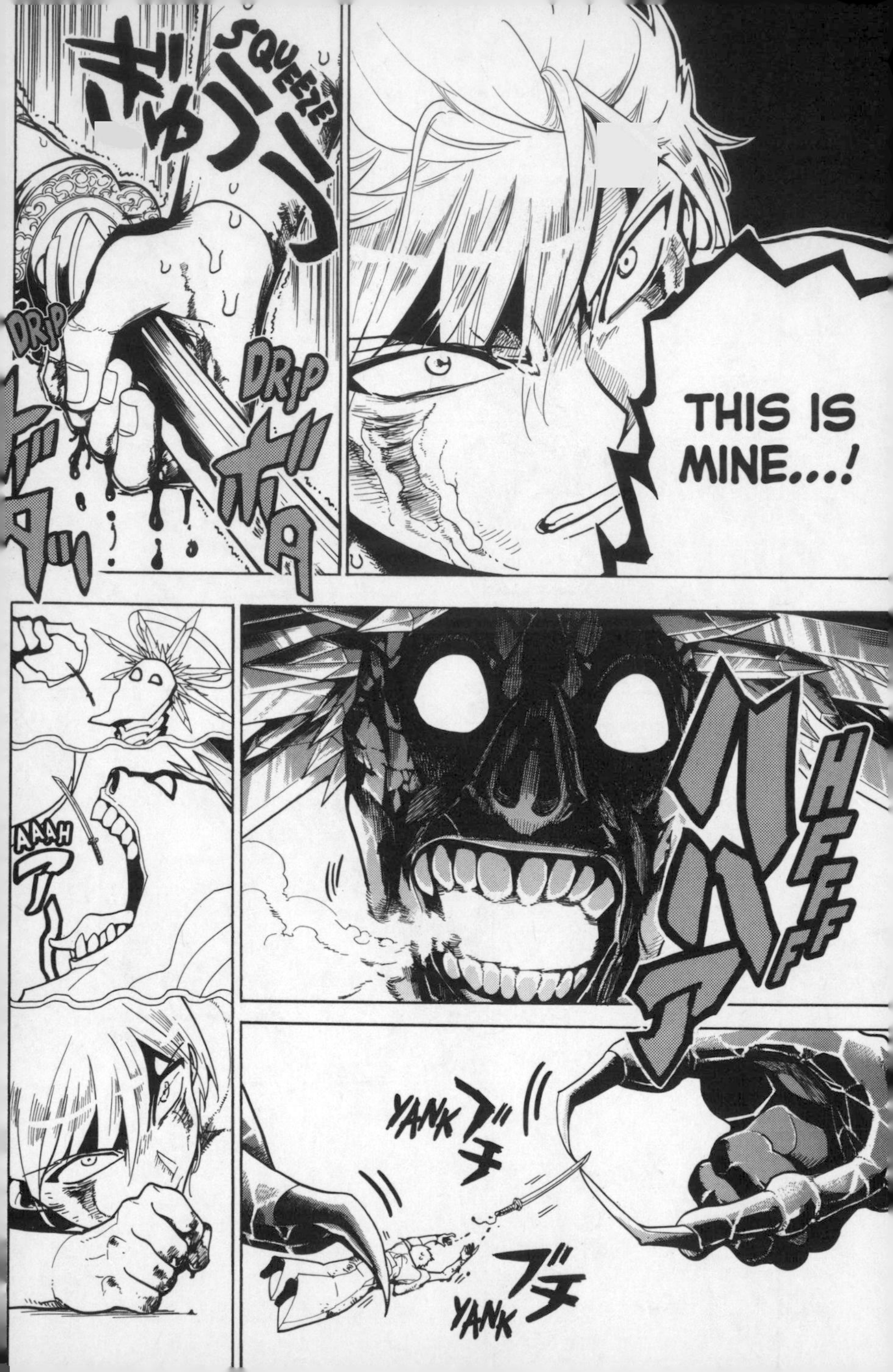
THIS IS MINE...!
SQUEEZE
DRIP
DRIP
HFFFF
AAAH
YANK
YANK

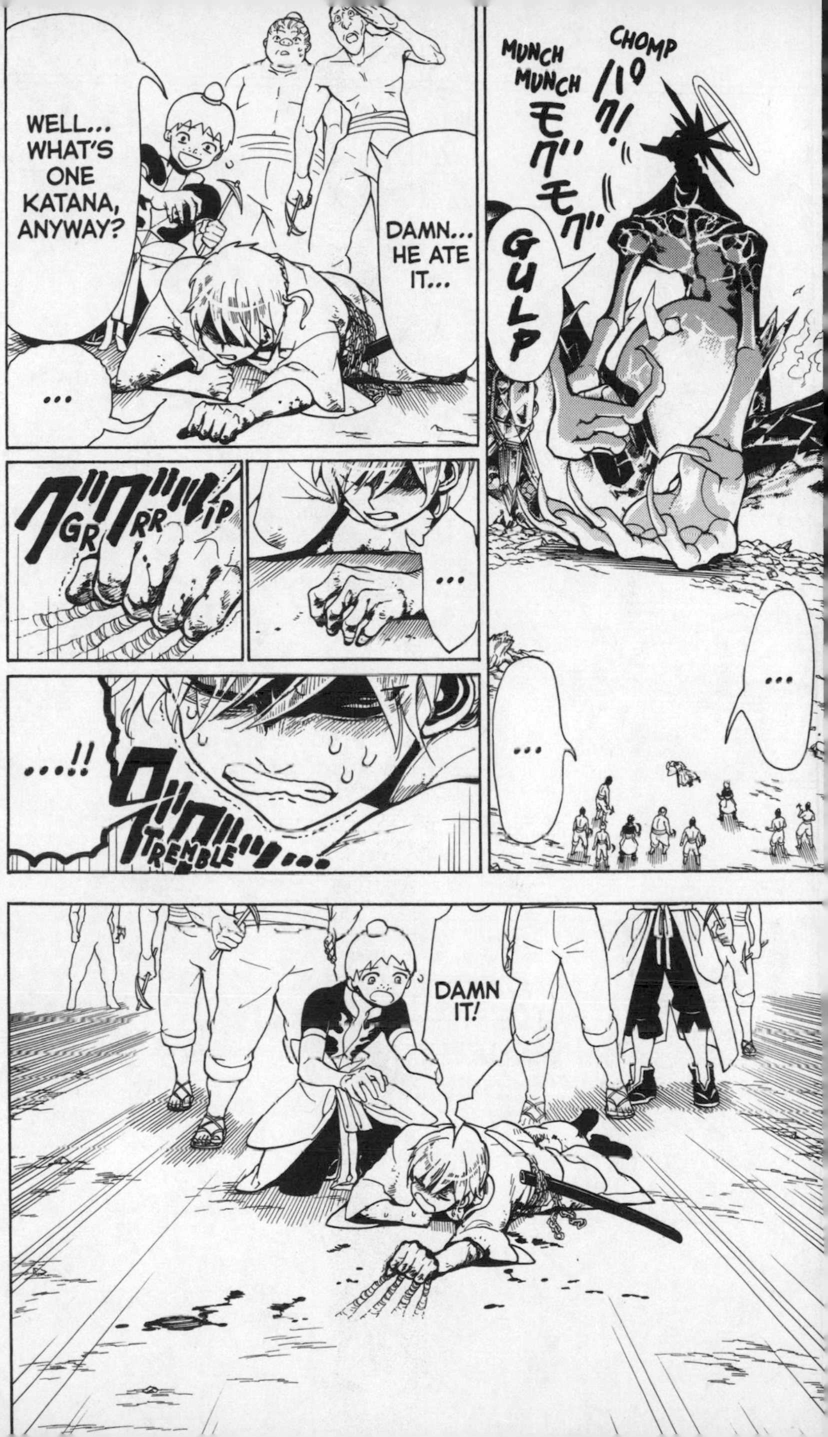
CHOMP
MUNCH MUNCH
GULP
...
...
DAMN... HE ATE IT...
WELL... WHAT'S ONE KATANA, ANYWAY?
...
...
GRRRIP
...!!
TREMBLE...
DAMN IT!

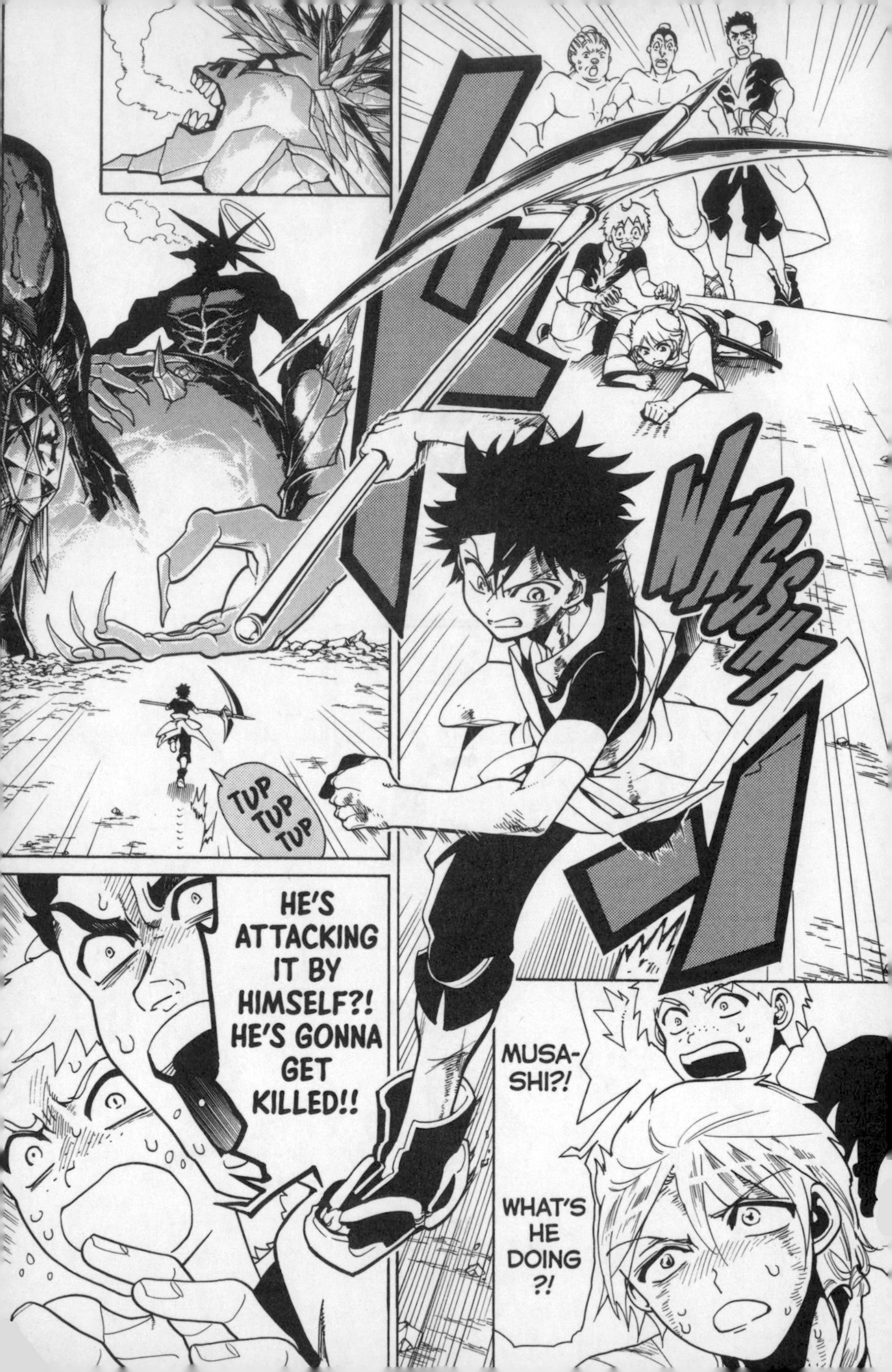
WHSSHT
TUP TUP TUP
MUSA-SHI?!
WHAT'S HE DOING ?!
HE'S ATTACKING IT BY HIMSELF?! HE'S GONNA GET KILLED!!

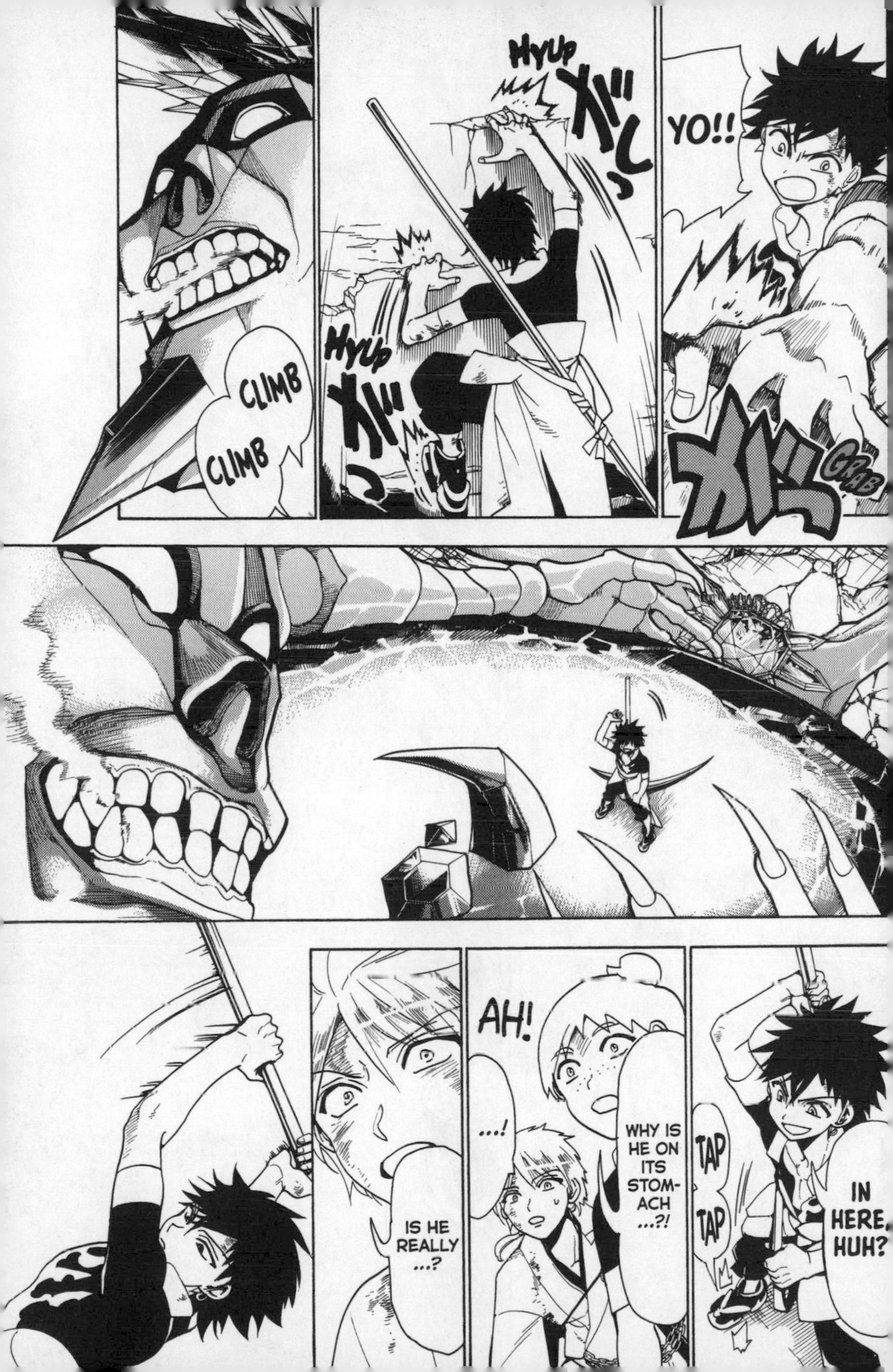
YO!!
GRAB
HYUP
HYUP
CLIMB
CLIMB
TAP
TAP
IN HERE, HUH?
AH!
WHY IS HE ON ITS STOMACH ...?!
...!
IS HE REALLY ...?

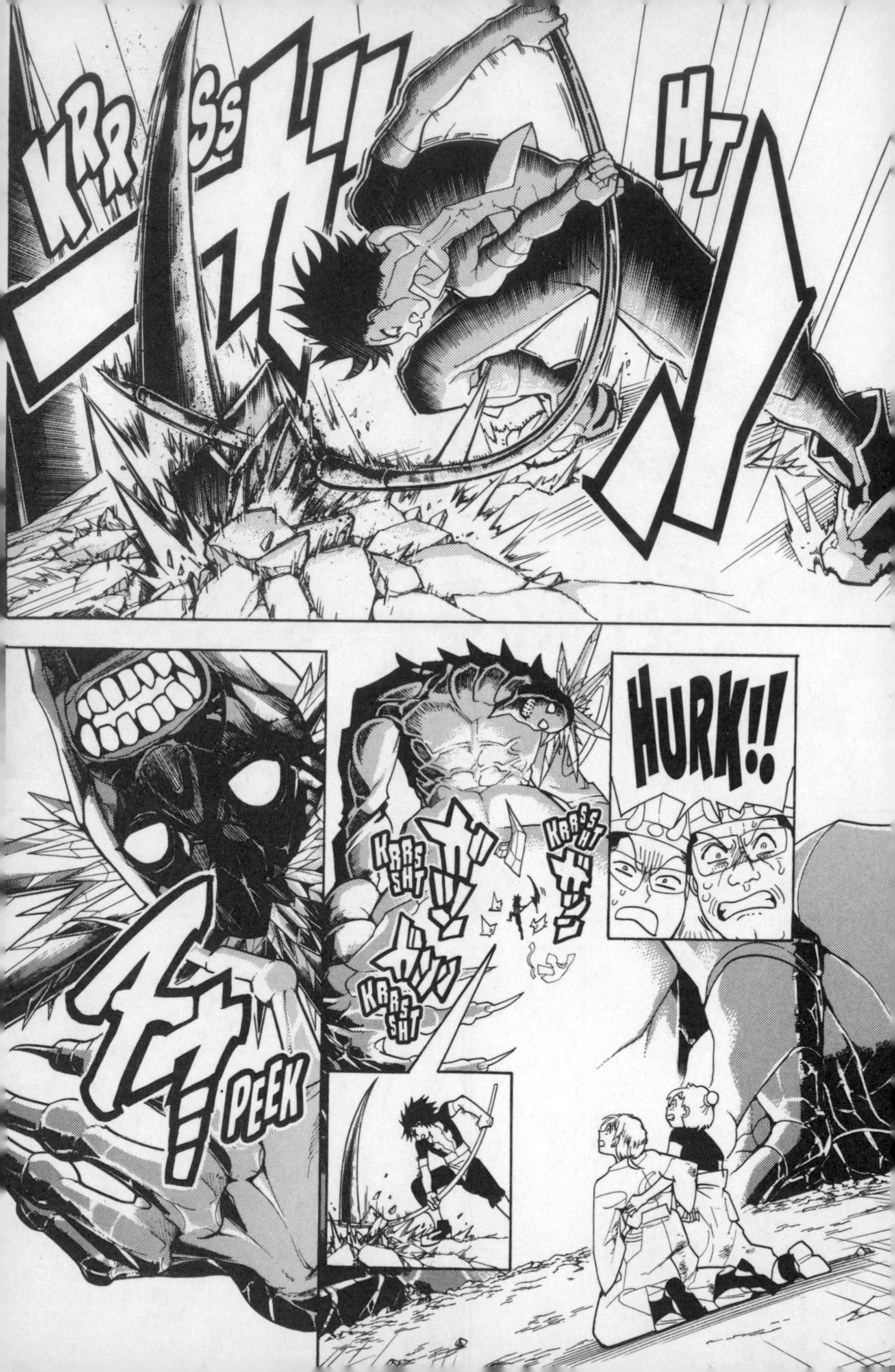
KRRSSHT
HURK!!
KRRSSHT
KRRSSHT
KRRSSHT
PEEK

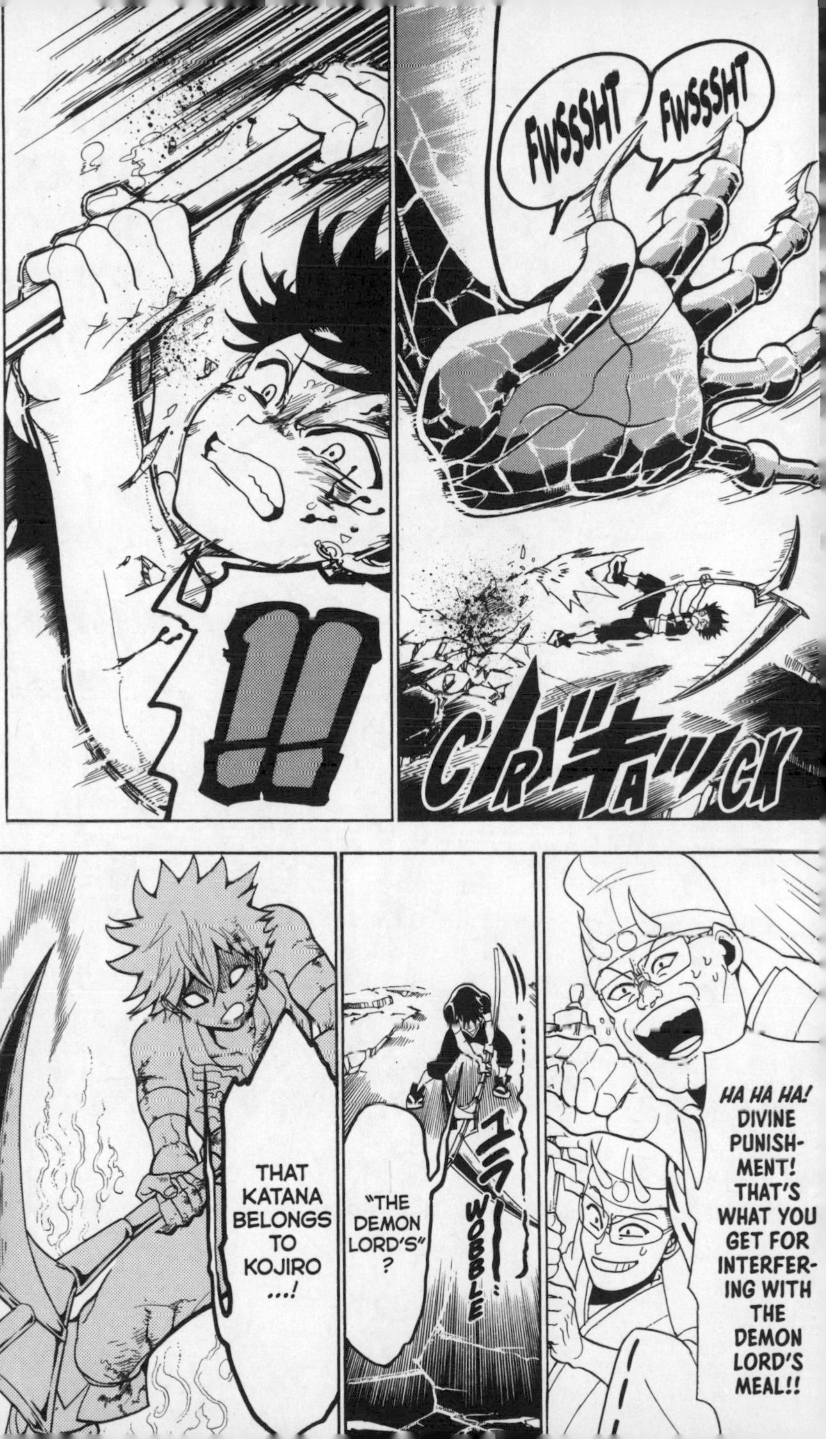

FWSSSHT
FWSSSHT
CRACK
!!
HA HA HA! DIVINE PUNISHMENT! THAT'S WHAT YOU GET FOR INTERFERING WITH THE DEMON LORD'S MEAL!!
WOBBLE
"THE DEMON LORD'S"?
THAT KATANA BELONGS TO KOJIRO ...!

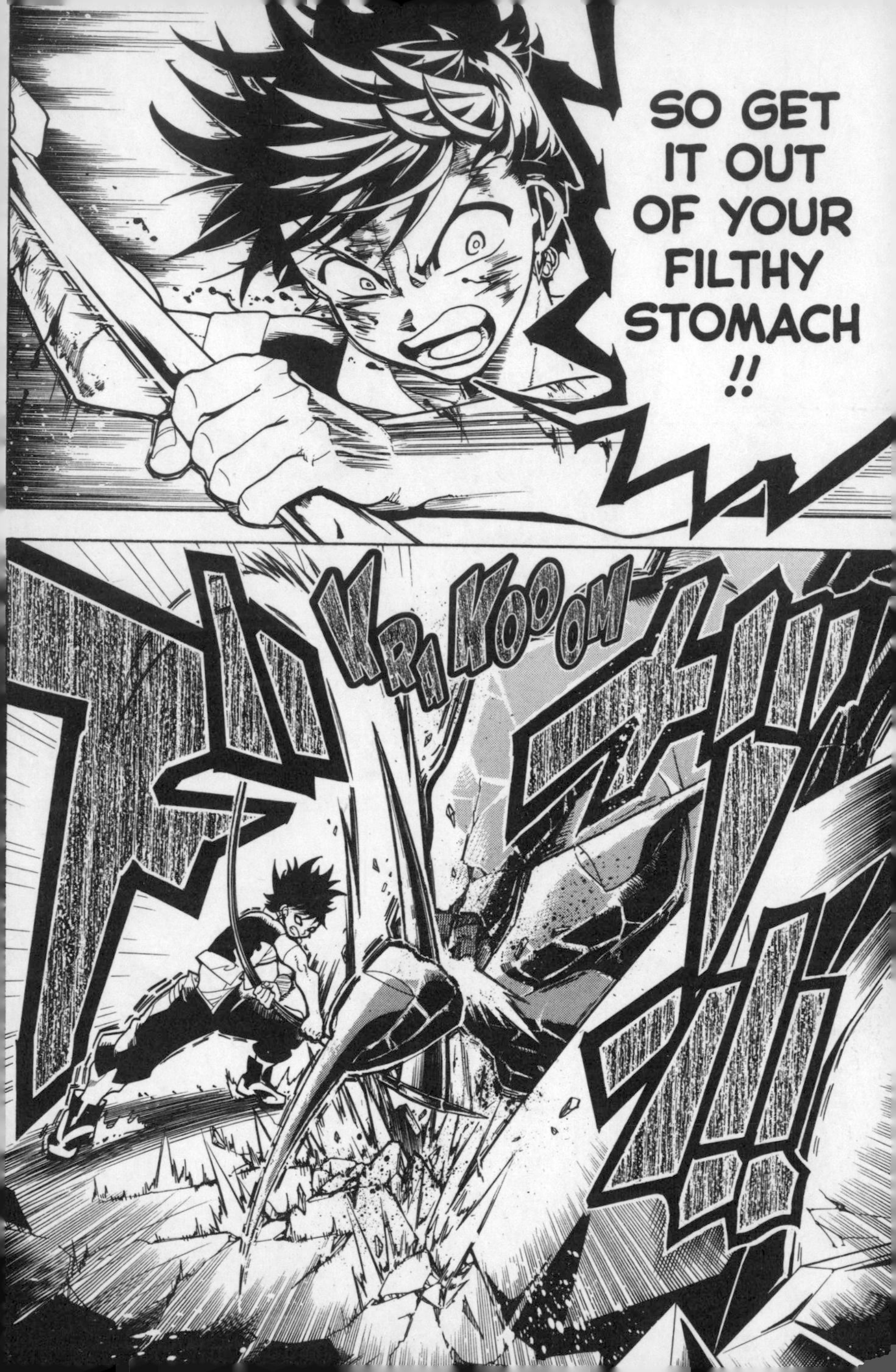
SO GET IT OUT OF YOUR FILTHY STOMACH !!
KRIKOOOM

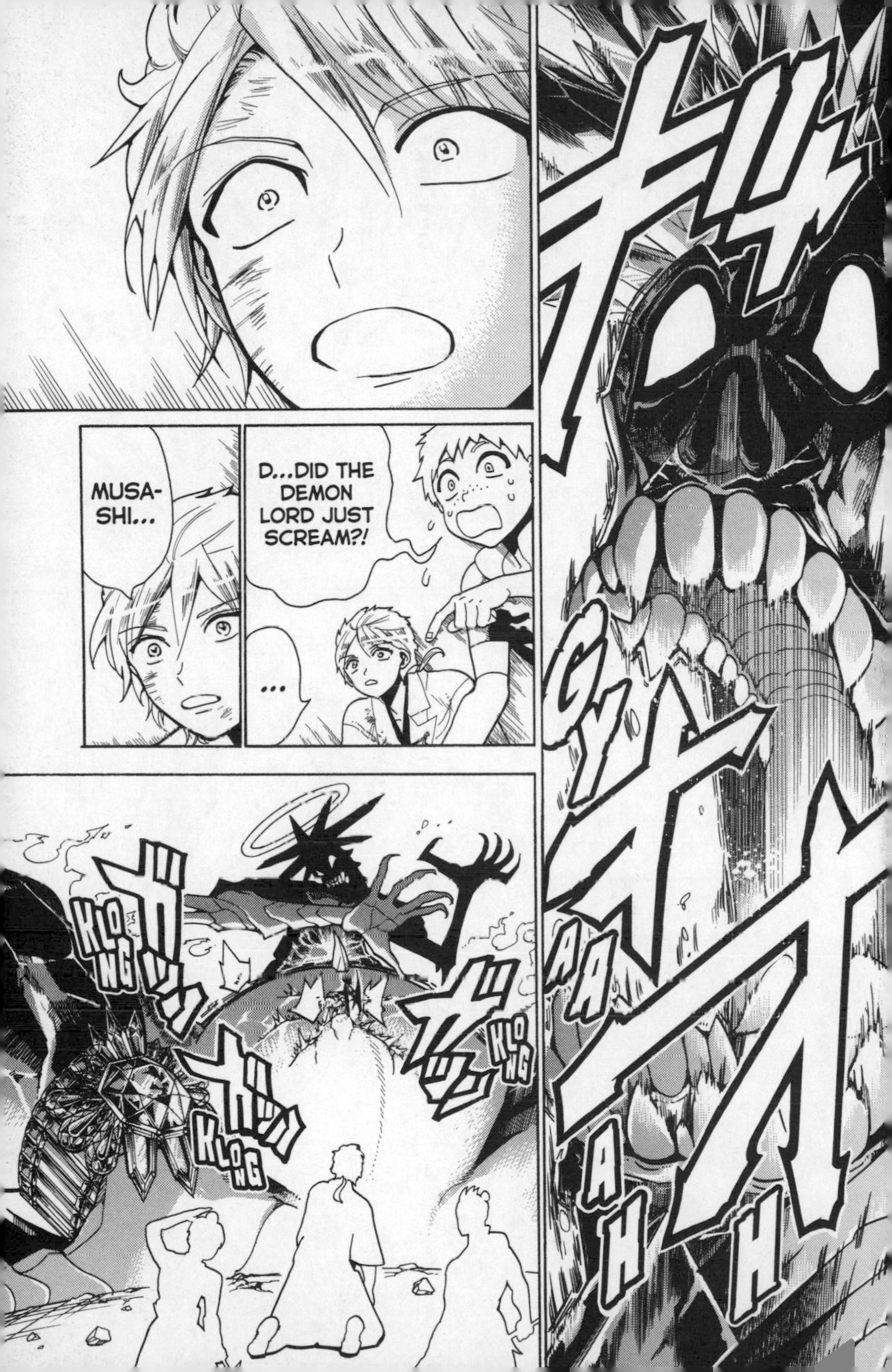

GYAAAHH
D...DID THE DEMON LORD JUST SCREAM?!
...
MUSA-SHI...
KLONG
KLONG
KLONG

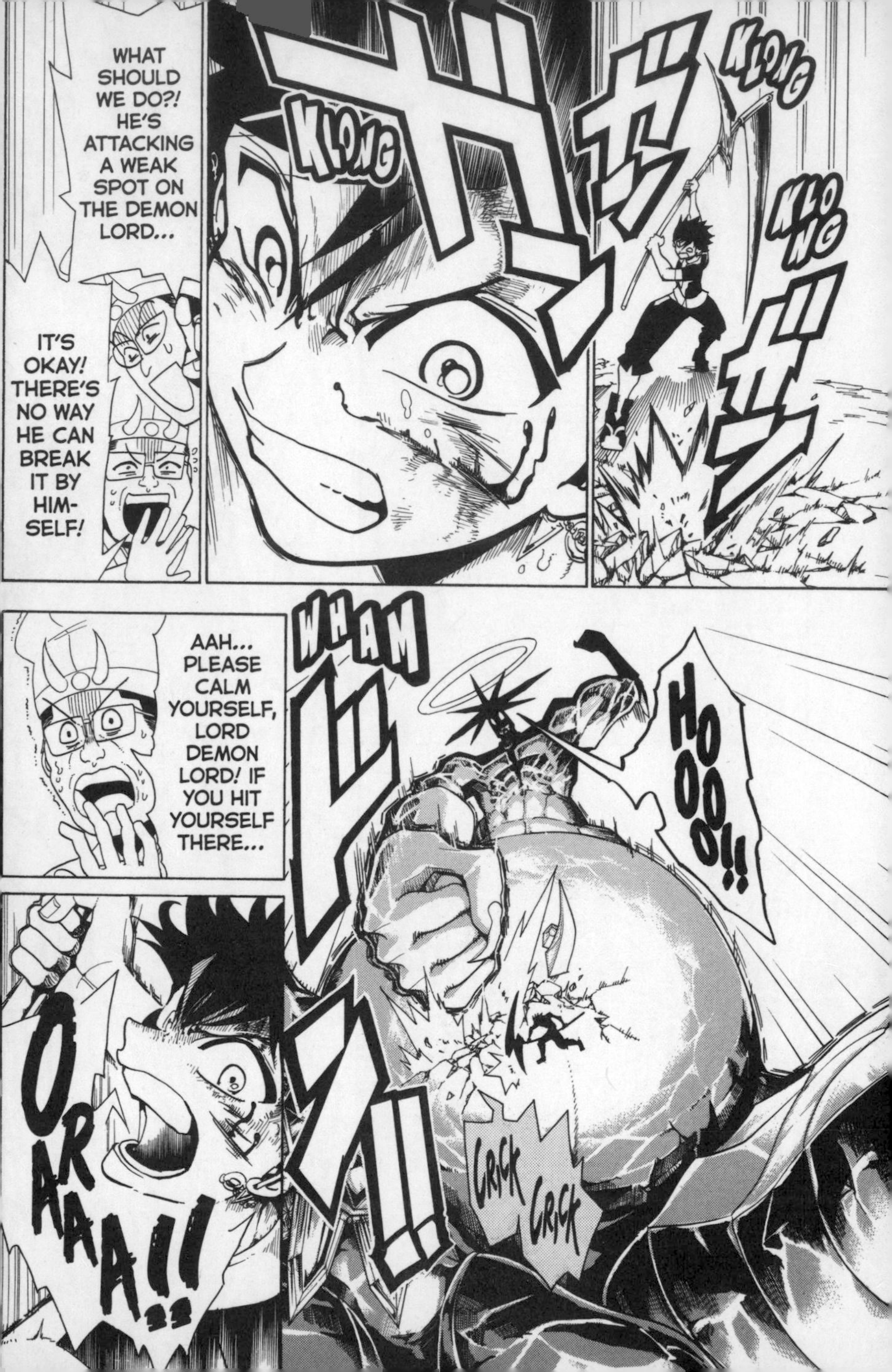
KLONG
KLONG
KLONG
WHAT SHOULD WE DO?! HE'S ATTACKING A WEAK SPOT ON THE DEMON LORD...
IT'S OKAY! THERE'S NO WAY HE CAN BREAK IT BY HIM-SELF!
WHAM
HOOOOO!!
CRCK
CRCK
AAH... PLEASE CALM YOURSELF, LORD DEMON LORD! IF YOU HIT YOURSELF THERE...
ORAAAA!!

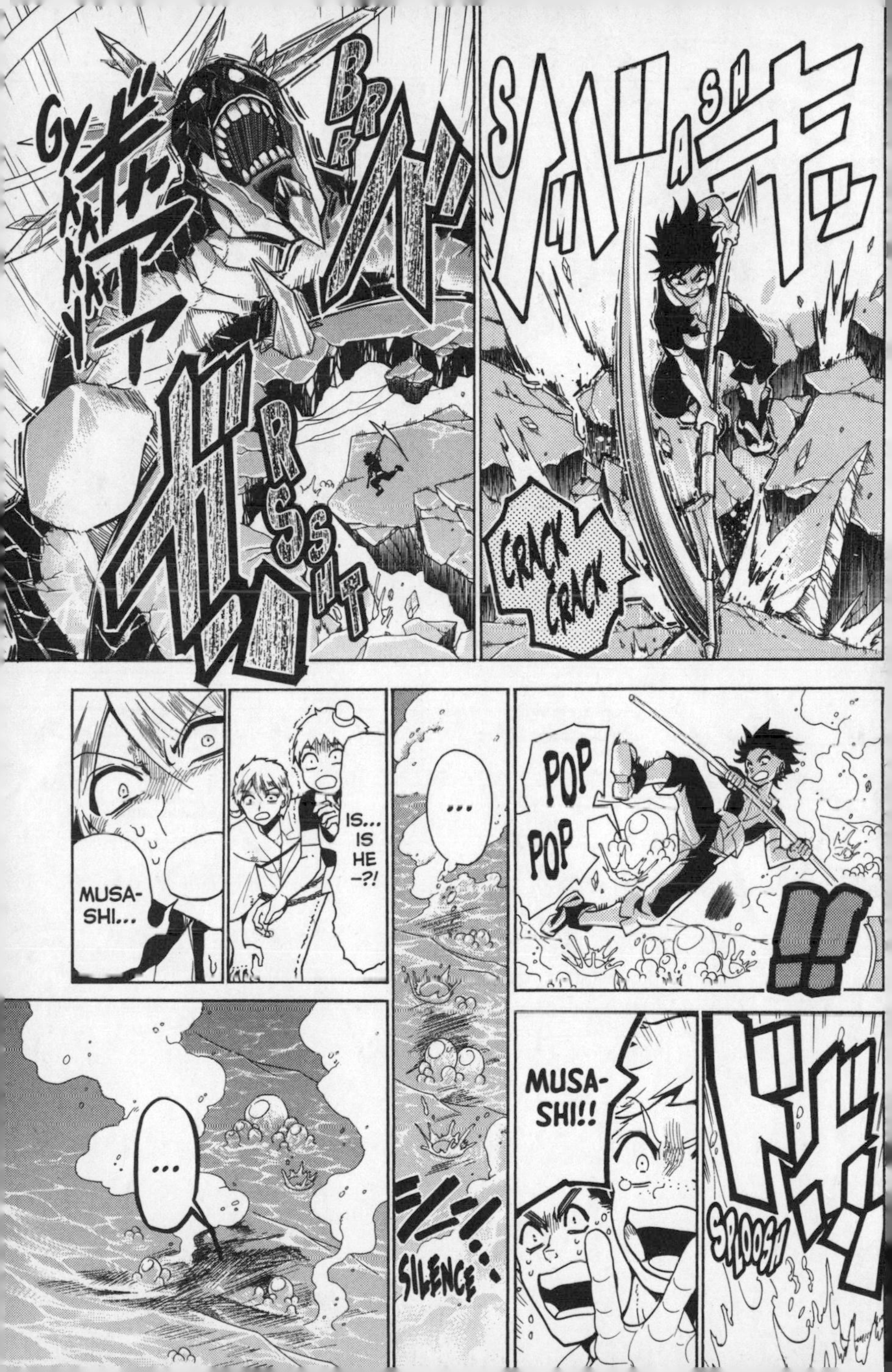

SMASH
CRACK CRACK
GYAAAY
BRR
RRSSHT
POP POP
MUSA-SHI!!
SPLOOSH
...
SILENCE
IS... IS HE—?!
MUSA-SHI...
...

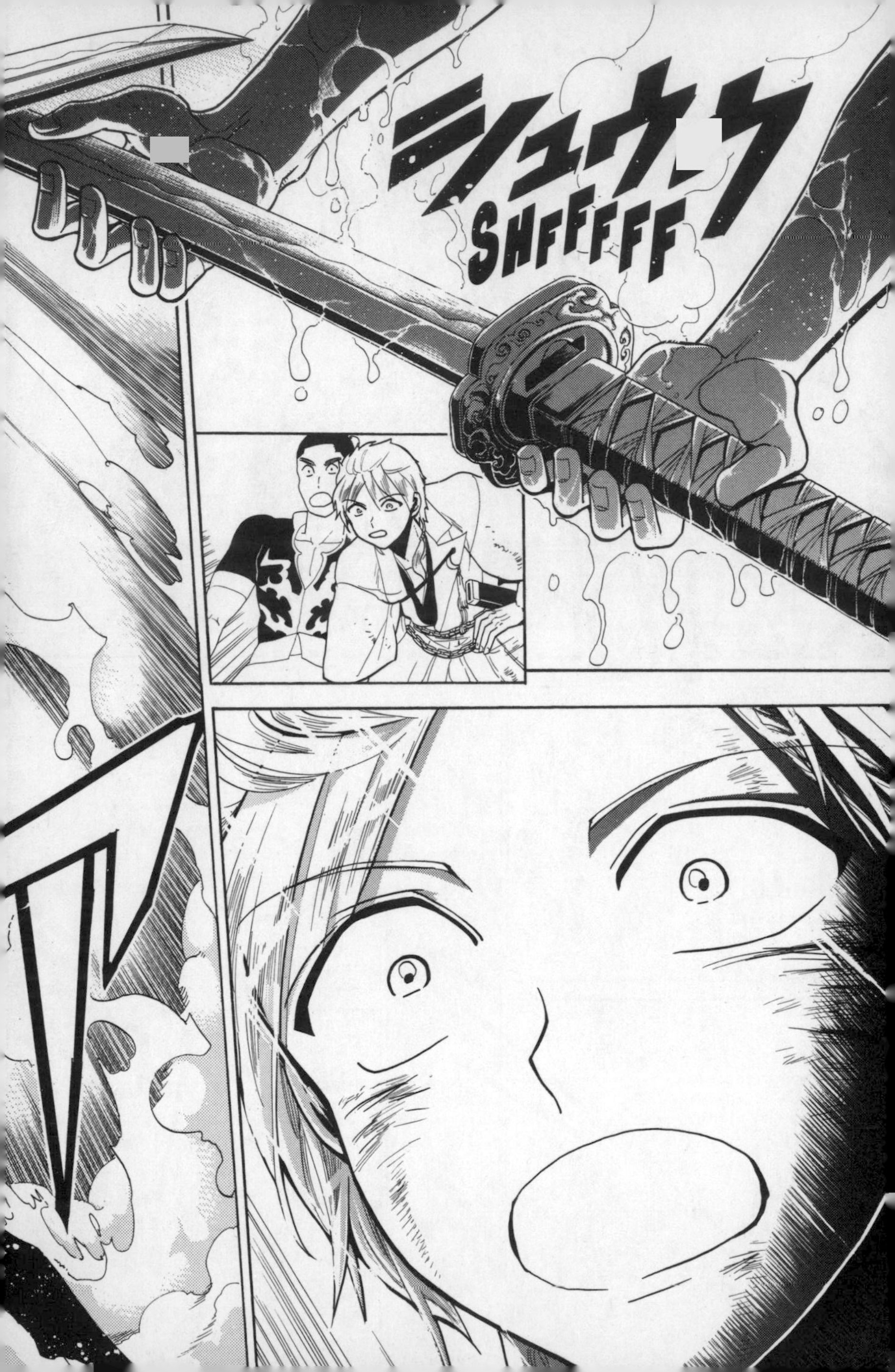
シュウ
SHFFFFF

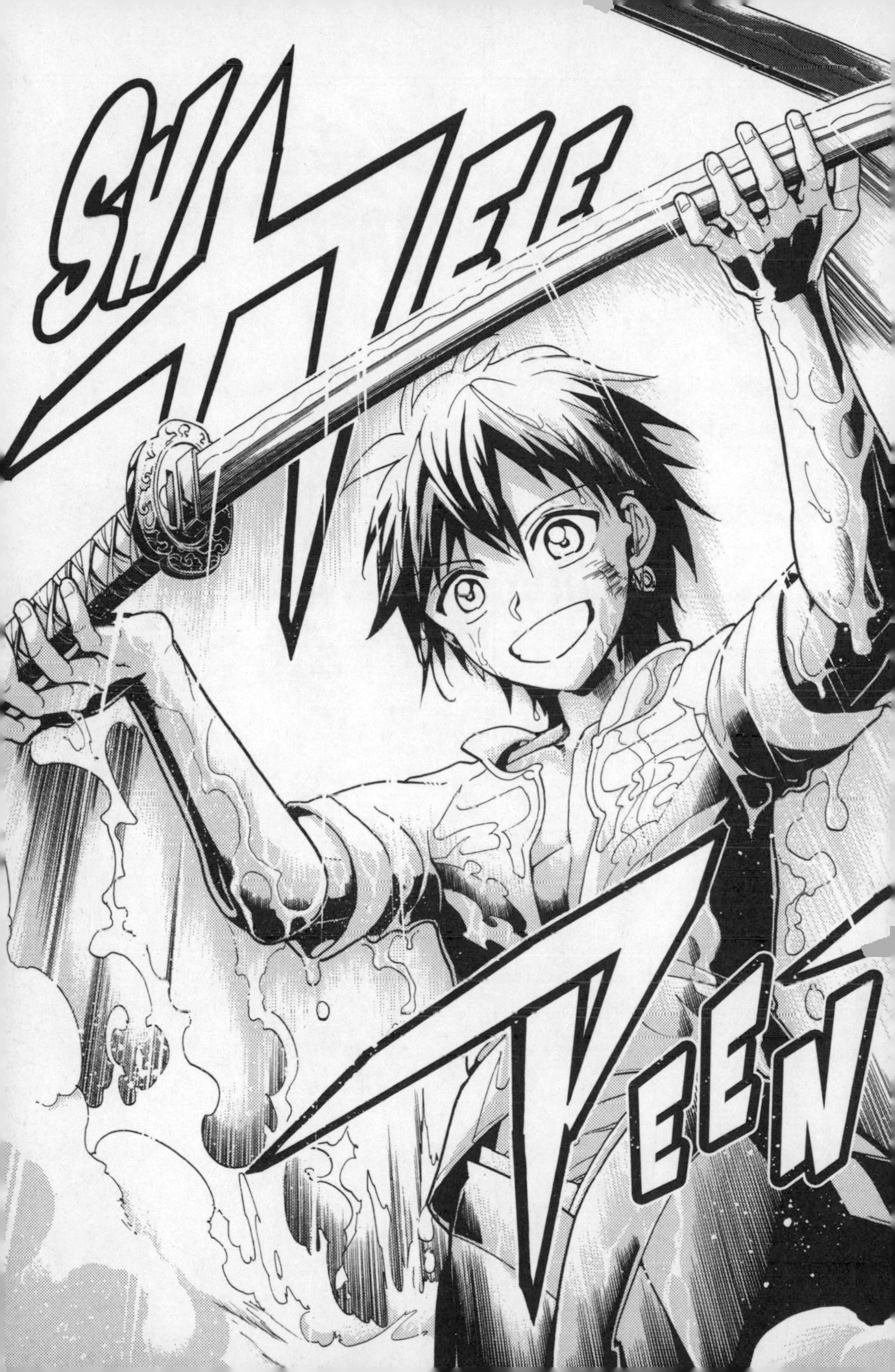
SHEE
EEN

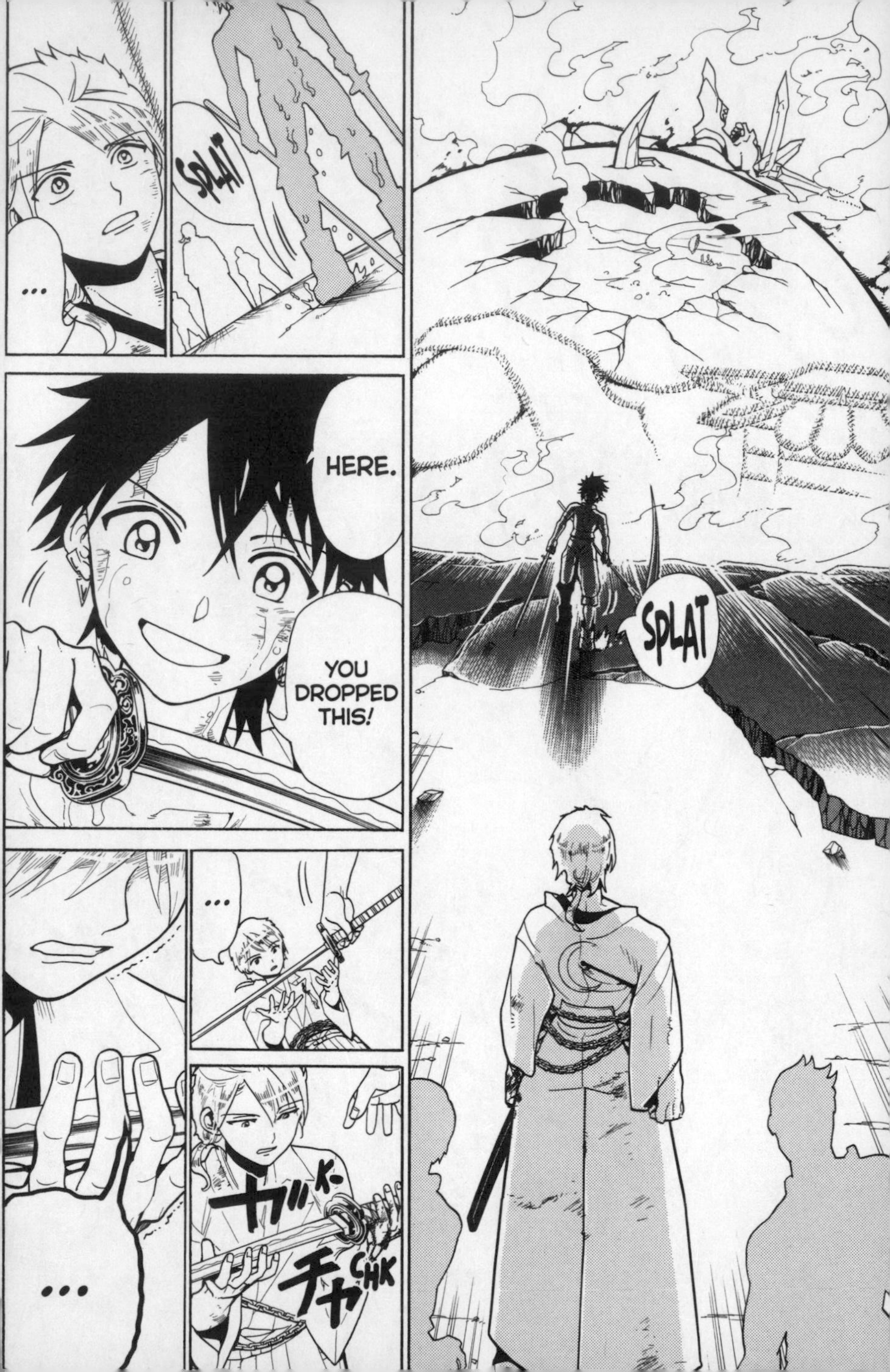
SPLAT
SPLAT
...
HERE.
YOU DROPPED THIS!
...
K-
CHK
...

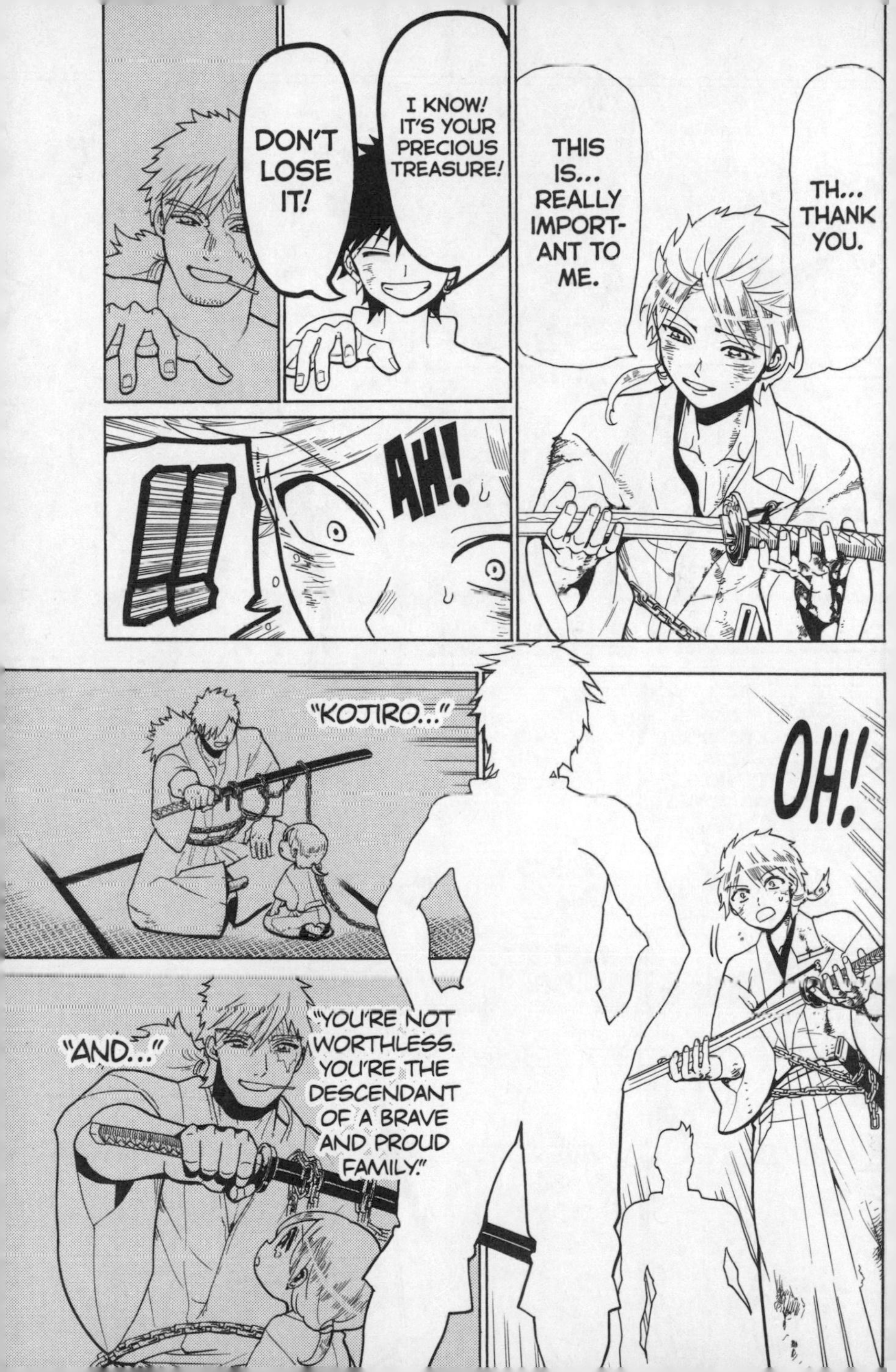
TH... THANK YOU.
THIS IS... REALLY IMPORT-ANT TO ME.
I KNOW! IT'S YOUR PRECIOUS TREASURE!
DON'T LOSE IT!
AH!
!!
OH!
"KOJIRO..."
"YOU'RE NOT WORTHLESS. YOU'RE THE DESCENDANT OF A BRAVE AND PROUD FAMILY."
"AND..."

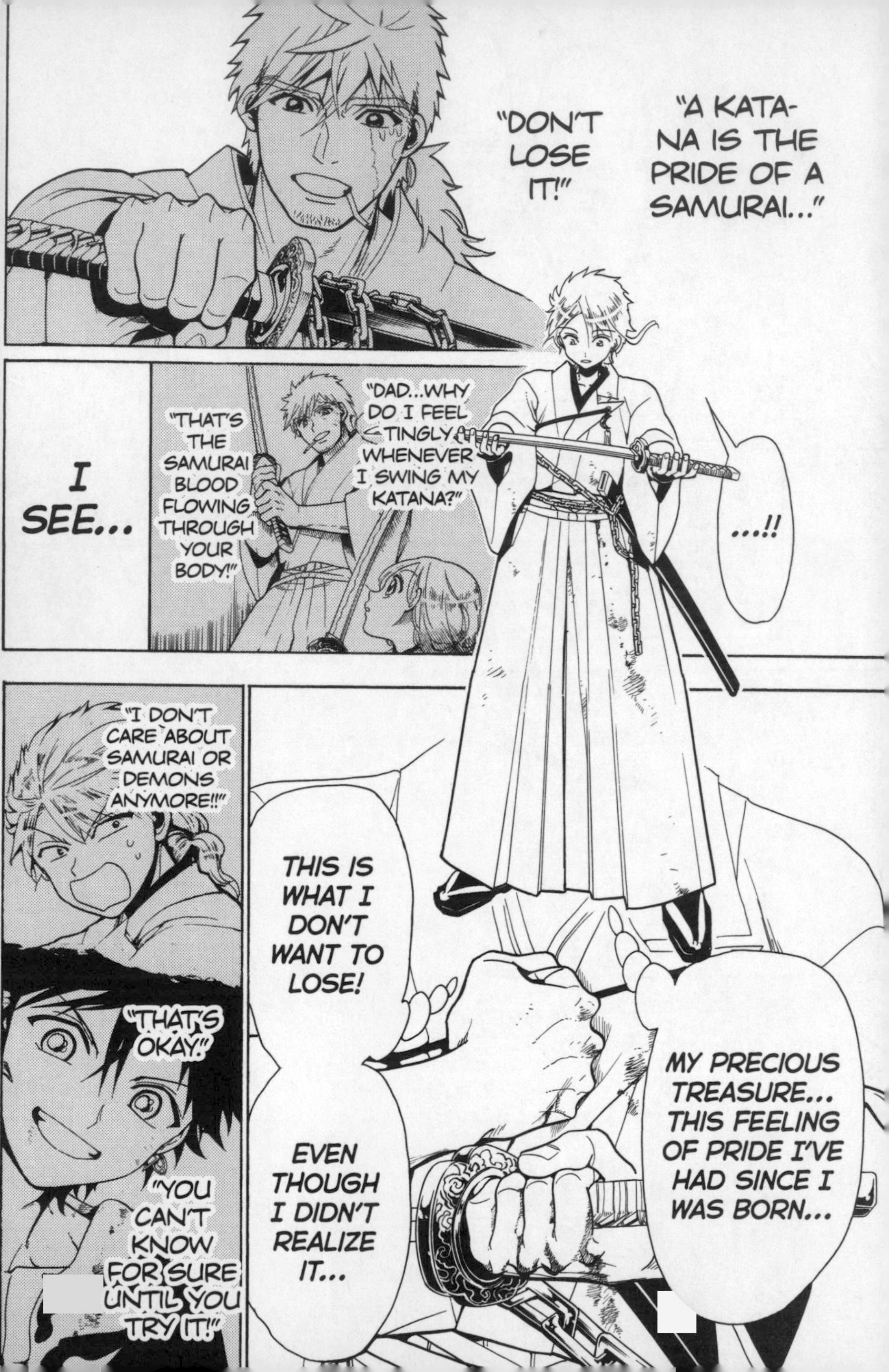
"A KATA-NA IS THE PRIDE OF A SAMURAI..."
"DON'T LOSE IT!"
...!!
"DAD...WHY DO I FEEL TINGLY WHENEVER I SWING MY KATANA?"
"THAT'S THE SAMURAI BLOOD FLOWING THROUGH YOUR BODY!"
I SEE...
MY PRECIOUS TREASURE... THIS FEELING OF PRIDE I'VE HAD SINCE I WAS BORN...
EVEN THOUGH I DIDN'T REALIZE IT...
THIS IS WHAT I DON'T WANT TO LOSE!
"I DON'T CARE ABOUT SAMURAI OR DEMONS ANYMORE!!"
"THAT'S OKAY."
"YOU CAN'T KNOW FOR SURE UNTIL YOU TRY IT!"

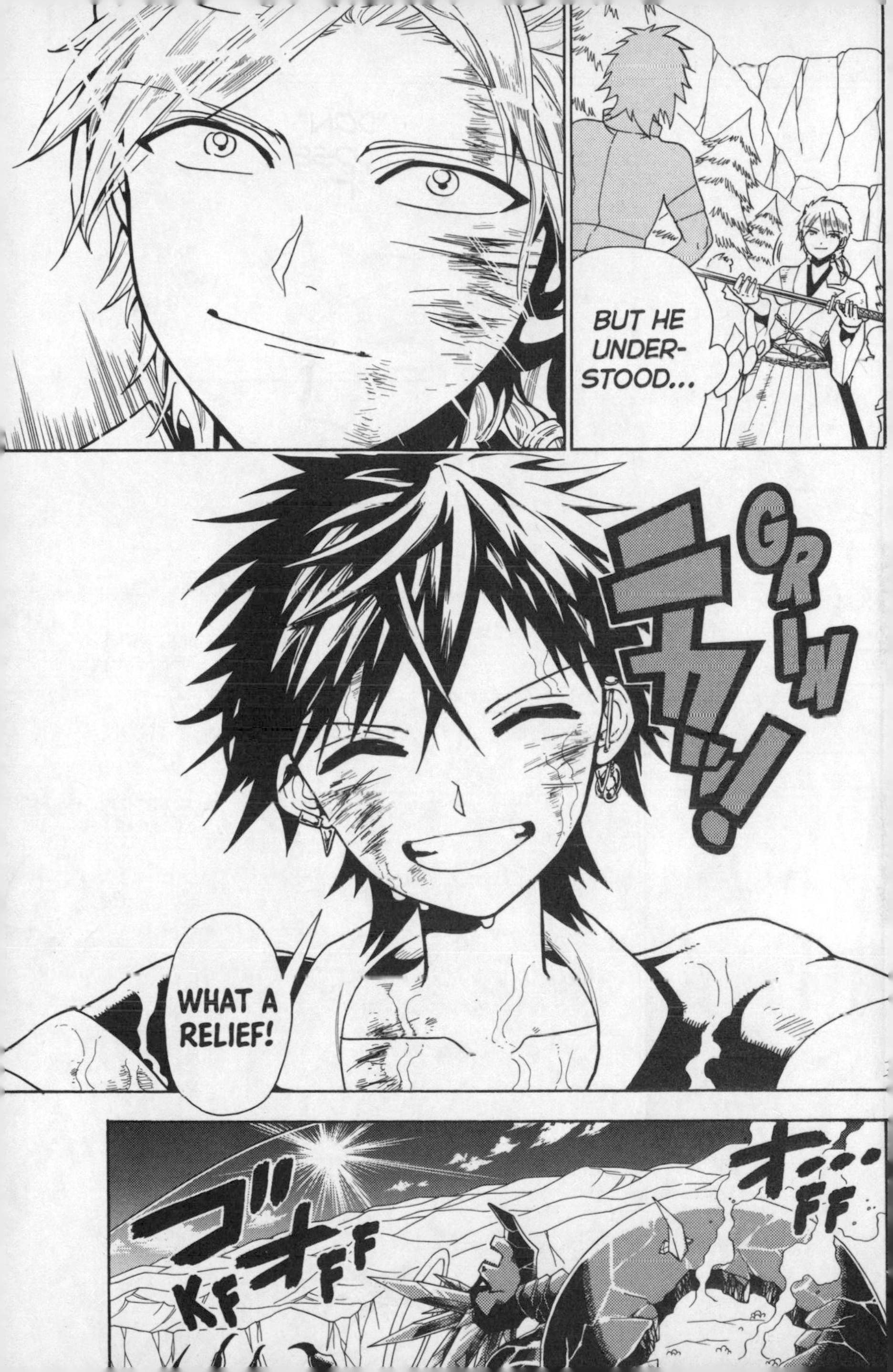
BUT HE UNDER-STOOD...
ニカッ!
GRIN
WHAT A RELIEF!
オ…
FF
ゴオ
KFFF

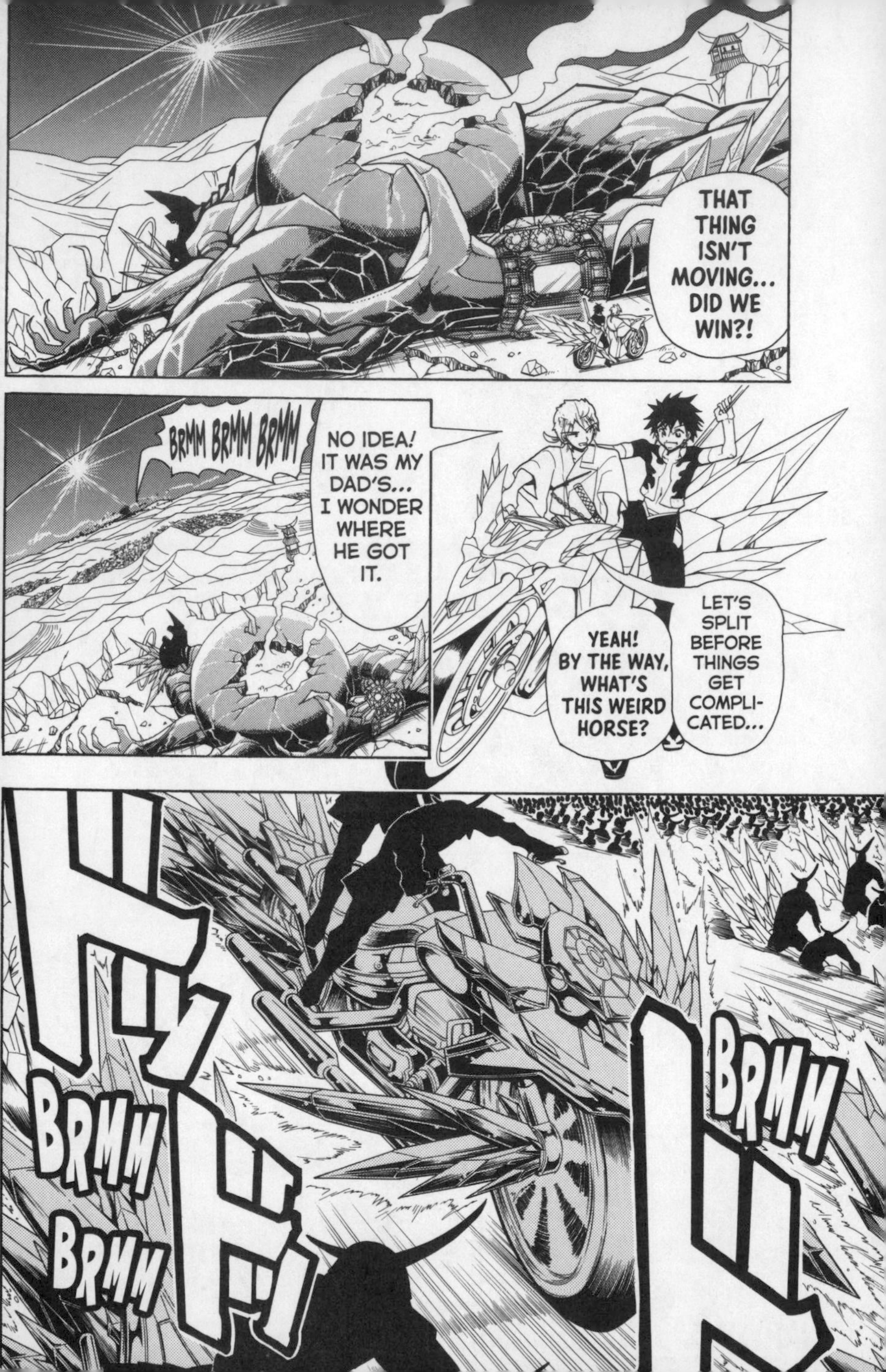
THAT THING ISN'T MOVING... DID WE WIN?!
LET'S SPLIT BEFORE THINGS GET COMPLI-CATED...
YEAH! BY THE WAY, WHAT'S THIS WEIRD HORSE?
NO IDEA! IT WAS MY DAD'S... I WONDER WHERE HE GOT IT.
BRMM BRMM BRMM
BRMM
BRMM
BRMM

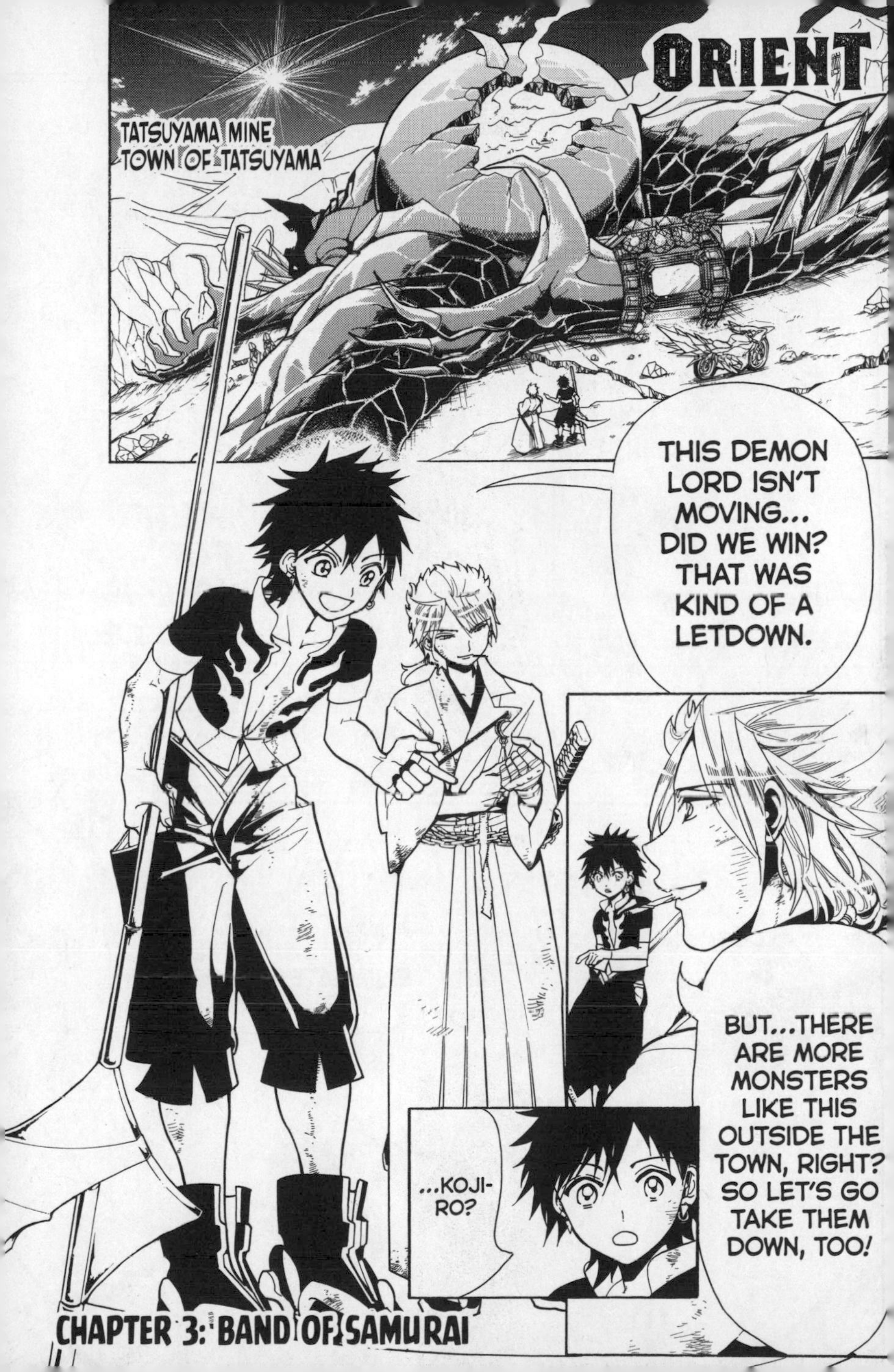
ORIENT
TATSUYAMA MINE
TOWN OF TATSUYAMA
THIS DEMON LORD ISN'T MOVING... DID WE WIN? THAT WAS KIND OF A LETDOWN.
BUT...THERE ARE MORE MONSTERS LIKE THIS OUTSIDE THE TOWN, RIGHT? SO LET'S GO TAKE THEM DOWN, TOO!
...KOJI-RO?
CHAPTER 3: BAND OF SAMURAI

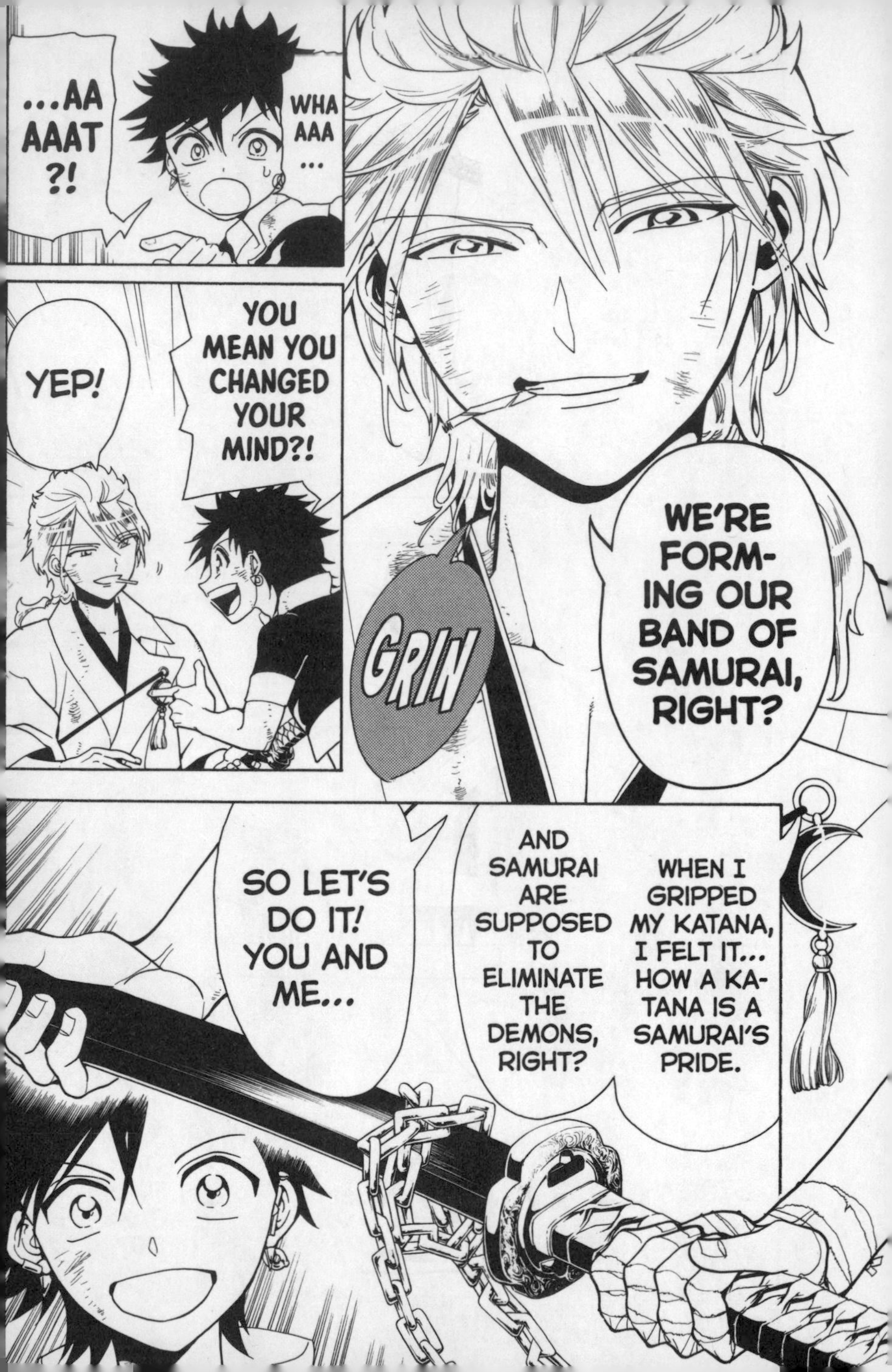

WE'RE FORMING-ING OUR BAND OF SAMURAI, RIGHT?
GRIN
WHA AAA ...
...AA AAAT ?!
YOU MEAN YOU CHANGED YOUR MIND?!
YEP!
WHEN I GRIPPED MY KATANA, I FELT IT... HOW A KA-TANA IS A SAMURAI'S PRIDE.
AND SAMURAI ARE SUPPOSED TO ELIMINATE THE DEMONS, RIGHT?
SO LET'S DO IT! YOU AND ME...

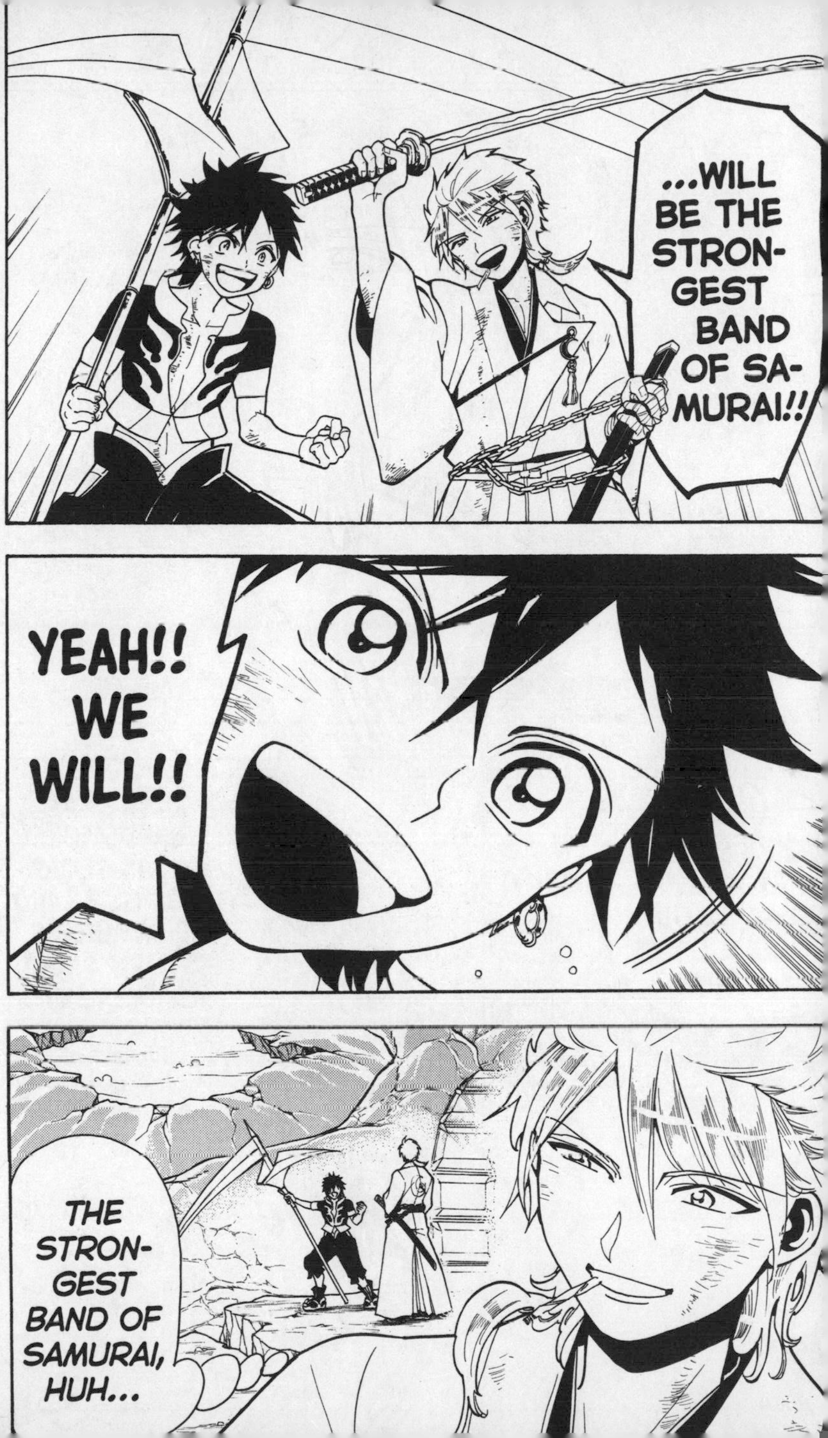
...WILL BE THE STRON-GEST BAND OF SA-MURAI!!
YEAH!! WE WILL!!
THE STRON-GEST BAND OF SAMURAI, HUH...

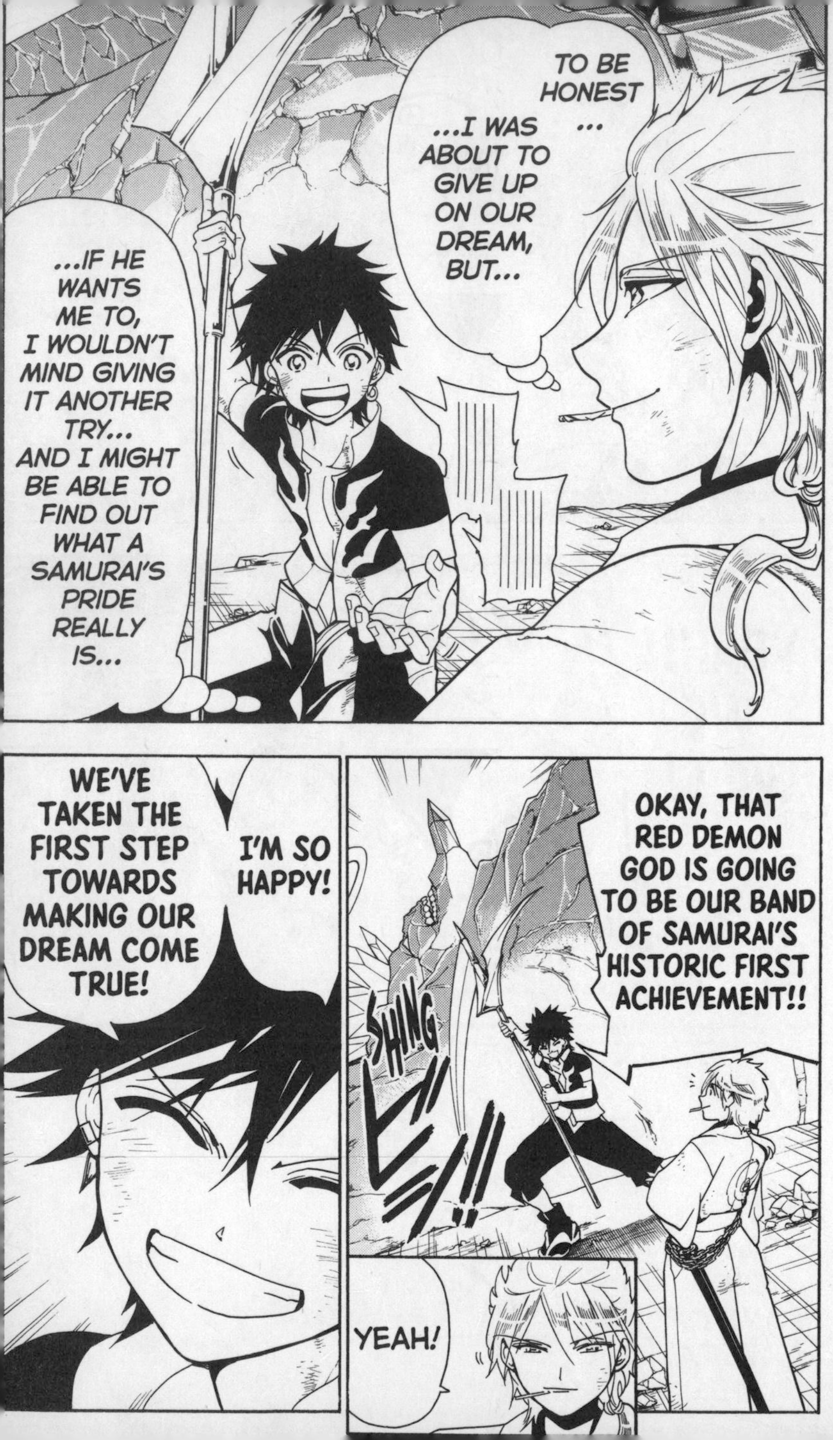
TO BE HONEST ...
...I WAS ABOUT TO GIVE UP ON OUR DREAM, BUT...
...IF HE WANTS ME TO, I WOULDN'T MIND GIVING IT ANOTHER TRY... AND I MIGHT BE ABLE TO FIND OUT WHAT A SAMURAI'S PRIDE REALLY IS...
OKAY, THAT RED DEMON GOD IS GOING TO BE OUR BAND OF SAMURAI'S HISTORIC FIRST ACHIEVEMENT!!
SHING
YEAH!
I'M SO HAPPY!
WE'VE TAKEN THE FIRST STEP TOWARDS MAKING OUR DREAM COME TRUE!

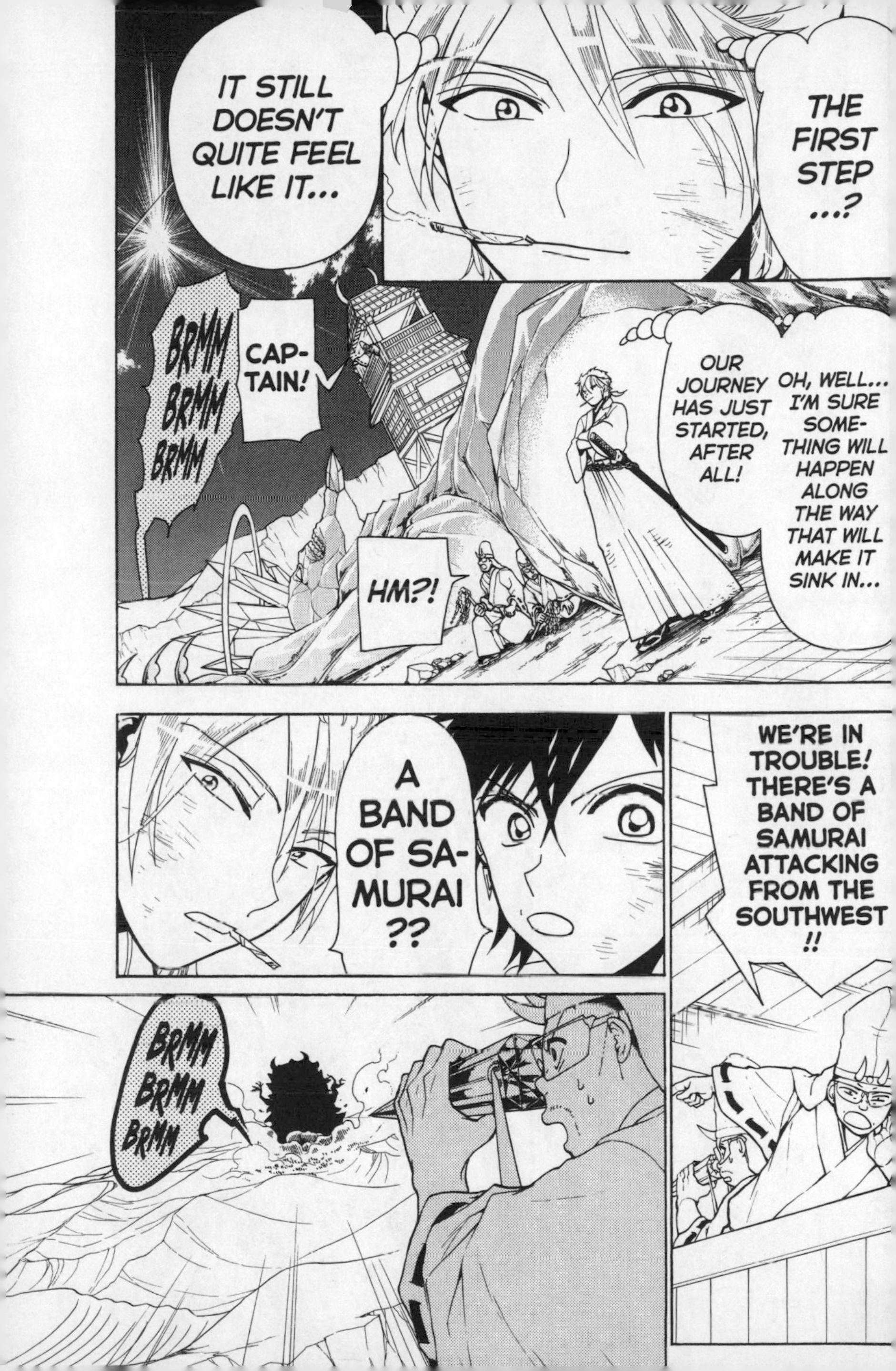
THE FIRST STEP ...?
IT STILL DOESN'T QUITE FEEL LIKE IT...
OH, WELL... I'M SURE SOME-THING WILL HAPPEN ALONG THE WAY THAT WILL MAKE IT SINK IN...
OUR JOURNEY HAS JUST STARTED, AFTER ALL!
CAP-TAIN!
BRMM BRMM BRMM
HM?!
WE'RE IN TROUBLE! THERE'S A BAND OF SAMURAI ATTACKING FROM THE SOUTHWEST !!
A BAND OF SA-MURAI ??
BRMM BRMM BRMM

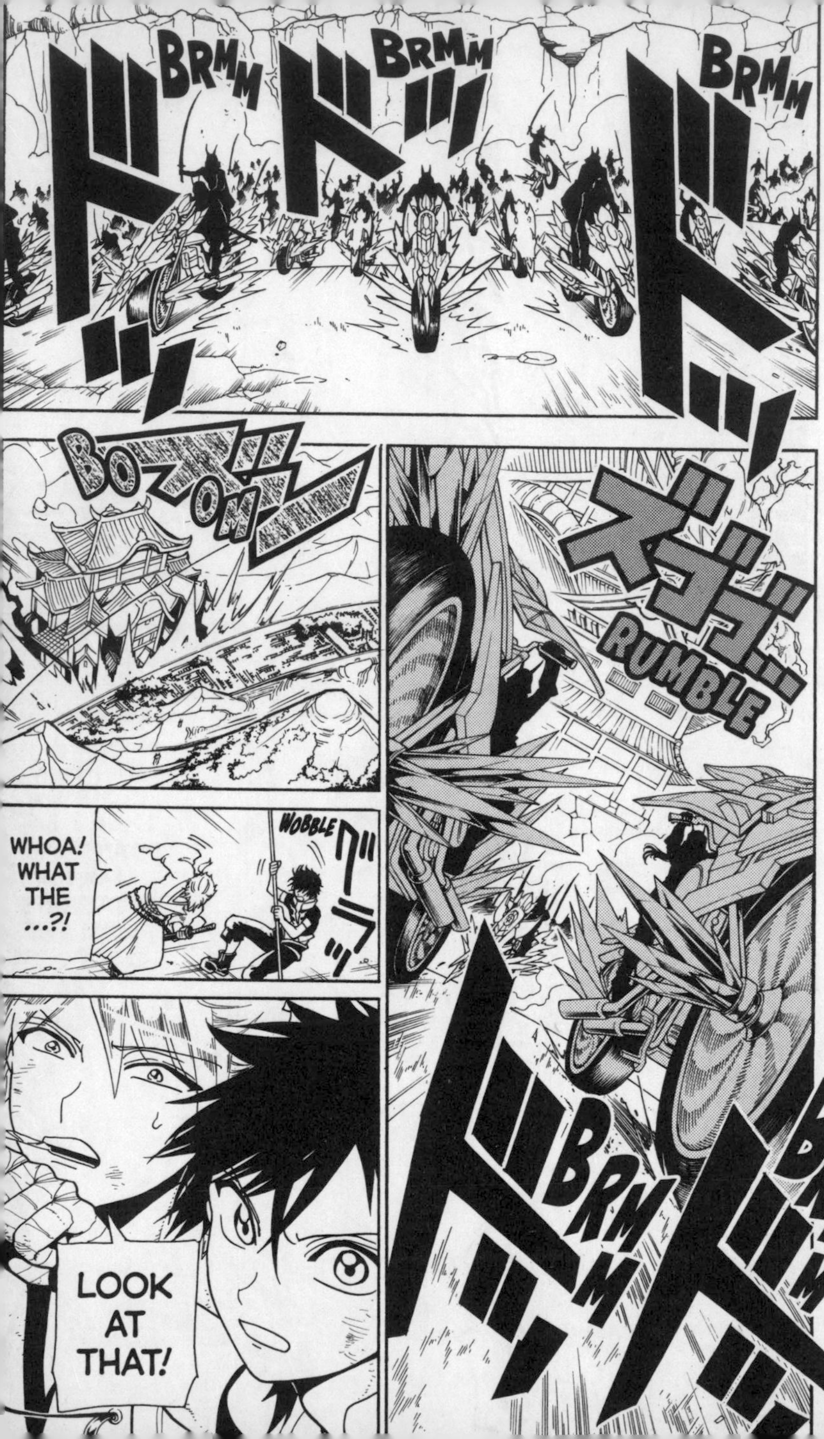
BRMM
BRMM
BRMM
RUMBLE
BRMM
BRMM
BOOM
WOBBLE
WHOA! WHAT THE ...?!
LOOK AT THAT!

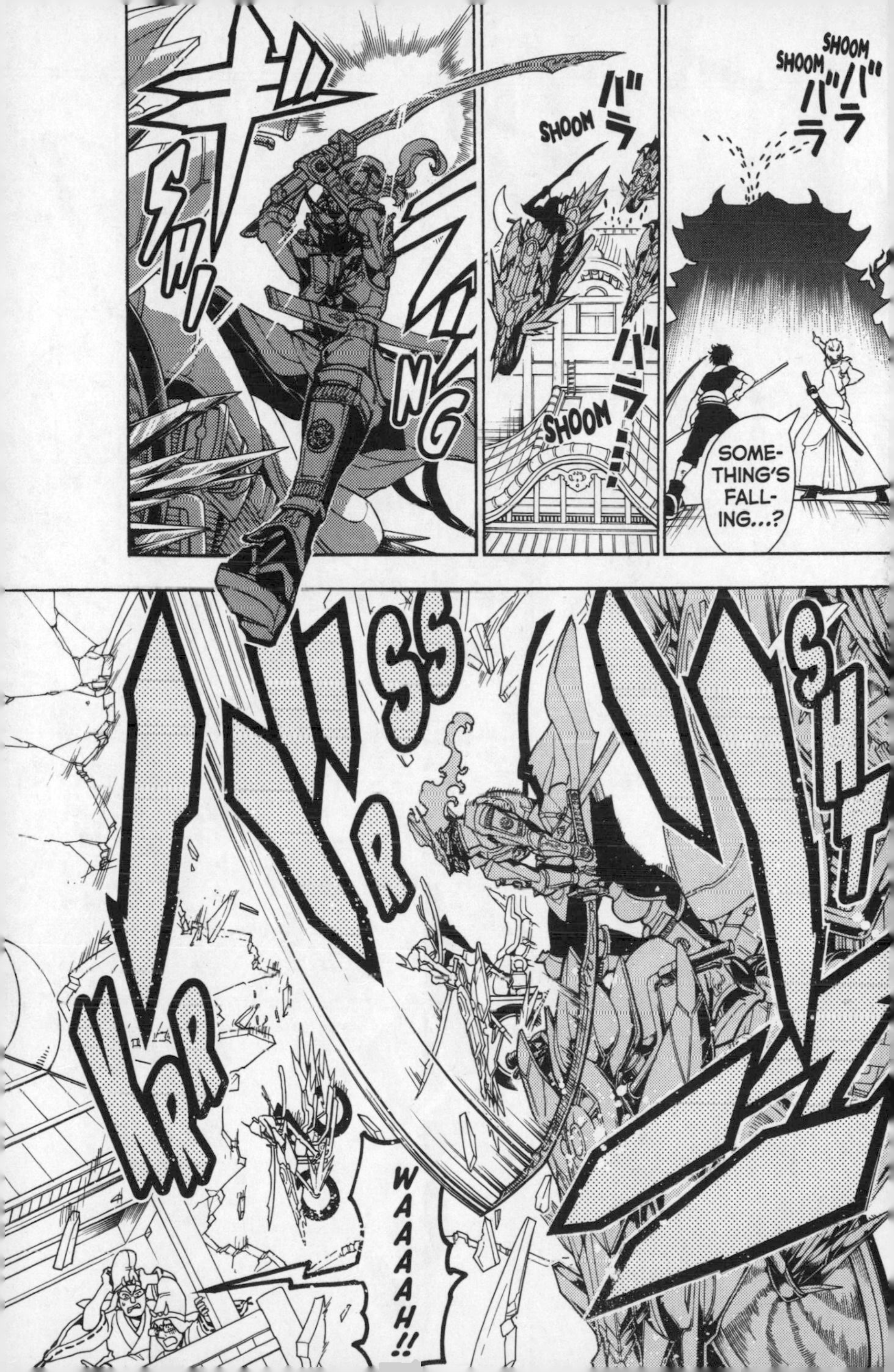
SHOOM
SHOOM
バラ
バラ
SOME-THING'S FALL-ING...?
SHOOM
バラ
SHOOM
バラ……
SHING
WAAAAAH!!

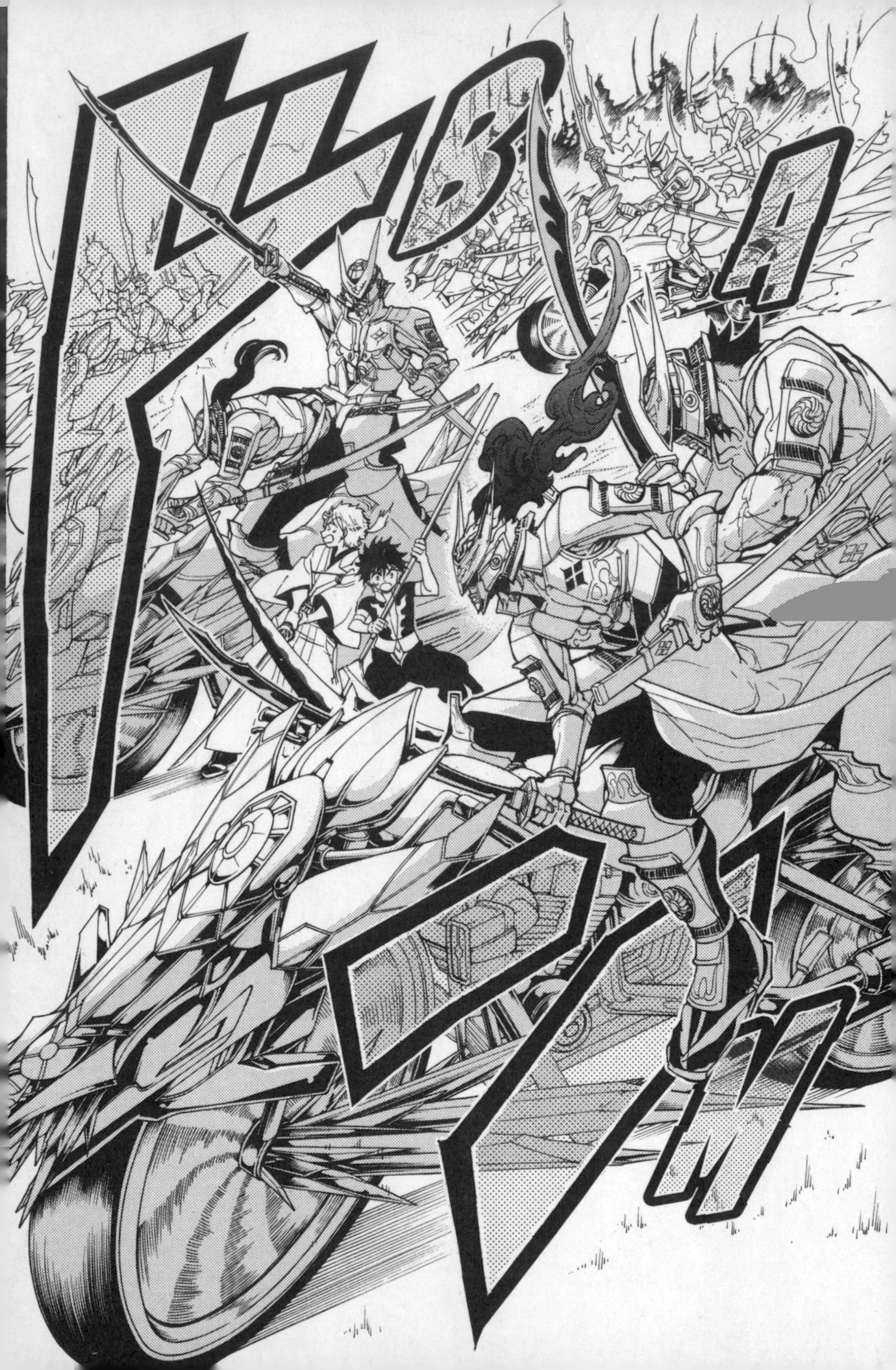

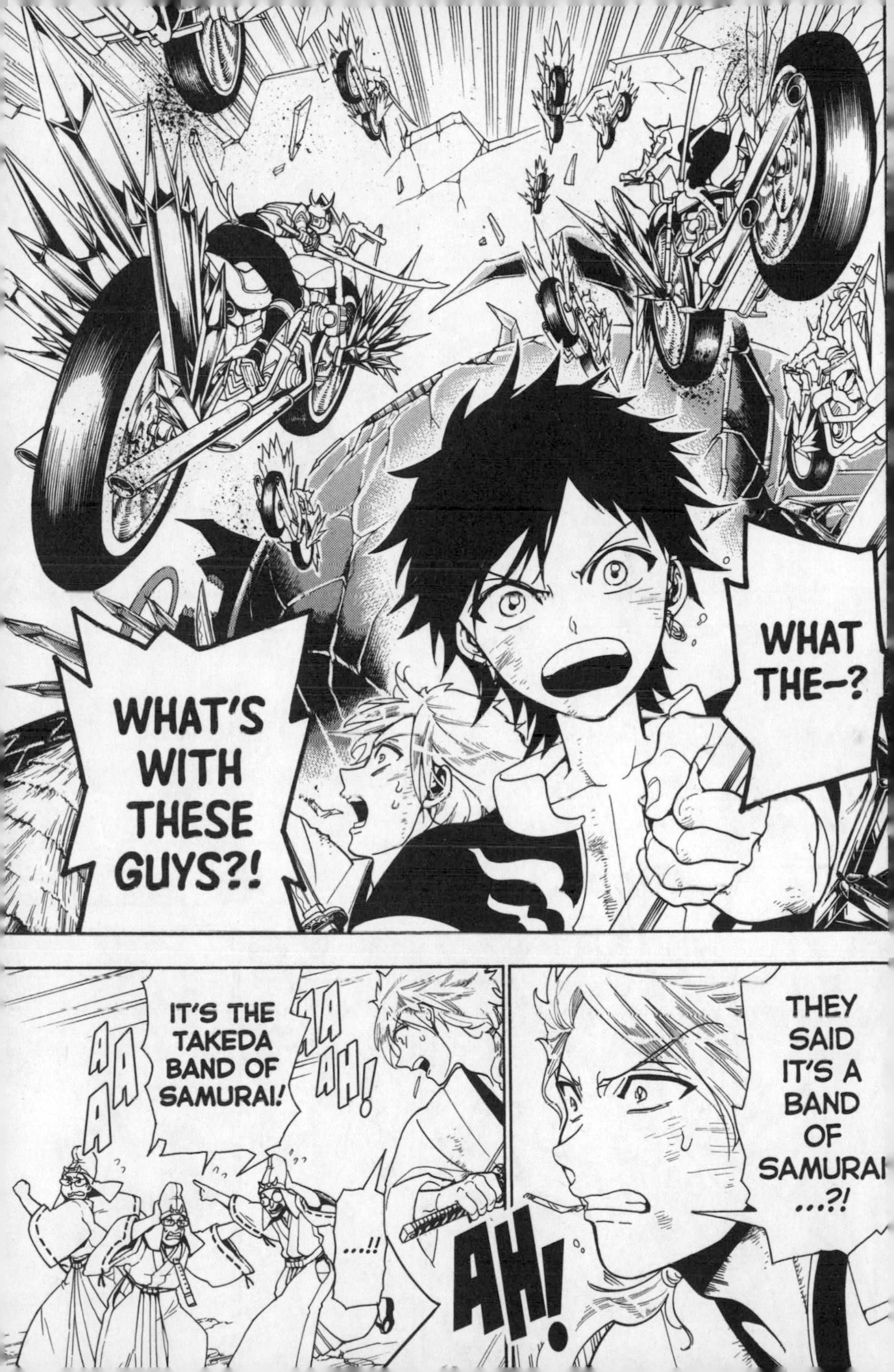
WHAT THE–?
WHAT'S WITH THESE GUYS?!
THEY SAID IT'S A BAND OF SAMURAI ...?!
AH!
AAAH!
IT'S THE TAKEDA BAND OF SAMURAI!
AAAA
...!!

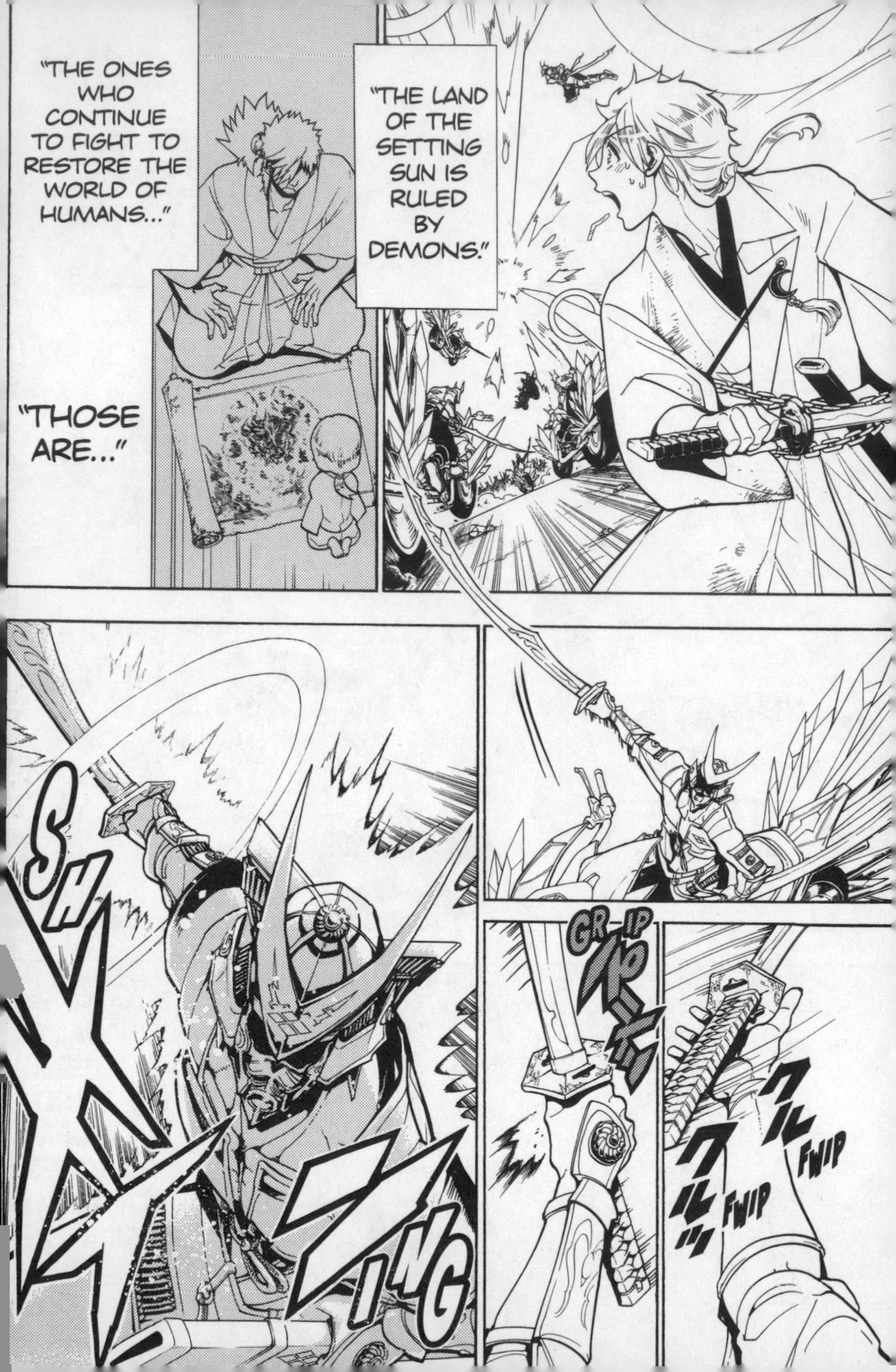
"THE LAND OF THE SETTING SUN IS RULED BY DEMONS."
"THOSE ARE..."
"THE ONES WHO CONTINUE TO FIGHT TO RESTORE THE WORLD OF HUMANS..."
FWIP
FWIP
GR-IP
SHING

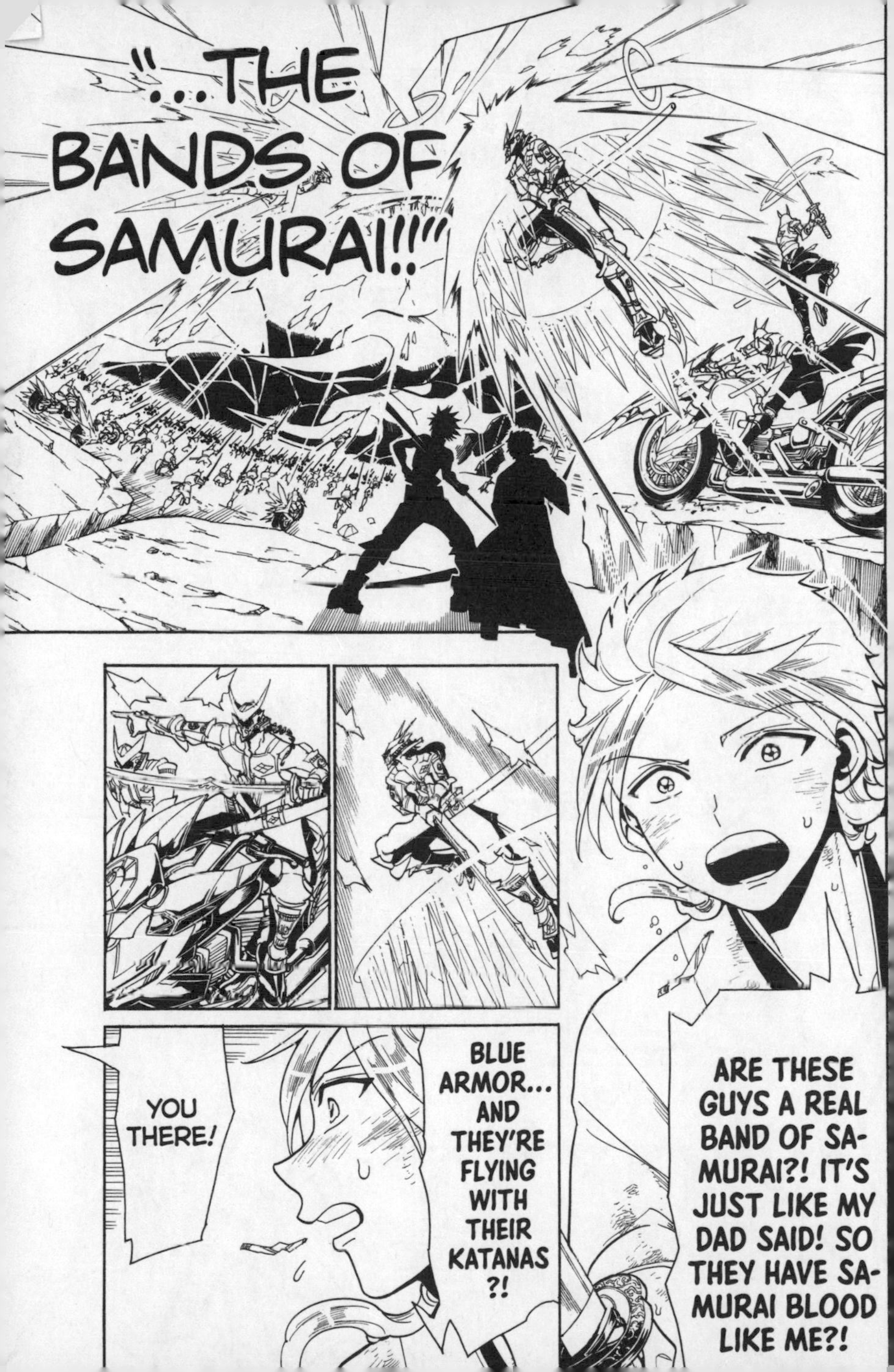
"...THE BANDS OF SAMURAI!!"
ARE THESE GUYS A REAL BAND OF SA-MURAI?! IT'S JUST LIKE MY DAD SAID! SO THEY HAVE SA-MURAI BLOOD LIKE ME?!
BLUE ARMOR... AND THEY'RE FLYING WITH THEIR KATANAS?!
YOU THERE!

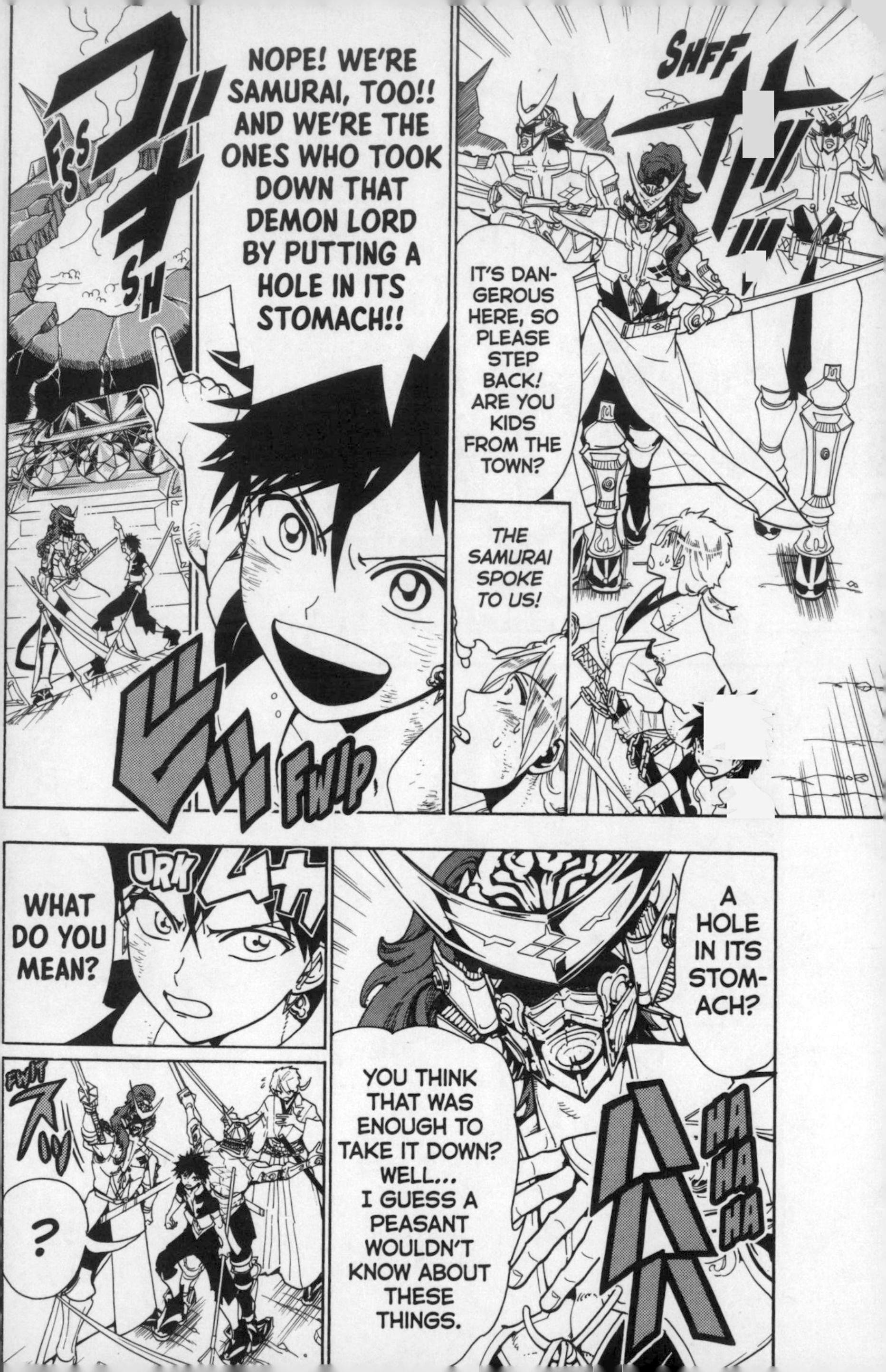
SHFF
IT'S DAN-GEROUS HERE, SO PLEASE STEP BACK! ARE YOU KIDS FROM THE TOWN?
THE SAMURAI SPOKE TO US!
NOPE! WE'RE SAMURAI, TOO!! AND WE'RE THE ONES WHO TOOK DOWN THAT DEMON LORD BY PUTTING A HOLE IN ITS STOMACH!!
FSS
SH
FWIP
A HOLE IN ITS STOM-ACH?
HA HA HA
YOU THINK THAT WAS ENOUGH TO TAKE IT DOWN? WELL... I GUESS A PEASANT WOULDN'T KNOW ABOUT THESE THINGS.
URK
WHAT DO YOU MEAN?
FWIT
?

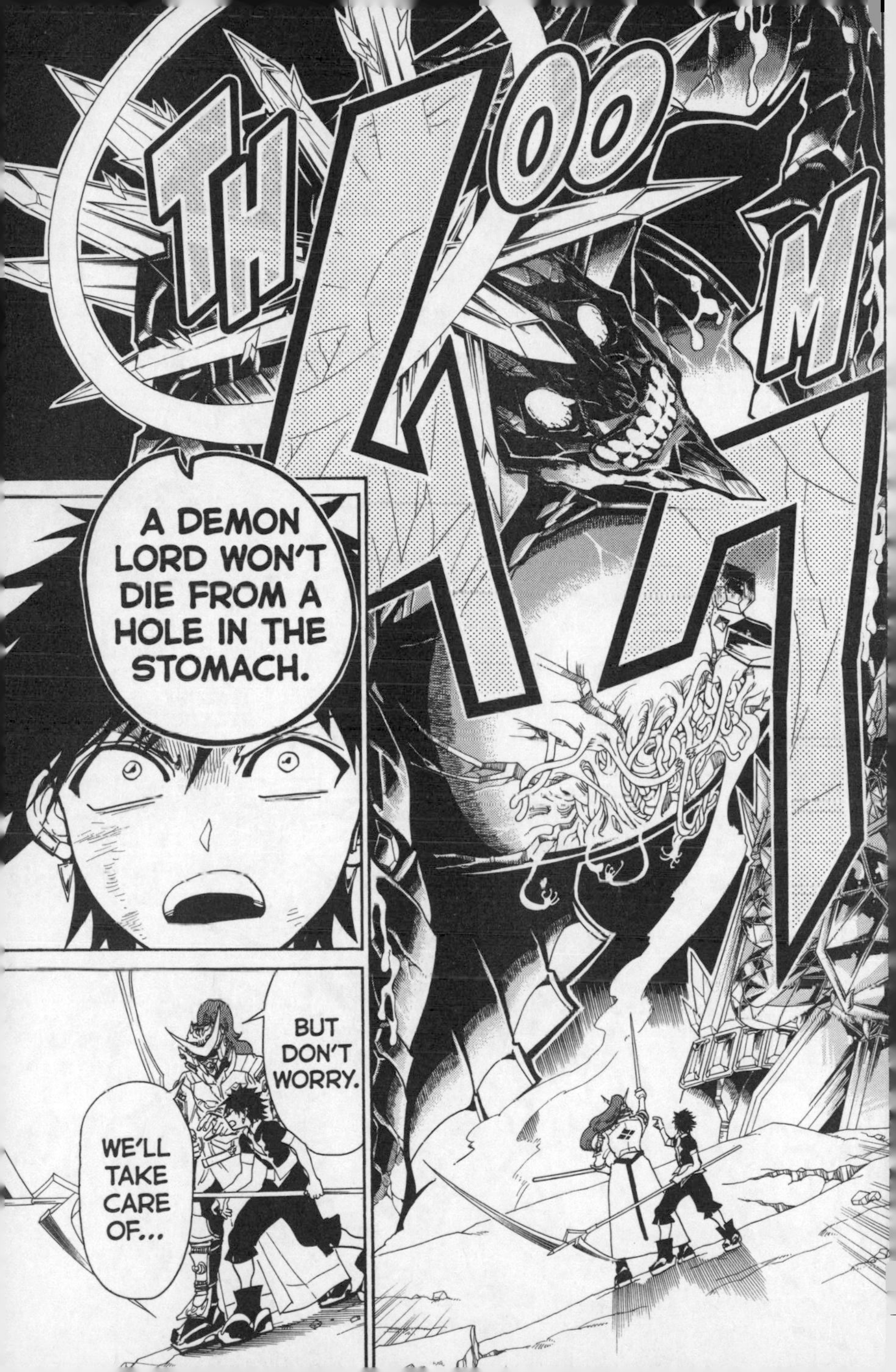
THOOOM
A DEMON LORD WON'T DIE FROM A HOLE IN THE STOMACH.
BUT DON'T WORRY.
WE'LL TAKE CARE OF...

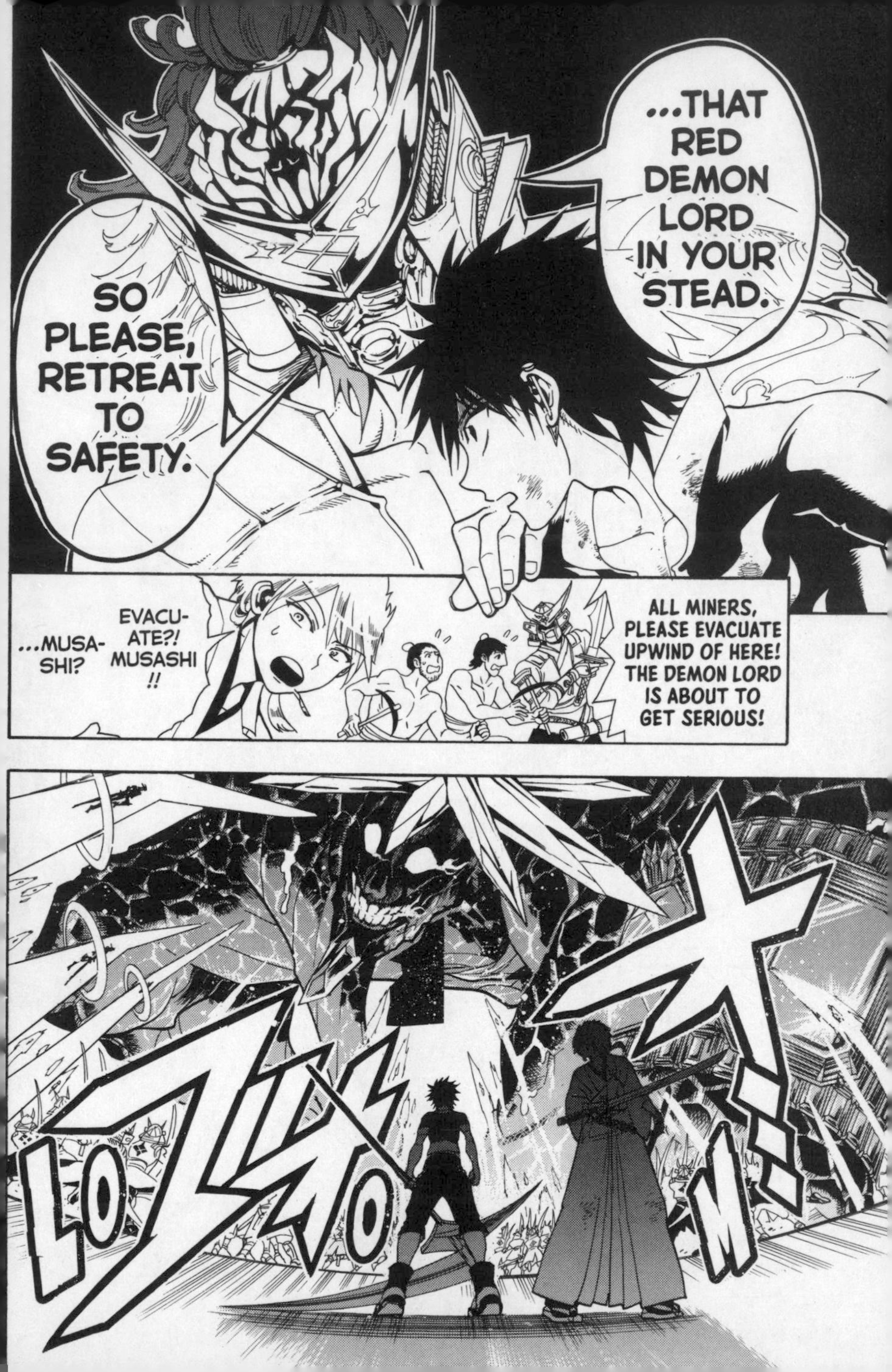
...THAT RED DEMON LORD IN YOUR STEAD.
SO PLEASE, RETREAT TO SAFETY.
ALL MINERS, PLEASE EVACUATE UPWIND OF HERE! THE DEMON LORD IS ABOUT TO GET SERIOUS!
EVACU-ATE?! MUSASHI!!
...MUSA-SHI?

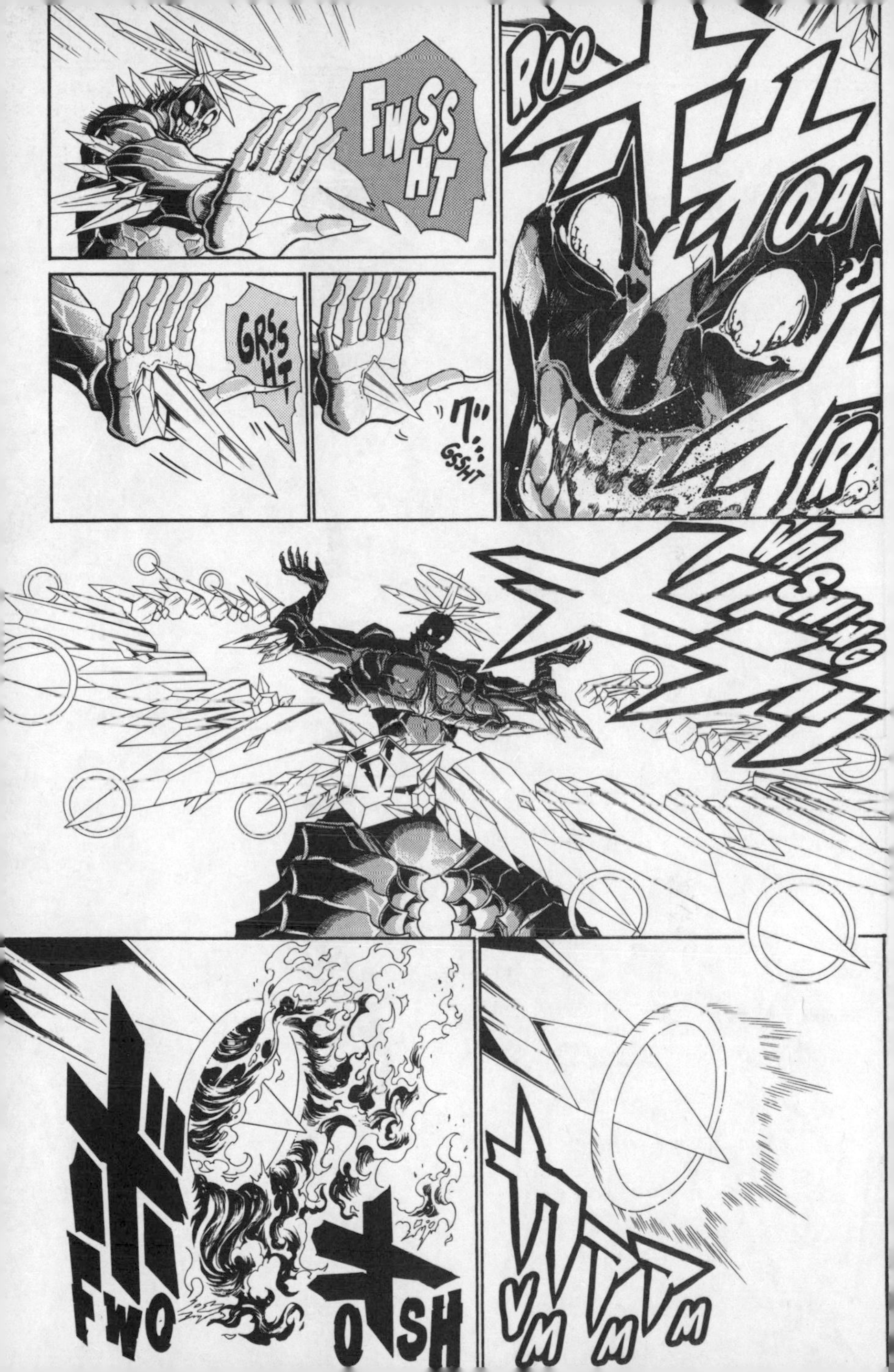
ROOOAR
FWSSHT
GSSHT
GRSSHT
WASHING
VM VM VM
FWOOSH

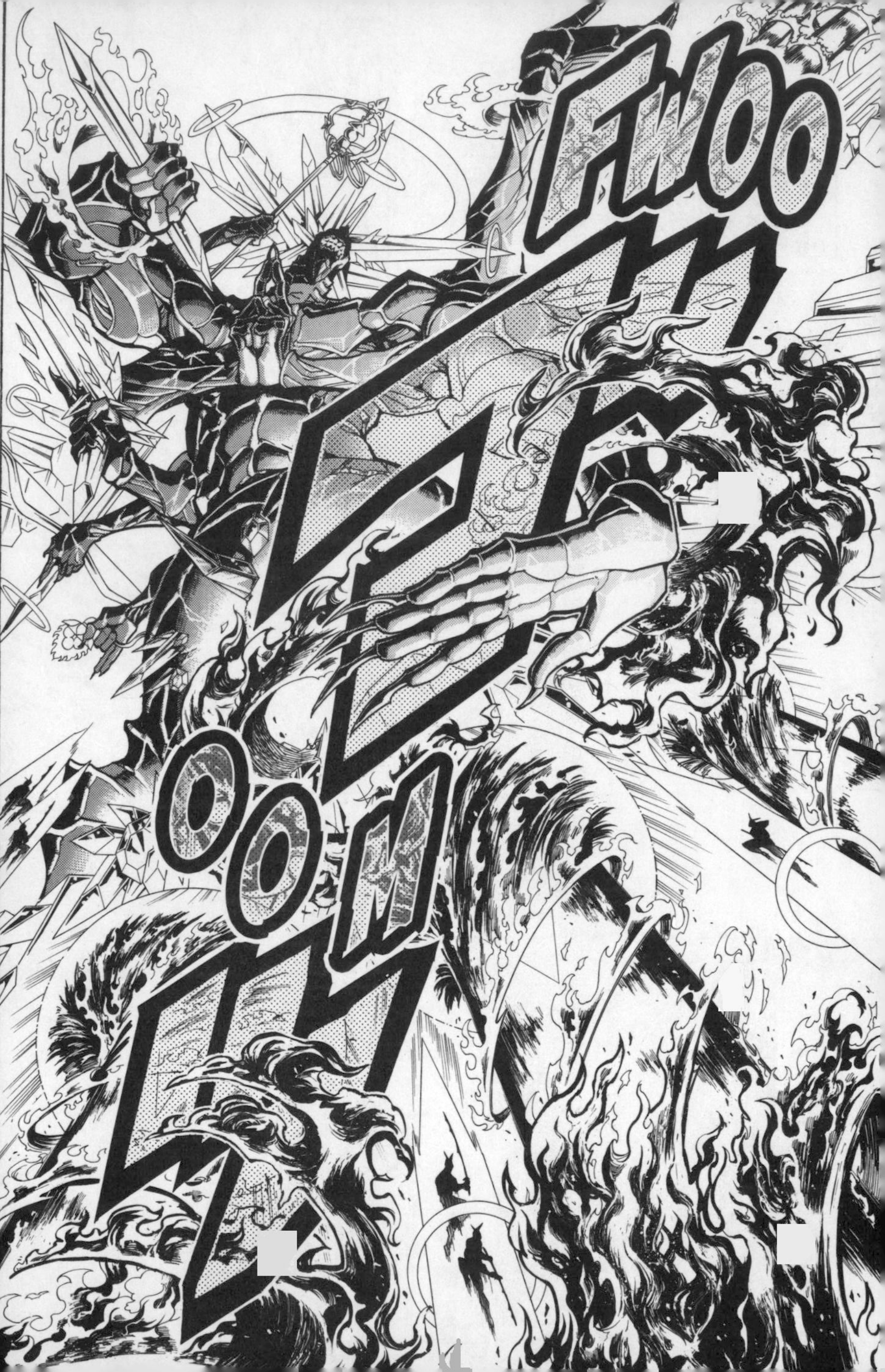
FWOOOOM

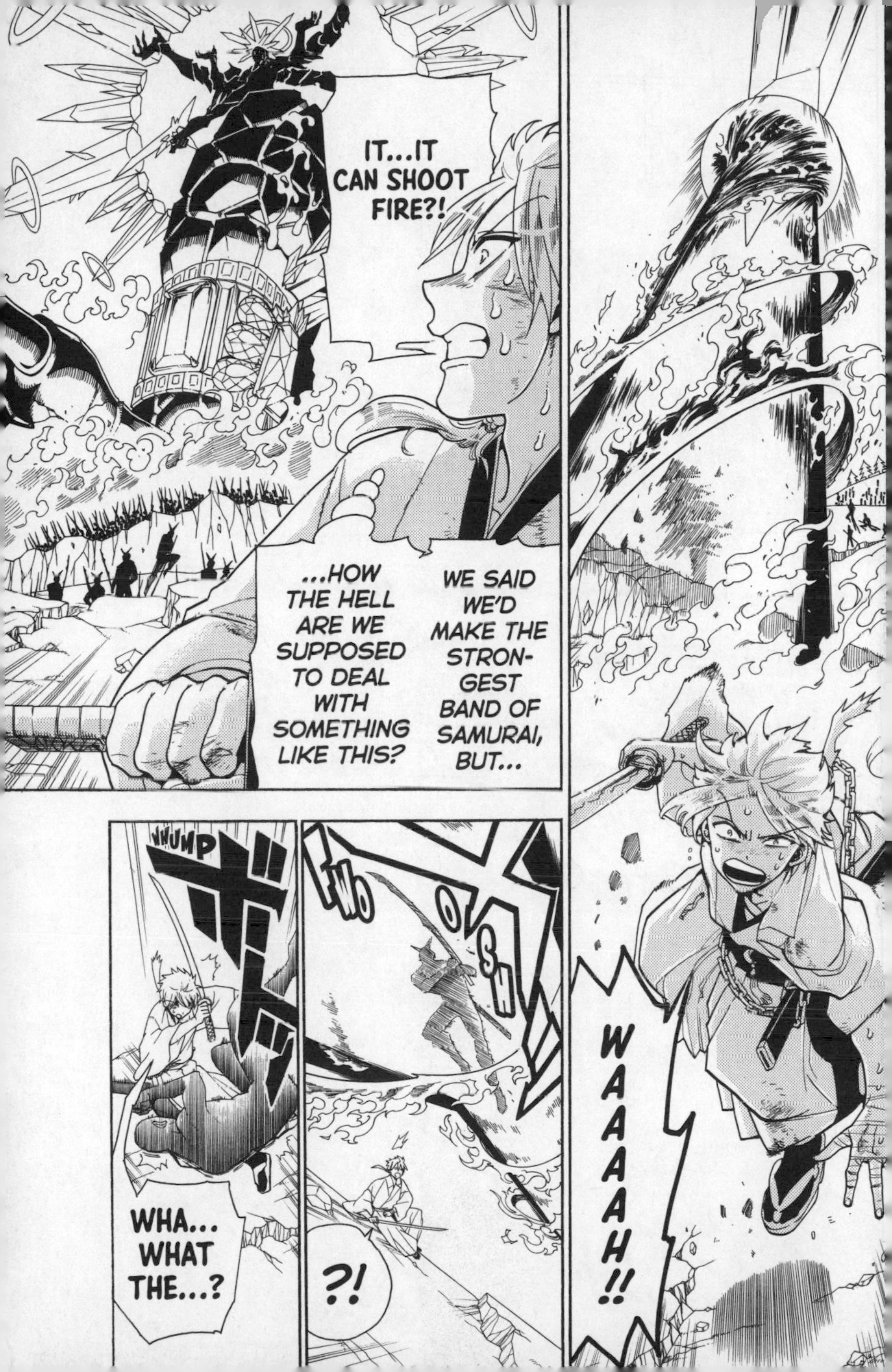
WAAAAAH!!
IT...IT CAN SHOOT FIRE?!
WE SAID WE'D MAKE THE STRON-GEST BAND OF SAMURAI, BUT...
...HOW THE HELL ARE WE SUPPOSED TO DEAL WITH SOMETHING LIKE THIS?
WHOOSH
?!
WHUMP
WHA... WHAT THE...?

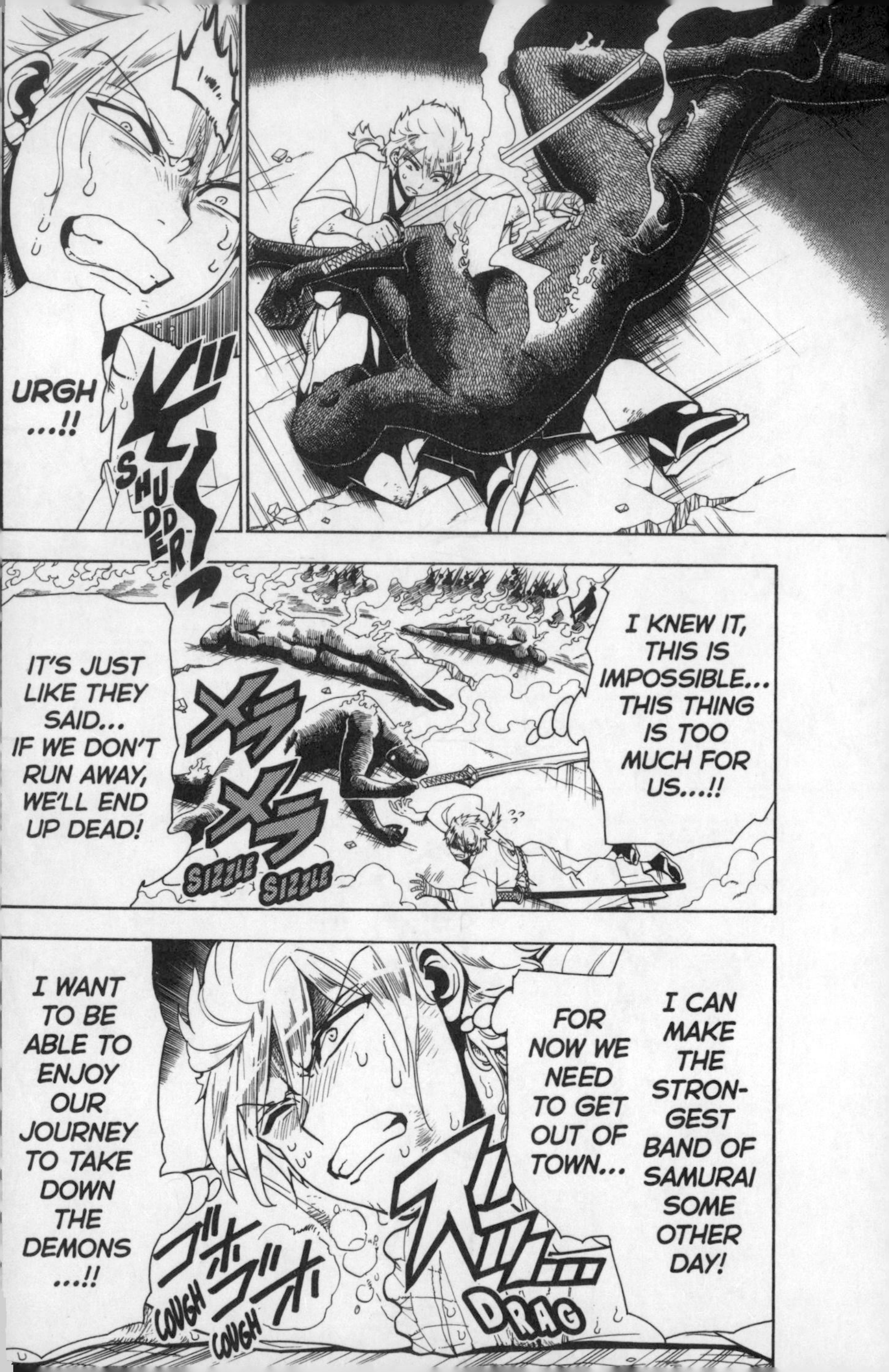
URGH ...!!
SHUDDER
I KNEW IT, THIS IS IMPOSSIBLE... THIS THING IS TOO MUCH FOR US...!!
IT'S JUST LIKE THEY SAID... IF WE DON'T RUN AWAY, WE'LL END UP DEAD!
メラメラ
SIZZLE SIZZLE
I CAN MAKE THE STRON- GEST BAND OF SAMURAI SOME OTHER DAY!
FOR NOW WE NEED TO GET OUT OF TOWN...
DRAG
I WANT TO BE ABLE TO ENJOY OUR JOURNEY TO TAKE DOWN THE DEMONS ...!!
COUGH COUGH

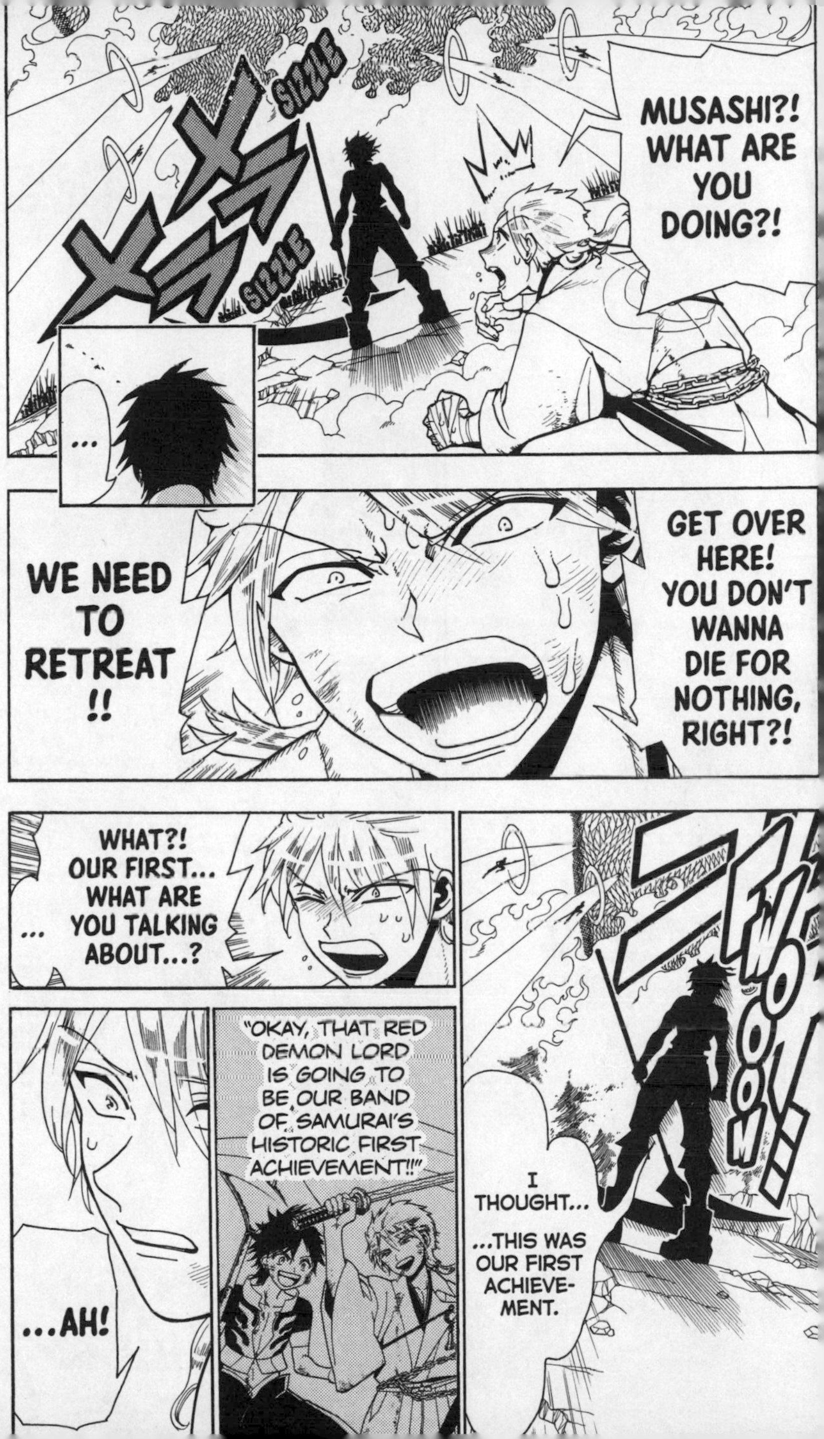
SIZZLE
SIZZLE
MUSASHI?! WHAT ARE YOU DOING?!
...
GET OVER HERE! YOU DON'T WANNA DIE FOR NOTHING, RIGHT?!
WE NEED TO RETREAT!!
FWOOOM!
I THOUGHT...
...THIS WAS OUR FIRST ACHIEVEMENT.
WHAT?! OUR FIRST... WHAT ARE YOU TALKING ABOUT...?
...
"OKAY, THAT RED DEMON LORD IS GOING TO BE OUR BAND OF SAMURAI'S HISTORIC FIRST ACHIEVEMENT!!"
...AH!

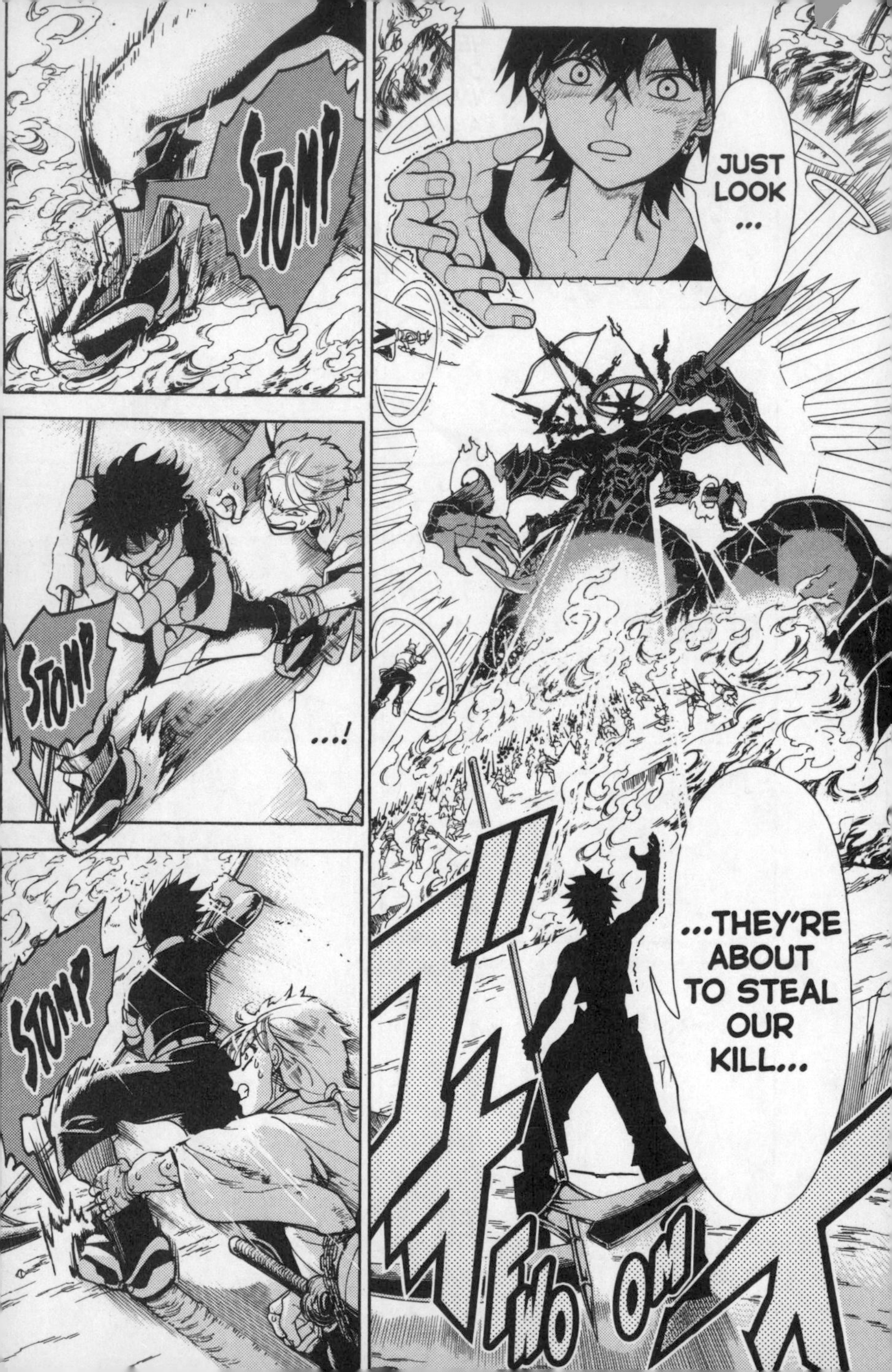
JUST LOOK ...
...THEY'RE ABOUT TO STEAL OUR KILL...
STOMP
STOMP
...!
STOMP

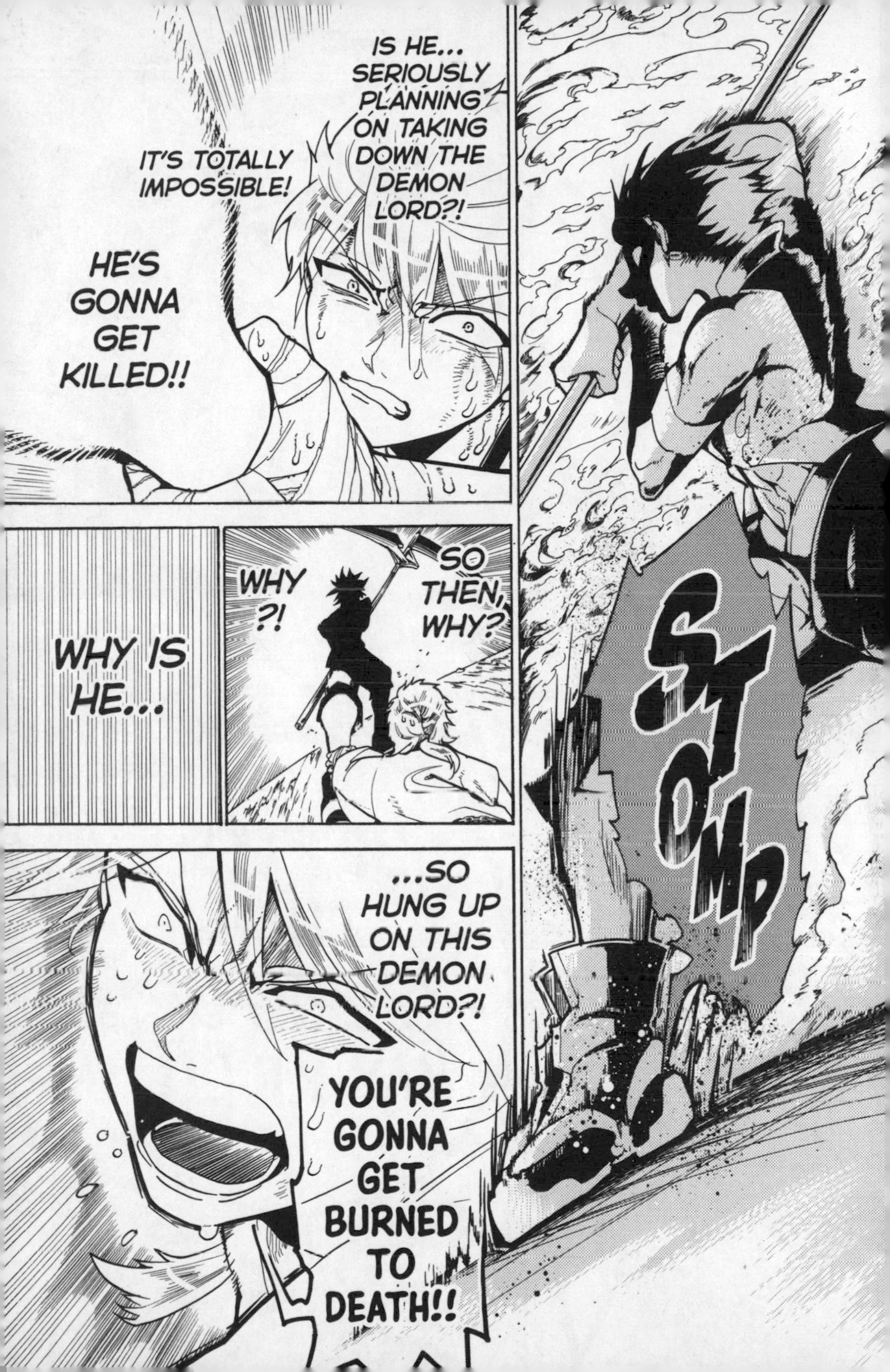
STOMP
IS HE... SERIOUSLY PLANNING ON TAKING DOWN THE DEMON LORD?!
IT'S TOTALLY IMPOSSIBLE!
HE'S GONNA GET KILLED!!
SO THEN, WHY?
WHY ?!
WHY IS HE...
...SO HUNG UP ON THIS DEMON LORD?!
YOU'RE GONNA GET BURNED TO DEATH!!

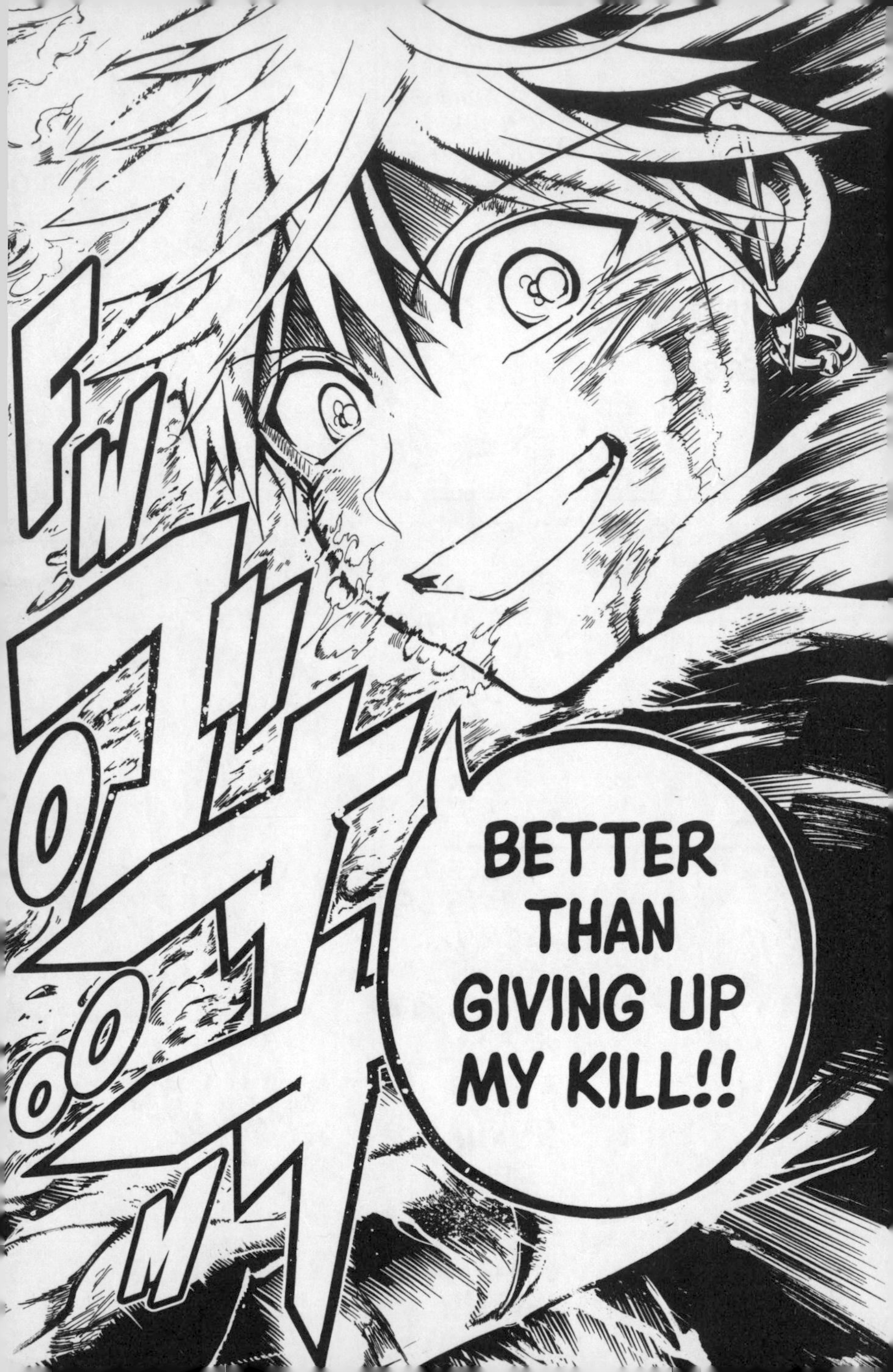
FWOOOM
BETTER THAN GIVING UP MY KILL!!

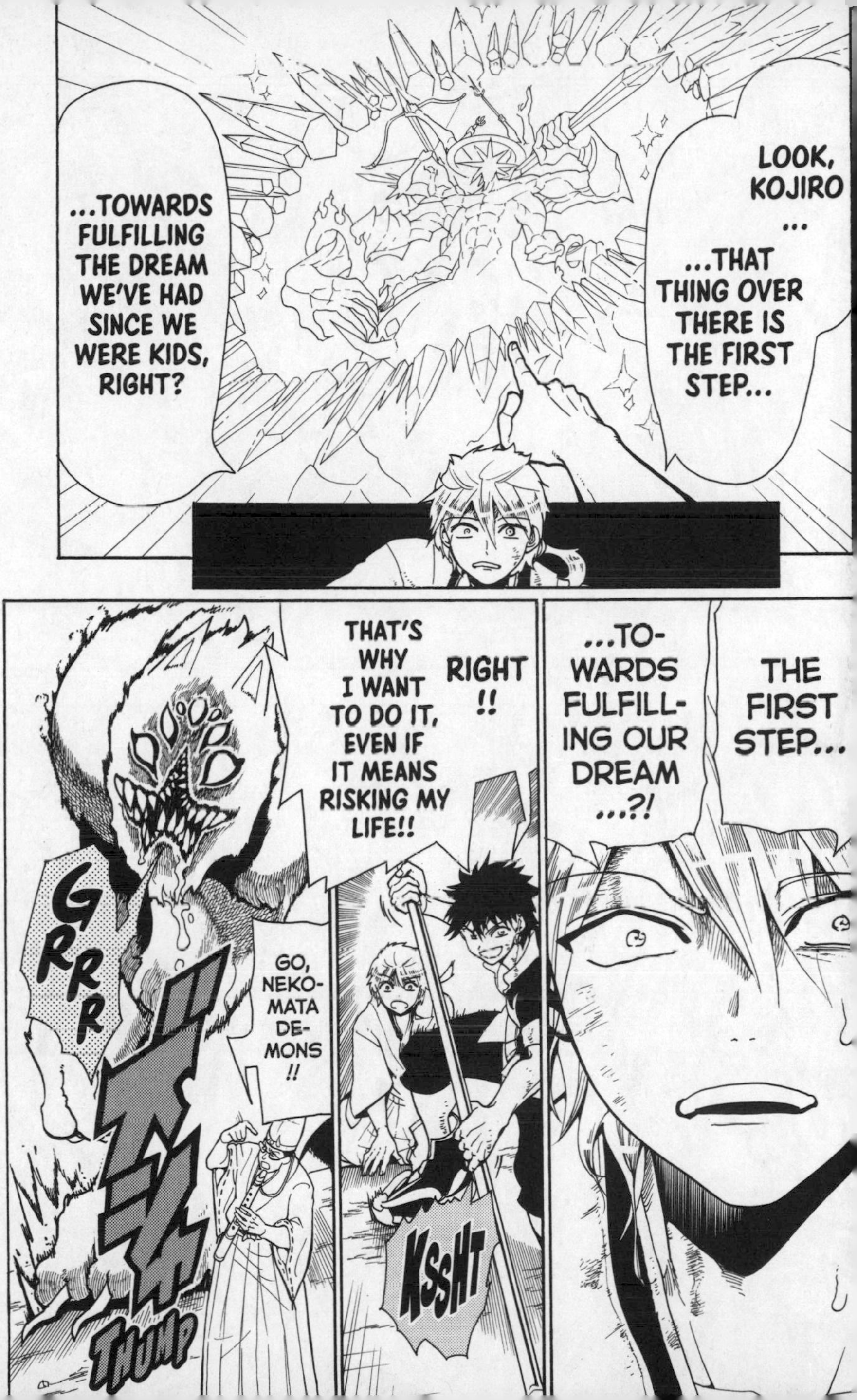
LOOK, KOJIRO ... ...THAT THING OVER THERE IS THE FIRST STEP...
...TOWARDS FULFILLING THE DREAM WE'VE HAD SINCE WE WERE KIDS, RIGHT?
THE FIRST STEP...
...TOWARDS FULFILLING OUR DREAM ...?!
RIGHT !!
THAT'S WHY I WANT TO DO IT, EVEN IF IT MEANS RISKING MY LIFE!!
GO, NEKOMATA DEMONS !!
KSSHT
GRRR
THUMP

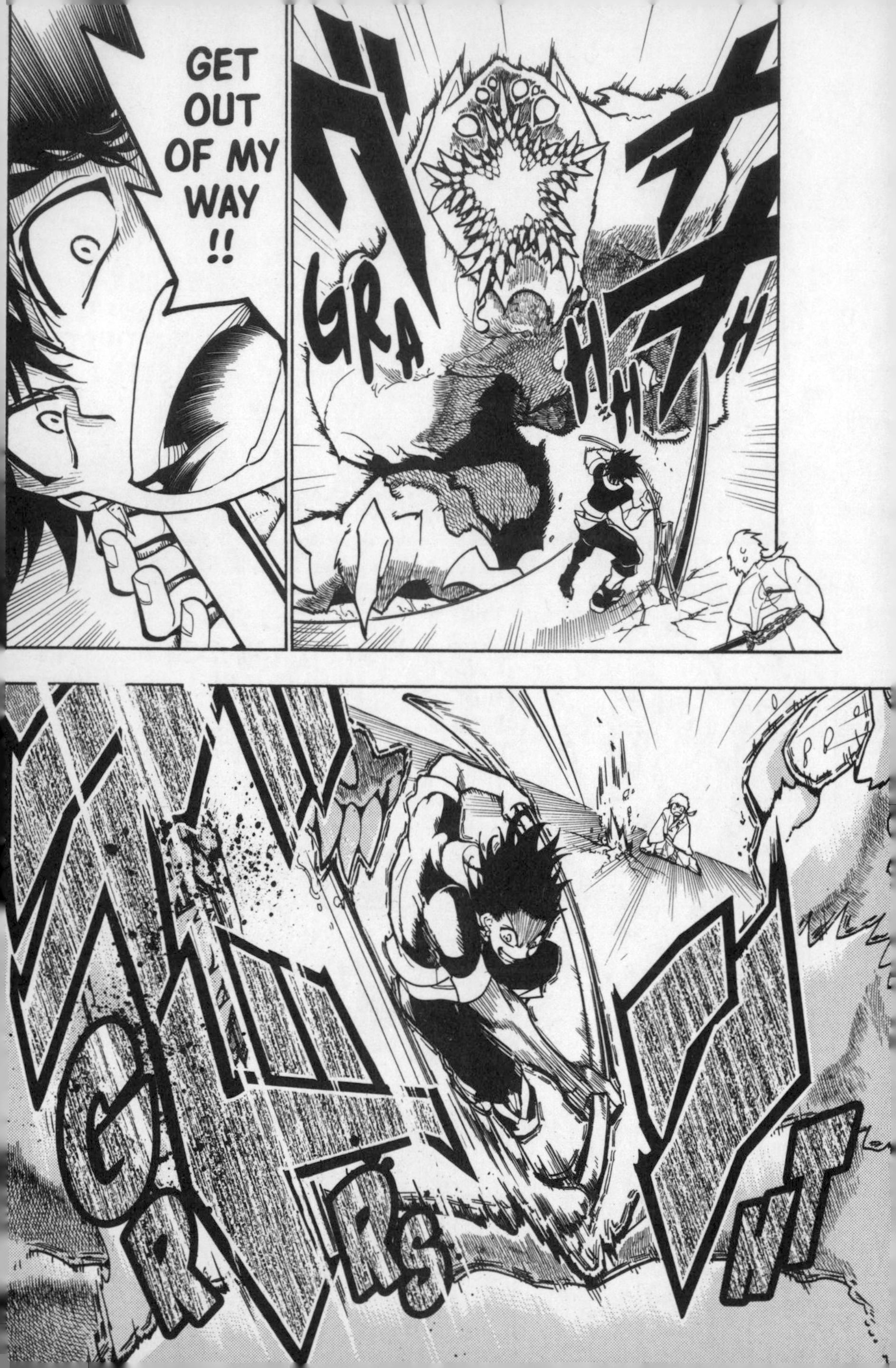
GRAHHHH
GET OUT OF MY WAY !!
CRRASH

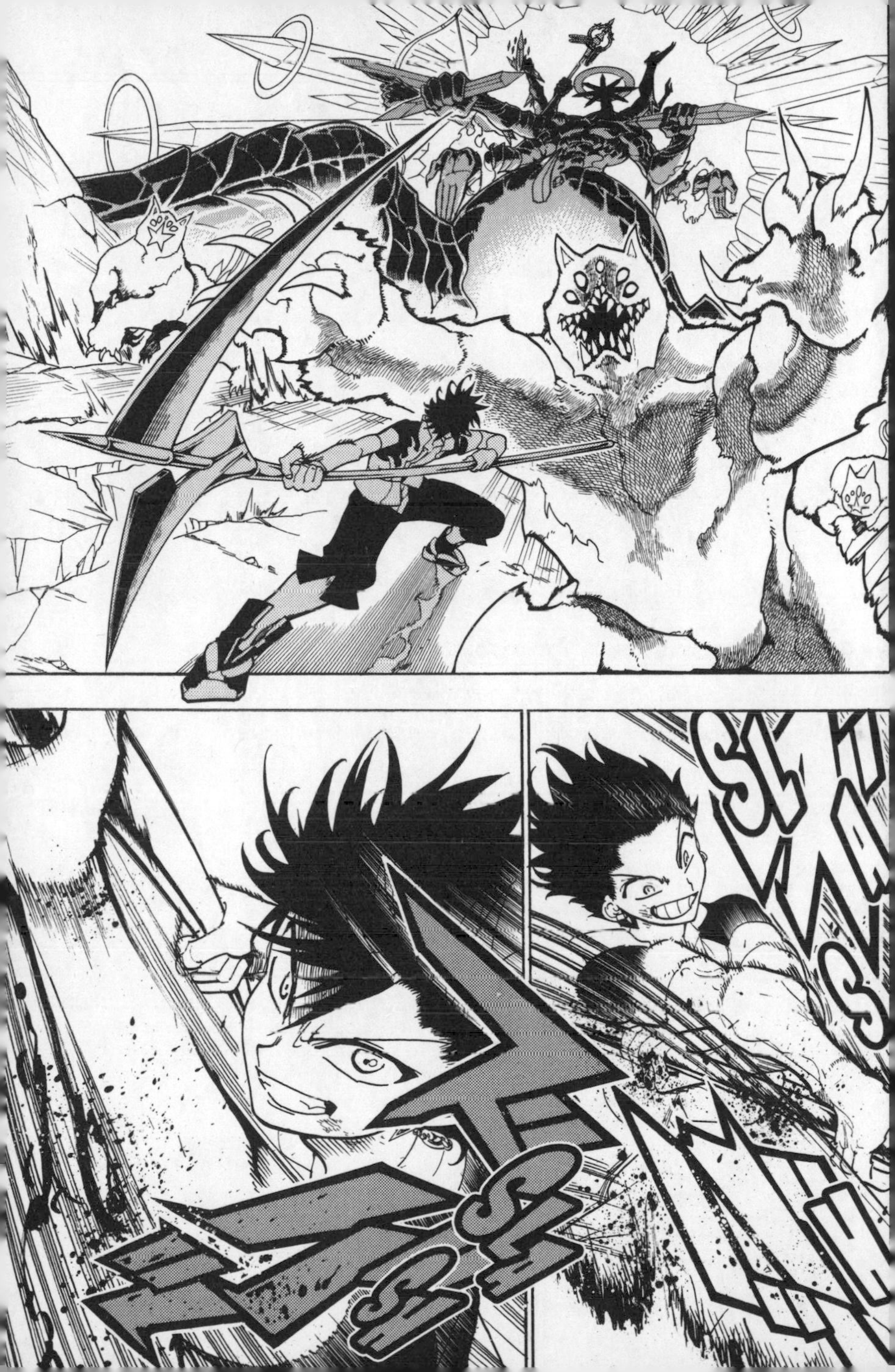

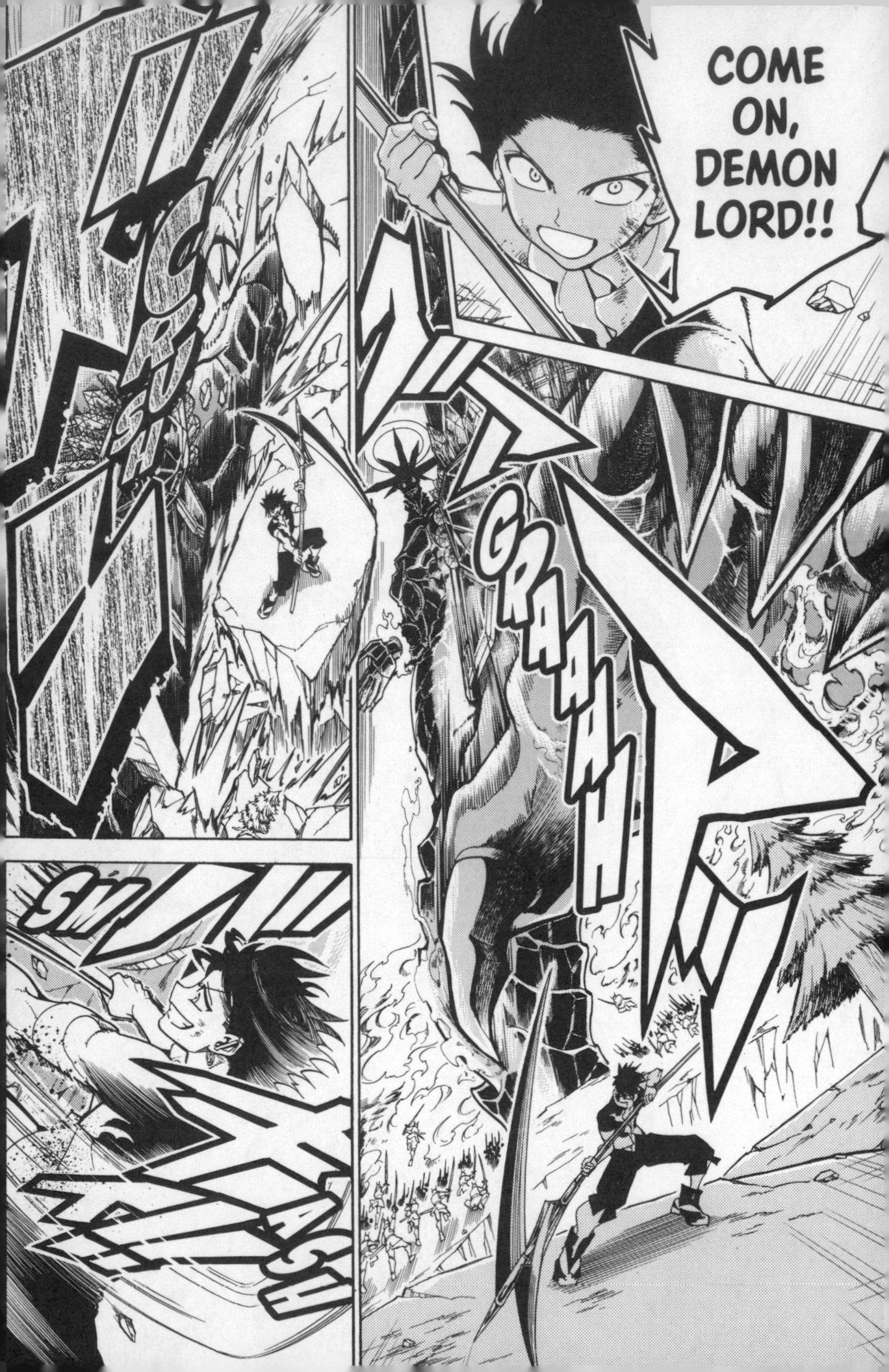
COME ON, DEMON LORD!!
GRAAAH
CRUSH
SMASH

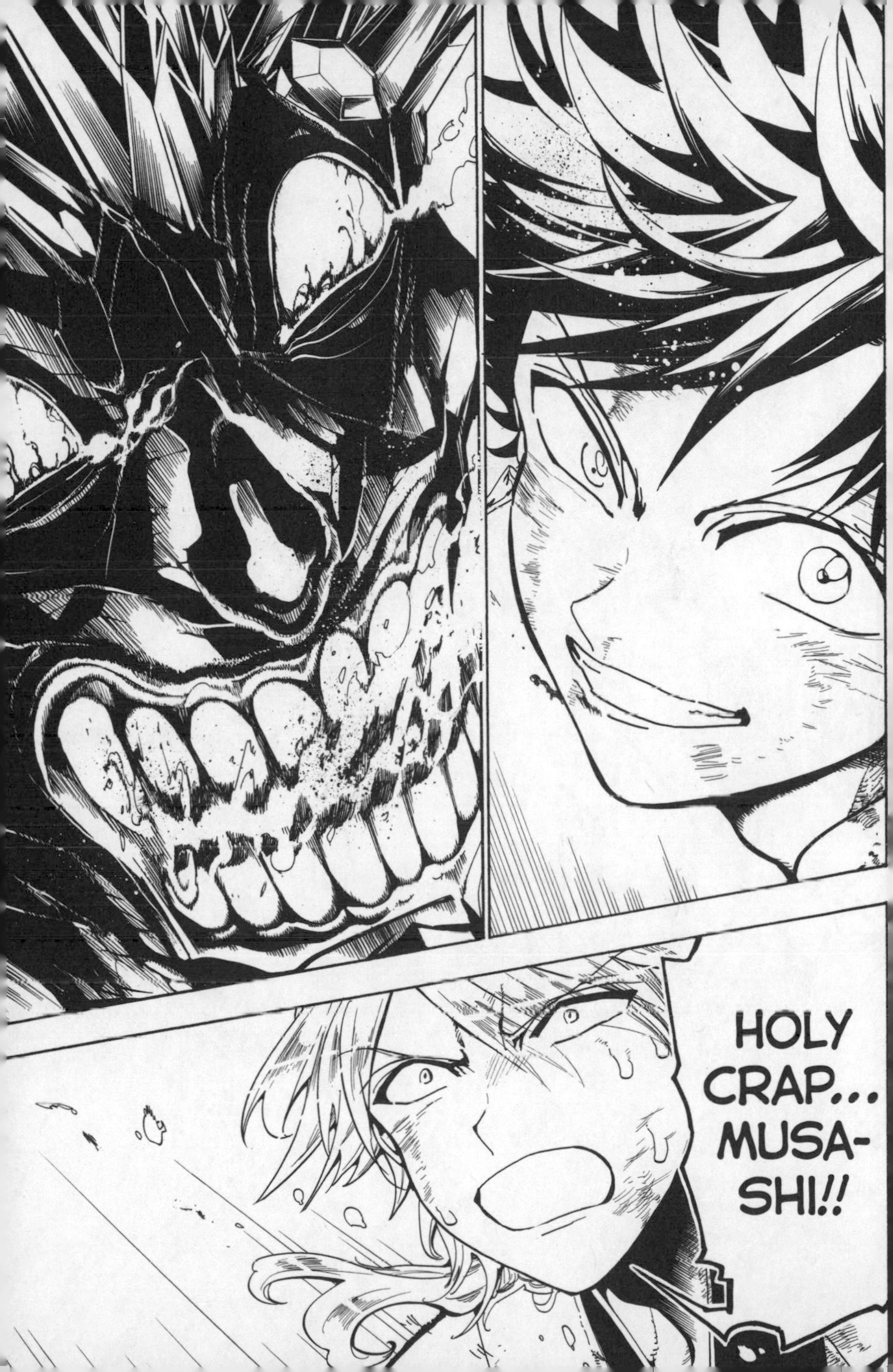
HOLY CRAP... MUSA-SHI!!

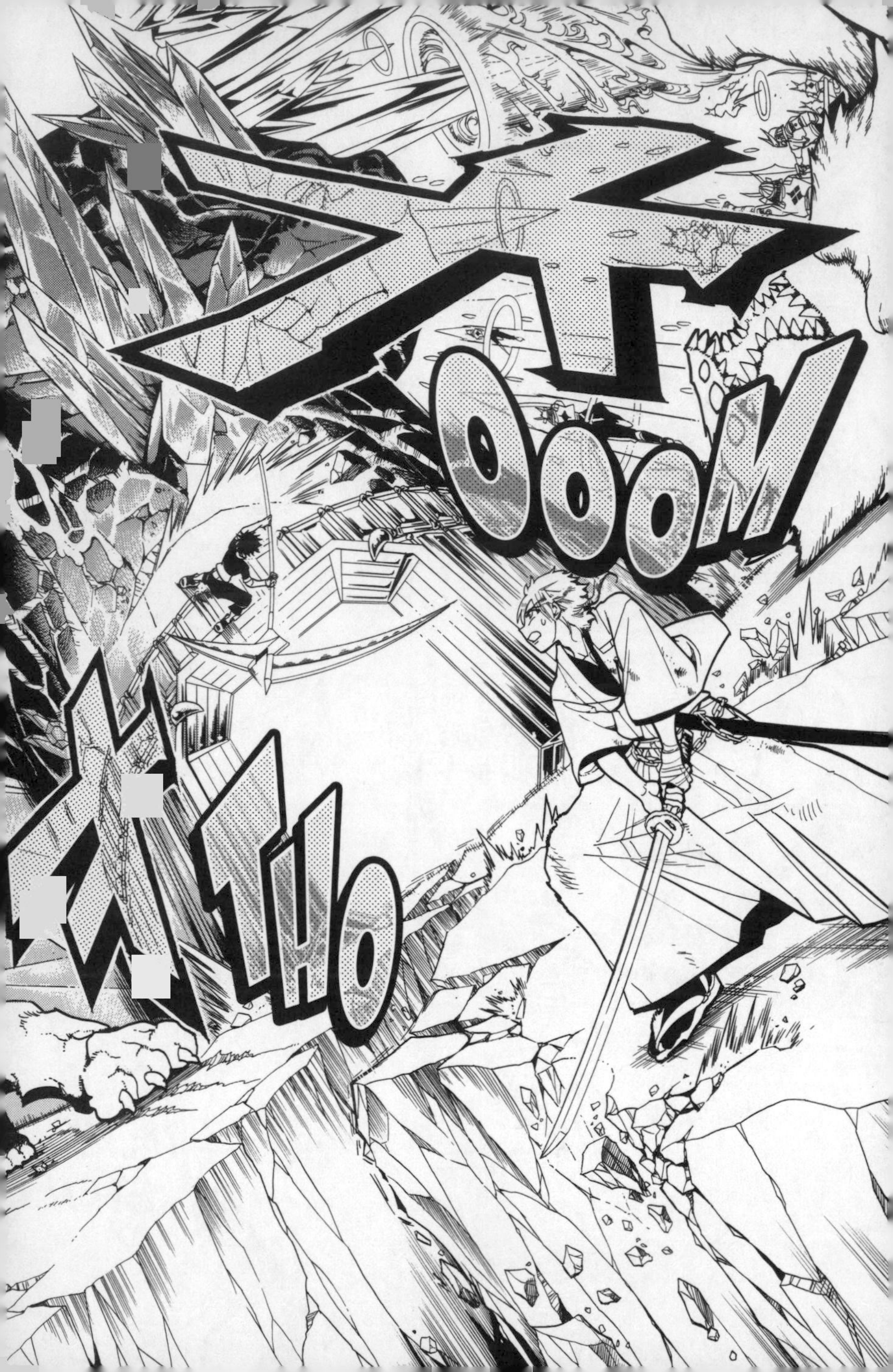

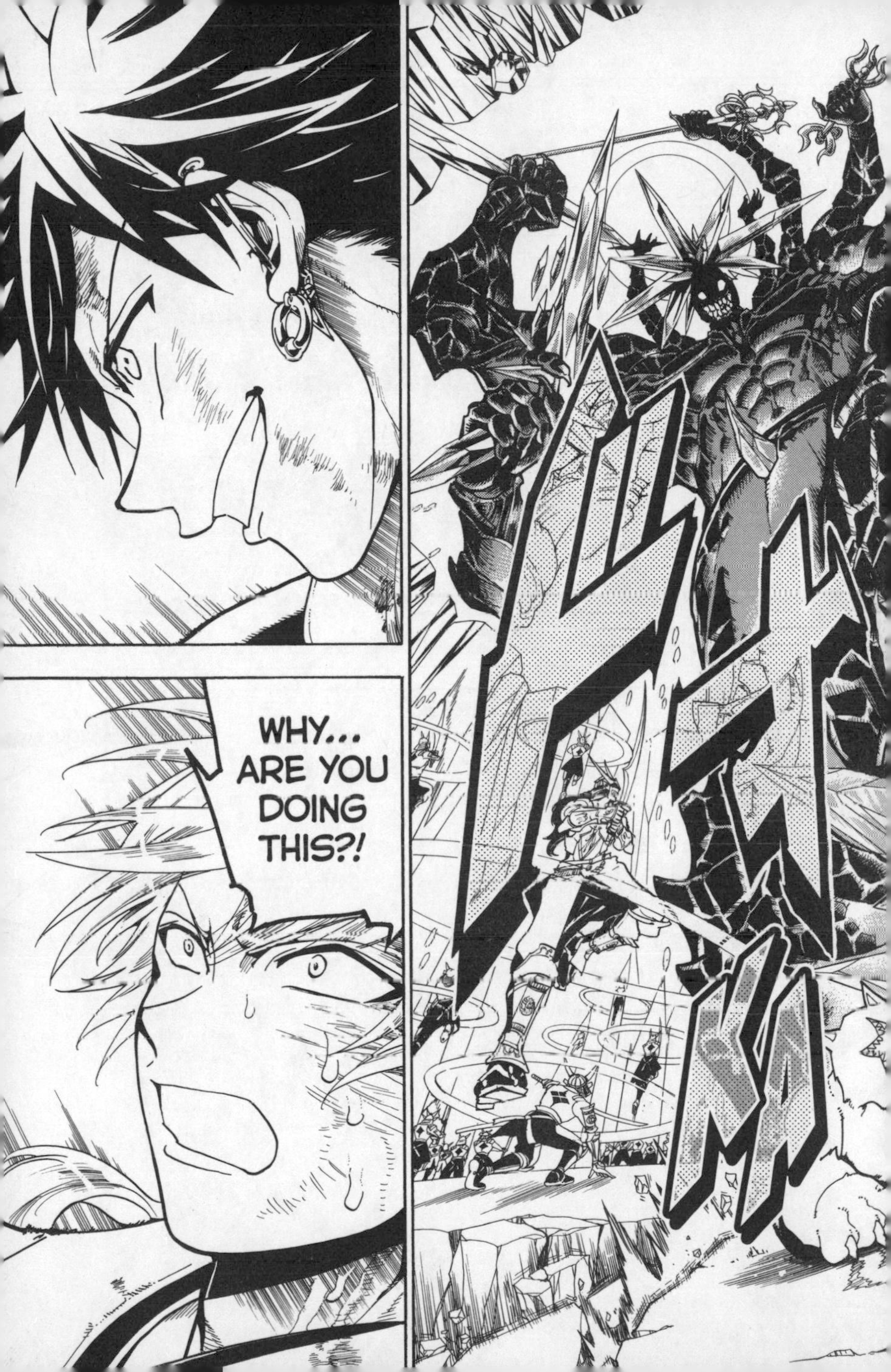
WHY... ARE YOU DOING THIS?!

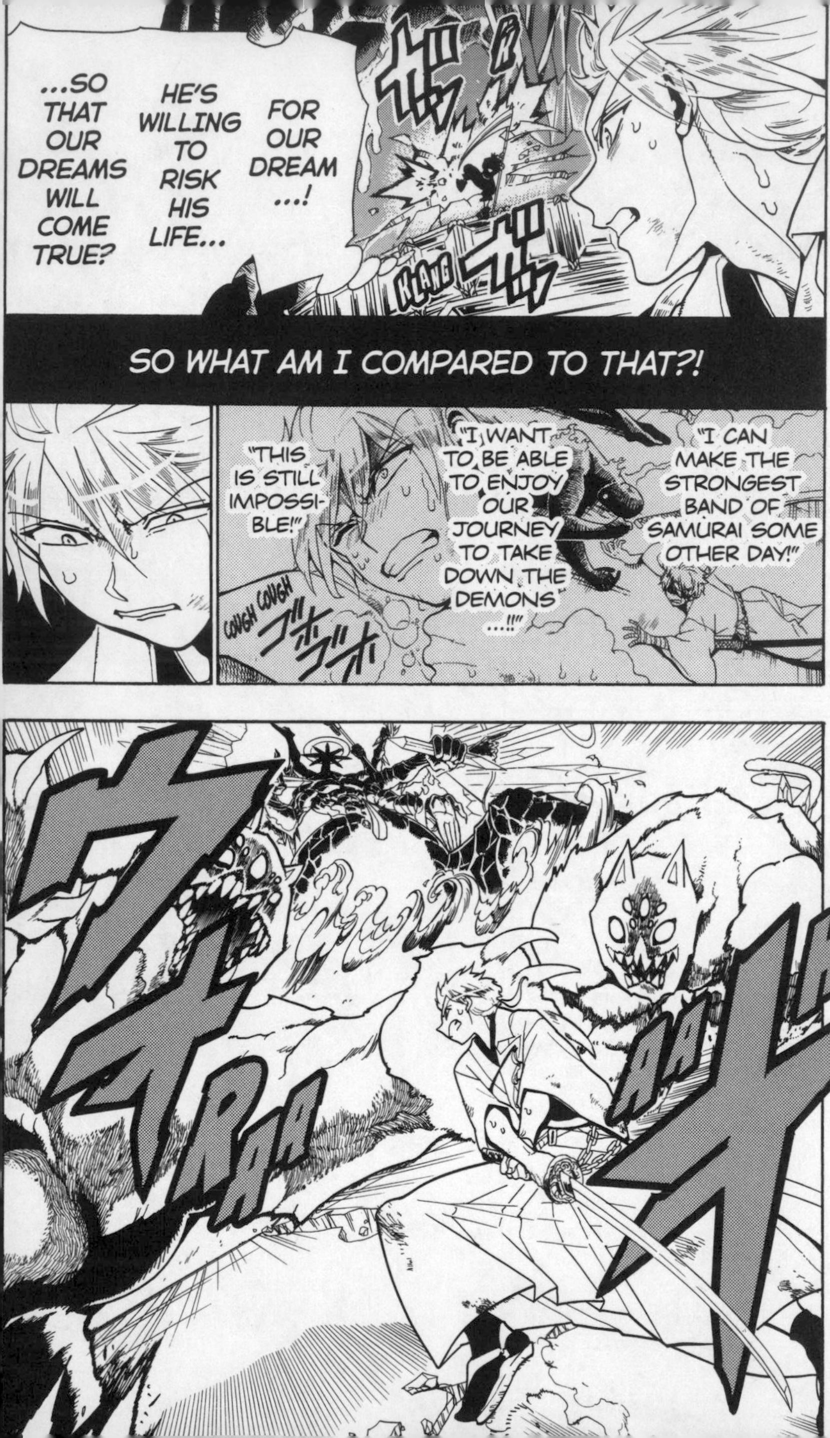
FOR OUR DREAM...!
HE'S WILLING TO RISK HIS LIFE...
...SO THAT OUR DREAMS WILL COME TRUE?
KLANG
SO WHAT AM I COMPARED TO THAT?!
"I CAN MAKE THE STRONGEST BAND OF SAMURAI SOME OTHER DAY!"
"I WANT TO BE ABLE TO ENJOY OUR JOURNEY TO TAKE DOWN THE DEMONS ...!!"
"THIS IS STILL IMPOSSIBLE!"
COUGH COUGH

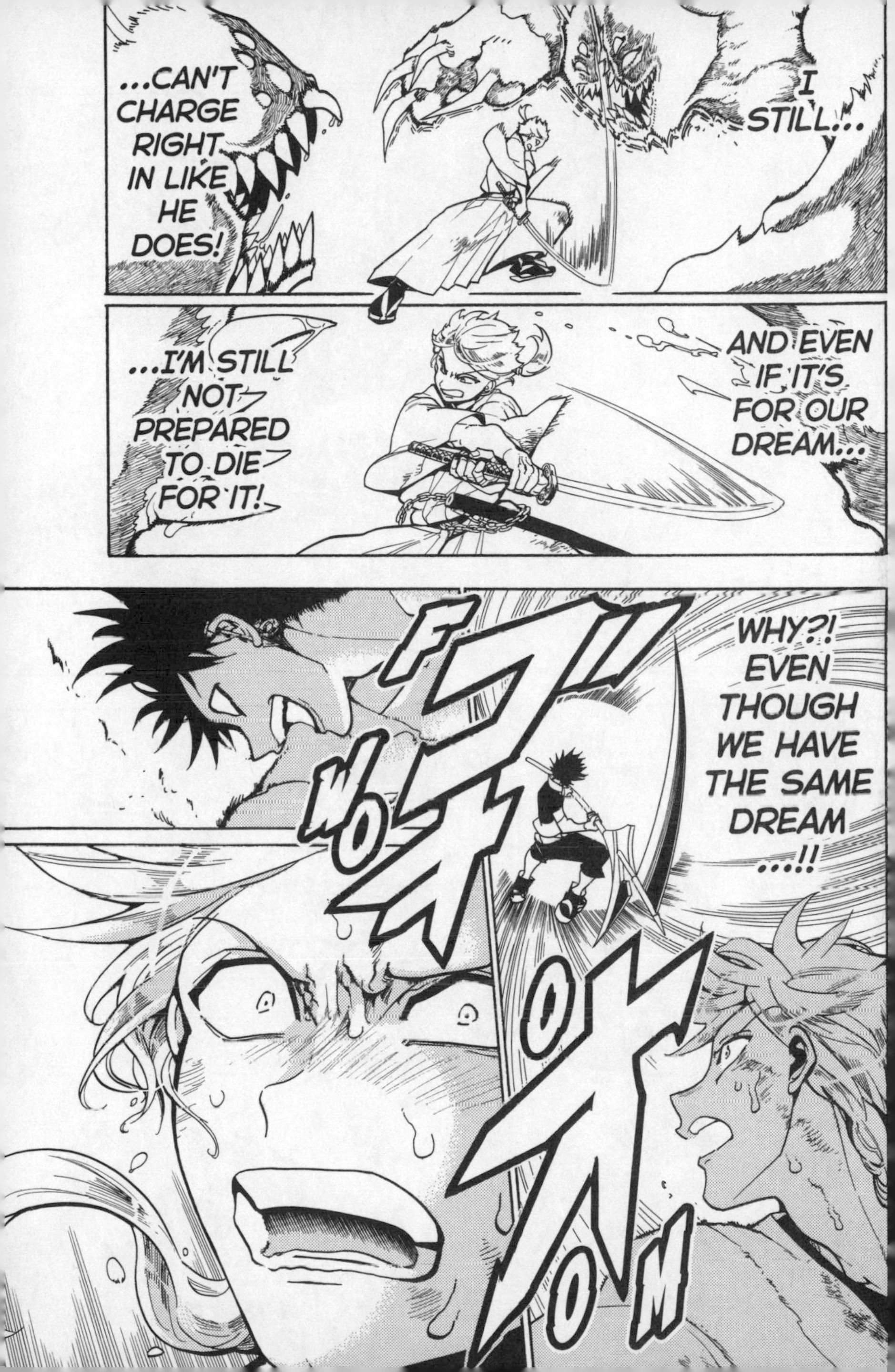
I STILL...
...CAN'T CHARGE RIGHT IN LIKE HE DOES!
AND EVEN IF IT'S FOR OUR DREAM...
...I'M STILL NOT PREPARED TO DIE FOR IT!
WHY?! EVEN THOUGH WE HAVE THE SAME DREAM ...!!
FWOOOM

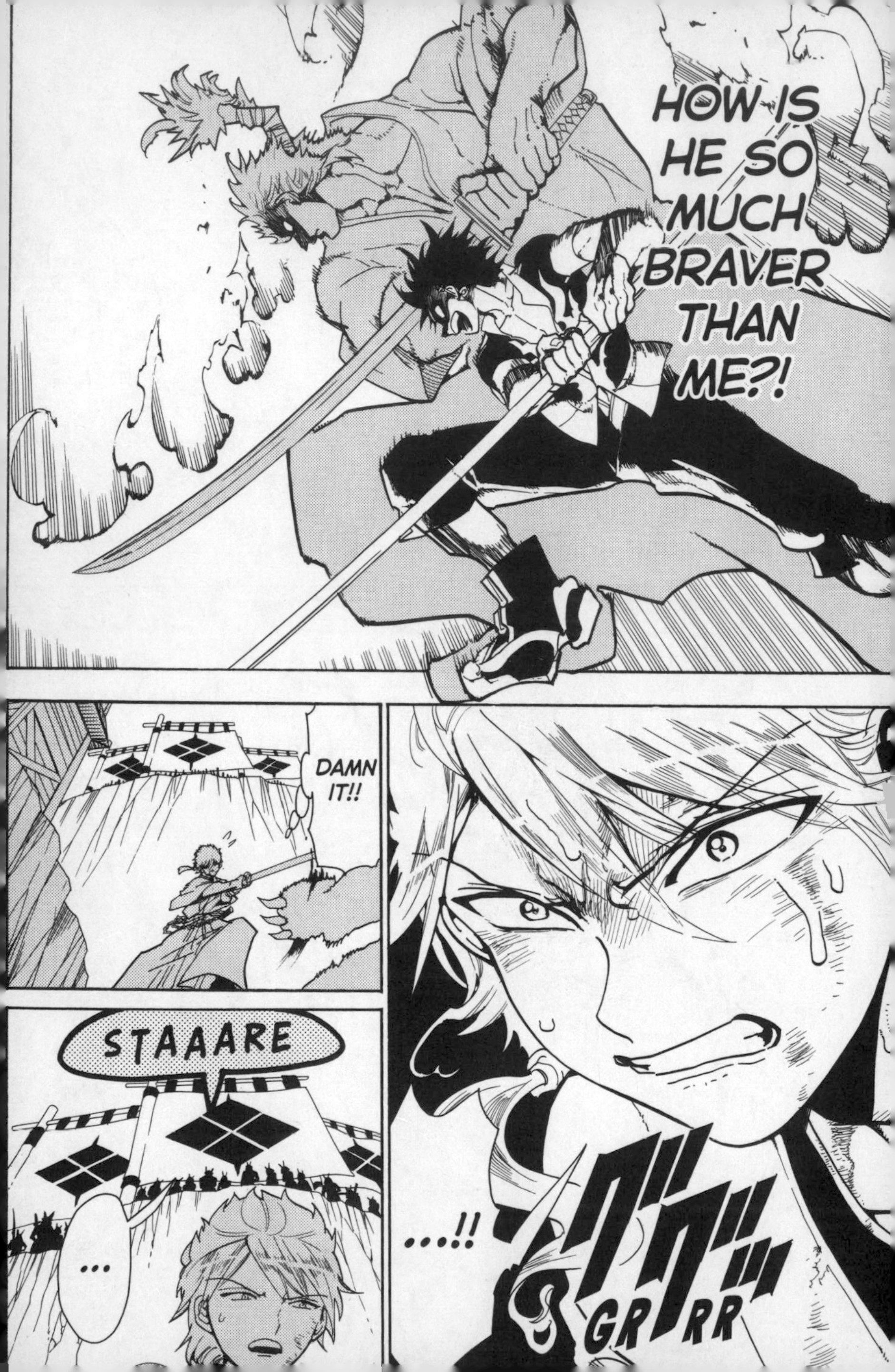
HOW IS HE SO MUCH BRAVER THAN ME?!
DAMN IT!!
...!!
GRRR
STAAARE
...

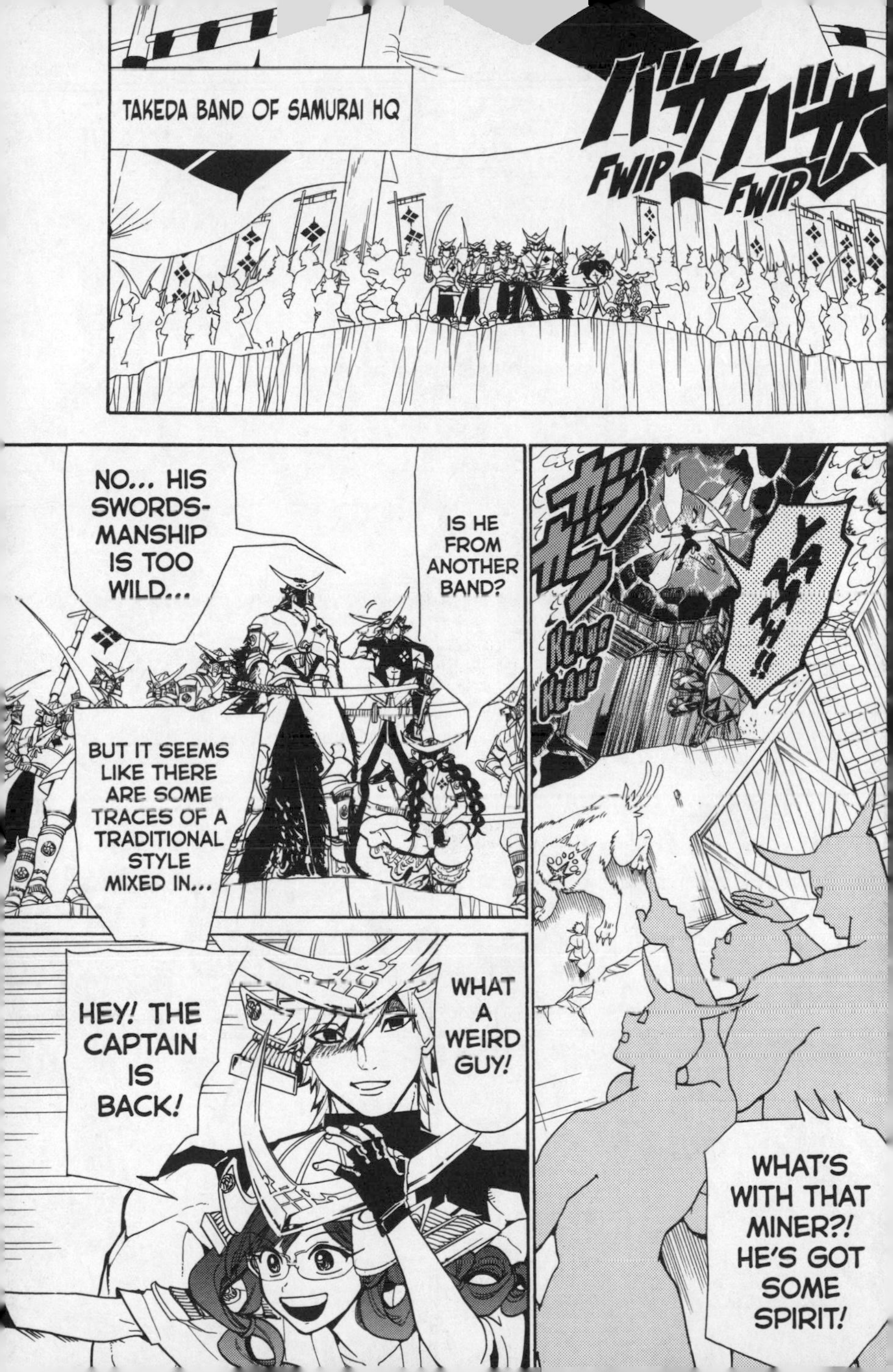

TAKEDA BAND OF SAMURAI HQ
バサバサ
FWIP FWIP
KLANG KLANG
YAAAHH!!
WHAT'S WITH THAT MINER?! HE'S GOT SOME SPIRIT!
IS HE FROM ANOTHER BAND?
NO... HIS SWORDS-MANSHIP IS TOO WILD...
BUT IT SEEMS LIKE THERE ARE SOME TRACES OF A TRADITIONAL STYLE MIXED IN...
WHAT A WEIRD GUY!
HEY! THE CAPTAIN IS BACK!

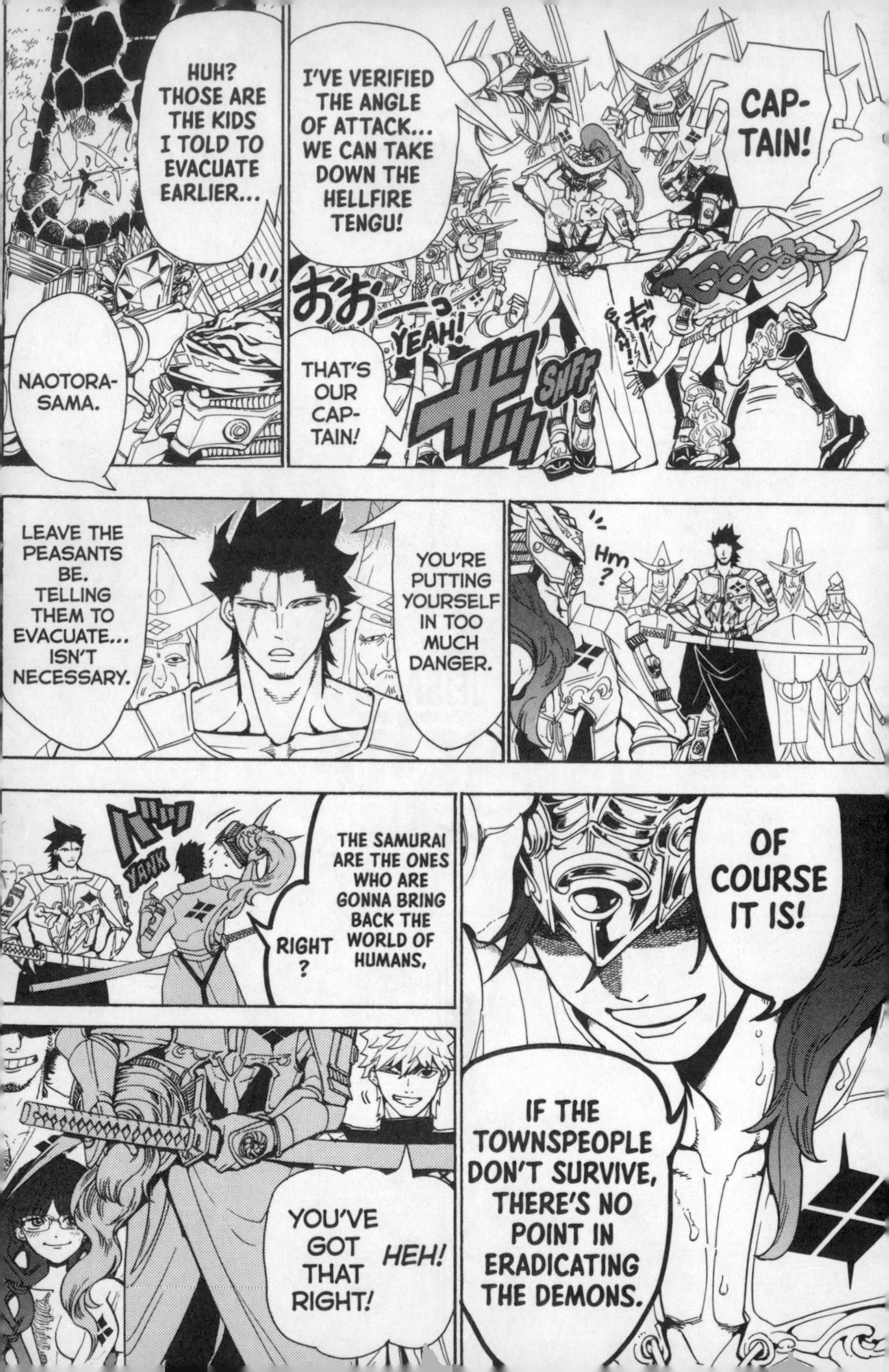
CAP-TAIN!
ギャー
GYAH!
I'VE VERIFIED THE ANGLE OF ATTACK... WE CAN TAKE DOWN THE HELLFIRE TENGU!
ザッ
SHFF
おおーっ
YEAH!
THAT'S OUR CAP-TAIN!
HUH? THOSE ARE THE KIDS I TOLD TO EVACUATE EARLIER...
NAOTORA-SAMA.
Hm?
YOU'RE PUTTING YOURSELF IN TOO MUCH DANGER.
LEAVE THE PEASANTS BE. TELLING THEM TO EVACUATE... ISN'T NECESSARY.
OF COURSE IT IS!
IF THE TOWNSPEOPLE DON'T SURVIVE, THERE'S NO POINT IN ERADICATING THE DEMONS.
THE SAMURAI ARE THE ONES WHO ARE GONNA BRING BACK THE WORLD OF HUMANS,
RIGHT?
バッ
YANK
HEH!
YOU'VE GOT THAT RIGHT!

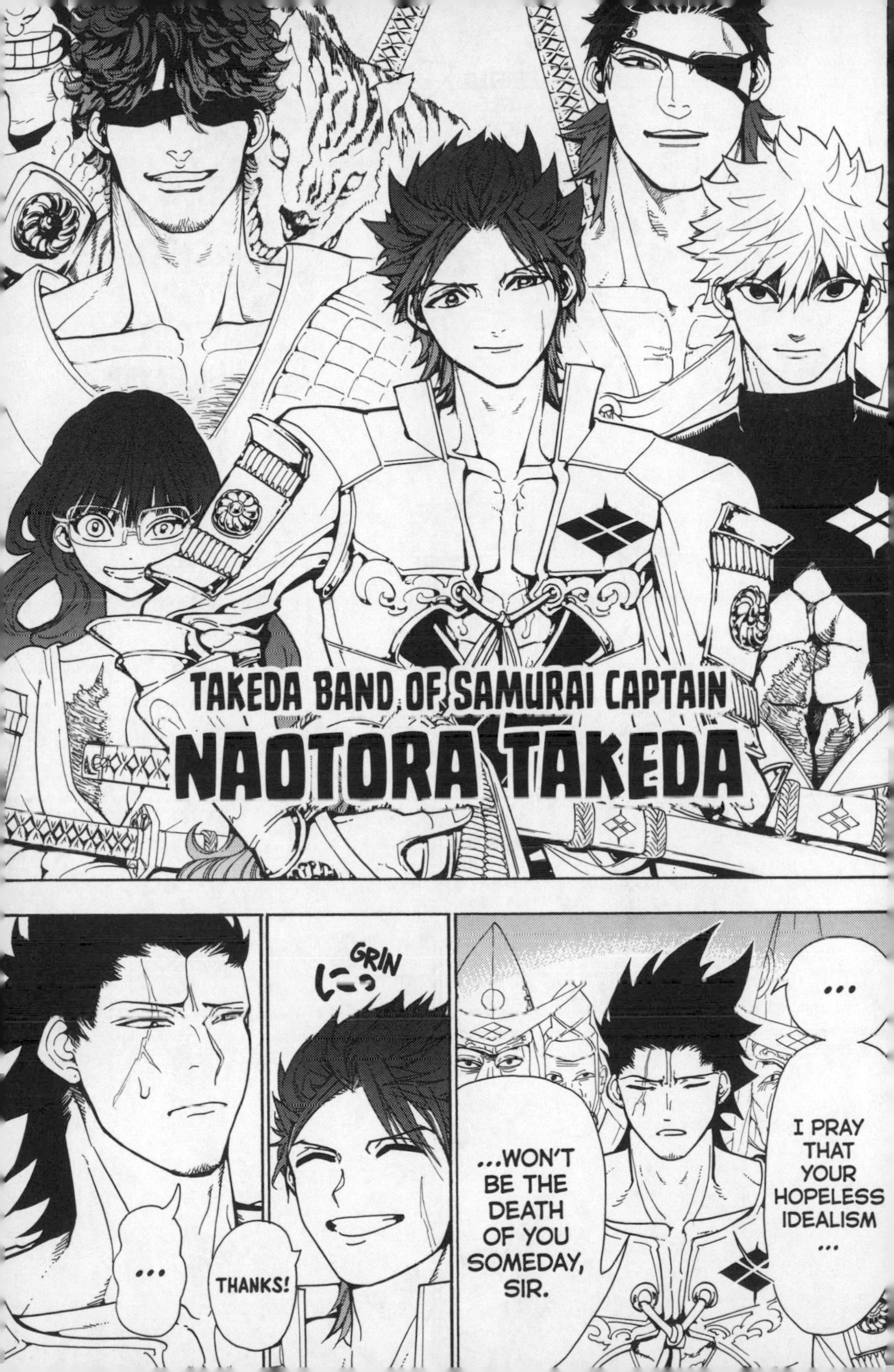
TAKEDA BAND OF SAMURAI CAPTAIN
NAOTORA TAKEDA
...
I PRAY THAT YOUR HOPELESS IDEALISM ...
...WON'T BE THE DEATH OF YOU SOMEDAY, SIR.
にっ
GRIN
THANKS!
...

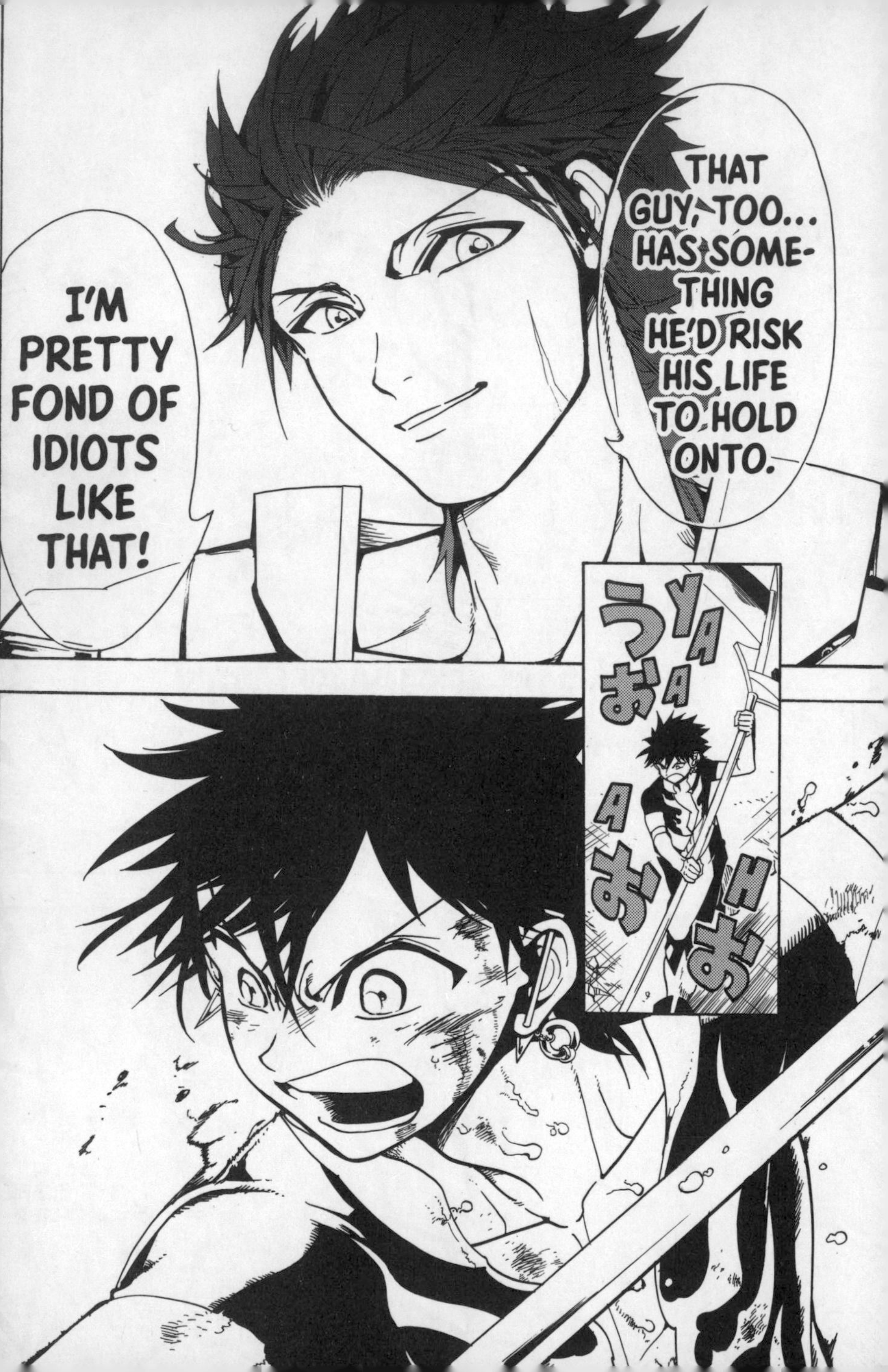
THAT GUY, TOO... HAS SOME-THING HE'D RISK HIS LIFE TO HOLD ONTO.
I'M PRETTY FOND OF IDIOTS LIKE THAT!
うおおお
YAAAH

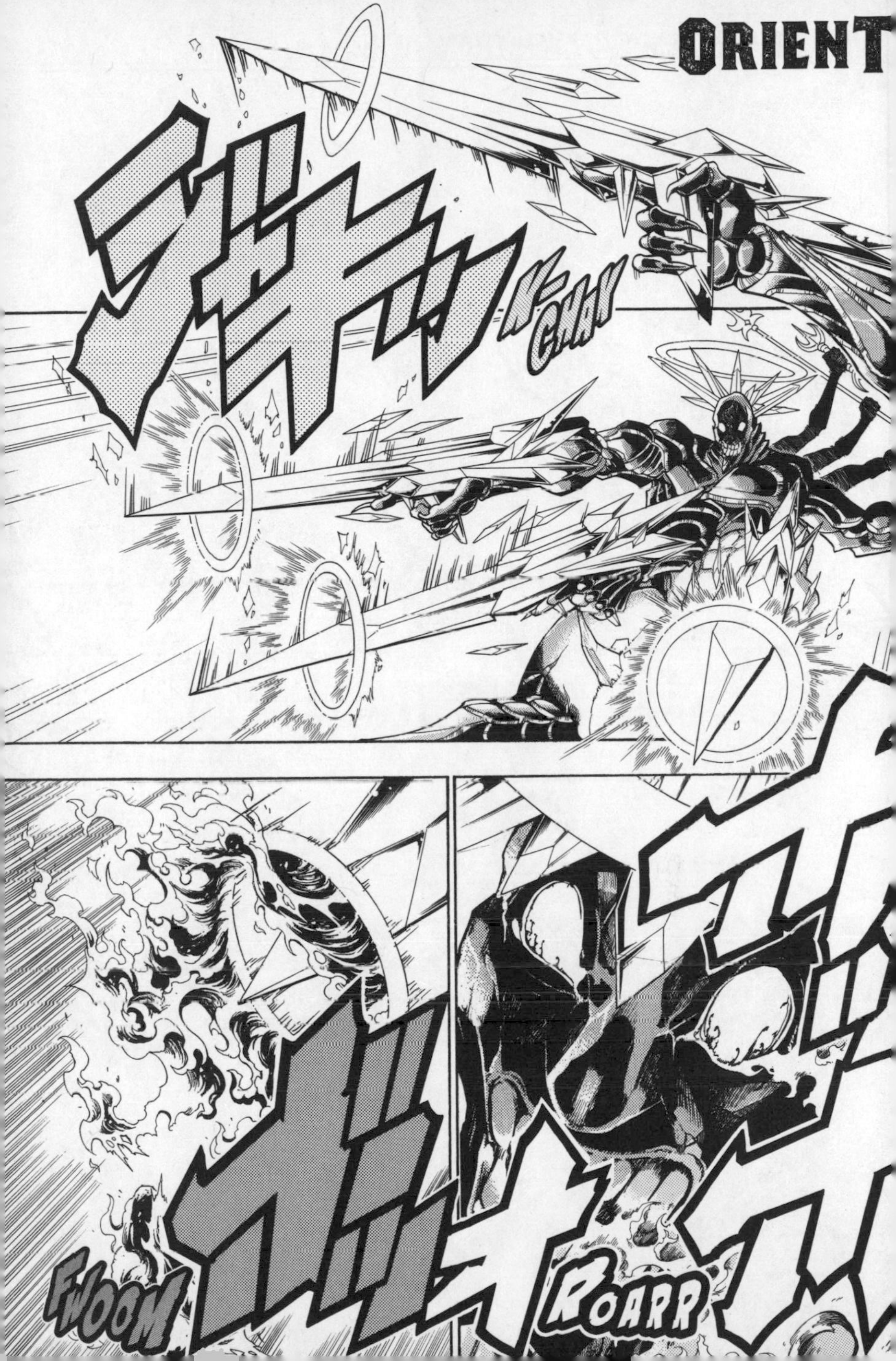
K-CHAK
ROARR
FWOOM

CHAPTER 4: AZURE HEAVEN CRANE WING

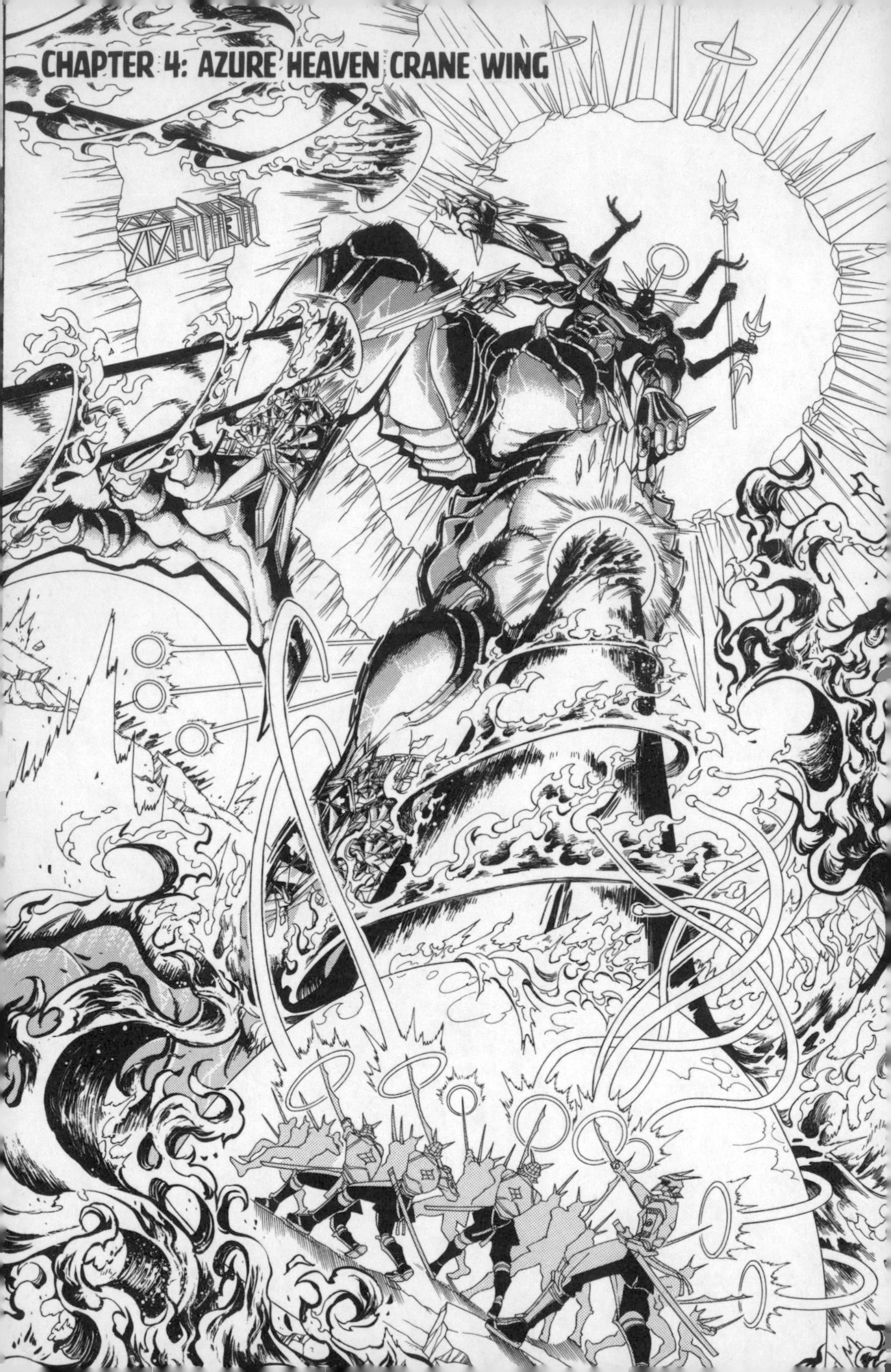

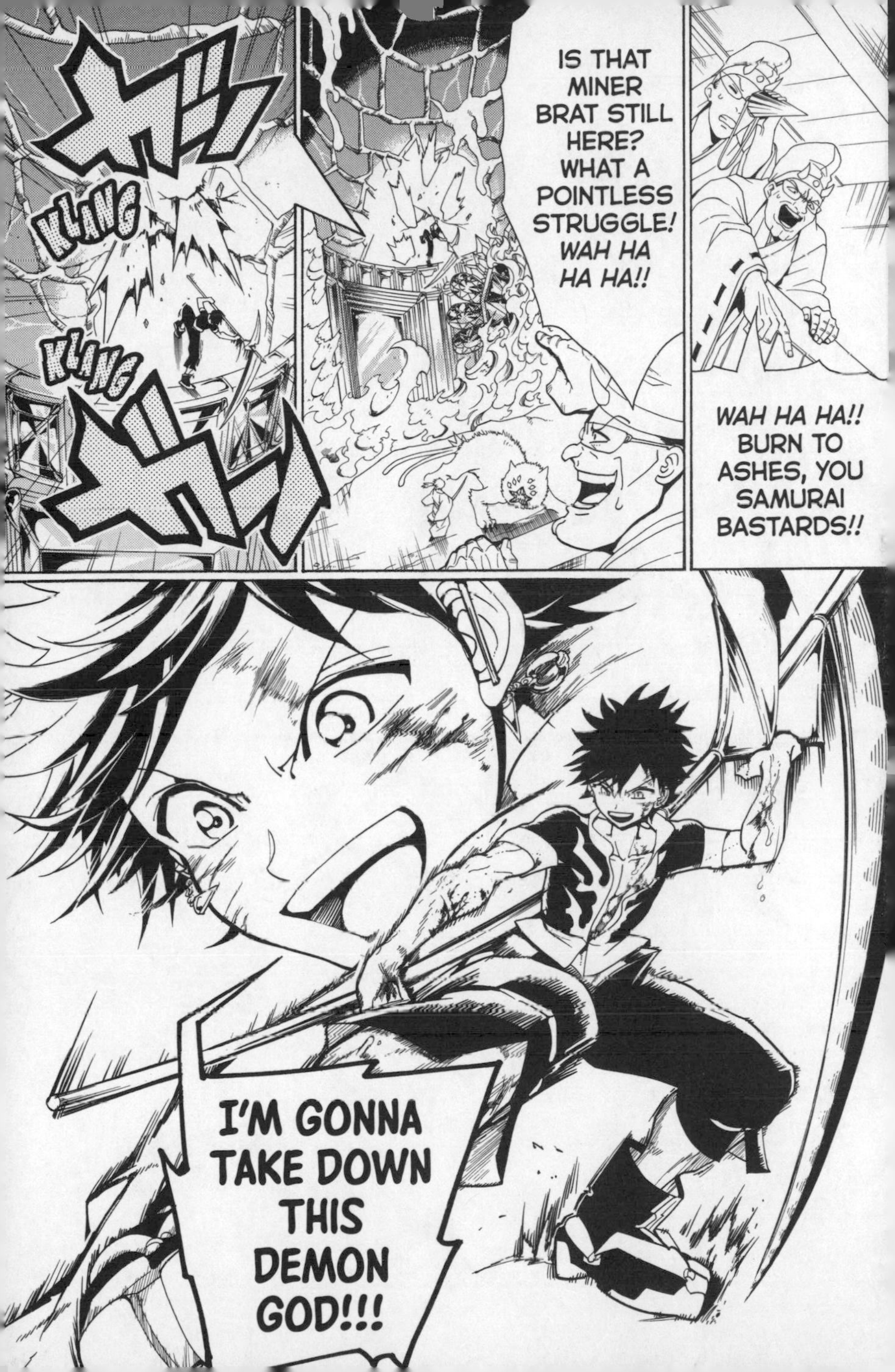

WAH HA HA!! BURN TO ASHES, YOU SAMURAI BASTARDS!!
IS THAT MINER BRAT STILL HERE? WHAT A POINTLESS STRUGGLE! WAH HA HA HA!!
KLANG
KLANG
I'M GONNA TAKE DOWN THIS DEMON GOD!!!

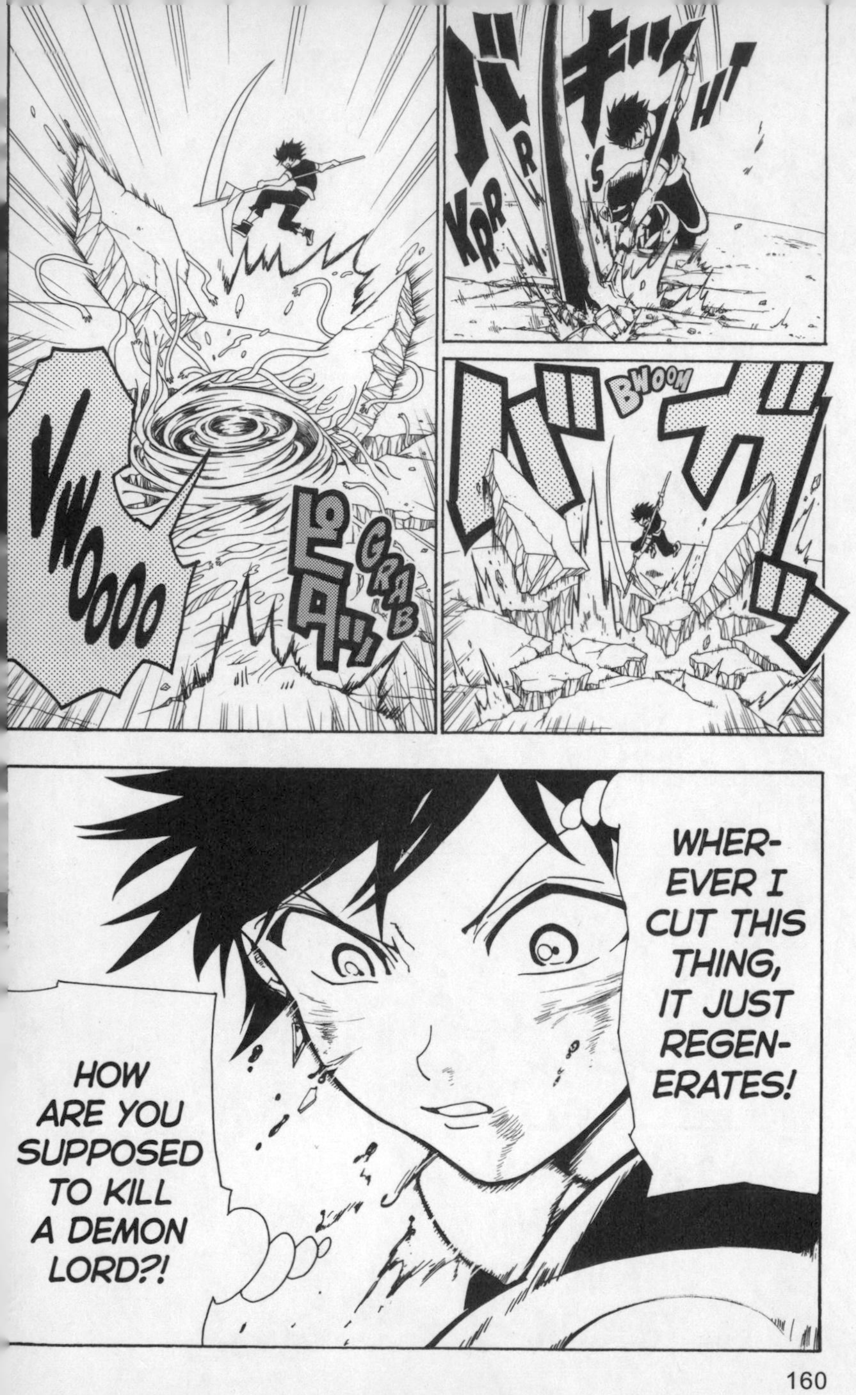
SHT
KRRRI
BWOOM
VWOOOO
GRAB
WHEREVER I CUT THIS THING, IT JUST REGENERATES!
HOW ARE YOU SUPPOSED TO KILL A DEMON LORD?!

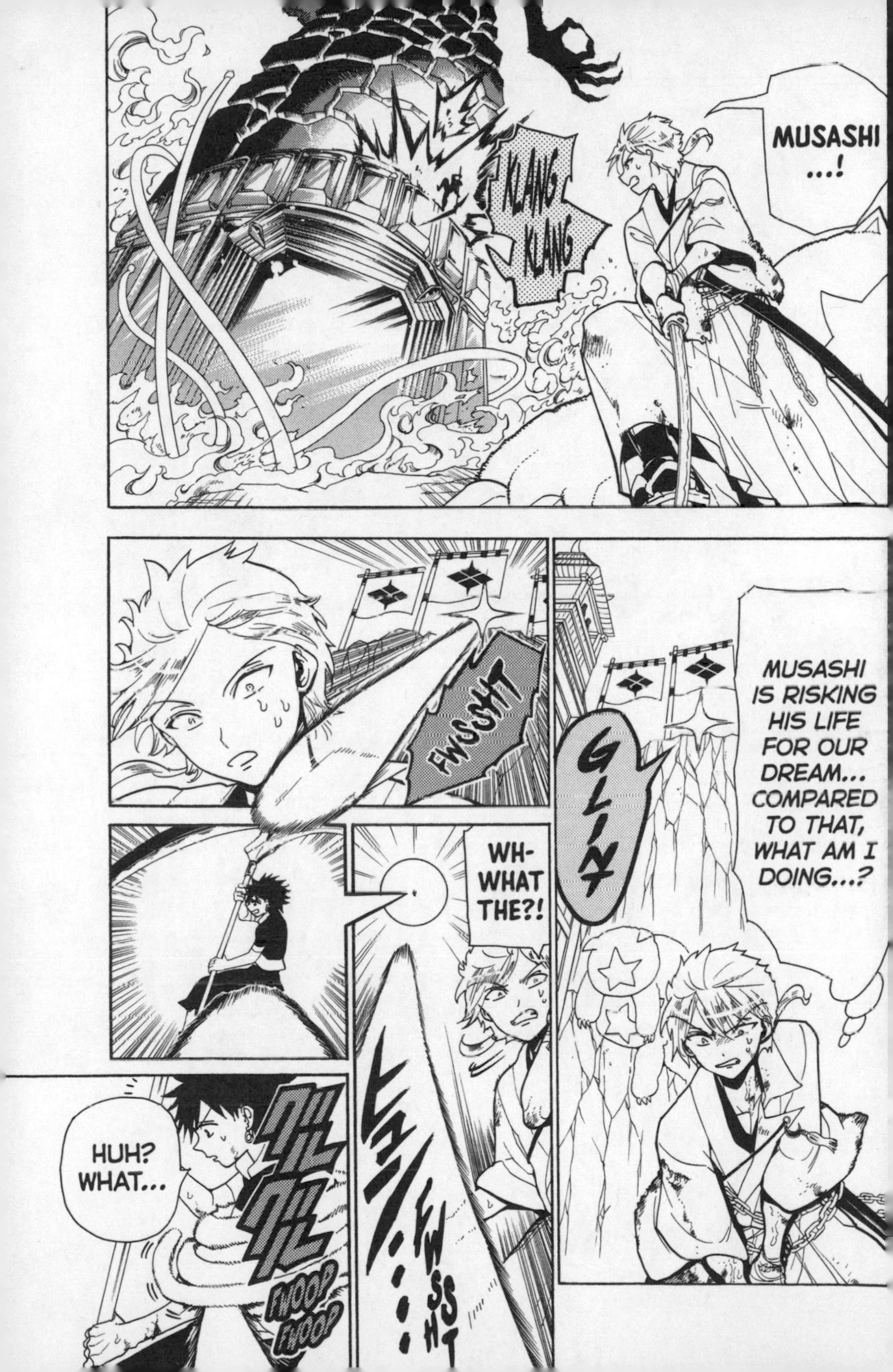
MUSASHI ...!
KLANG KLANG
MUSASHI IS RISKING HIS LIFE FOR OUR DREAM... COMPARED TO THAT, WHAT AM I DOING...?
GLINT
WH- WHAT THE?!
HUH? WHAT...
FWOOP FWOOP

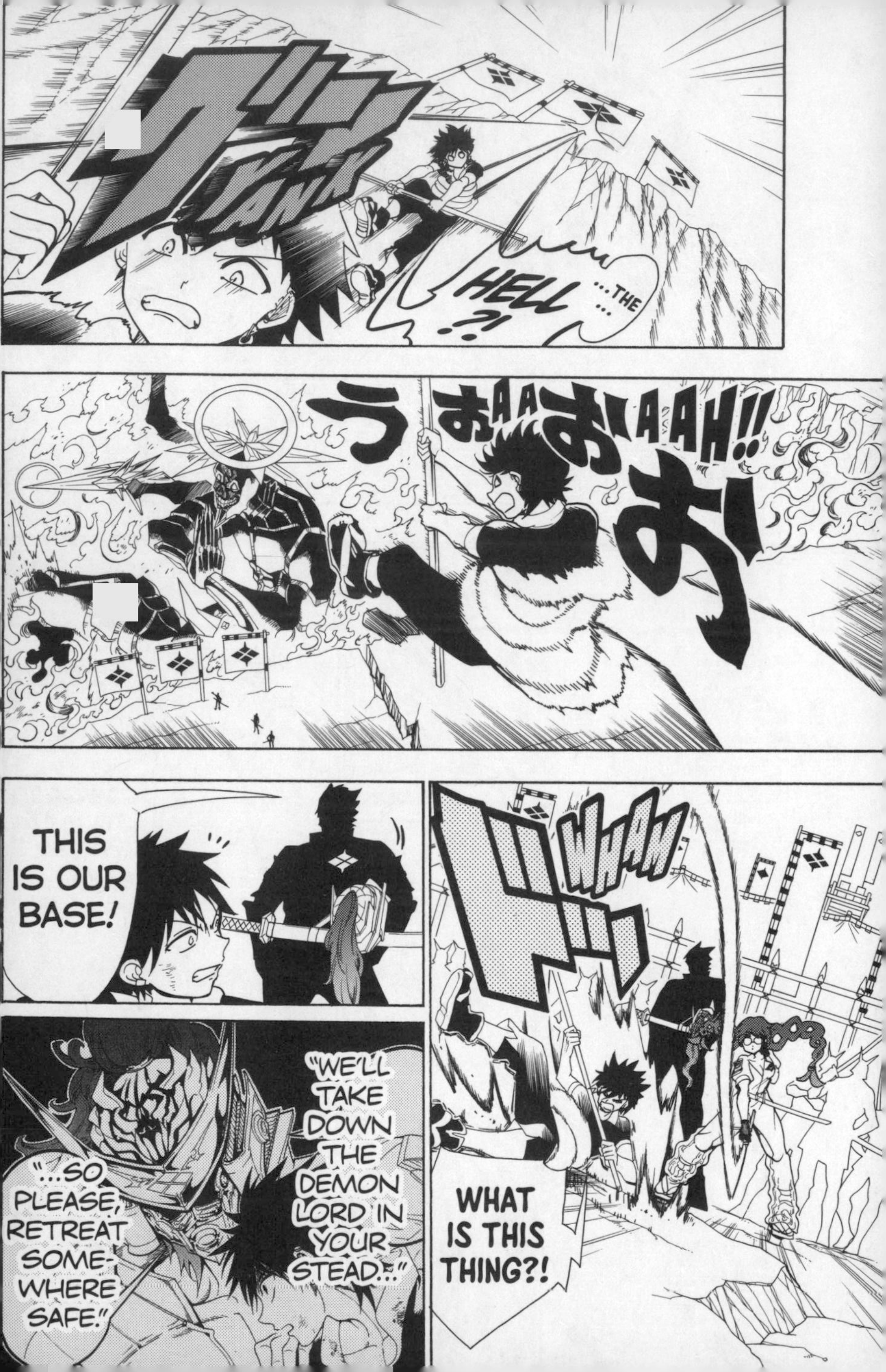

...THE ... HELL ?!
うおおお
AAAAH!!
WHAM
WHAT IS THIS THING?!
THIS IS OUR BASE!
"WE'LL TAKE DOWN THE DEMON LORD IN YOUR STEAD..."
"...SO PLEASE, RETREAT SOME-WHERE SAFE."

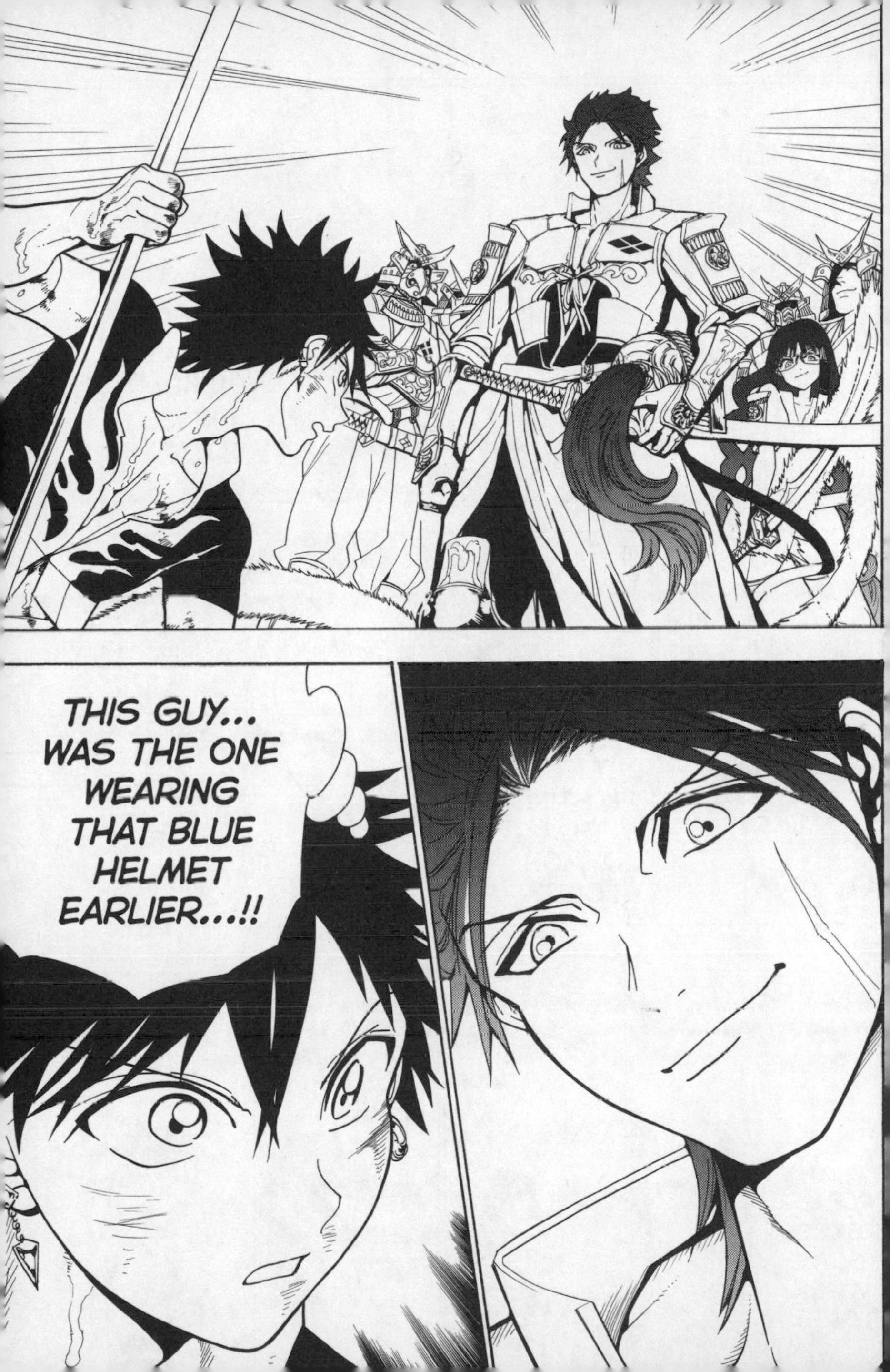
THIS GUY... WAS THE ONE WEARING THAT BLUE HELMET EARLIER...!!

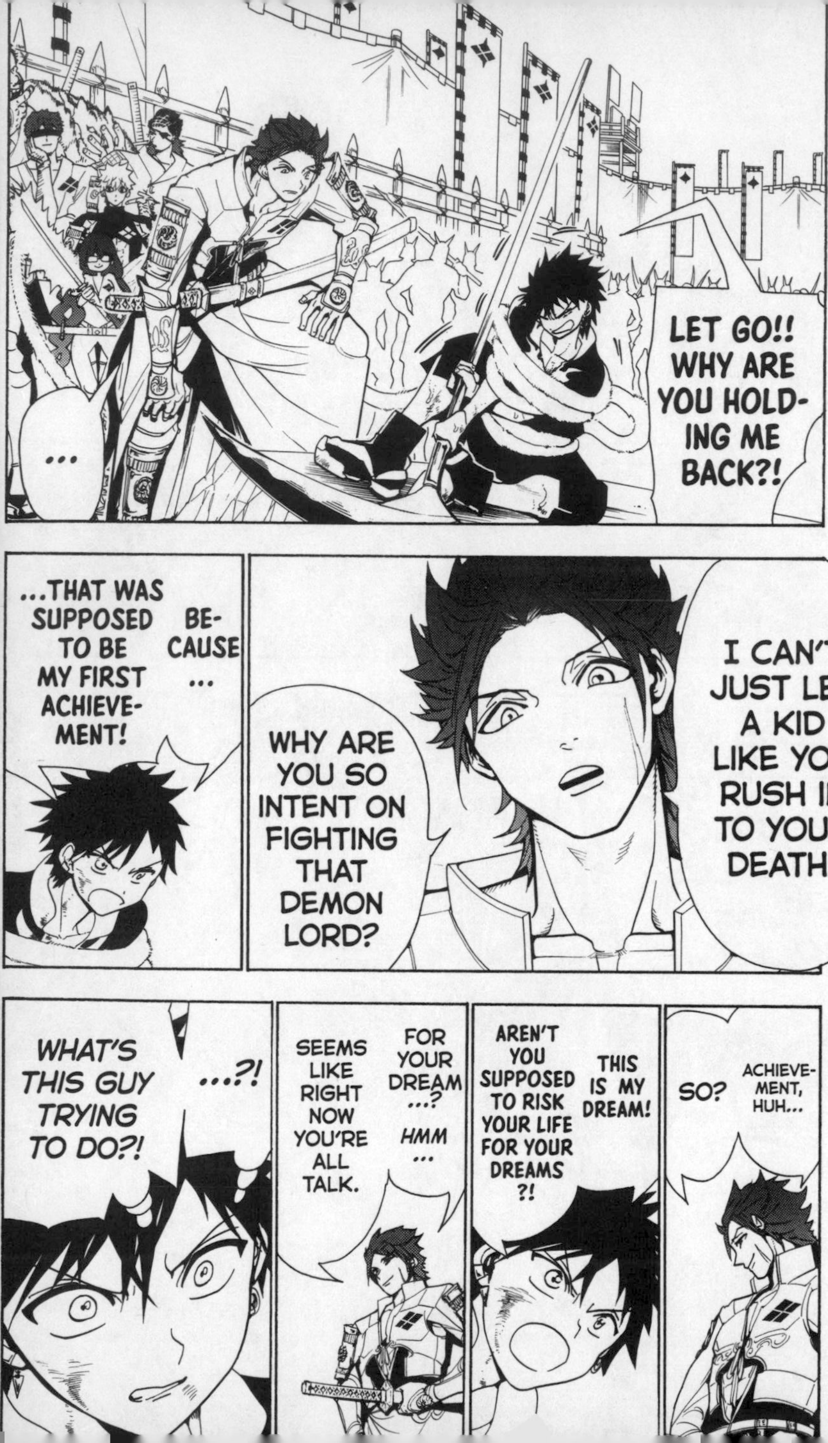
LET GO!! WHY ARE YOU HOLDING ME BACK?!
...
I CAN'T JUST LET A KID LIKE YOU RUSH IN TO YOUR DEATH.
WHY ARE YOU SO INTENT ON FIGHTING THAT DEMON LORD?
BECAUSE...
...THAT WAS SUPPOSED TO BE MY FIRST ACHIEVEMENT!
ACHIEVEMENT, HUH...
SO?
THIS IS MY DREAM!
AREN'T YOU SUPPOSED TO RISK YOUR LIFE FOR YOUR DREAMS?!
FOR YOUR DREAM...? HMM...
SEEMS LIKE RIGHT NOW YOU'RE ALL TALK.
...?!
WHAT'S THIS GUY TRYING TO DO?!

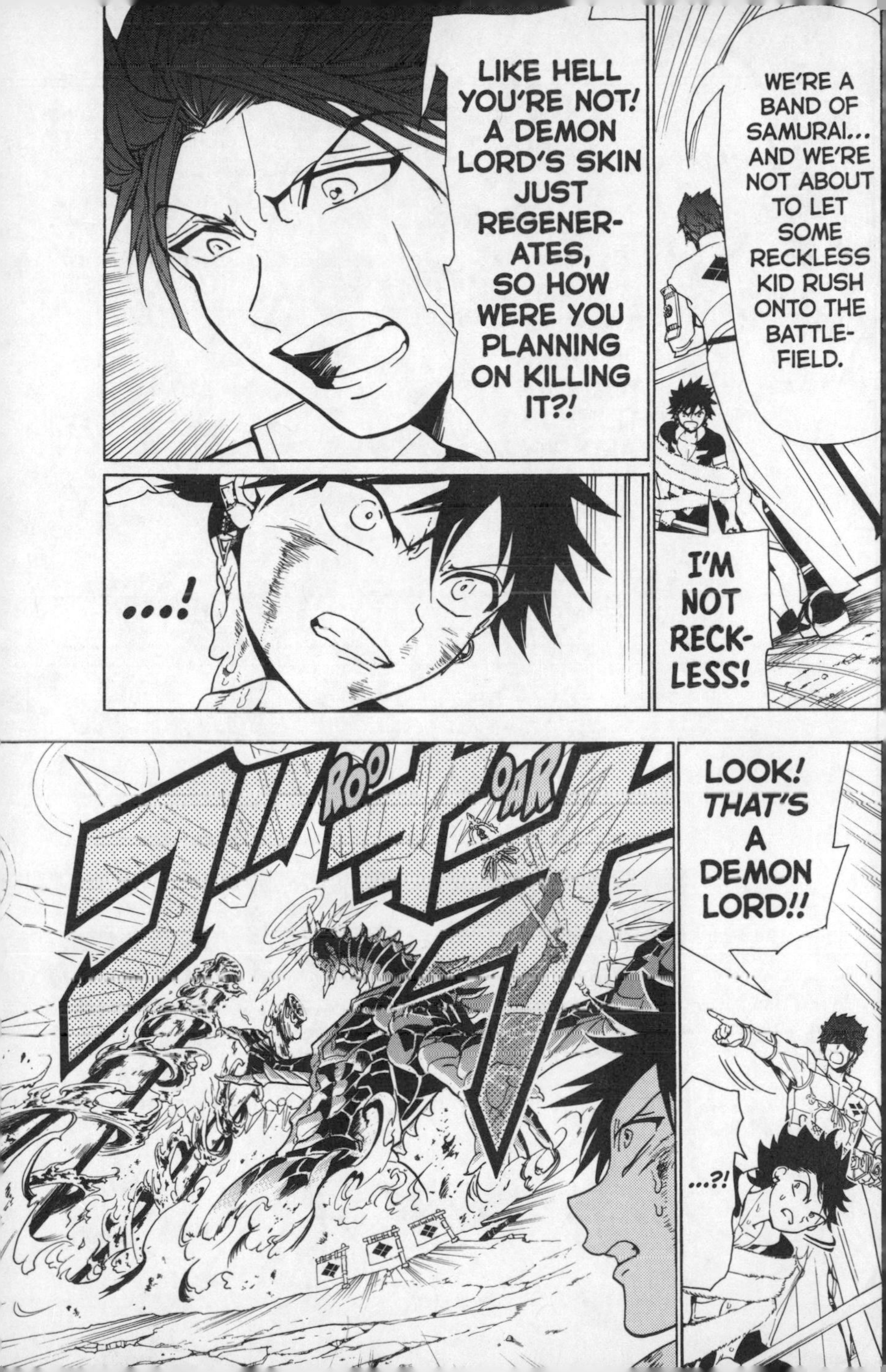
WE'RE A BAND OF SAMURAI... AND WE'RE NOT ABOUT TO LET SOME RECKLESS KID RUSH ONTO THE BATTLE-FIELD.
I'M NOT RECK-LESS!
LIKE HELL YOU'RE NOT! A DEMON LORD'S SKIN JUST REGENER-ATES, SO HOW WERE YOU PLANNING ON KILLING IT?!
...!
LOOK! THAT'S A DEMON LORD!!
...?!
ROOOAR

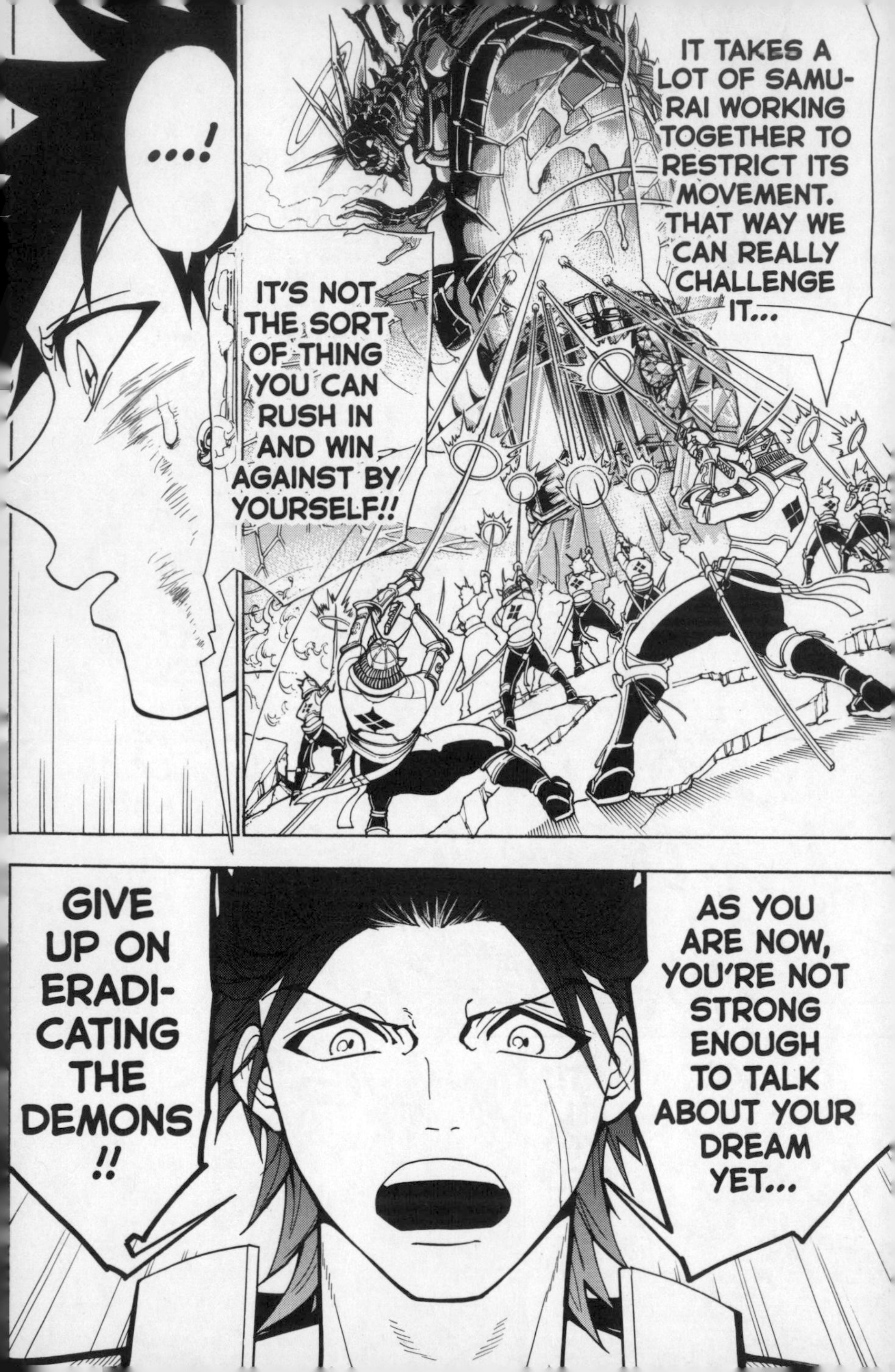
IT TAKES A LOT OF SAMU-RAI WORKING TOGETHER TO RESTRICT ITS MOVEMENT. THAT WAY WE CAN REALLY CHALLENGE IT...
IT'S NOT THE SORT OF THING YOU CAN RUSH IN AND WIN AGAINST BY YOURSELF!!
...!
AS YOU ARE NOW, YOU'RE NOT STRONG ENOUGH TO TALK ABOUT YOUR DREAM YET...
GIVE UP ON ERADI-CATING THE DEMONS!!

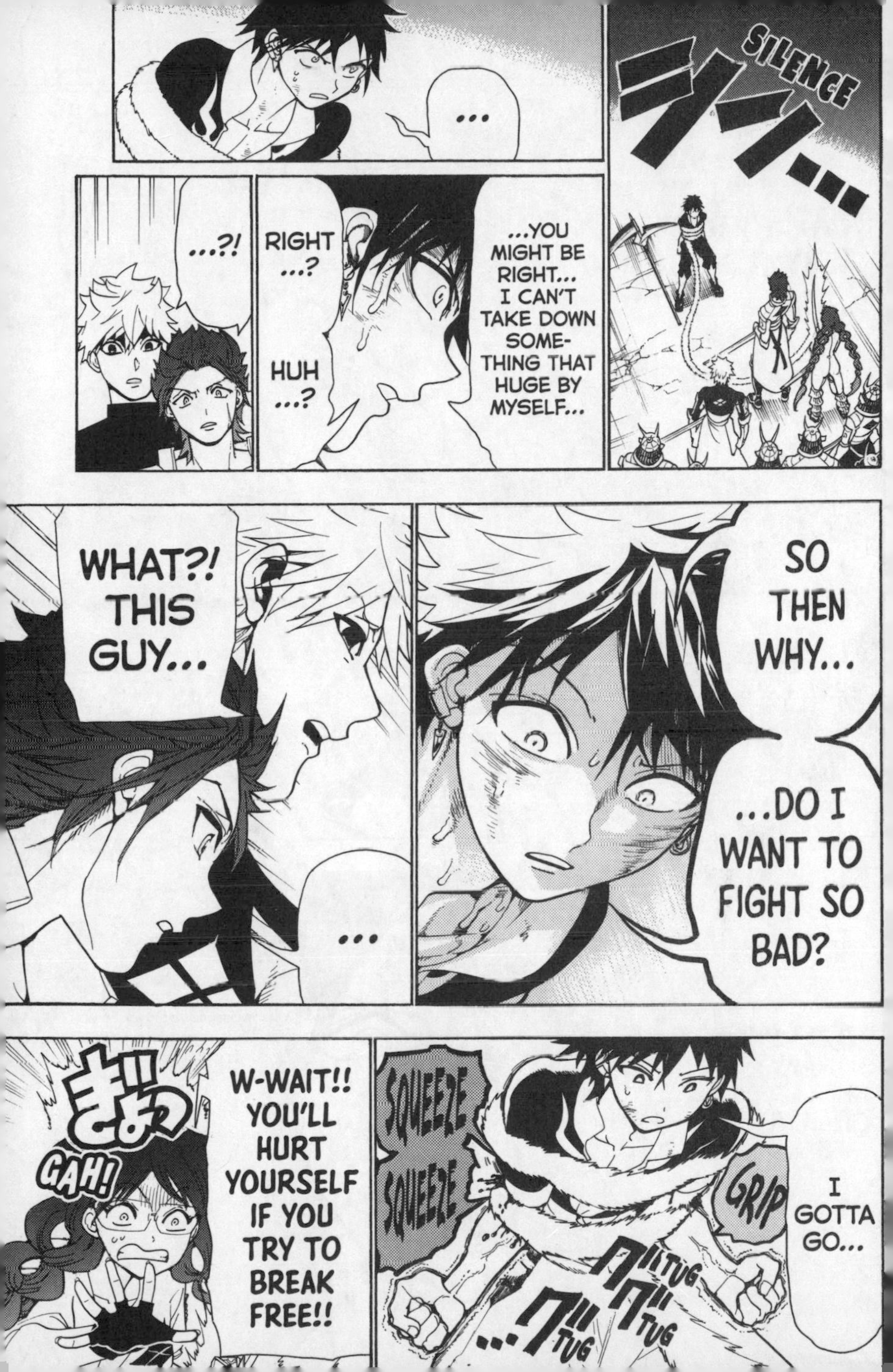
SILENCE
...
...YOU MIGHT BE RIGHT... I CAN'T TAKE DOWN SOMETHING THAT HUGE BY MYSELF...
RIGHT...?
HUH...?
...?!
SO THEN WHY...
...DO I WANT TO FIGHT SO BAD?
WHAT?! THIS GUY...
...
I GOTTA GO...
GRIP
SQUEEZE
SQUEEZE
TUG
TUG
TUG
TUG
W-WAIT!! YOU'LL HURT YOURSELF IF YOU TRY TO BREAK FREE!!
GAH!

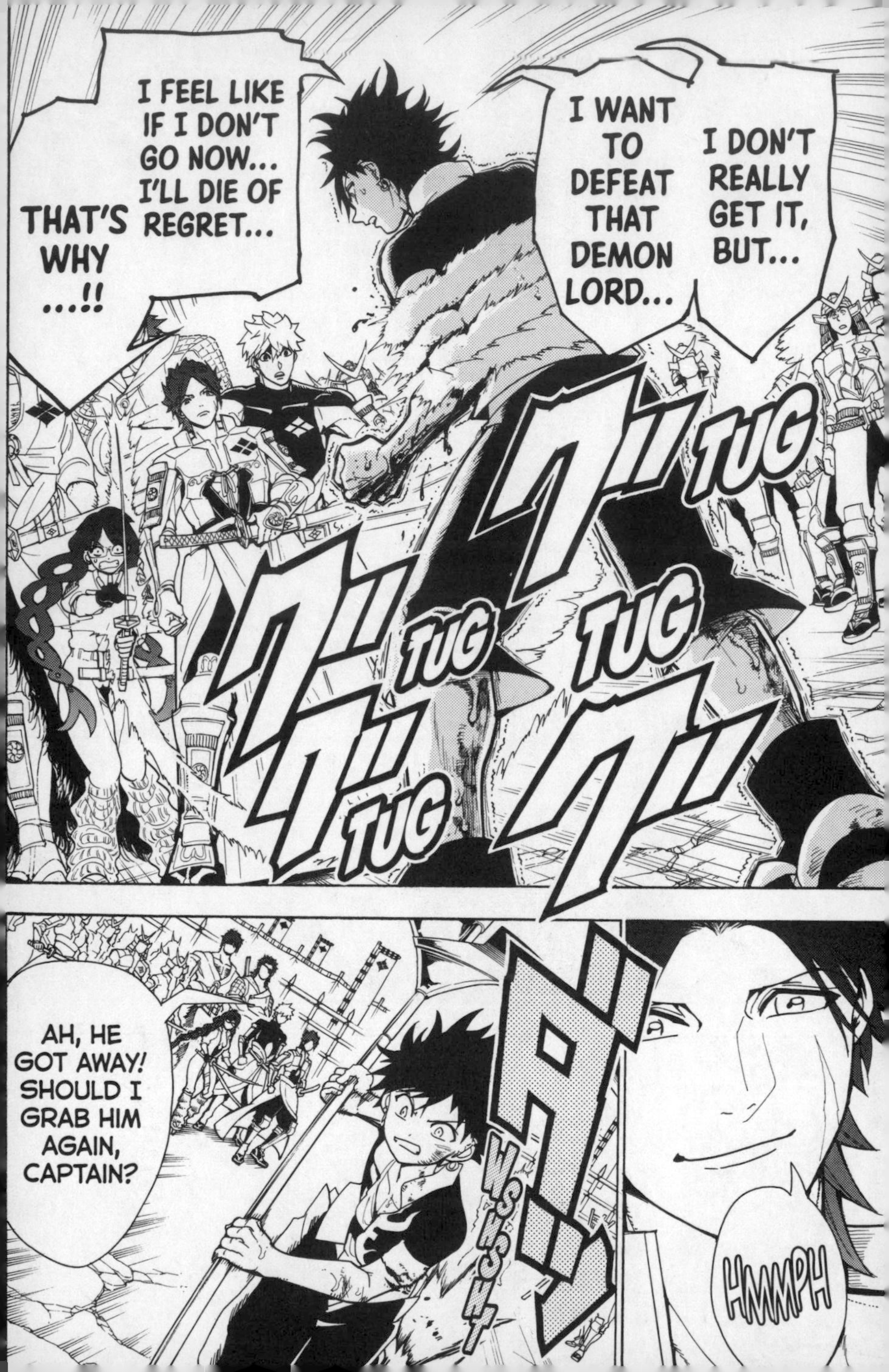
I DON'T REALLY GET IT, BUT...
I WANT TO DEFEAT THAT DEMON LORD...
I FEEL LIKE IF I DON'T GO NOW... I'LL DIE OF REGRET...
THAT'S WHY ...!!
TUG
TUG
TUG
TUG
WSSSHT
AH, HE GOT AWAY! SHOULD I GRAB HIM AGAIN, CAPTAIN?
HMMPH

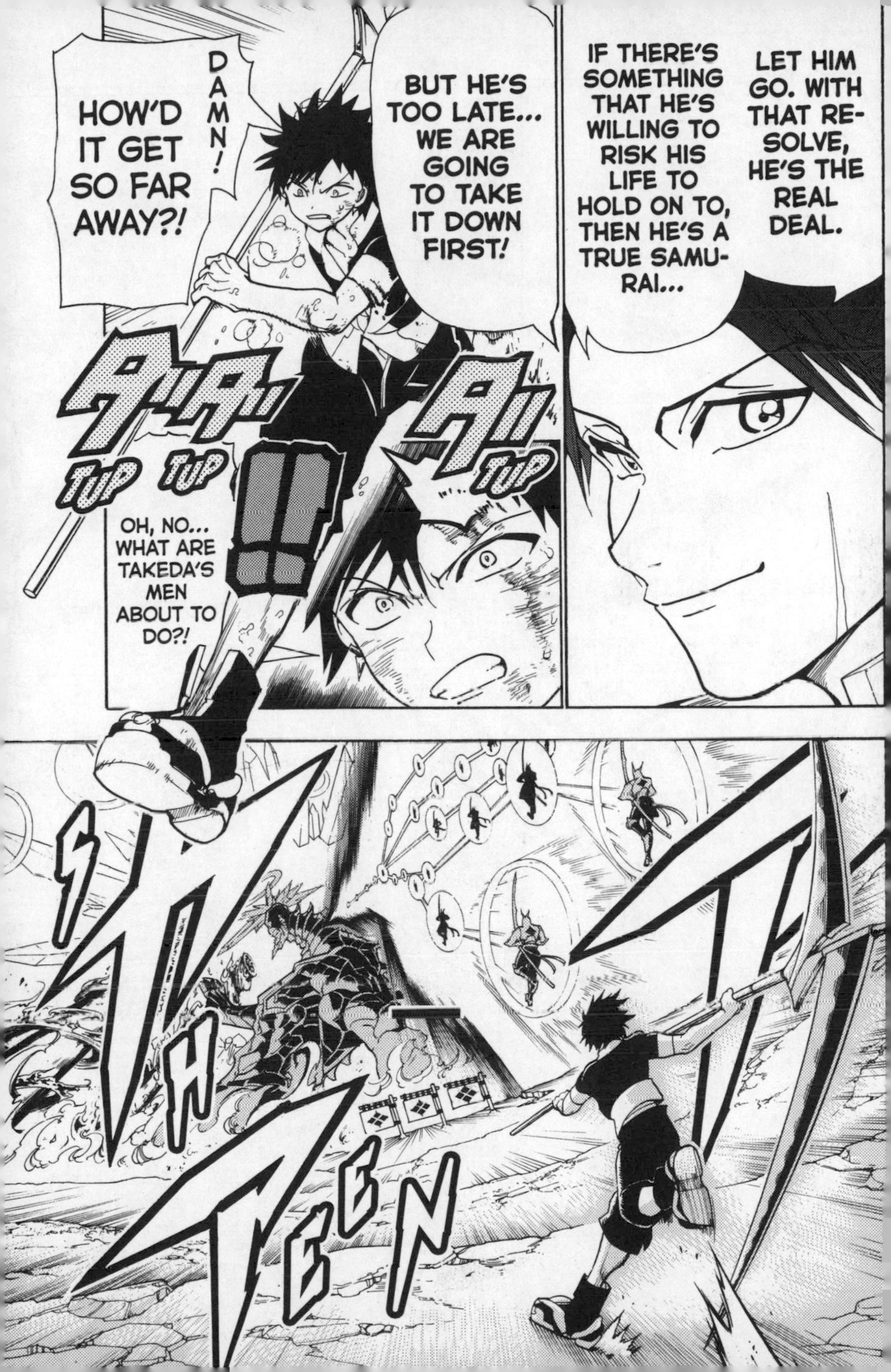
LET HIM GO. WITH THAT RE-SOLVE, HE'S THE REAL DEAL.
IF THERE'S SOMETHING THAT HE'S WILLING TO RISK HIS LIFE TO HOLD ON TO, THEN HE'S A TRUE SAMU-RAI...
BUT HE'S TOO LATE... WE ARE GOING TO TAKE IT DOWN FIRST!
DAMN!
HOW'D IT GET SO FAR AWAY?!
TUP
TUP TUP
!!
OH, NO... WHAT ARE TAKEDA'S MEN ABOUT TO DO?!

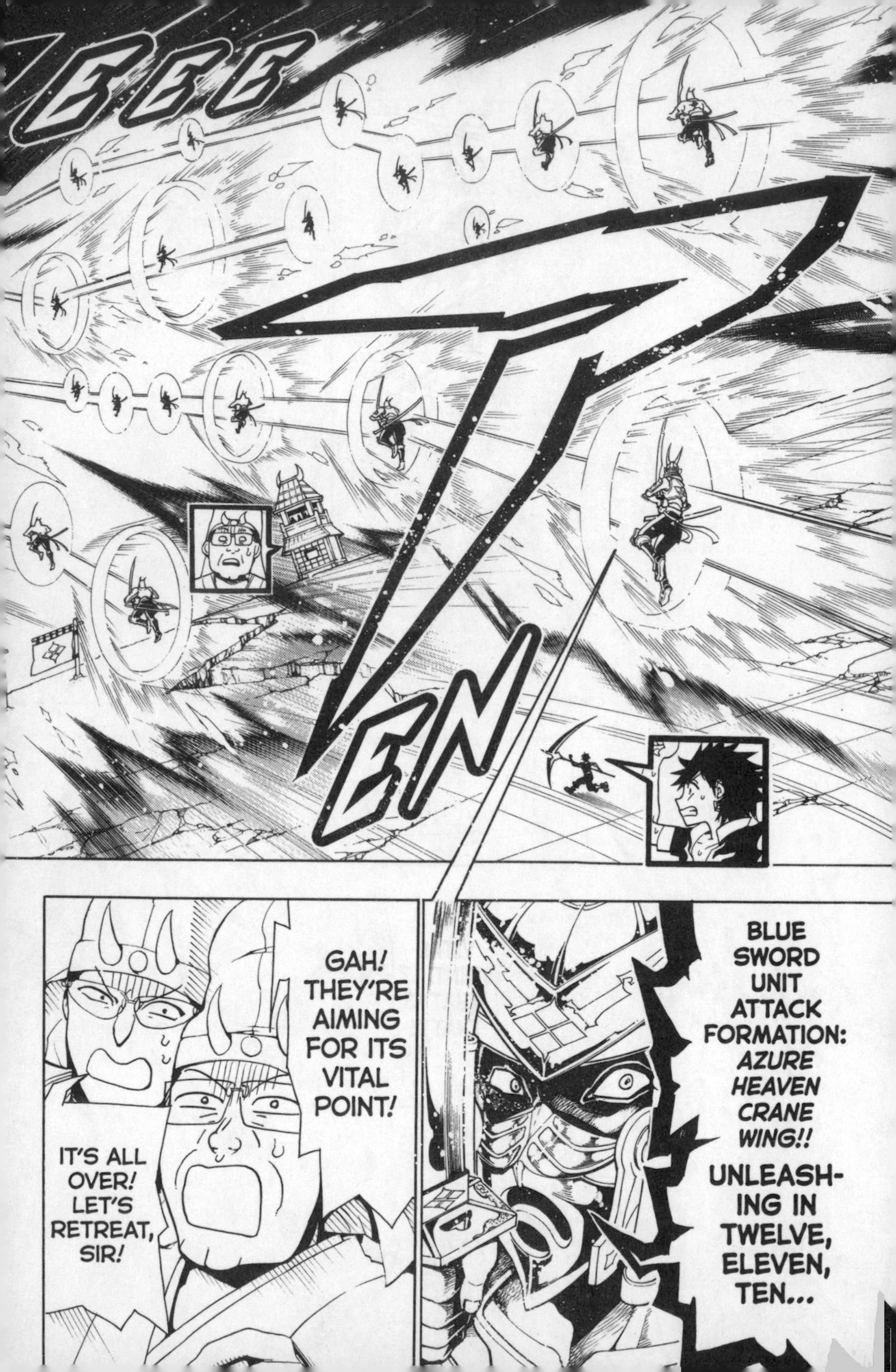
BLUE SWORD UNIT ATTACK FORMATION: *AZURE HEAVEN CRANE WING!!*
UNLEASHING IN TWELVE, ELEVEN, TEN...
GAH! THEY'RE AIMING FOR ITS VITAL POINT!
IT'S ALL OVER! LET'S RETREAT, SIR!

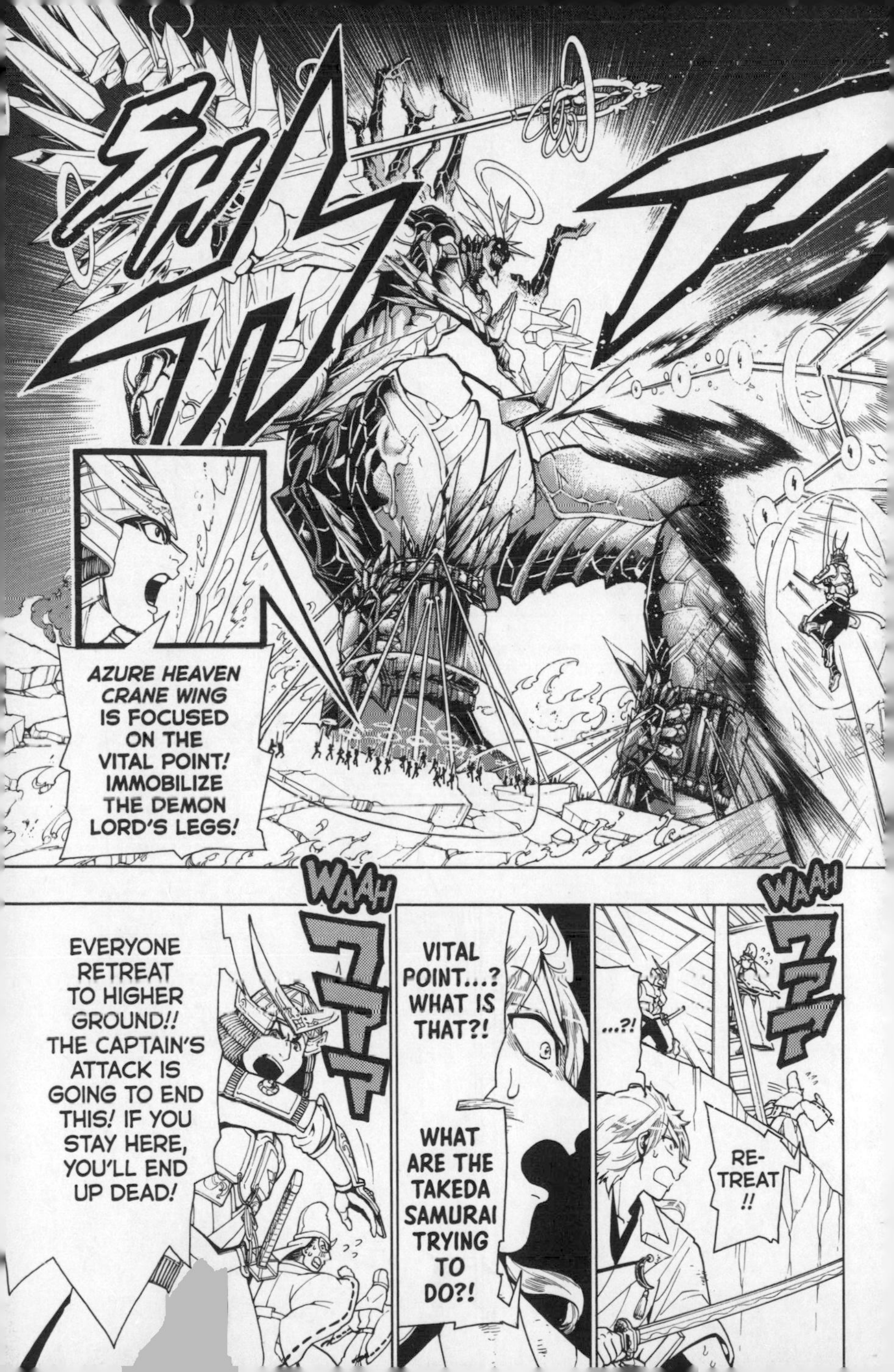
AZURE HEAVEN CRANE WING IS FOCUSED ON THE VITAL POINT! IMMOBILIZE THE DEMON LORD'S LEGS!
WAAH
...?!
RE-TREAT!!
VITAL POINT...? WHAT IS THAT?!
WHAT ARE THE TAKEDA SAMURAI TRYING TO DO?!
WAAH
EVERYONE RETREAT TO HIGHER GROUND!! THE CAPTAIN'S ATTACK IS GOING TO END THIS! IF YOU STAY HERE, YOU'LL END UP DEAD!

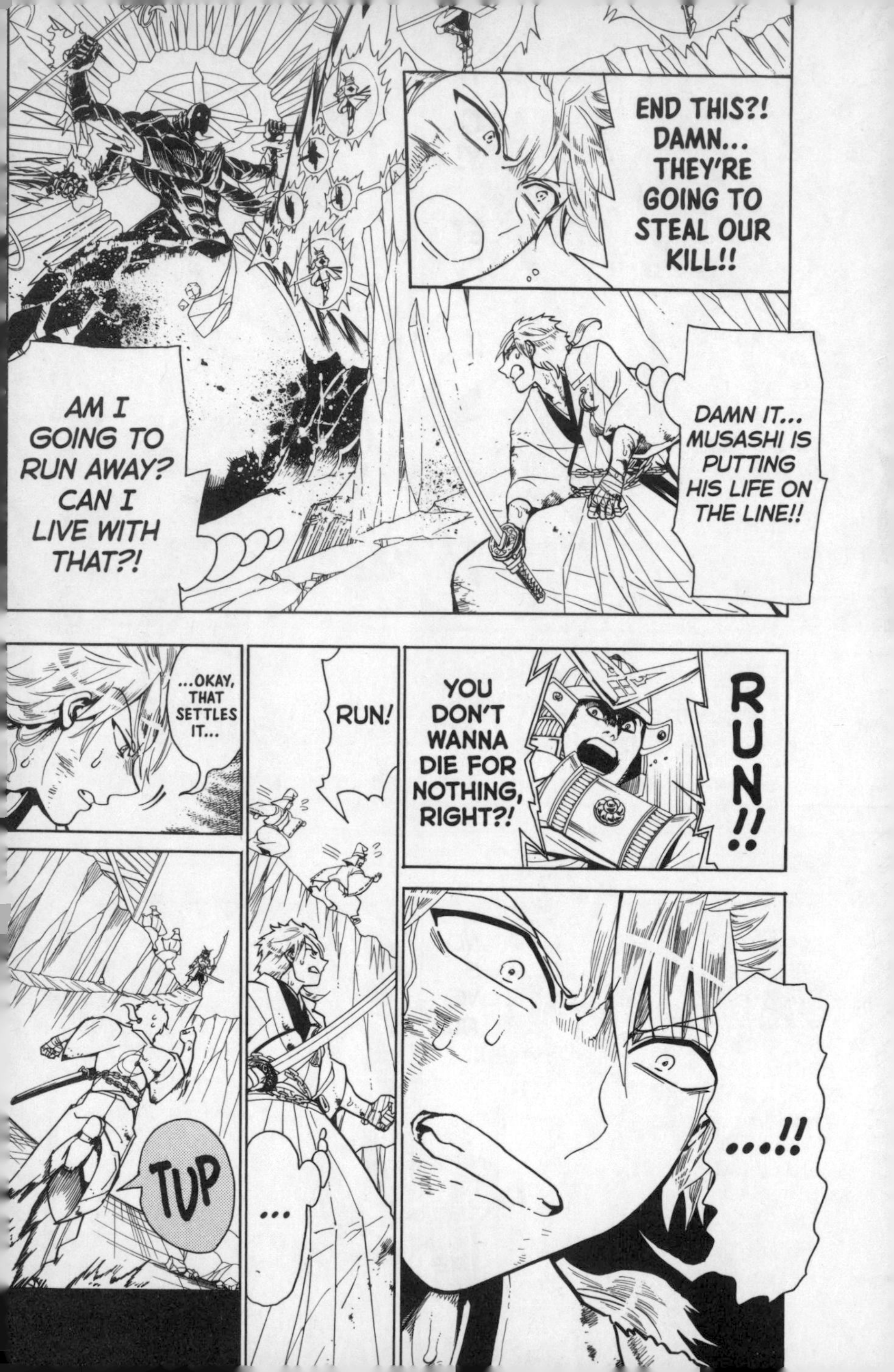
END THIS?! DAMN... THEY'RE GOING TO STEAL OUR KILL!!
DAMN IT... MUSASHI IS PUTTING HIS LIFE ON THE LINE!!
AM I GOING TO RUN AWAY? CAN I LIVE WITH THAT?!
RUN!!
YOU DON'T WANNA DIE FOR NOTHING, RIGHT?!
...!!
RUN!
...
...OKAY, THAT SETTLES IT...
TUP

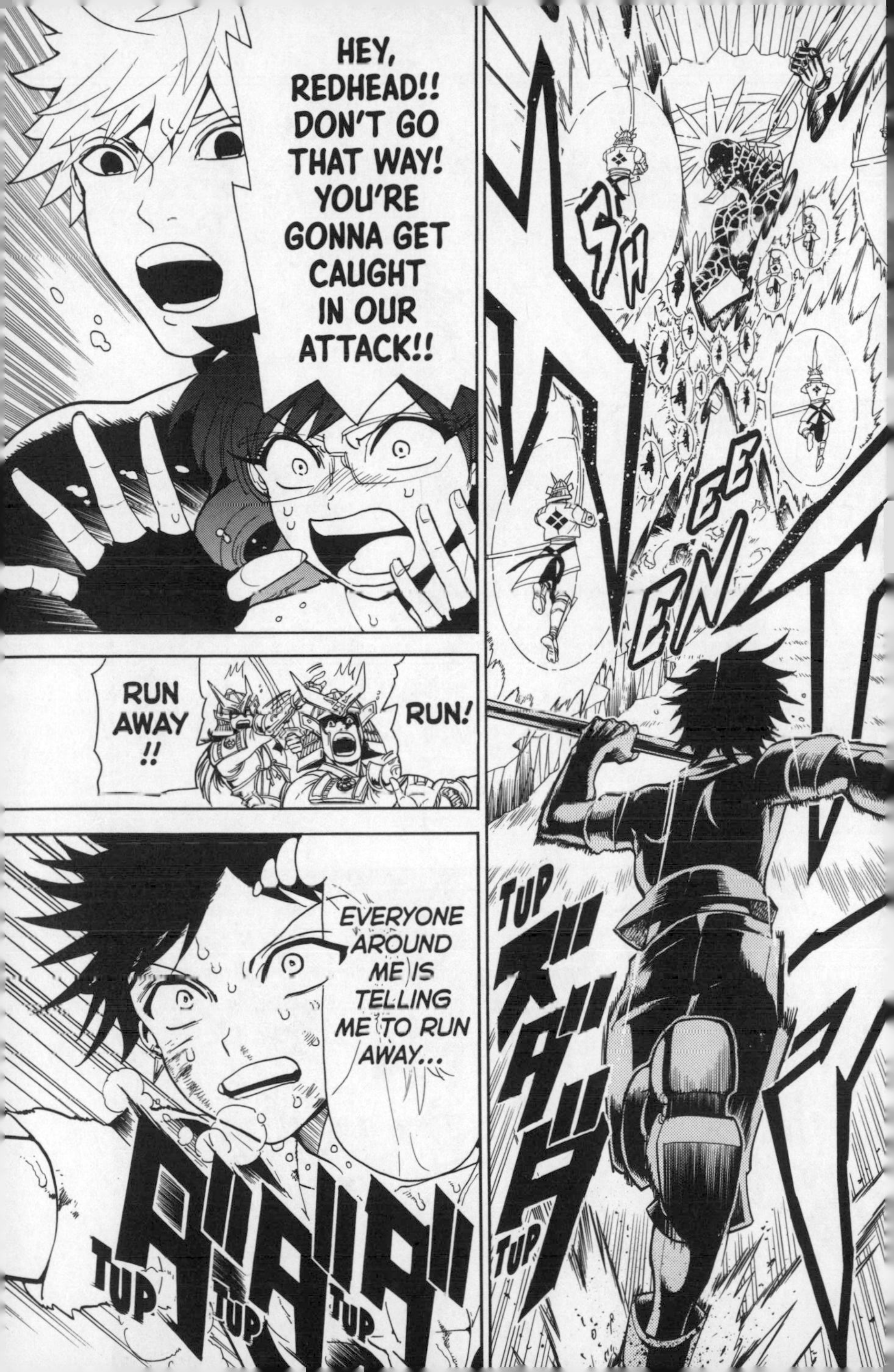
SH
EE
EN
TUP
TUP
HEY, REDHEAD!! DON'T GO THAT WAY! YOU'RE GONNA GET CAUGHT IN OUR ATTACK!!
RUN!
RUN AWAY!!
EVERYONE AROUND ME IS TELLING ME TO RUN AWAY...
TUP
TUP
TUP
TUP

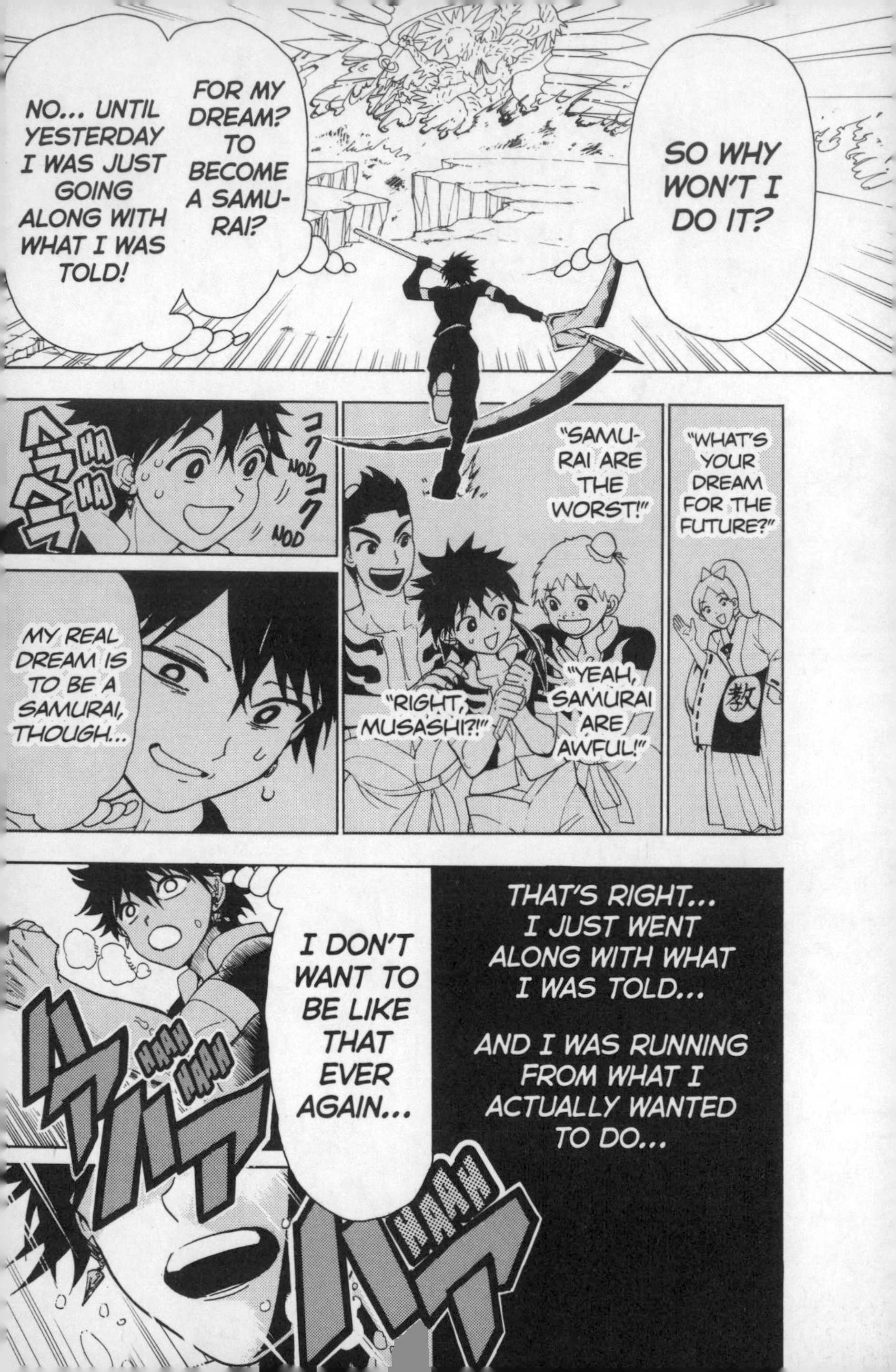
SO WHY WON'T I DO IT?
FOR MY DREAM? TO BECOME A SAMURAI?
NO... UNTIL YESTERDAY I WAS JUST GOING ALONG WITH WHAT I WAS TOLD!
"WHAT'S YOUR DREAM FOR THE FUTURE?"
"SAMURAI ARE THE WORST!"
"YEAH, SAMURAI ARE AWFUL!"
"RIGHT, MUSASHI?!"
NOD NOD
HA HA
MY REAL DREAM IS TO BE A SAMURAI, THOUGH...
THAT'S RIGHT... I JUST WENT ALONG WITH WHAT I WAS TOLD...
AND I WAS RUNNING FROM WHAT I ACTUALLY WANTED TO DO...
I DON'T WANT TO BE LIKE THAT EVER AGAIN...
HAAH HAAH
HAAH

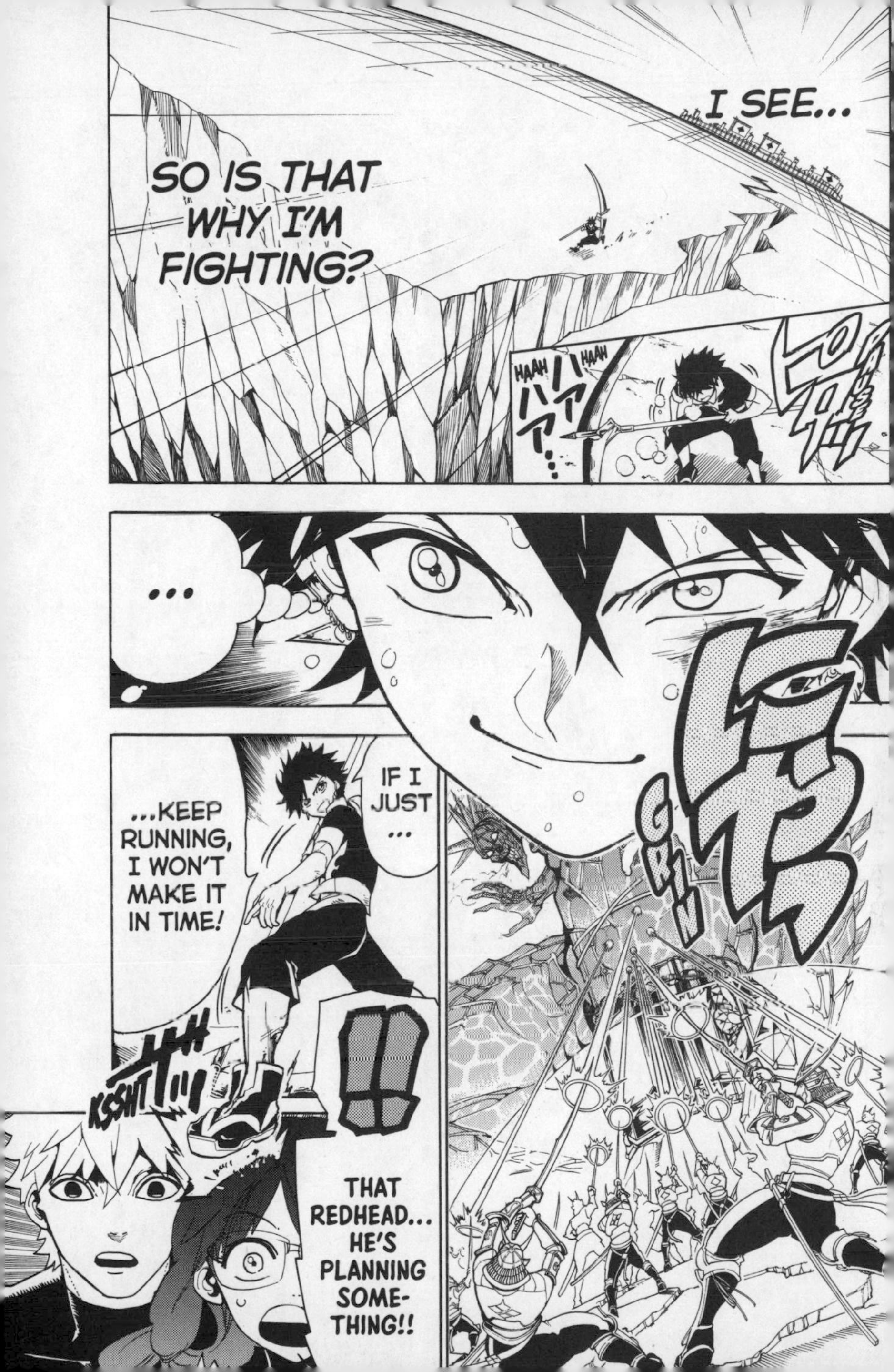

I SEE...
SO IS THAT WHY I'M FIGHTING?
HAAH
HAAH
...
GRIN
IF I JUST ...
...KEEP RUNNING, I WON'T MAKE IT IN TIME!
KSSHT
THAT REDHEAD... HE'S PLANNING SOME-THING!!

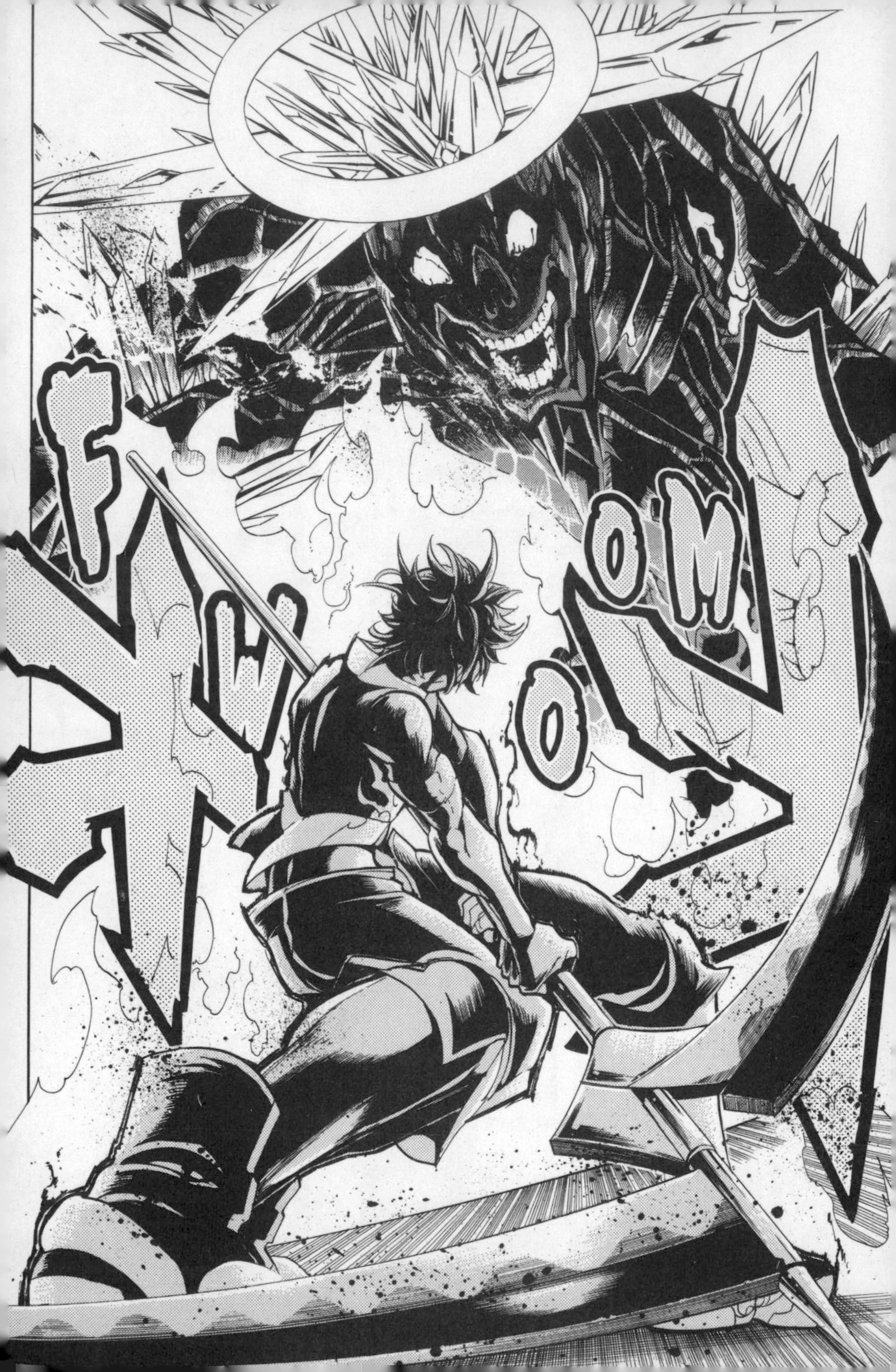
FWOOM

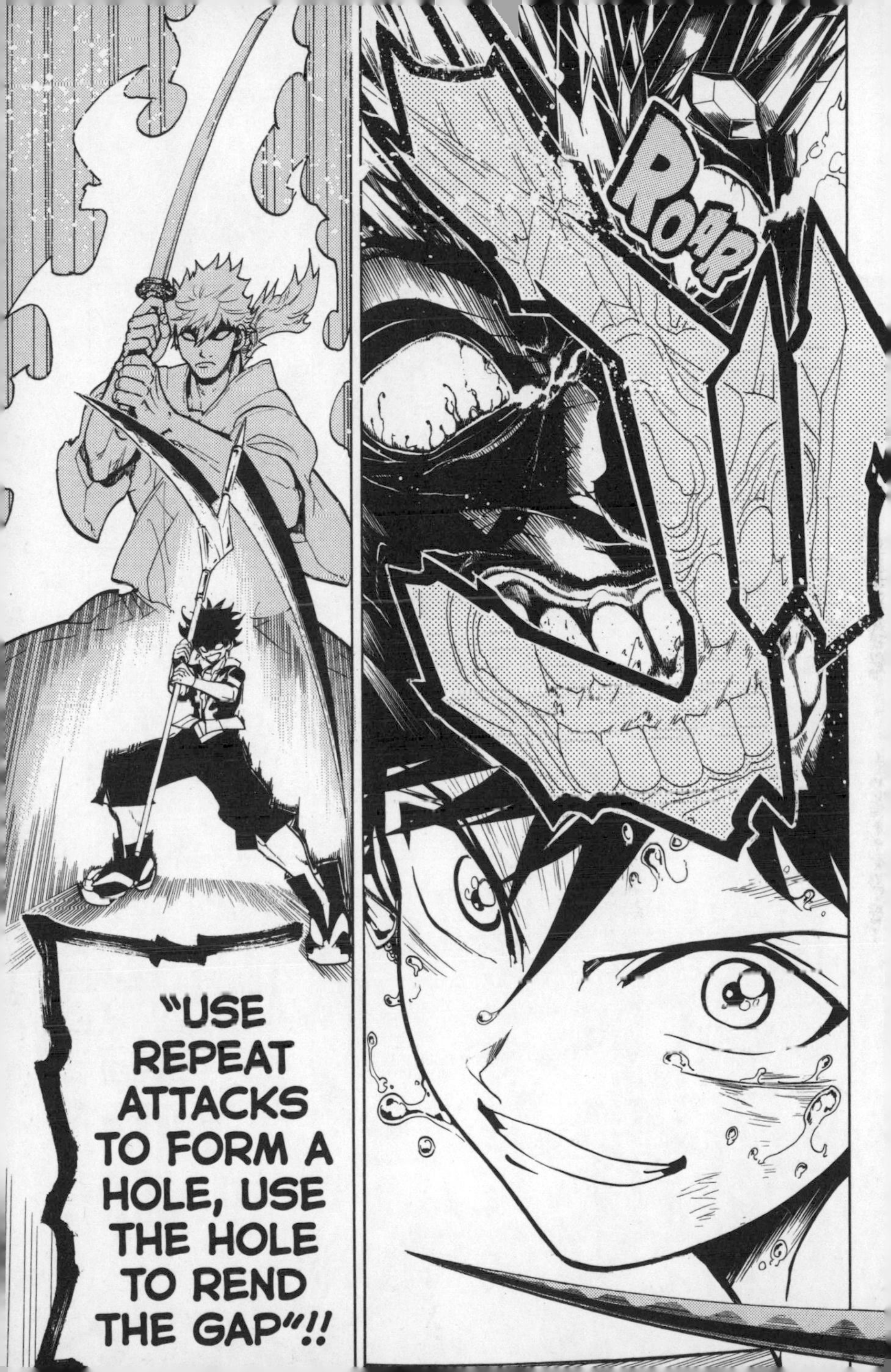
ROAR
"USE REPEAT ATTACKS TO FORM A HOLE, USE THE HOLE TO REND THE GAP"!!

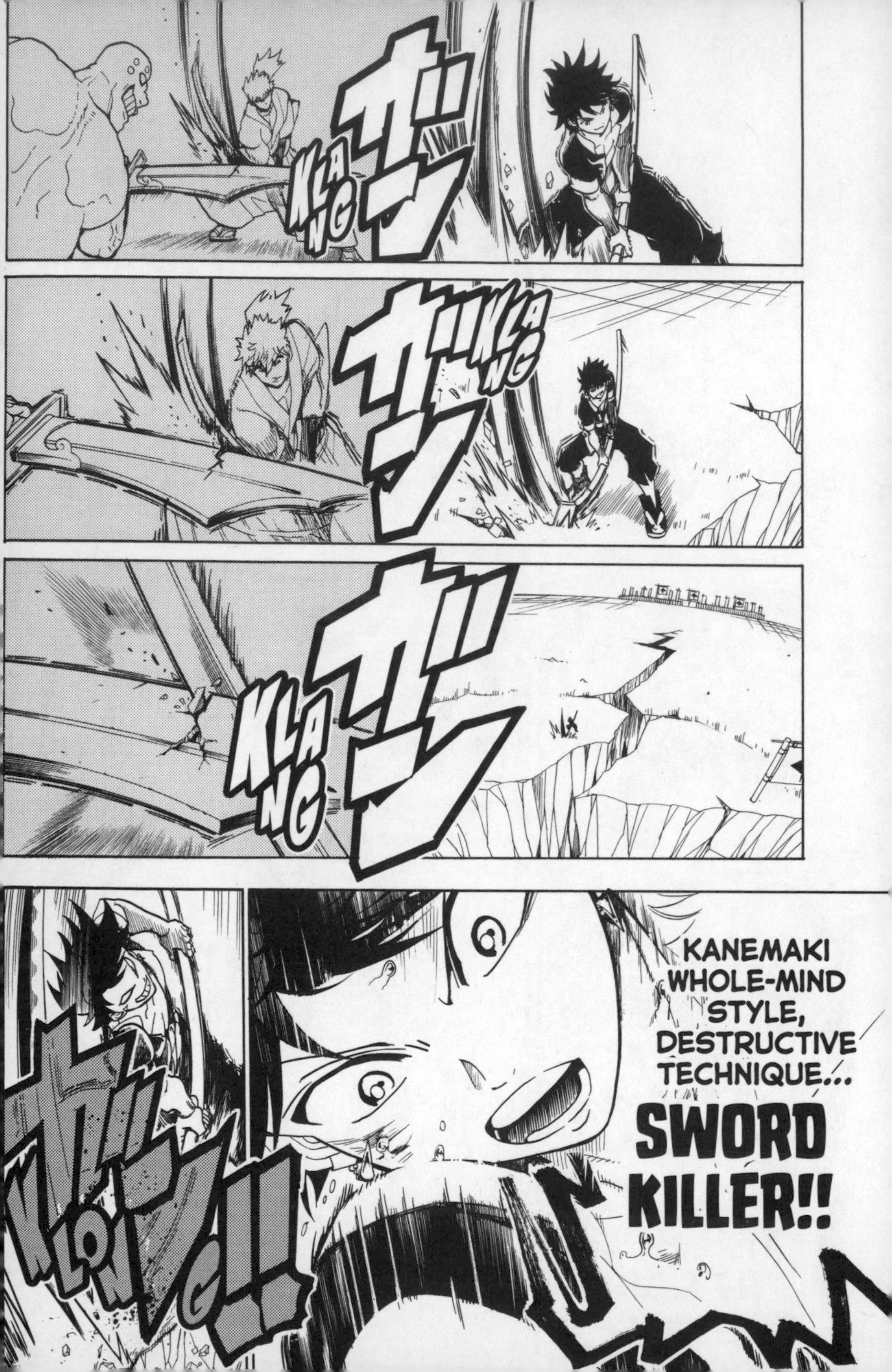
KLANG
KLANG
KLANG
KANEMAKI WHOLE-MIND STYLE, DESTRUCTIVE TECHNIQUE...
SWORD KILLER!!
KLONG!!

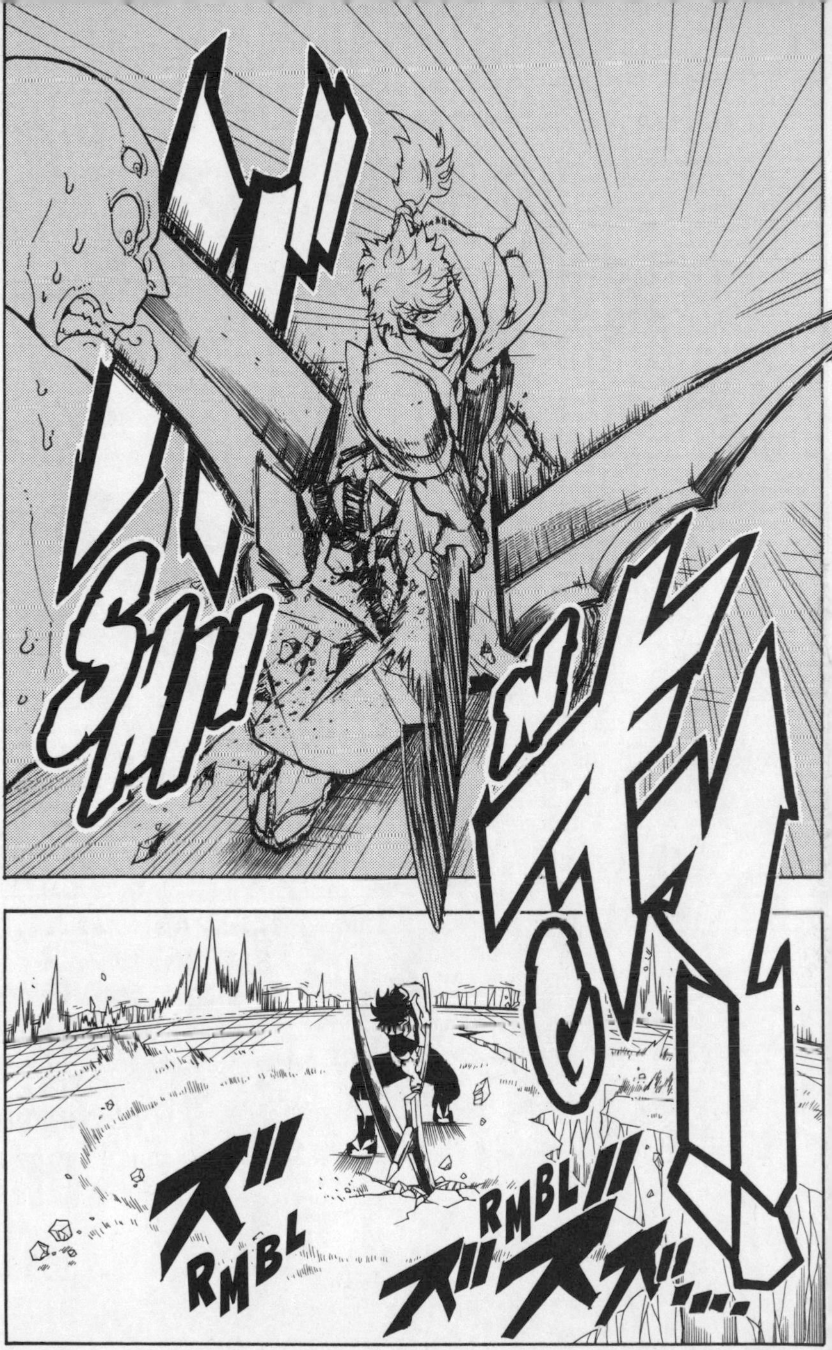
RMBL
RMBL!!

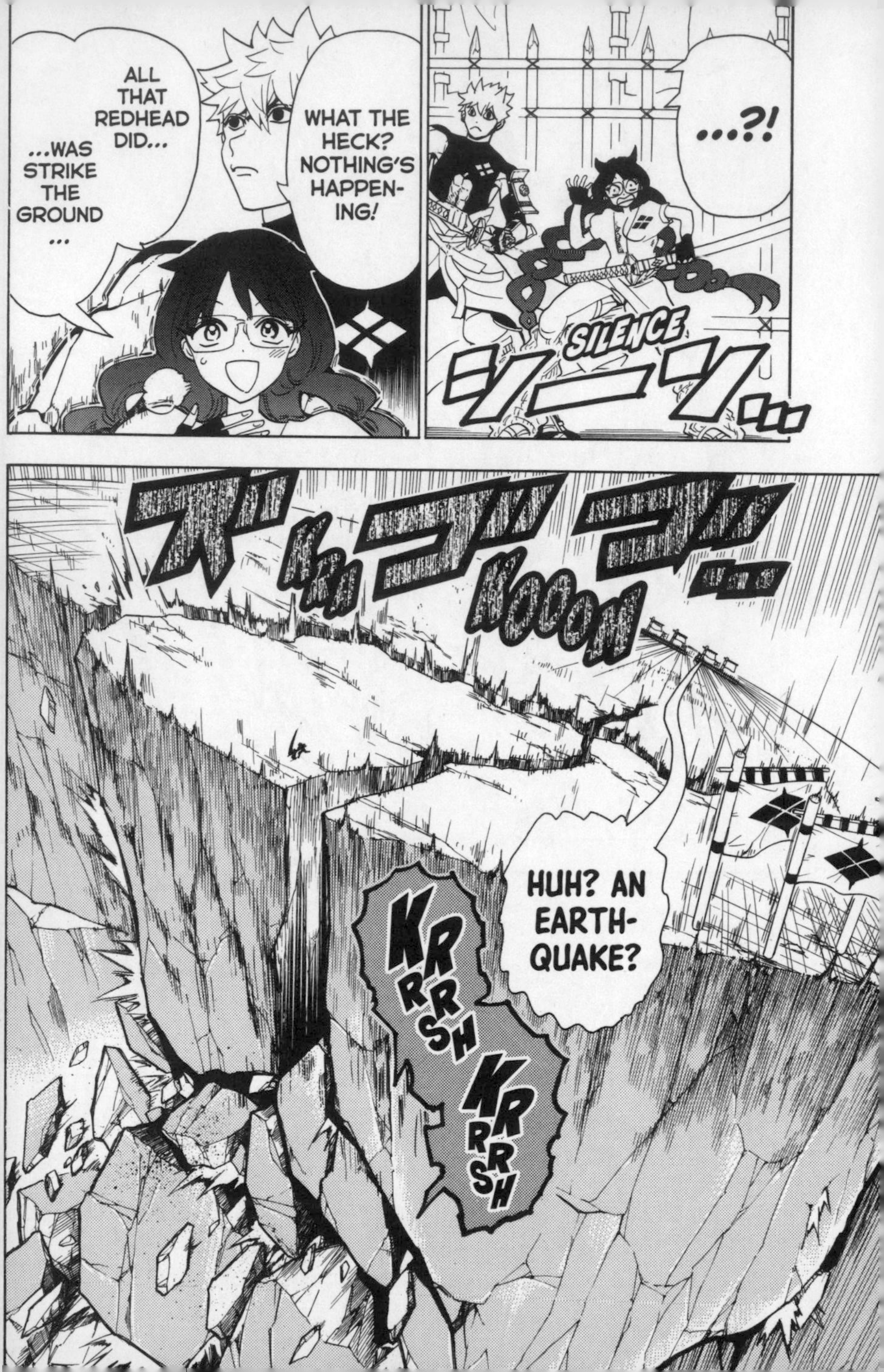
...?!
SILENCE
WHAT THE HECK? NOTHING'S HAPPENING!
ALL THAT REDHEAD DID...
...WAS STRIKE THE GROUND...
KOOOM
HUH? AN EARTHQUAKE?
KRRRSH
KRRRSH

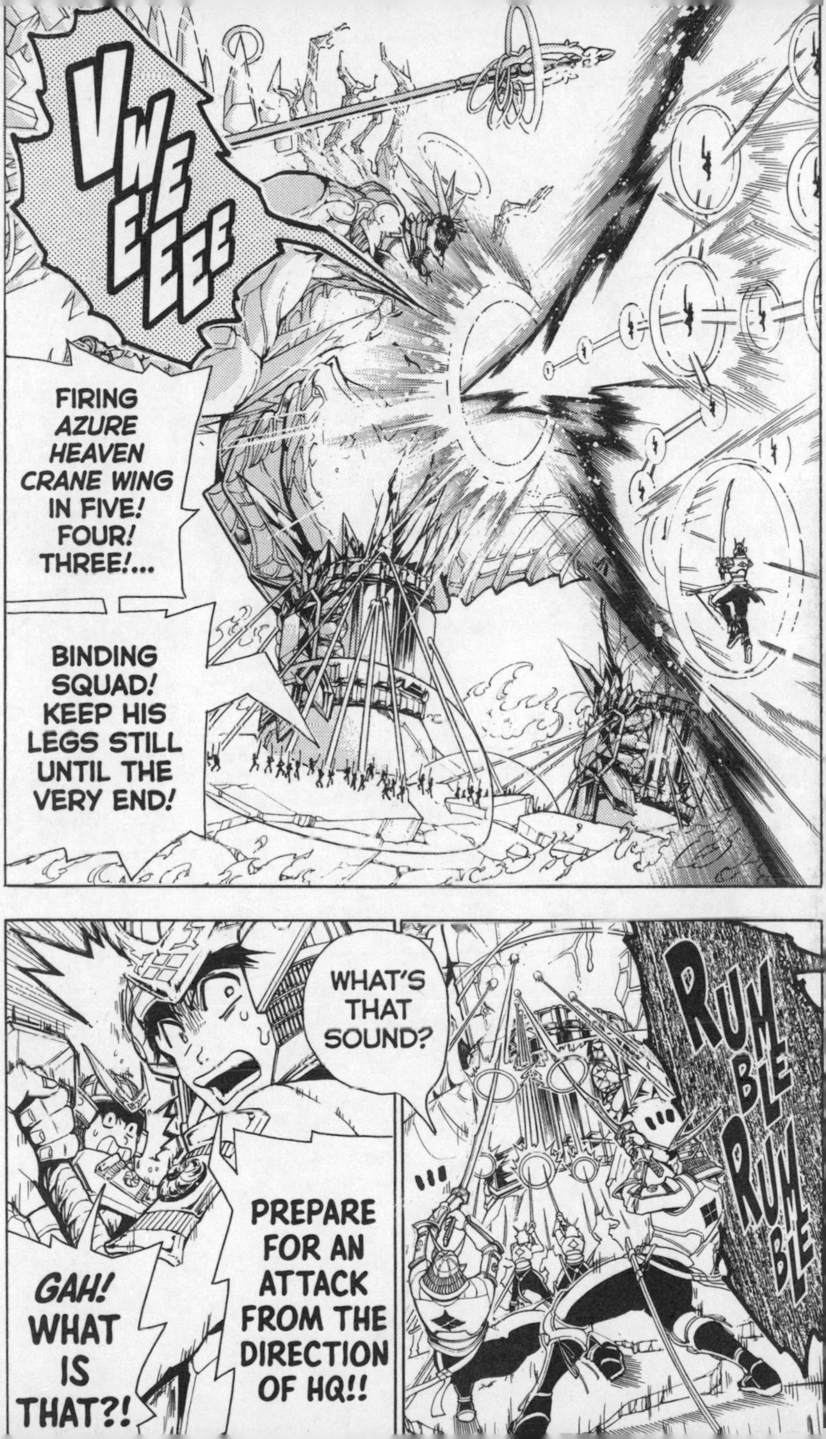
VWEEEEE
FIRING AZURE HEAVEN CRANE WING IN FIVE! FOUR! THREE!...
BINDING SQUAD! KEEP HIS LEGS STILL UNTIL THE VERY END!
RUMBLE RUMBLE
...
...
WHAT'S THAT SOUND?
PREPARE FOR AN ATTACK FROM THE DIRECTION OF HQ!!
GAH! WHAT IS THAT?!

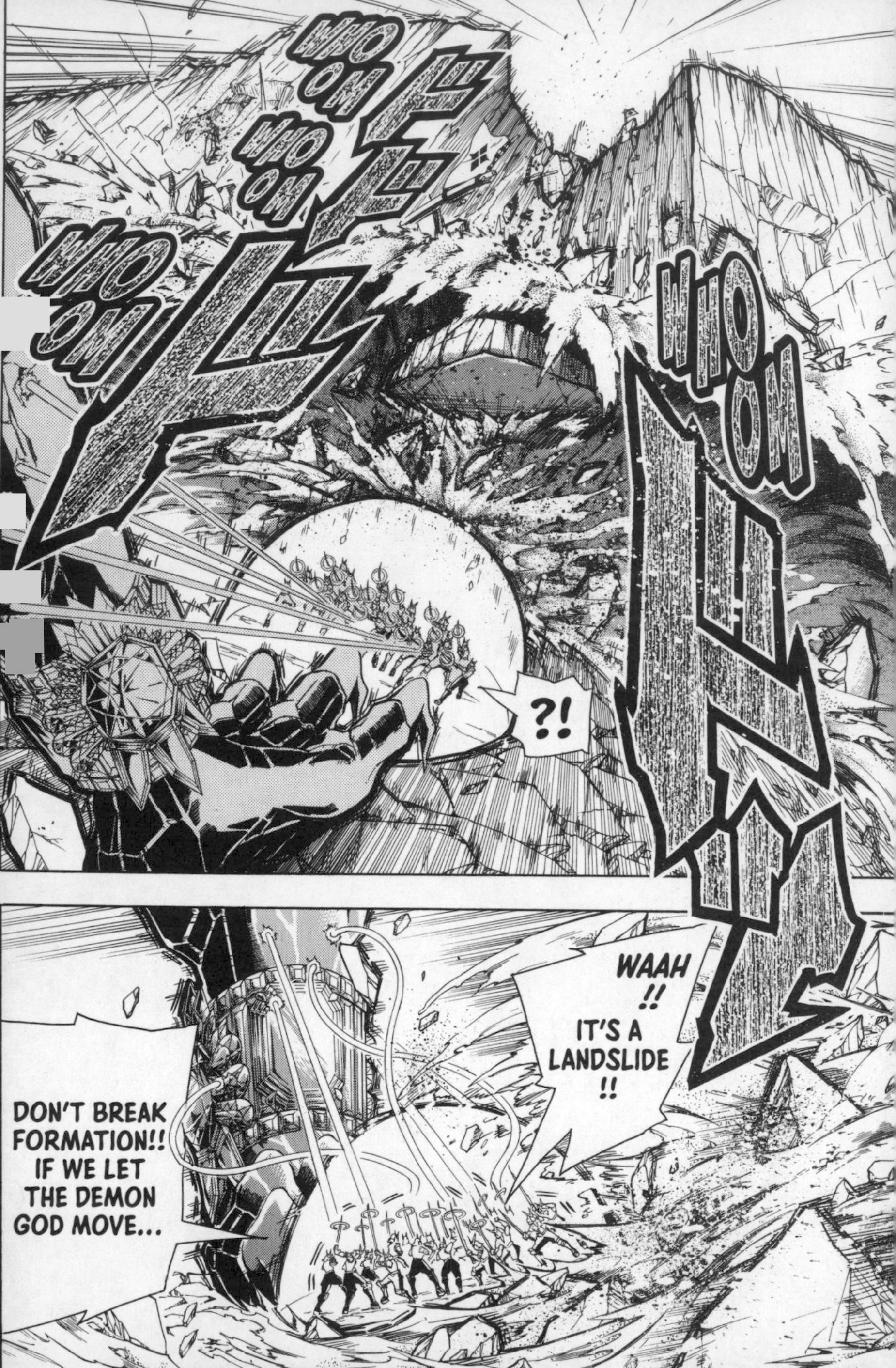
WHOOM
WHOOM
WHOOM
WHOOM
?!
WAAH!! IT'S A LANDSLIDE!!
DON'T BREAK FORMATION!! IF WE LET THE DEMON GOD MOVE...

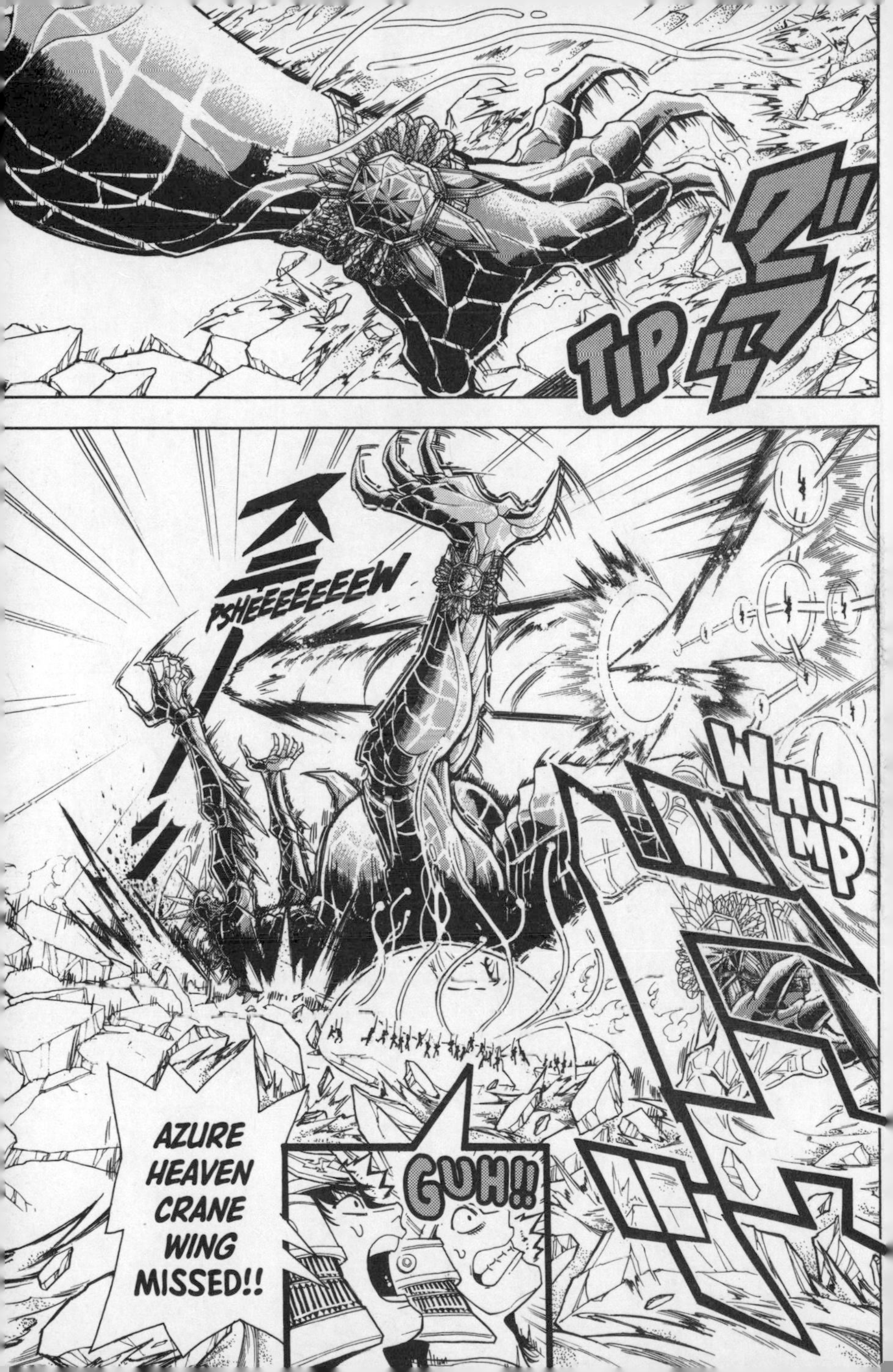
TIP
WHUMP
PSHEEEEEEEEW
GUH!!
AZURE HEAVEN CRANE WING MISSED!!

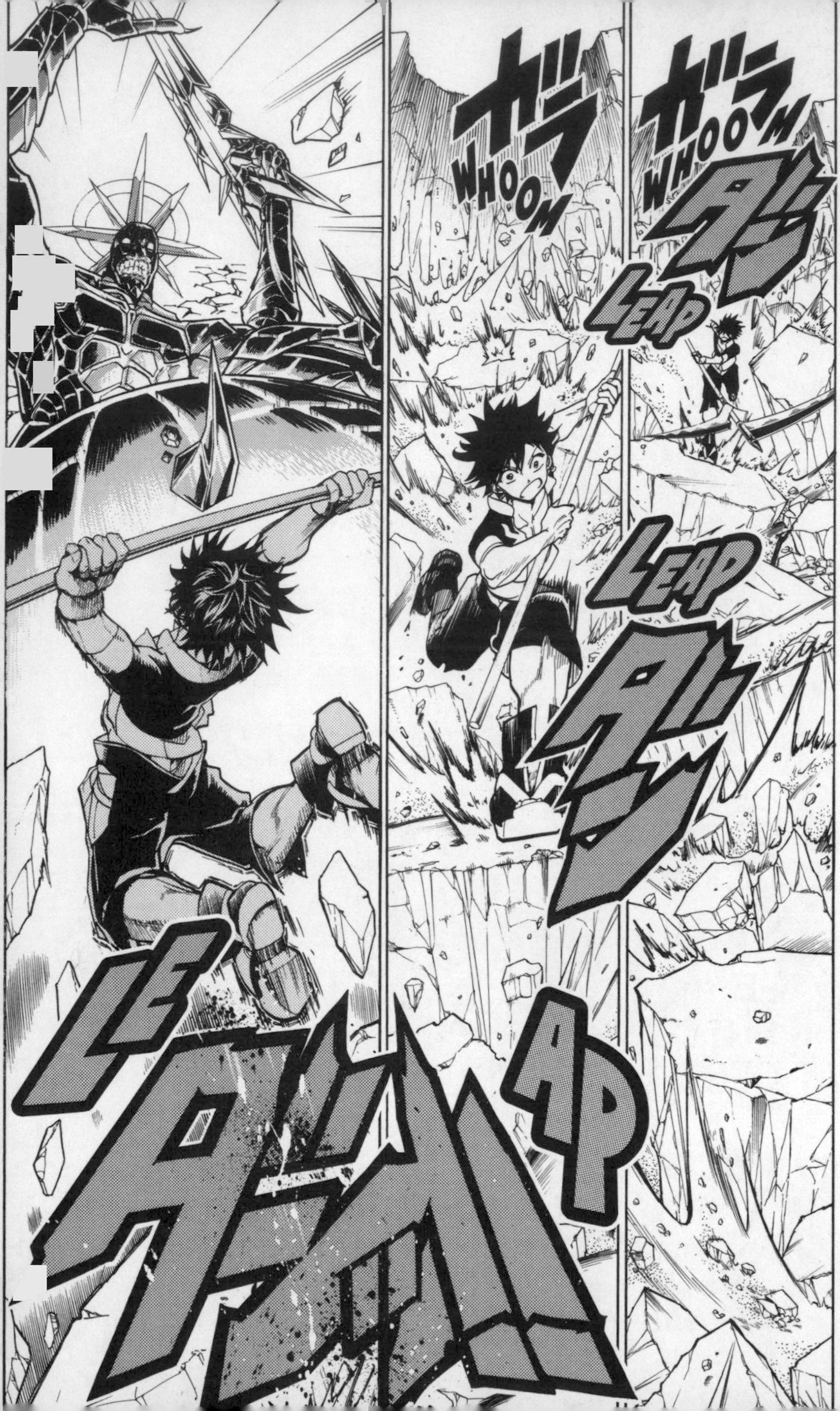
WHOOM
LEAP
WHOOM
LEAP
LEAP

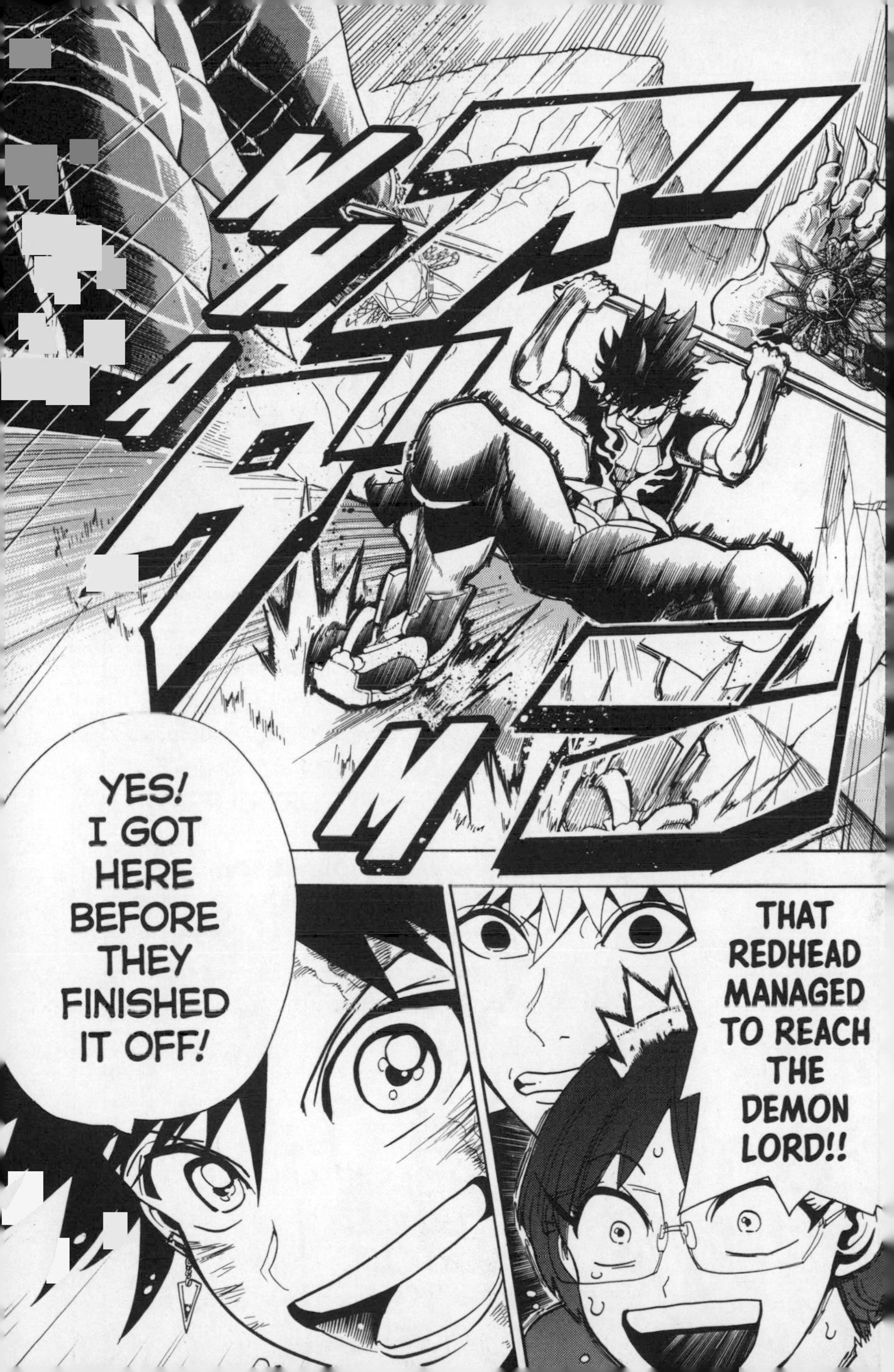
WHAM
THAT REDHEAD MANAGED TO REACH THE DEMON LORD!!
YES! I GOT HERE BEFORE THEY FINISHED IT OFF!

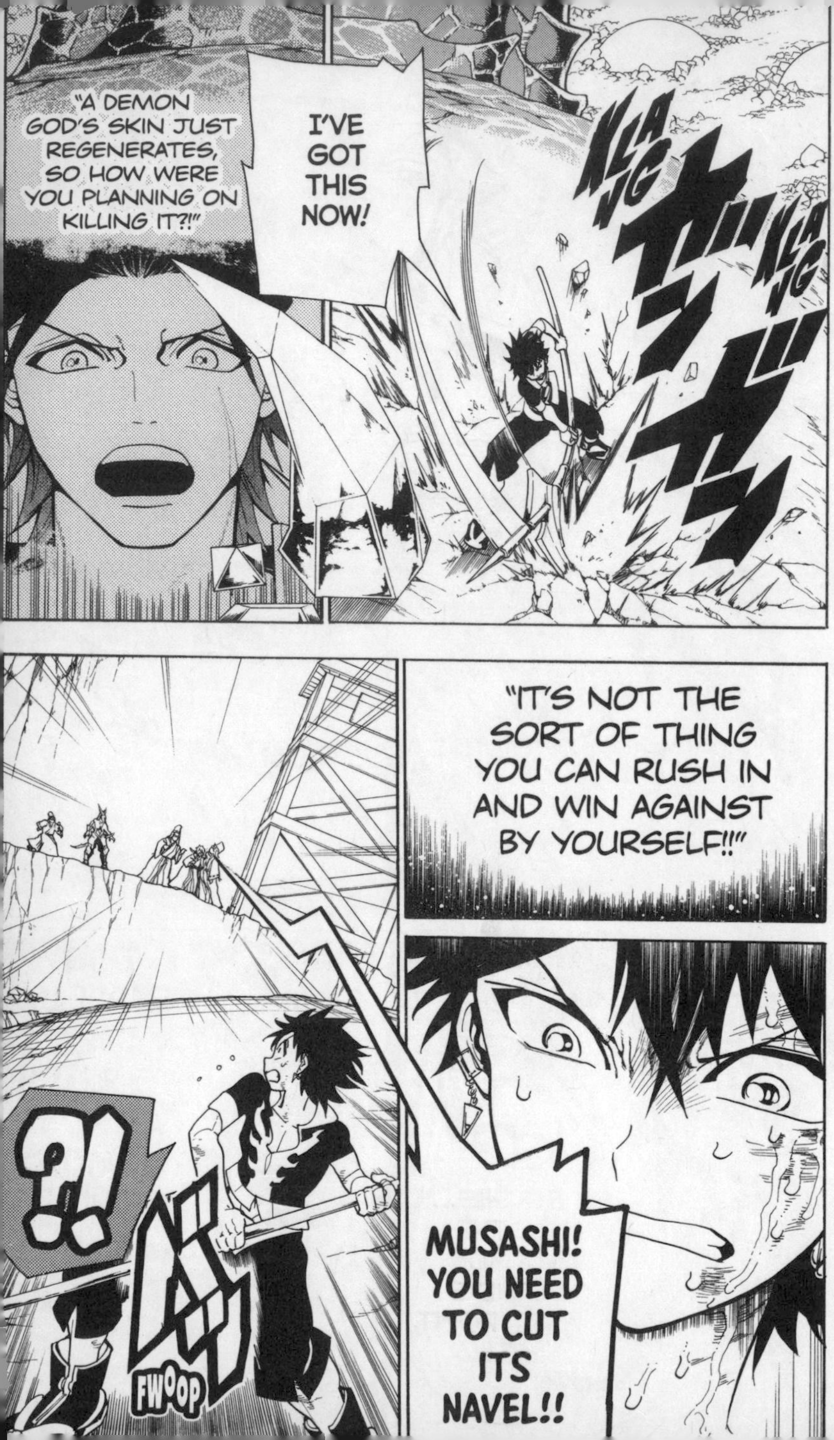
KLANG
KLANG
I'VE GOT THIS NOW!
"A DEMON GOD'S SKIN JUST REGENERATES, SO HOW WERE YOU PLANNING ON KILLING IT?!"
"IT'S NOT THE SORT OF THING YOU CAN RUSH IN AND WIN AGAINST BY YOURSELF!!"
MUSASHI! YOU NEED TO CUT ITS NAVEL!!
?!
FWOOP

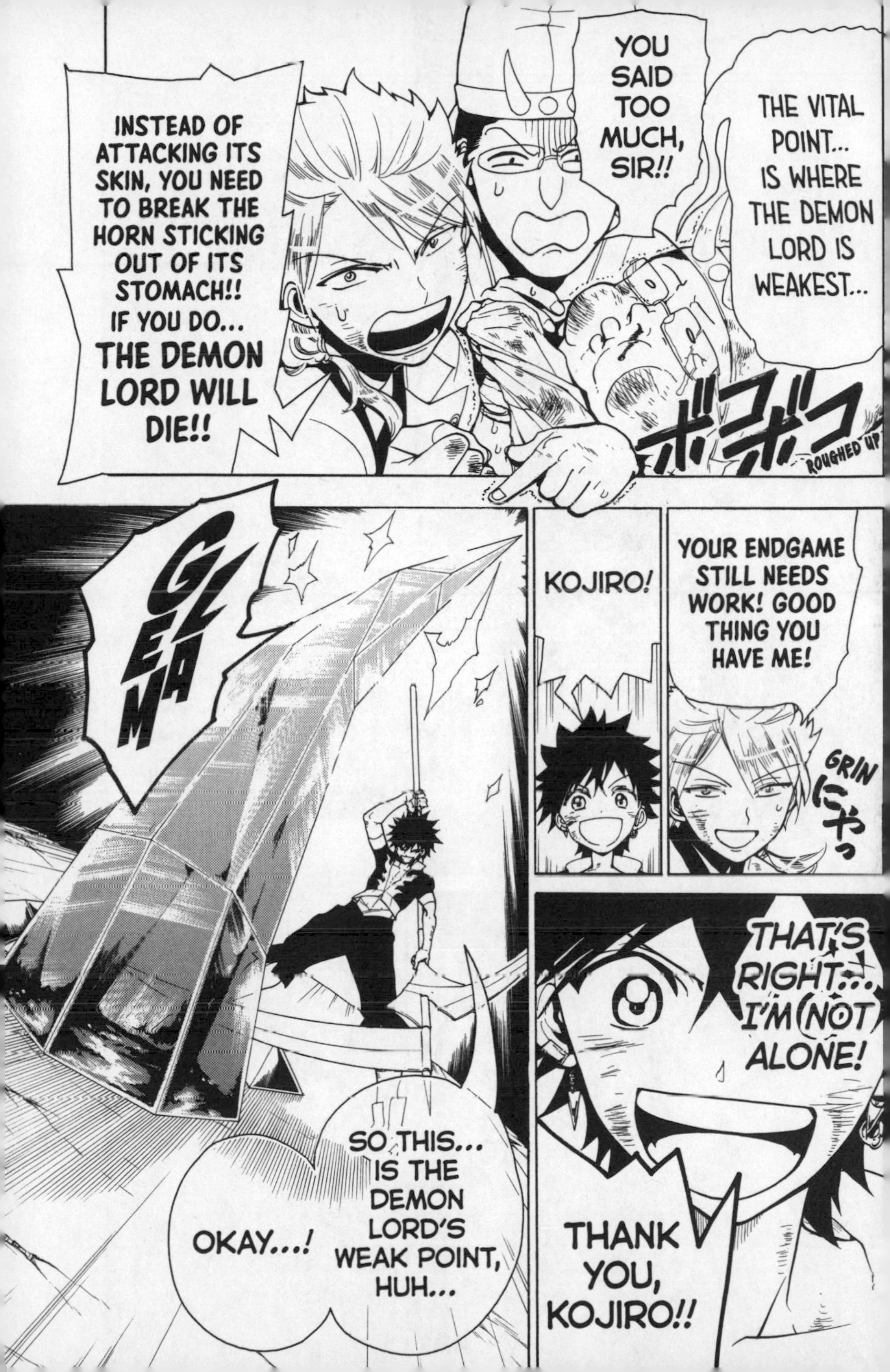
THE VITAL POINT... IS WHERE THE DEMON LORD IS WEAKEST...
YOU SAID TOO MUCH, SIR!!
INSTEAD OF ATTACKING ITS SKIN, YOU NEED TO BREAK THE HORN STICKING OUT OF ITS STOMACH!! IF YOU DO... THE DEMON LORD WILL DIE!!
ボコボコ
ROUGHED UP
YOUR ENDGAME STILL NEEDS WORK! GOOD THING YOU HAVE ME!
KOJIRO!
GRIN
にやっ
THAT'S RIGHT... I'M NOT ALONE!
THANK YOU, KOJIRO!!
GLEAM
SO THIS... IS THE DEMON LORD'S WEAK POINT, HUH...
OKAY...!

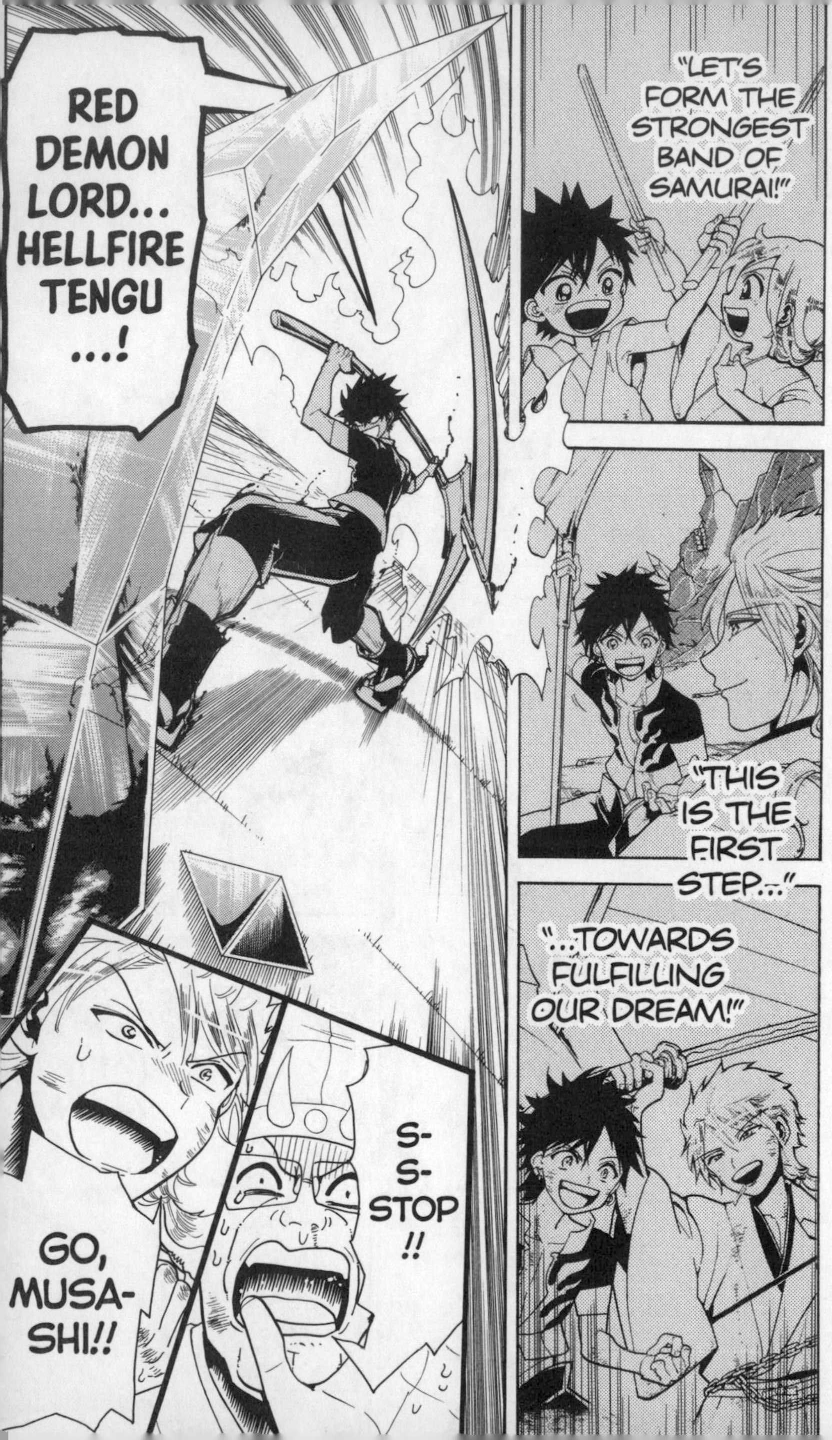
"LET'S FORM THE STRONGEST BAND OF SAMURAI!"
"THIS IS THE FIRST STEP..."
"...TOWARDS FULFILLING OUR DREAM!"
RED DEMON LORD... HELLFIRE TENGU ...!
S-S-STOP!!
GO, MUSASHI!!

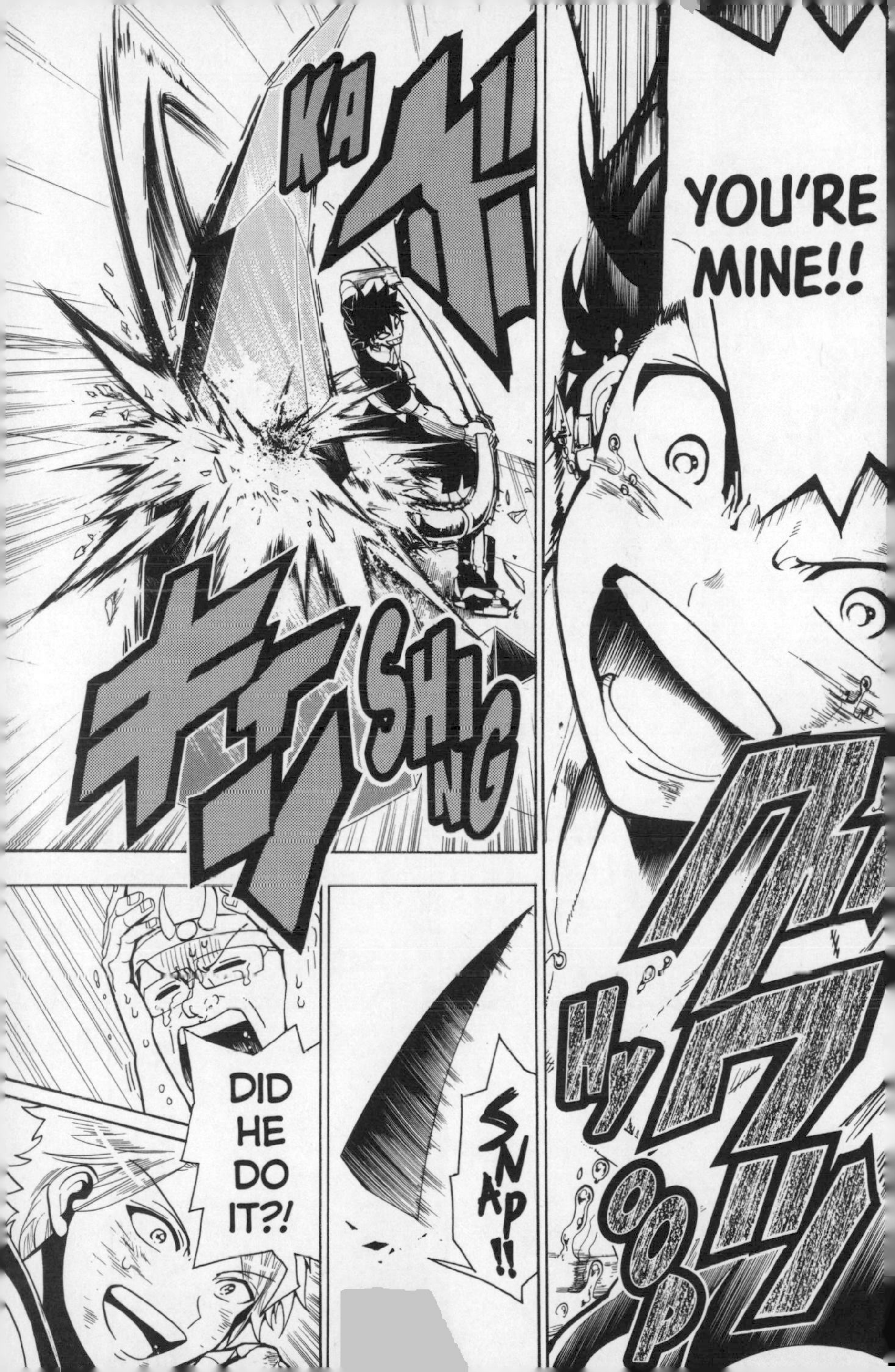
YOU'RE MINE!!
HyooP
KA
SHING
SNAP!!
DID HE DO IT?!

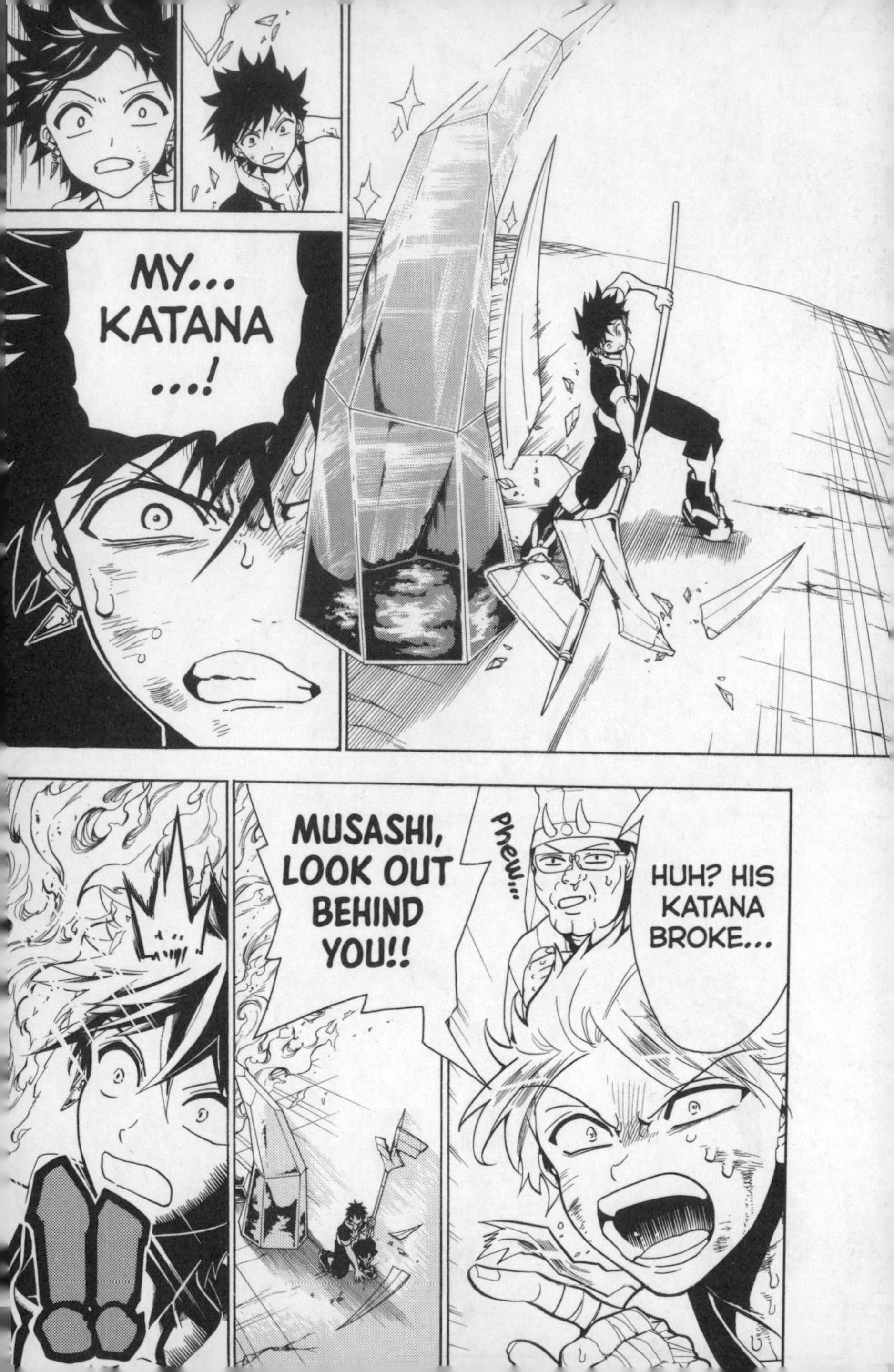
MY... KATANA ...!
HUH? HIS KATANA BROKE...
Phew...
MUSASHI, LOOK OUT BEHIND YOU!!

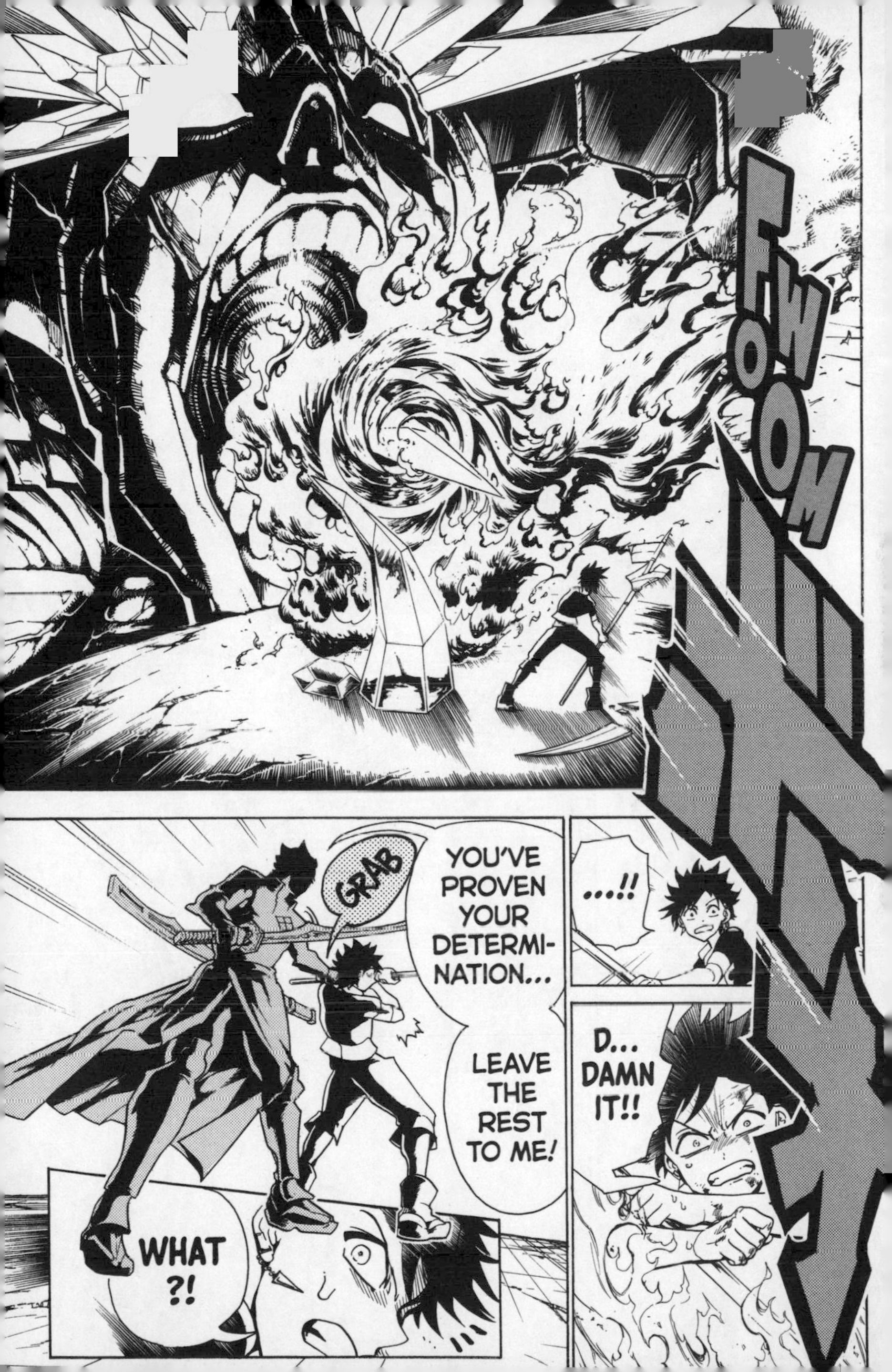
FWOOM
...!!
D... DAMN IT!!
GRAB
YOU'VE PROVEN YOUR DETERMINATION...
LEAVE THE REST TO ME!
WHAT ?!

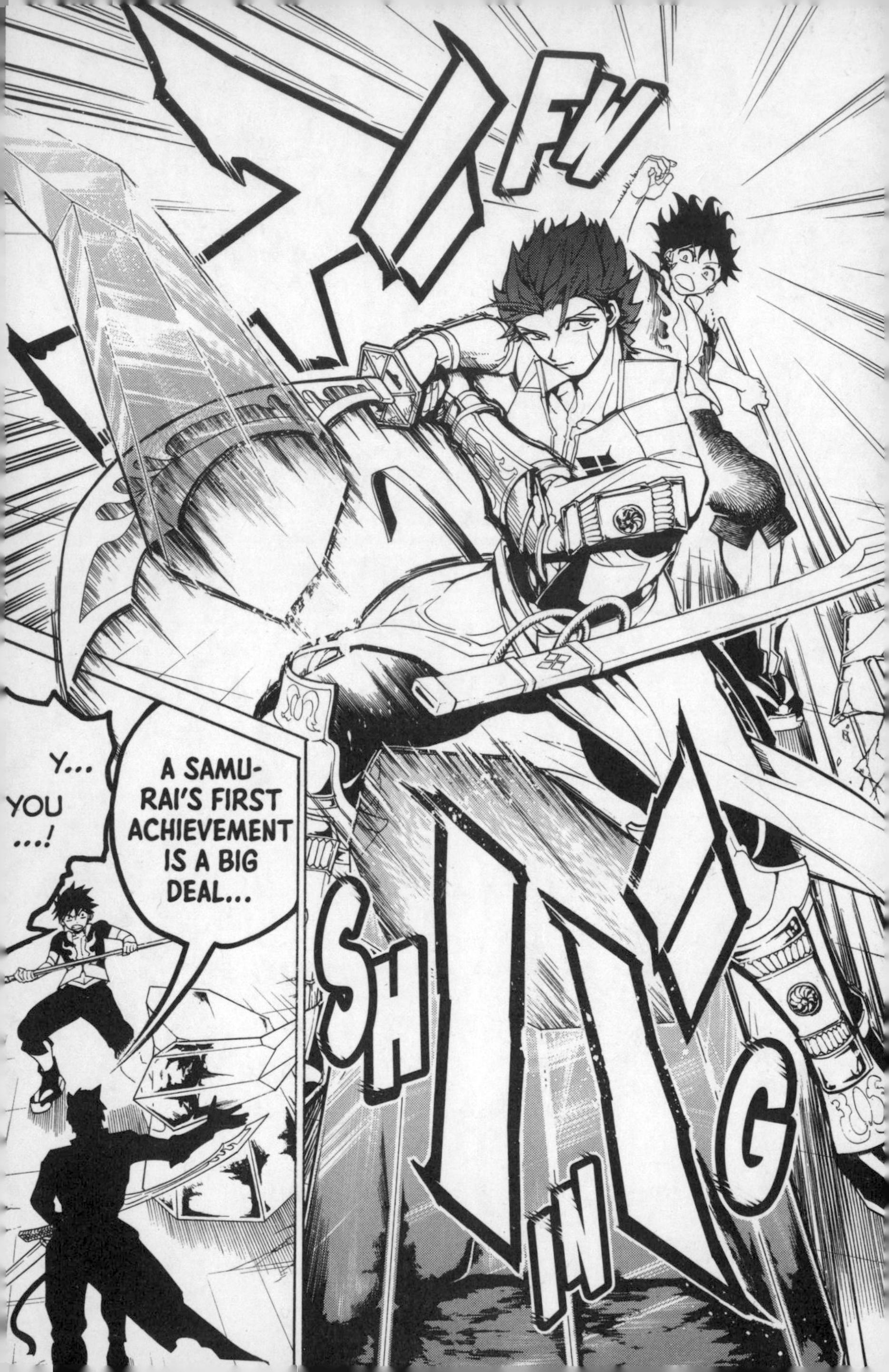

FWN
A SAMU-RAI'S FIRST ACHIEVEMENT IS A BIG DEAL...
Y... YOU ...!
SHING

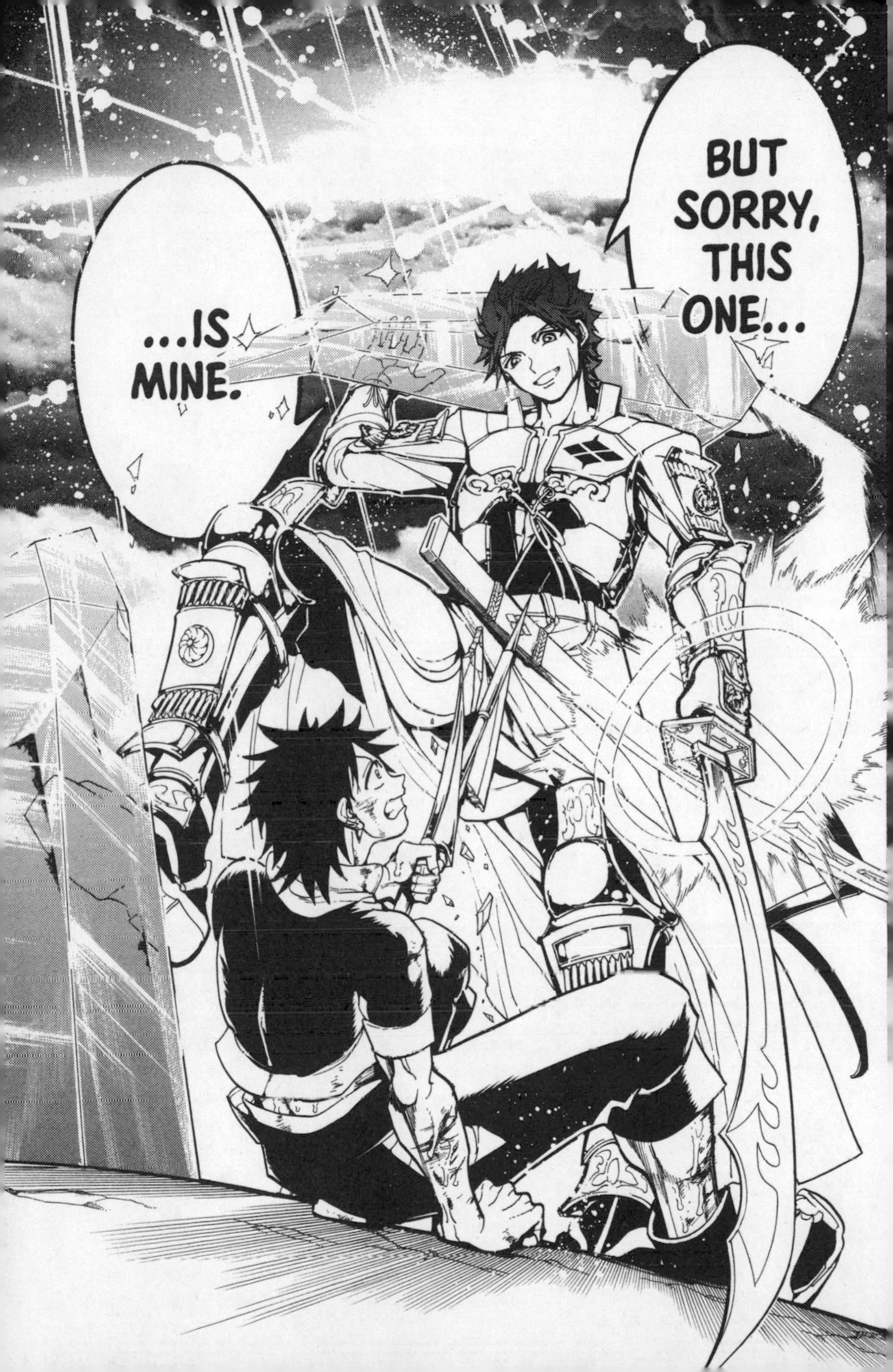
BUT SORRY, THIS ONE...
...IS MINE.

Pg. 4, Land of the Setting Sun

This term is *hi no moto* in the original Japanese. It literally means the root or source of the sun, which is a play on one of the ancient names for Japan. The modern term for Japan, *nihon* or *nippon,* uses the same Chinese character but omits the *no* (of), and so the pronunciation of the two characters change. To approximate the play on the ancient term for Japan, we've used a variation of a now outdated name for Japan, "The Land of the Setting Sun."

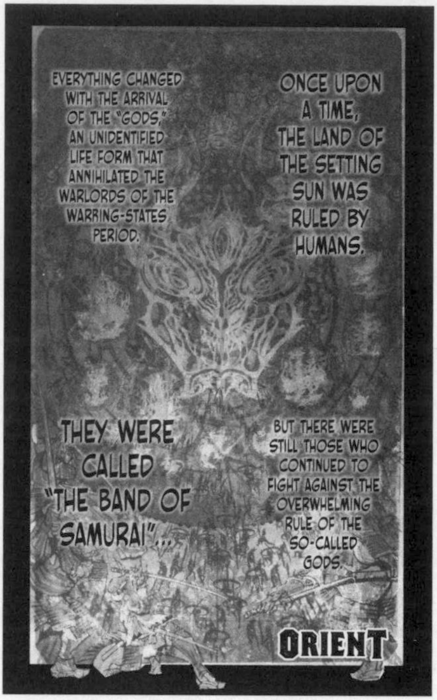
ONCE UPON A TIME, THE LAND OF THE SETTING SUN WAS RULED BY HUMANS.
EVERYTHING CHANGED WITH THE ARRIVAL OF THE "GODS," AN UNIDENTIFIED LIFE FORM THAT ANNIHILATED THE WARLORDS OF THE WARRING-STATES PERIOD.
BUT THERE WERE STILL THOSE WHO CONTINUED TO FIGHT AGAINST THE OVERWHELMING RULE OF THE SO-CALLED GODS.
THEY WERE CALLED "THE BAND OF SAMURAI"...
ORIENT

Pg. 4, Gods

This term is *kishin* in the original Japanese. In premodern tales and other literature from Japan, this term can mean either a benevolent or evil deity. We have chosen the term "gods" in the mythological sense, to encompass the ambiguity meant by the term in Japanese.

Pg. 4, Samurai

In the Japanese, this term is *bushi*, which means warrior within a variety of contexts in premodern and modern Japan. This term can be used interchangeably with samurai. However, this word often more specifically refers to a system of warriors within the feudal system in medieval and early modern Japan. Since the manga contains references to the period of early modern Japan (see below), we have opted for the term that would be most recognizable to English language readers.

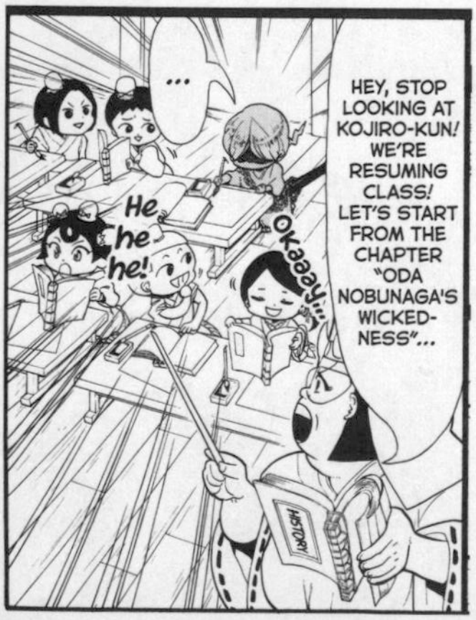
HEY, STOP LOOKING AT KOJIRO-KUN! WE'RE RESUMING CLASS! LET'S START FROM THE CHAPTER "ODA NOBUNAGA'S WICKED-NESS"...
...
He he he!

Pg. 73, Oda Nobunaga

In the lead-up to the Edo Period, a relatively long period of stable rule across the Japanese archipelago from 1603 – 1868, there were three important warlords who each played a part in conquering and consolidating lands held by rival feudal lords.The first one of these conquerors was Oda Nobunaga. He was subsequently defeated and his mantle as unifier of Japan taken up by Toyotomi Hideyoshi, who was then succeeded by Tokugawa Ieyasu in the Battle of Sekigahara in 1600. The Tokugawa Clan, which ruled from Edo (now called Tokyo) until the late 1800s, demonized the previous "unifiers" to glorify their own role in this history, so including Oda Nobunaga in this text places the story in an alternate version of the Edo Period.

ORIENT

Young characters and steampunk setting, like *Howl's Moving Castle* and *Battle Angel Alita*

Beyond the Clouds © 2018 Nicke / Ki-oon

A boy with a talent for machines and a mysterious girl whose wings he's fixed will take you beyond the clouds! In the tradition of the high-flying, resonant adventure stories of Studio Ghibli comes a gorgeous tale about the longing of young hearts for adventure and friendship!

The boys are back, in 400-page hardcovers that are as pretty and badass as they are!

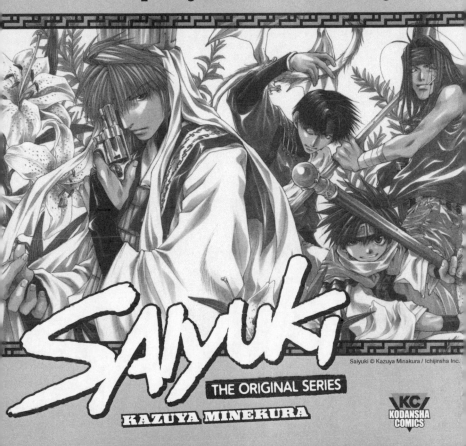

Saiyuki © Kazuya Minekura / Ichijinsha Inc.

SAIYUKI
THE ORIGINAL SERIES
KAZUYA MINEKURA

"AN EDGY COMIC LOOK AT AN ANCIENT CHINESE TALE." —YALSA

Genjo Sanzo is a Buddhist priest in the city of Togenkyo, which is being ravaged by yokai spirits that have fallen out of balance with the natural order. His superiors send him on a journey far to the west to discover why this is happening and how to stop it. His companions are three yokai with human souls. But this is no day trip — the four will encounter many discoveries and horrors on the way.

FEATURES NEW TRANSLATION, COLOR PAGES, AND BEAUTIFUL WRAPAROUND COVER ART!

CAN A FARMER SAVE THE WORLD? FIND OUT IN THIS FANTASY MANGA FOR FANS OF *SWORD ART ONLINE* AND *THAT TIME I GOT REINCARNATED AS A SLIME*!

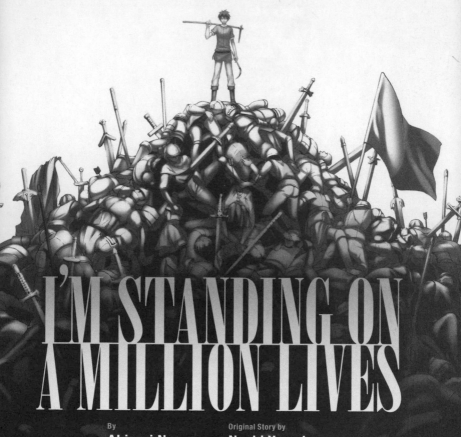

I'M STANDING ON A MILLION LIVES

By
Akinari Nao

Original Story by
Naoki Yamakawa

Yusuke Yotsuya doesn't care about getting into high school—he just wants to get back home to his game and away from other people. But when he suddenly finds himself in a real-life fantasy game alongside his two gorgeous classmates, he discovers a new world of possibility and excitement. Despite a rough start, Yusuke and his friend fight to level up and clear the challenges set before them by a mysterious figure from the future, but before long, they find that they're not just battling for their own lives, but for the lives of millions...

KC
KODANSHA
COMICS

MAGIC KNIGHT RAYEARTH
25TH ANNIVERSARY EDITION
CLAMP

A BELOVED CLASSIC MAKES ITS STUNNING RETURN IN THIS GORGEOUS, LIMITED EDITION BOX SET!

This tale of three Tokyo teenagers who cross through a magical portal and become the champions of another world is a modern manga classic. The box set includes three volumes of manga covering the entire first series of *Magic Knight Rayearth*, plus the series's super-rare full-color art book companion, all printed at a larger size than ever before on premium paper, featuring a newly-revised translation and lettering, and exquisite foil-stamped covers. A strictly limited edition, this will be gone in a flash!

PERFECT WORLD

Rie Aruga

A TOUCHING NEW SERIES ABOUT LOVE AND COPING WITH DISABILITY

An office party reunites Tsugumi with her high school crush Itsuki. He's realized his dream of becoming an architect, but along the way, he experienced a spinal injury that put him in a wheelchair. Now Tsugumi's rekindled feelings will butt up against prejudices she never considered — and Itsuki will have to decide if he's ready to let someone into his heart...

"Depicts with great delicacy and courage the difficulties some with disabilities experience getting involved in romantic relationships... Rie Aruga refuses to romanticize, pushing her heroine to face the reality of disability. She invites her readers to the same tasks of empathy, knowledge and recognition."
—Slate.fr

"An important entry [in manga romance]... The emotional core of both plot and characters indicates thoughtfulness... [Aruga's] research is readily apparent in the text and artwork, making this feel like a real story."
—Anime News Network

KC KODANSHA COMICS

A SMART, NEW ROMANTIC COMEDY FOR FANS OF *SHORTCAKE CAKE* AND *TERRACE HOUSE!*

A romance manga starring high school girl Meeko, who learns to live on her own in a boarding house whose living room is home to the odd (but handsome) Matsunaga-san. She begins to adjust to her new life away from her parents, but Meeko soon learns that no matter how far away from home she is, she's still a young girl at heart — especially when she finds herself falling for Matsunaga-san.

SAINT ☆ YOUNG MEN

A LONG AWAITED ARRIVAL IN PREMIUM 2-IN-1 HARDCOVER

After centuries of hard work, Jesus and Buddha take a break from their heavenly duties to relax among the people of Japan, and their adventures in this lighthearted buddy comedy are sure to bring mirth and merriment to all!

"Brilliant...the physical comedy and facial expressions will make you literally LOL."

—Sam Humphries (host of *DC Daily*; writer, *Green Lanterns, Legendary Star-Lord*)

The beloved characters from *Cardcaptor Sakura* return in a brand new, reimagined fantasy adventure!

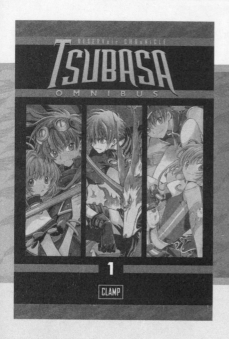

"[*Tsubasa*] takes readers on a fantastic ride that only gets more exhilarating with each successive chapter." —Anime News Network

In the Kingdom of Clow, an archaeological dig unleashes an incredible power, causing Princess Sakura to lose her memories. To save her, her childhood friend Syaoran must follow the orders of the Dimension Witch and travel alongside Kurogane, an unrivaled warrior; Fai, a powerful magician; and Mokona, a curiously strange creature, to retrieve Sakura's dispersed memories!

One of CLAMP's biggest hits returns in this definitive, premium, hardcover 20th anniversary collector's edition!

CLAMP

1 Chobits

20TH ANNIVERSARY EDITION

Chobits © CLAMP-ShigatsuTsuitachi CO.,LTD./Kodansha Ltd.

"A wonderfully entertaining story that would be a great installment in anybody's manga collection."
— Anime News Network

"CLAMP is an all-female manga-creating team whose feminine touch shows in this entertaining, sci-fi soap opera."
— Publishers Weekly

Poor college student Hideki is down on his luck. All he wants is a good job, a girlfriend, and his very own "persocom"—the latest and greatest in humanoid computer technology. Hideki's luck changes one night when he finds Chi—a persocom thrown out in a pile of trash. But Hideki soon discovers that there's much more to his cute new persocom than meets the eye.

A Kodansha Comics Trade Paperback Original
Orient 1 copyright © 2018 Shinobu Ohtaka
English translation copyright © 2020 Shinobu Ohtaka

All rights reserved.

Published in the United States by Kodansha Comics, an imprint of
Kodansha USA Publishing, LLC, New York.

Publication rights for this English edition arranged through
Kodansha Ltd., Tokyo.

First published in Japan in 2018 by Kodansha Ltd., Tokyo.

ISBN 978-1-64651-141-9

Printed in the United States of America.

www.kodanshacomics.com

9 8 7 6 5 4 3 2 1
Translation: Nate Derr
Lettering: Daniel Park
Editing: Jesika Brooks, Nathaniel Gallant
Kodansha Comics edition cover design by Phil Balsman
YKS Services LLC/SKY Japan, INC.

Publisher: Kiichiro Sugawara

Director of publishing services: Ben Applegate
Associate director of operations: Stephen Pakula
Publishing services managing editor: Noelle Webster
Assistant production manager: Emi Lotto, Angela Zurlo
Logo and character art ©Kodansha USA Publishing, LLC